Death and Life

Death and Life

*Resurrection, Restoration, and Rectification
in Paul's Letter to the Galatians*

Andrew K. Boakye

FOREWORD BY
Peter Oakes

⌬PICKWICK *Publications* · Eugene, Oregon

DEATH AND LIFE
Resurrection, Restoration, and Rectification in Paul's Letter to the Galatians

Copyright © 2017 Andrew K. Boakye. All rights reserved. Except for brief quotations in critical publications or reviews, no part of this book may be reproduced in any manner without prior written permission from the publisher. Write: Permissions, Wipf and Stock Publishers, 199 W. 8th Ave., Suite 3, Eugene, OR 97401.

Pickwick Publications
An Imprint of Wipf and Stock Publishers
199 W. 8th Ave., Suite 3
Eugene, OR 97401

www.wipfandstock.com

PAPERBACK ISBN: 978-1-4982-9000-5
HARDCOVER ISBN: 978-1-4982-9002-9
EBOOK ISBN: 978-1-4982-9001-2

Cataloguing-in-Publication data:

Names: Boakye, Andrew K. | foreword by Oakes, Peter.

Title: Death and life : resurrection, restoration, and rectification in Paul's letter to the Galatians / Andrew K. Boakye.

Description: Eugene, OR: Pickwick Publications, 2017 | Includes bibliographical references and index.

Identifiers: ISBN 978-1-4982-9000-5 (paperback) | ISBN 978-1-4982-9002-9 (hardcover) | ISBN 978-1-4982-9001-2 (ebook)

Subjects: LSCH: Bible. Galatians—Criticism, interpretation, etc. | Jesus Christ—Resurrection. | Paul, the Apostle, Saint. | Jews—Restoration.

Classification: BS2655.E7 B6 2017(print) | BS2655.E7 (ebook)

Manufactured in the U.S.A.   02/06/24

This book is dedicated to Chienye "CHI-CHI" Boakye, who has carried my burdens, thereby fulfilling the Law of Christ (Gal 6:2).

And to Dad, Mum, Raymond and Lynette, who have never grown tired of doing good (Gal 6:9).

Contents

Foreword by Peter Oakes | xi

1   Introduction: Outline and Setting the Scene | 1

   Thesis Outline. · 1
   Methodological Considerations · 16
   Setting the Scene: Resurrection in Galatians · 22
   Revivification in Ancient Literature · 30
   The Exodus as Resurrection · 45
   Ezekiel 37:1–14 as Principal "Restoration as Resurrection" Text · 60
   Summary of Introductory Issues · 76

2   Revivification Text One—Galatians 1:1–5: Resurrection as Paradigm in Galatians | 77

   Scholarly Comment on Gal 1:1–5 · 77
   Co-textual Analysis: Gal 1:1 in Relation to 1:2–4 · 81

3   Revivification Text Two—Galatians 2:19–20: Paul's Autobiography of Rectification | 93

   Context: Opening Comments/Significance of Unit Gal 2:15–21 · 94
   Galatians 1:13–20; 2:1–9; 2:11–14—Three Connected Narratives Concluded by 2:15–21 · 96
   Co-Text: Gal 2:15–21 as Riposte to Events of Gal 1:13–20; 2:1–9; 2:11–14 · 102
   Intertextual Resonances: Galatians 2:19–20 and Ezekiel 37 · 112
   Summary: Gal 2:19–20—Christ Lives in Me. · 117

4 Revivification Text Three—Galatians 3:21: The Law Cannot Generate Life | 120

    Context: Life as Headline for Restoration Blessing · 120
    Co-Text: Gal 3:10–14 · 120
    The Deuteronomic Context of Galatians—A Survey · 122
    Exegesis of Gal 3:10–14 · 131
    Co-Text: Gal 3:15–18 · 139
    Exegesis of Gal 3:19–25 · 140
    Juxtaposition of Gal 3:22–25 and 2:19–21 · 143
    Intertextual Resonances: "Life" in Galatians and the Prophets · 148
    Summary: Gal 3:21—Rectification as Endowment of Life in Galatians · 157

5 Revivification Text Four—Galatians 5:24–25: The Crucifixion of the Flesh | 159

    Context of Gal 5:24–25; 6:8; 6:14–15: Flesh and Spirit · 159
    Co-Text: Gal 5:24–25—Crucifixion and Life · 164
    Intertextual Resonances: Spirit and Life · 166
    Intertextual Resonances: Gal 5:24–25, Spirit Internalization and the New Covenant · 171
    Summary: Gal 5:24–25—Life by Virtue of Spirit · 184

6 Revivification Text Five—Galatians 6:8: The Spirit and Eternal Life | 186

    Contextual and Co-Textual Issues—Gal 6:1–6 · 187
    Exegesis of Gal 6:7–8 · 188
    Sowing to the Flesh/Spirit · 191
    Intertextual Resonances: The Spirit of Life—Gal 6:8 and Ezek 37 · 194
    Summary: Gal 6:8—Life Now, Life Everlasting · 195

7 Revivification Text Six—Galatians 6:14–15: A Newly Created Cosmos | 196

    Context: Closing Sentiments of Galatians · 196
    Co-Text: Gal 6:12–13 · 198
    Exegesis of Gal 6:14–15 · 199
    Intertextual Resonances · 202
    Summary: Gal 6:14–15—The Eschatological People of God · 212

8   Thesis Conclusions and Summation | 214

    Outline of Argument and Controlling Theory of Thesis · 214

Bibliography | 219
Author Index | 239
Subject Index | 243
Scripture Index | 251

Foreword

It is a pleasure to commend this book by my recent PhD student, Andrew Boakye, This is an excellent study that begins from a counter-intuitive premise. Whereas Galatians scholarship has frequently drawn attention to the virtual absence of the topic of resurrection in Galatians after 1:1, Boakye sees it as central. He does this by linking it to the material on death and life in the letter. This, in turn, he links to the role of the life-giving Spirit in the restoration rhetoric of prophets such as Ezekiel. This series of moves enables Boakye to demonstrate the existence of a "revivification" motif running through Galatians and playing a key role in the argument.

Boakye defines and defends the key conceptual move in the thesis by looking at ways in which a range of ancient texts relate together issues of life, death, revivification and restoration, an argument culminating in consideration of Ezekiel 37. He then covers six Galatians texts relating to death and life, reading each text co-textually and intertextually.

Boakye strongly links 1:1 with 2:19–20 to argue that Christ is the paradigm of the death-to-life experience of the believers, seen in 2:19–20 in the case of Paul. This makes the resurrection in 1:1 a statement of God's identity of the kind that prefaces the Decalogue. Galatians 3:21 is the starting point for arguing that "rectification" is seen in terms of giving of life, an argument reinforced by the links between parts of Galatians 3–4 and the restoration prophecies of Jeremiah and Ezekiel. Chapters 4–5 use discussion of 5:24–25 and 6:8 to show the intimate connection between the role of the Spirit and death/life issues. Finally, Boakye links the death/life idea into the rhetorical climax of the new creation in 6:14–15.

The argument is persuasively made. It certainly influenced me at points in the writing of my commentary. Readers will find this book a very good contribution to the understanding of Galatians and of ideas about life in Paul's theology.

—Peter Oakes, University of Manchester, May 2016

1

Introduction

Outline and Setting the Scene

Thesis Outline

This investigation aims to ascertain the basis for which Paul's response to the implied crisis in the Galatian Jesus communities took the shape and form it did in the epistle. A cursory reading of Galatians uncovers several wider concerns relating to Israel's unfolding history that Paul deemed necessary to incorporate within his polemic—Israel's relation to the Gentile world, to Abraham, Torah and Spirit. In addressing the issues within the Galatian churches by recourse to these elements of Israel's religious history, Paul clearly saw the difficulties there as a practical manifestation of disagreements over these concerns within Israel.

The difficulties arose because certain Jewish believers (Gal 1:6) questioned Paul's rendition of the gospel.[1] To these rogue teachers, Israel's future still had Torah at its centre, so Gentiles desiring a share in that future were not exempt from its demands. Paul vociferously objected; however, the language and ideas by which he expressed his discord in Galatians imply a more thoroughgoing proposition than simply "Gentiles do not need to

---

1. The attempts of some writers to recast Paul's interlocutors as other than Jewish Christ-believers are to be rejected. Schmithals's inventive treatment suggests that the opponents are Jews who have abandoned Torah in favour of the arcane secrets of gnostic cults. See Schmithals, *Paul and the Gnostics*. Cf. the critique of Schmithals in Wilson, "Gnostics: In Galatia?" 358–67. Equally creative is Nanos's suggestion that Gal 1:6 is an ironic use of εὐαγγέλιον, where the "good news" is actually that Gentiles can enjoy the protections Rome afforded to the Jews if they became proselytes. In this reading, Paul's opponents are Jews and not Jewish Christ believers. See Nanos, *Irony of Galatians*. For a survey of scholarly views on the motives of Paul's opponents, see Gregerman, "Counter-Mission," 1–24.

Judaize to be counted among God's people." The present volume will consider what motivated Paul to employ the vocabulary of *life* and *living* in conjunction with the language of *death* and *crucifixion* in Galatians to both rebut the Torah-centered gospel and simultaneously convey how God acted to restore his relationship with mankind.[2]

Scholarly theories surrounding Paul's literary-polemic approach in Galatians, with certain themes clearly predominant, are convoluted. There is generous consensus on some issues and wide divergence on others. Most agree that a serious "Law-related" problem instigated Paul's response; if, however, there is a core element to Paul's retort, commentators exhibit little concurrence on what this might be.[3] In what follows, a possible inroad will unfold.

Navigating a way into Galatians is an imprecise science; Cosgrove helpfully suggests that readers "join the conversation" at Gal 3:1–2, for, this only did Paul wish to inquire about.[4] Methodologically, he argues that the first unit that addresses the Galatian problem with directness and specificity is the question of 3:2.[5] Cosgrove is broadly correct and my reading proceeds by suggesting that the question of Gal 3:19 is a corollary of the one in 3:2, which brings the two key elements of the problem to the fore—the manifestation of the Spirit and the place of the Law. No scholarly investigation of Galatians of any influence has left these components untreated, but innovative hermeneutic strategies have produced divergent outcomes regarding them, as the following scholars demonstrate.

By employing Aristotelian categorization, H. D. Betz postulated that Galatians fits the form of apologetic letter.[6] Betz adjudged Galatians to be a form of *forensic* rhetoric, noting how Quintillian's literary divisions make good sense of much of the epistle.[7] For Betz, however, Paul's letter is not

---

2. The interplay of this imagery is the basis for *revivification* in this project. Revivification is the enlivening of that which is in a state of death. As such, resurrection is form of revivification (see table in concluding chapter).

3. This is exemplified by Tolmie's superb summary of research in Galatians from 2000 to 2010. See Tolmie, "Research," 118–57.

4. The issue being the basis of receiving the Spirit.

5. Cosgrove, *Cross and the Spirit*, 5–6.

6. Betz, *Galatians*, 14–25; cf. Betz, "Literary Composition," 4.

7. The method was criticized for making questionable assumptions about Paul's rhetorical training and the somewhat "ill-fit" of Galatians 5–6 within Betz's scheme. See further Kennedy, *New Testament Interpretation*, 148–50; Hester, "Placing the Blame," 281–307; cf. Aune, *New Testament in Its Environment*, 203; Anderson Jr., *Rhetorical Theory*, 167.

For a helpful critique of Betz, see Kern, *Rhetoric and Galatians*, 106–9. Some argue that Paul was fully trained in Hellenistic rhetoric, as C. Forbes, "Comparison," 23.

primarily defending his *apostleship*, as several commentators suggest. Rather, Betz states that:

> ... Paul goes directly to the root of the matter. As his strategy of defence he has chosen to defend the gift of the Spirit to the Galatians ... The Spirit was ... God's self-manifestation among and within human beings.[8]

The Spirit in Betz's reading is outside human control and cannot be manipulated or averted.[9] The ecstatic Spirit experience of the Galatian Gentiles was evidence of their salvation without works of Law; his opponents said that such a thing should never happen, but it *did* happen. As such, the Spirit proved the non-essentiality of the Law.

For J. Louis Martyn, it is the apocalyptic thrust of Galatians that governs its interpretation. As such, the key questions it addresses are "what time is it?" and "in what cosmos do we actually live?"[10] Martyn answers in terms of Spirit:

> It is the time after the apocalypse of the faith of Christ, the time, therefore, of God's making things right by Christ's faith, the time of the presence of the Spirit of Christ, and thus the time in which the invading Spirit has decisively commenced the war of liberation from the powers of the present evil age.[11]

He further argues that the Spirit institutes and constitutes a new state of affairs.[12] In this new state of affairs, the dualisms upon which the old world rested are replaced. Sin still remains a genuine power that must be opposed, but it is not opposed by Law; it is opposed by the Spirit of the crucified Christ.[13]

In the work of J. D. G. Dunn, there is primarily a social quandary at issue in Galatians. The letter is Paul's first sustained attempt to deal with "covenantal nomism," because the Law is being used

---

For an alternative position, see Weima, "What Does Aristotle Have to Do with Paul?" 458–68. See further Aune, "Paul," 343; Russell, "Rhetorical Analysis," 341–58.

8. Betz, *Galatians*, 28–29.

9. Ibid 29.

10. Martyn, *Galatian*, 23; Martyn, "Apocalyptic Gospel," 258.

11. Martyn, "Apocalyptic Gospel," 258. See the critique of Martyn's position by Sigurd Grindheim, "Not Salvation History," 91–108. Grindheim argues that the concept of a new era is not temporal, but rather depicts a transfer from the old domain of slavery to the new domain of sonship.

12. Martyn, *Galatians*, 323.

13. Martyn, "Apocalyptic Gospel," 259.

> ... both to identify Israel as the people of the covenant and to mark them off as distinct from the (other) nations.[14]

Dunn's concern to highlight the issue of Israel's national identity in Galatians is valid; however, it must go further insofar as the letter deals with the entire complex identity transformation process, which this project associates with life coming from death. Dunn writes:

> ... Paul confirms that the reception of the Spirit was equivalent in his thought to being reckoned righteous—two ways of describing the same positive relationship with God through which his blessing flows.[15]

Fee goes beyond the aforementioned scholars in a way that is more commensurate with this volume, by acknowledging that the eschatological people of God are Spirit people.[16] In this he cites Gal 5:25, observing that for Paul, therefore, to get saved means first of all to receive the Spirit.[17]

What these scholars (and scholarship more generally) overlook, is a pervasive *Spirit-life soteriology* throughout Galatians. The present work launches from two related ideas; the first is that the opening of Galatians focuses attention on the resurrection of Jesus and the work of God in raising him. The second, connected idea is that the language of "death/crucifixion" and "life" that permeates the text demonstrates that this focus on the God of resurrection undergirds the argument. Jesus was crucified and God raised him; God's people are those who have shared in the crucifixion, and, through the Spirit, shared in the risen life of Jesus; God's new world has itself suffered crucifixion and been newly created.

The language of this narrative in Galatians reflects both the language and essential story of Ezekiel 36–37 and the associated narrative of New Covenant in Jeremiah—a story of Spirit revivifying the dead people of God, securing their liberation, and revitalizing their receptiveness to the divine commands. Paul insists that God never invested the Law with the power to revivify. It is the mediation of Jesus' risen life by the Spirit, a life Paul saw enshrined in Israel's scripture, as the soteriological centre of Galatians that sets this reading apart from other approaches to Galatians.

---

14. Dunn, *Jesus, Paul and the Law*, 223; Dunn, "Works of the Law," 528.
15. Dunn, *Galatians*, 179.
16. Fee, *Empowering Presence*, 855.
17. Ibid.

Review of Scholarship

The present work is aligned with scholarship which sees in the New Testament (NT) evidence that the Messianic age brings to bear the blessings of the restoration from exile codified in Israel's prophetic traditions.[18] It also resonates with scholars who acknowledge the centrality of Jesus' resurrection in the inception of the New Covenant people of God, especially as expounded by Paul.

Pauline scholarship touching on these interests exhibits a curious trend. Scholars sensitive to the importance of exile and restoration in Paul seldom have much to say about resurrection; those who do, seldom have much to say about Galatians. In what follows, the stances of scholars who have commented on exile/new Exodus motifs and/or resurrection theology in Paul are reviewed.

Scott Hafemann

The outstanding contribution of Scott J. Hafemann in building on the ground-breaking work of James Scott is his attention to the epochal nature of Israel's history. For Hafemann, Paul's reflections on exile distinguish between two epochs of redemptive history.[19] His major work on Galatians has focused on Galatians 3–4 to this end.

He highlights the deficiencies of reading Gal 4:1–2 as the generic application of an illustration from the legal practice of testamentary guardianship over minors.[20] Where Paul *does* apply secular legal arguments as a defence (e.g., Gal 3:15–18) he is explicit. Hafemann points out that the testamentary guardianship position does not seem to reflect any known law.[21] Rather, he follows Scott in seeing the backdrop of Gal 4:1–7 as the first and second Exodus typology used in Old Testament (OT)/Post-Biblical Judaism to picture Israel's restoration from exile.[22]

As such, there is a basic harmony between type (Israel's redemption to divine sonship at the foreordained time of the Exodus) and antitype

---

18. The theme is prevalent elsewhere in the NT. See McComiskey, "Exile and the Purpose," 59–85; Pitre, "Ransom For Many," 41–68; Wright, *New Testament and the People of God*, 278; Fuller, *Restoration of Israel*," 197–267; for an extensive bibliography, see Evans, "Aspects of Exile," 300–28.

19. Hafemann, "Paul and the Exile," 368.

20. Ibid., 334.

21. Neither does 3:15–18, but Paul's audience may not have shared our ignorance.

22. Scott provides six lexical arguments in support of the "Exodus" reading of Gal 4:1–2. See Scott, *Adoption as Sons of God*, 126–45.

(believers' redemption to divine sonship at the foreordained time of the second Exodus).[23] W. N. Wilder similarly sees the Exodus story as the implied narrative to which Paul glancingly refers in Galatians 5–6.[24] S. C. Keesmaat correctly suggests that Paul's description of the Galatians' story has the same narrative flow as the story of the Exodus.[25] She continues that Paul also

> ... tells the story of God's salvation of the Galatians in such a way that the Exodus of Israel becomes paradigmatic for their redemption in Christ.[26]

Hafemann takes up Scott's position carefully. He notes, for example, that the only key term Scott can point to linking the Exodus narratives with Galatians is νήπιος in Hos 11:1; other terms from Gal 4:1–2 are applied to the Exodus by pointing to only general conceptual parallels and applying προθεσμία (Gal 4:2) to the 430 years of 3:17 instead of the period of Law.[27] Others have been more critical of Scott's lexical connections.[28]

In Hafemann's work, Paul is not so much using "Exodus language," but using Exodus imagery to describe Israel's history as a child in one long period of slavery for as long as it may exist (ἐφ' ὅσον χρόνον)—in other words, until she receives her inheritance. The stance is different from the traditional argument based on secular forensic praxis, but the net effect is not *much* different—for Hafemann, it is the epochal nature of salvation history that cannot be neglected.

The problem in Galatia, as Hafemann reckons it, is the agitators' failure to recognize the eschatological implications of demanding Gentile adherence to Torah.[29] Their disregard for the true purpose of the Torah is wreaking havoc on God's eschatological calendar. The scripture shut up "all things under sin" (3:22), hence, 4:8–9 suggests Gentiles are under the same condemnation. Τὰ στοιχεῖα in 4:3 suggests that Israel's life under the curse of the Law is part of humanity's existence in this world under the cursed elements of this present evil age (1:4). Israel under the curse for her perennial rebellion is equivalent to the world under slavery to idolatry. Israel having been adopted at the first Exodus rebelled as a "youth," rendering her a slave in regard to inheritance. Therefore, she received the inheritance at the same

---

23. Hafemann, "Paul and Exile," 335.
24. Wilder, *Echoes*, 75 (see entire section 75–199).
25. Keesmaat, "Paul and His Story," 135.
26. Ibid., 135–36.
27. Hafemann, "Paul and Exile," 335–36.
28. Goodrich, "Guardians, not Taskmasters," 255–62.
29. Hafemann, "Paul and Exile," 352.

time as the Gentiles, who were adopted at the second Exodus—this is the correct "order of things."[30] Paul's emphasis on status as Abraham's heirs in 3:26–29 and 4:1–7 is to raise the issue of inheritance (3:29; 4:5, 7), which points to the eschatological transition from the present evil age to what Cosgrove calls "realized heirship."[31]

Hafemann's reading of Gal 4:21–30 is consistent with this emphasis on the contrasting periods of Israelite history; Gal 4:21–25 reflects the present state of Israel. From Paul's eschatological perspective, being in or out of the covenant is represented by Isaac/Ishmael—to be born according to flesh is to be left to one's own devices under the power of sin; birth according to the Spirit is receiving the Spirit as per the Abrahamic promise. Here, as in 3:17—4:5, Paul shows that the Sinai covenant did not fulfil the promises to Abraham, but rather adjudicated over a people who like Ishmael stood outside the covenant.[32] For Hafemann the key issue of 4:21–30 is that it evidences Israel's present rejection of God's word—a rejection consistent with her traditional stubbornness. Once more, for Hafemann, Paul is making a clear distinction between two epochs of redemptive history.

Hafemann has clearly done some considerable reflection on the convoluted issues in 2 Corinthians. Eventually, these ruminations became *Paul, Moses, and the History of Israel: The Letter/Spirit Contrast and the Argument from Scripture in 2 Corinthians 3*. Here, Hafemann adopts a similar salvation-history approach to the one through which he reads Galatians 3–4. This publication ambitiously attempts to articulate the continuity between Paul's gospel and Moses' Law, and in particular, the contentious letter/Spirit contrast. In his critiques of some scholarly treatments of the quandary, Hafemann suggests that

> . . . one must entertain anew the possibility that the arguments from Scripture in 2 Cor. 3:3b and 3:6a may provide the backdrop for understanding the meaning of the letter/Spirit contrast in this context, rather than prejudice the exegesis of this passage by deciding in advance that Paul could not have derived his thinking from the OT passages to which he explicitly alludes.[33]

---

30. During the "youth" of Israel, Gentiles were excluded from the covenant—now in the period of inheritance, Gentiles are being incorporated. The age of the Sinai covenant is the age of this world, where "Gentile sinners" were excluded from the people of God (Gal 2:15); the age of the New Covenant is the new age of new creation where Gentiles as Gentiles are incorporated into God's people.

31. Cosgrove, *Cross and the Spirit*, 51, 69.

32. Hafemann, "Paul and Exile," 358.

33. Hafemann, *Paul, Moses, History of Israel*, 156.

The term "letter" does not point to a critique of Torah, for the hearts of the people, and not the structure of the covenant relationship between God and his people *per se*, have now been changed by the work of Christ and the power of the Spirit.[34] Hafemann contends that the New Covenant texts in Jeremiah 31 and Ezekiel 36 attest to the maintenance of Torah in the age of Spirit. Indeed:

> From its very beginning . . . the old covenant of the Law without the Spirit implicitly looked forward to the time when the Law would encounter a people whose hearts had been changed and empowered to keep God's covenant.[35]

"Letter" implies Torah in the absence of Spirit. Spirit is the energy behind Law keeping, which the Israelites lacked before the age of the Spirit; the problem lay not in Moses or the Law but in Israel's hard heartedness, a motif he sees in Galatians 3–4, 2 Corinthians 3, and Romans 9–11.

Hafemann's analyses are hard to fault; however, the neglect of attention to resurrection in his treatments of Galatians is palpable. Scott himself expressed concerns at how little scholarly attention is given to the Assyrian exile compared to the Babylonian exile.[36] It seems that the key "conceptual parallel" (Hafemann's term) within biblical portraits of exile and restoration is resurrection. Hosea 6:1–3 exemplifies such resurrection imagery in the context of restoration from Assyria. When one further considers the death-life language associated with exile and restoration in Deuteronomy 30, the resurrection metaphor in Ezek 37:1–14 and the significance of resurrection to Galatians, Hafemann is too hasty to dismiss such "conceptual parallels." He is correct that Hos 11:1–4 is a judgment text—Israel is about to be enslaved in Assyria just like she was in Egypt.[37] Later, we will suggest why the Exodus would have been read as a resurrection image, together with the other two great freedom-from-captivity narratives in Israel's scriptures. Coupled with Paul's encounter of a resurrection, the meagre lexical interface between the Exodus narratives and Galatians 4 need not *over*-concern us.

Also, it should be noted that Gal 4:21–30 goes well beyond establishing a contrast between periods of history, which even according to Hafemann has already been established earlier in Galatians 4. Though this contrast is present, the chief contrast is between the births of Abraham's sons. Isaac's birth by Spirit into freedom, compared to Ishmael born according to flesh

---

34. Ibid., 440–41.
35. Ibid., 442.
36. Scott, "Exile and Restoration," 1.
37. Hafemann, "Paul and Exile," 338.

into slavery, is the critical distinction in the text. It reflects rectification by faith in opposition to the false attempt to be rectified by works of Law.

Whilst I am in virtually complete agreement with Hafemann's position on the continuity of the Law and Gospel in the out-working of New Covenant prophecy, he has not pursued these ideas in Galatians, where the kernel of these ideas lie.

Rodrigo Morales

The chief concern of Morales's monograph is to demonstrate the centrality of Spirit in the restoration eschatology of Galatians. The Spirit, in bringing forth the eschatological blessing of life, achieved what the Law could not (Gal 3:21). Morales's work is primarily a pneumatology of Galatians—as I wrote in a review of his work:

> Spirit is a lead actor in the drama of Biblical/Post-Biblical restoration eschatology, and the images and ideas employed in the associated texts have influenced Paul's understanding of the Spirit in Galatians. These images include creation, Exodus, peace, righteousness, fatherhood, covenant, heart, resurrection, renewal of heart, filial relationship with God and in particular the undoing of curse.[38]

Morales is sensitive to some of the revivification imagery in Galatians, but resurrection is not his key theme and he does not develop the ideas. Nonetheless, he accurately rehearses:

> If the result of redemption from the curse is (eschatological) life, then naturally the result of the curse is death . . . In Paul's first statements about the Law in the epistle (2:15–21) he speaks in terms of death and life. . . . Again later in the epistle he speaks of the problem with the Law in terms of life (3:21b) . . . This verse is crucial, in that Paul explicitly states what the problem with the Law is and why his followers should not submit to it: it has no power to give life.[39]

Where Morales is most persuasive is in his understanding of the curse of the Law ultimately as *death*. He too builds upon J. M. Scott and N. T. Wright, and this work draws a similar conclusion based on an understanding of the blessing/curse language in Deuteronomy, though the analysis differs significantly. Indeed, as the resurrection imagery clarifies, exile is death.

38. Boakye, Review of *Spirit*, 83.
39. Morales, *Spirit*, 106.

Morales was criticized for making Spirit the central issue of Galatians. S. Grindheim notes that the chief contrast in Galatians is between faith and works of the law, not between the Spirit and the Law.[40] Similarly, Schreiner, whilst acknowledging Morales's actual objectives, accuses him of saying wrongly and too quickly that the Spirit is the central issue of the letter, ignoring the programmatic nature of Gal 2:15–21, where justification and the cross come to the forefront.[41] Scholars can often draw sharp distinctions between the conceptual paradigms in Paul's polemics—distinctions it is doubtful Paul himself would make. However, if justification is indeed a process whereby believers experience death to one sphere of existence and are made alive with the risen life of Jesus through Spirit, the contrasts of faith with Law and Spirit with Law are so inextricably bound that prioritising either is always going to be risky.

Morales is broadly convincing; his equation of flesh with Law in Galatians 5–6 is difficult to fully accept, though his treatment of what is often reduced to the paranaetic section of Galatians with his reading of Galatians 1–4 is a cogent one. However, the life-death imagery must be pushed further. It was not solely Paul's reflection on Jewish texts that led him to employ these ideas as Morales claims. Rather, the resurrection of Jesus led him to reread the exilic texts and develop the concept of rectification as revivification.

N. T. Wright

To many, N. T. Wright is the *de facto* target of Reformed antagonism at the New Perspective movement.[42] Matt Kennedy of the *Stand Firm* Christian network once accused New Perspective scholars of undermining the gospel, pointing to a series of lectures by D. A. Carson to this effect, which isolate Wright as the chief culprit.[43] It seems Wright's insistence that the gospel is unconcerned with Evangelicalism's preoccupation with "individual salvation" has inflamed passions.[44] Wright's position is nonetheless influential, impacting supporters and detractors with equal impetus.

40. Grindheim, Review of *Spirit*.
41. Schreiner, Review of *Spirit*.
42. See Wright, *Justification*, 12.

43. See http://www.standfirminfaith.com/?/sf/page/29216; Carson gave a series of lectures on the New Perspective in January 2008 available on *The Gospel Coalition* http://thegospelcoalition.org/index.php?%2Fresources%2Fname-index%2Fa%2Fda_carson%2Ftopic%2FNew+Perspective.

44. Wright opines: "It is a measure of how far the church has travelled from Paul's vision that Romans has often been read as a book about individual salvation rather than as a treatise on the nature of the people of God." See Wright, *Climax*, 252; his chief

However, it is his proposition that many first century Jews believed they were still in exile, even after the restoration from Babylon, which concerns us here. The paucity of direct NT evidence of such a state of affairs has made it difficult for many scholars to accept his view. M. Thompson's sentiments are typical:

> Theologically, though Wright's approach integrates many texts and makes for good preaching, one wishes that we had more explicit evidence in the NT for the exile motif to be as important and pervasive as Wright claims it to be.[45]

More recently, Philip Alexander, former head of Jewish studies at the University of Manchester, defended Wright's stance in a joint presentation of the Second Temple Judaism seminar of the British New Testament Conference (Edinburgh, 2015). He argued persuasively that the earliest Jesus communities read the Christ event and the advent of the Spirit in light of reworked traditions about an extended exile and a delay in the promised divine return.

Wright points to texts like *Psalms of Solomon* 11 as evidence that the theme of hope of freedom from exile was still vibrant in the first century. This Psalm speaks of return from exile, drawing on the great restoration texts in Deutero-Isaiah.[46] He adds other key ancient texts as evidence that the Deutero-Isaianic hopes remained unaddressed, including *1QH* 18.14–15; *11QMelch*; of such texts he claims it is clear that, within the Second-Temple period, some Jews at least were still looking earnestly for a fulfilment of the Isaianic promises.[47] Their return from Babylon had not brought about that independence and prosperity which the prophets had foretold.[48]

I heartily agree with Wright that Galatians attests to the restoration promises finding fulfillment.[49] Of Paul's statements in Gal 4:1–11, Wright suggests that in sending his son God has redeemed his people from bondage to false gods, and by sending his Spirit made them truly his children. In this way the people have come to know God and be known by him (Gal 4:9).[50] This for Wright brings the great promises of Isaiah 40–55 to fulfilment; the true God has been revealed and the idols of the nations exposed

---

critic, John Piper, aired his views in Piper, *Future of Justification*.

45. Thompson, *New Perspective*, 12.

46. Isa 40:9; 52:7.

47. Wright, "Gospel and Theology in Galatians," 225; cf. Wright, *The New Testament & the People of God*, 270.

48. Wright, *Climax*, 141.

49. Wright, "Letter to the Galatians," 216.

50. Ibid., 227.

as phony. Furthermore, I follow his lead in connecting the curse of the Law in Galatians with exile and death based on the context of Deuteronomy, particularly chapters 27–30. However, Wright determines that resurrection is a minor theme in Galatians—in this I think Wright acknowledges the obvious without probing the necessary. Like many, Wright observes the close link between rectification and resurrection in Romans, where passages like Rom 4:25 make it far more explicit. Wright points out:

> Resurrection is, therefore, as in much contemporary Jewish thought, the ultimate "justification": those whom God raises from death, as in [Rom.] 8:11 are thereby declared to be his covenant people.[51]

He does however, correctly acknowledge:

> Paul refers here movingly to his own journey of death and new life, *not for its own sake but in order to explain that this is true of all who belong to the Messiah*. He now shares, participates, finds himself caught up in, the Messiah's death and resurrection: he is "crucified with the Messiah."[52]

Resurrection, as will be shown, is no minor theme, but paradigmatic for rectification in Galatians.

Michael Gorman

The analysis presented in this volume is in strong overall agreement with Michael J. Gorman that justification is by crucifixion, specifically co-crucifixion, understood as participation in Christ's act of covenant fulfilment.[53] He argues that co-crucifixion leads to co-resurrection, which draws those of faith into a cruciform lifestyle, for which Jesus was template and Paul was example. Gorman shows with great exegetical acuity how, because God's nature is cruciform, Jesus' self-giving act took the shape it did. He equates being "in Christ" with "inhabiting the cruciform God."

His argument is both sound and, pastorally, a sharp upward call. I wish to suggest two lines of critique, the import of which will be manifest in the argument of this book. Co-resurrection is explicit in certain Deutero-Pauline texts; however, Paul treats believers' experience of co-crucifixion as pre-cursory for eschatological salvation. As such, Paul carefully reserves

---

51. Wright, *Climax*, 203.
52. Wright, *Faithfulness*, 859 (emphasis mine).
53. Gorman, *Inhabiting*, 43–44.

his traditional resurrection lexicon for his Judgment discourses. In 1 Cor 15:35–50, Paul explains how in a corporeal sense the difference between the believer and Jesus will only be resolved at the Parousia. Rectification is a first stage event which foreshadows the finality.

In personal conversation with Gorman, he pointed out that most 20th century interpreters of Paul were afraid to speak of present resurrection, but more recently scholars like A. J. M. Wedderburn and J. Daniel Kirk variously argue for present as well as future resurrection.[54] Nonetheless, the nervousness of earlier readers of Paul is not unwarranted. Believers will not fully participate in this risen life until the eschaton, but rectification is the initial endowment of that life; it is the "already but not yet life." Paul narrates the deliverance he experienced as co-crucifixion with Christ in order that he might live to God (Gal 2:19). He claims neither to have been *raised* nor, in the undisputed Pauline corpus, ever says believers were raised before the eschaton. Lexically we observe the following.

Of the forty-one uses of ἐγείρω in Paul, twenty-four refer to the resurrection of Jesus. Of the seventeen that do not, ten are in conjunction with the raising of the dead at the judgment in 1 Corinthians 15, one in Rom 9:17 (citing Exod 9:16) refers to Pharaoh being "raised" to the position of king, and one in 2 Cor 1:9 is a divine title. Only five of the references to ἐγείρω refer to the raising up of believers—two of these occur in the future indicative (1 Cor 6:14 and 2 Cor 4:14) and clearly refer to the eschaton. This leaves Col 2:12; 3:1; Eph 2:6; all three employ the compound verb συνεγείρω and point to a raising *with* Christ, which has already occurred. No undisputed Pauline text speaks of Christians being raised in the here and now.[55] However, as early as the penning of Colossians and Ephesians, Pauline devotees saw a profound correlation between Jesus' resurrection and the experience of believers.

Jesus brought the end into the present by *his* resurrection, but Paul's assertion that the risen life he lives to God he lives "in the flesh" (Gal 2:20) suggests that his risen life is demonstrably inferior to Jesus' risen life. This may appear pedantic, but the distinction certainly seems critical enough to speak of the now-time *revivification* of believers and only their end-time *resurrection*.

Secondly, Gorman, quite correctly, treats both eschatology and ethics as "resurrection shaped" in Paul—it is because of "co-resurrection" that the life of believers will be characterized by Christ-like faith and love as

---

54. See Wedderburn, *Baptism*, 1–2; Kirk, *Unlocking*, 108–9.
55. Cf. 2 Tim 2:18.

they are guided by the Spirit.⁵⁶ He even speaks of Paul's ministry in terms of "inhabiting the God of life-in-death and power-in-weakness," claiming this is the heart of Paul's cruciform spirituality.⁵⁷ The reasoning is largely persuasive, but for this very reason might we better comprehend both the church's ethical program and Paul's ministry career as "resurrectiform", or more accurately, *reviviform*?⁵⁸

The resurrection as God's action in Christ is only where Paul's death-life story in Galatians begins. Paul's revivification language points to a much more pervasive death-life narrative. Paul's over-vaunted problem with the Law is explained in revivification terms in Galatians (3:21) as is his post-conversion ethnic categorisation (2:19–20; 6:14–16; cf. 3:28). *Reconciliation* in Paul's ministry is described using revivification imagery in Romans and 2 Corinthians.⁵⁹ In 2 Corinthians Paul's ministry gives rise to "the aroma of life and death." As Gorman himself points out, justification is depicted in terms of resurrection in Galatians and Romans.⁶⁰ God is the God of resurrection in Galatians (1:1).⁶¹ In Rom 5:12–21, sin and righteousness are contrasted as death and life—moving from the rule of one to the other is "resurrection." It seems that precisely because power comes from weakness (Gal 2:19; 2 Cor 12:9), life from death (Gal 5:24–25; 2 Cor 4:11) and victory from suffering (Gal 3:4; Rom 8:17), emphasizing crucifixion over resurrection creates a hierarchy that Paul never intended.⁶²

David M. Stanley

From the outset, D. M. Stanley's 1961 monograph seeks to probe more deeply into Paul's resurrection theology than simply making a case for its importance; resurrection is, for Stanley, what enabled Paul to arrive at the definitive expression of his conception of Christian salvation.⁶³ He attempts

---

56. Gorman, *Inhabiting*, 117.

57. Ibid., 150–52.

58. My own terms.

59. In Rom 14:7–9, reconciliation between believers is a by-product of Jesus' resurrection.

60. Ibid., 74–79.

61. Cf. Rom 4:17.

62. Sublimely captured by S. Finlan, who writes that we leave out half of Paul's message if we see it as only cruciform; Finlan coins the term "anastiform." See Finlan, "Theosis in Paul," 74–75. Cf. Minear, who also emphasizes "death" while marginalizing "life" in Paul; see Minear, "Pauline Thoughts on Dying," 91.

63 Stanley, *Resurrection*, 1.

this through an examination of the Pauline kerygma contained in all of the canonical Pauline texts and at key moments in Acts.[64]

He zeroes in on the absence of direct resurrection language in Galatians, and explains this by suggesting that Paul's resurrection theology was the same as that of his opponents.[65] This is perhaps unremarkable; what seems less reasonable, especially in light of his opening statements, is the treatment of key texts in Galatians, which he relegates to dress rehearsals for Romans. By Stanley's reckoning, the life of Christ in Gal 2:20 will be restated with a greater nicety of precision in Rom 8:11, 15.[66] He further suggests that the themes of life and justification will only be united into a complete synthesis in Romans.[67] Aside from whether we get a "complete synthesis" in Romans, it is difficult to imagine that anything but the paucity of overt resurrection vocabulary in Galatians lies behind Stanley's critique. The five-fold references to "live" in 2:19–20 go completely unmentioned. The absence of any handling at all of Gal 5:24–25 betrays a sense of disconnection between the concepts of Spirit and life which are utterly central to Paul's resurrection testimony.

Terrance Callan

The most relevant section of Terrance Callan's study is the third and longest chapter on salvation. His thesis statement is that dying and rising with Christ as part of the body of Christ is central both to Paul's understanding of Jesus as Saviour and to his understanding of Christian life.[68] As such, for Callan, the absence of any mention of resurrection on occasions where Paul writes of the salvific death of Jesus (e.g., Rom 3:23–25) is not cause for concern. The resurrection of Jesus should be understood as belonging together with his death as part of a single salvific action.[69]

Like myself, Callan carefully stops short of speaking of a current "resurrection" of believers—for Callan the risen life is an "ongoing death and resurrection with Christ."[70]

My main criticism of Callan, which Betz made more generally of Tannehill's (more thorough) monograph with a virtually identical title, is that

64. Ibid., 39.
65. Ibid., 148.
66. Ibid., 151.
67. Ibid., 151–52.
68. Callan, *Dying*, 8.
69. Ibid., 85.
70. Ibid., 128.

his presentation of dying and rising with Christ in Galatians seems exegetically divorced from the wider context of Galatians and the implied arguments of Paul's opponents.[71]

Methodological Considerations

Discourse Analysis

Despite the limitations of Betz's over-specificity, he was correct to draw attention to rhetoric itself. Though commentators are not unanimous in their assessment of the *Sitz im Leben* of Galatians, a few things seem fairly clear. Firstly, Galatians is certainly a counter-thesis aimed at establishing loyalty to Paul's position over and against an opposing one. Secondly, Paul's appeal to Jewish scripture reveals a core historical narrative to which he is beholden. What Paul believes is happening amongst the communities has its origin in Israel's redemptive history, though it is neither a clean break nor a smooth transition from Israel's past. Thirdly, the recurrence of certain key terms, particularly in light of their appearances in related contexts in other Pauline epistles, suggests Paul's response was not just concocted *ex nihilo* to combat the Galatian crisis. Without over-systematizing Paul's theological framework, terms like "Spirit," "life/live," "Law," "faith/believe," "rectify," "died/crucified," and "flesh" appear integral to a fabric of thought by which Paul comprehended the work of God in Christ.

As such, in approaching the text of Galatians, it seems to me that one of the driving questions must be how this particular collocation of words in context advances Paul's rhetorical objectives.[72] A sufficient reading strategy must consider seriously *why* Paul chose to argue the case in the way he did, given his own circumstances, those of his audience and those more widely of Israel.

This project posits that Gal 1:1–5 emphasizes God's action in raising Jesus (1:1); the presence throughout the epistle of five further texts regarding the rectification of humanity in terms of life-coming-from-death, suggests that the revelation of the crucified/risen Christ "in" Paul was the origin of this stance (2:19–20; 3:21; 5:24–25; 6:8; 6:14–15). This reading of Galatians centralizes these six texts, asking how they cohere to the surrounding text and the letter as a whole. This notion of linguistic cohesiveness has been ably defined by Reed as

---

71. Betz, Review of *Dying and Rising*, 350.
72. Nida, "Role of Context," 20.

> ... the means by which an immediate linguistic context meaningfully relates to a preceding context and/or a context of situation (i.e., meaningful relationships between text, co-text and context). Linguistic cohesiveness provides speakers with the means to produce a "message" (i.e., theme) from individual and sometimes unrelated words and phrases.[73]

As such, this investigation deploys an adaptation of Reed's approach to *discourse analysis*, which incorporates the roles of the author, the audience and the text in communicative events.[74] Though relatively embryonic in NT studies, discourse analysis is broadly understood as a method of determining the way in which words, phrases, clauses, sentences, paragraphs and whole compositions are joined to achieve an author's purpose.[75] The discourse, in this case Galatians, comprises (1) the linguistic units surrounding a sentence (co-text); (2) the immediate situation (context of situation); (3) the wider cultural background of the text (cultural context).[76]

For the purposes of this analysis, consideration will be given to the context and co-text before moving to the *intertexts* which influenced Paul's polemical trajectory. Like Reed, Halliday, *et al.* the focus in this thesis is upon how linguistic units "function" to create cohesion. There is an effective cumulative effect of meaning as units open windows on each other. This corresponds to what Easley refers to as the relationship between microstructure and macrostructure in discourse units; the logical dependence of sentences on the other sentences in a paragraph and the interrelationship between the paragraphs.[77]

The approach here is driven by what Galatians suggests Paul has invested into the key terms, so they come together to give what Lemke calls "text-meaning"; the word choices and clause formations lead to meanings the words alone often cannot.[78] To illustrate what Paul invests in the terms, consider his employment of ζάω language in Galatians. For "live" could simply denote "existence," e.g., "he lived a long time." It could imply conforming to a standard, as in the phrase "he lived up to expectations." Furthermore, it could point to the reality of an experience as implied by the phrase "he made my life a living hell," or mark something that continues, as in the phrase "his legacy lives on."

---

73. Reed, "Cohesiveness of Discourse," 29.
74. Reed, "Discourse Analysis as New Testament Hermeneutic," 229.
75. Black, "Discourse Analysis, Synoptic Criticism," 91.
76. Reed, "Discourse Analysis," 225.
77. Easley, *User-Friendly Greek*, 115–16.
78. Lemke, "Semantics and Social Values," 48.

Galatians exhibits a far more sharply nuanced use of the term, shaped by the co-textual and contextual dynamics of the corresponding pericopae. For example, in Gal 5:25, Paul implies that believers live πνεύματι ("in" or "by" Spirit). The co-text demands that those so living are "of Christ", having crucified the flesh. Therefore, those living πνεύματι should order their steps (στοιχέω) by Spirit. This introduces an avalanche of lexico-semantic connections; in what sense does "flesh" function? In what sense is flesh "crucified"? How does this relate to the literal crucifixion of Jesus' literal flesh? How does "of Christ" here impact on those "of Christ" in 3:29, who are said to be "Abraham's seed" and "heirs according to promise"? What is the significance of the benediction in 6:16 which is upon those who "order their steps by this canon" (the only other use of στοιχέω in Galatians)?

These co-textual and contextual nuances are seen elsewhere in Galatians and, indeed, elsewhere in Paul; sometimes they draw elements of narratives from Israel's history into re-contextualized formulations pertinent to Paul's rhetoric. So, for example, when Paul writes that the Israelites were "baptized into Moses in the Red Sea" (1 Cor 10:2) this is clearly an attempt to connect the experience of the Corinthian disciples with that of Israel. Paul seeks to create a new narrative which receives semantic impetus from his creative use of the term *baptized*, which has obvious theological import for Paul in general and in 1 Corinthians in particular (1 Cor 1:13, 14, 15, 16, 17; 12:13; 15:29). Baptism acts as a conceptual prism—a transformational drama which occurs in a moment of passing through water. Those authors reflecting on the Exodus treated it as the creation of Israel as a distinct people of God—Exod 3:10; Num 22:5; Deut 4:20; 1 Kgs 8:51; 1 Chr 17:21; Ps 80:8; Ps 114:1. Paul is armed with his own paradigm of identity transformation in his baptism theology, exemplified in 1 Cor. 12:13 (which is also seen in 1 Cor 10:17 and 1 Cor 10:32), and thus is able to present a commentary on Exodus 13–14 and 16–17. It is precisely because the Exodus was its own "passing through the waters" that Paul can refer to it as a baptism.[79]

The apostle's objective is that the Corinthian believers, instructed in the socio-theological and soteriological ramifications of baptism, would reflect on the former "baptism" narrative (the Exodus) in light of their own baptism narrative (baptism into the body of Christ believers as 12:13 implies) in order to discern a new narrative (being an obedient people through the corrective steps outlined in 1 Cor 10:7–12 as opposed to a stubborn people who fell in the desert as 10:5). In Galatians, it is not baptism, but *resurrection,* acting as the conceptual prism. Paul speaks of rectification in terms of death/crucifixion and life because he understands it as a transformative act

---

79. See the very helpful discussion in Soards, *1 Corinthians*, 200–202.

that results from participation in the death-life act of the Christ event. With the death and resurrection of Jesus in the interpretive foreground, Paul employs the language and themes employed by Ezekiel and Jeremiah in order to articulate rectification for the Galatians. Just as passing through water makes baptism and Exodus twin concepts from which Paul can draw theological and practical capital, death and life make Judah's restoration from captivity and Jesus' resurrection twin concepts by which he does the same. This leads to another issue pertinent to how this study will unfold.

The interpretive focus of Pauline studies has shifted numerous times even in the years following Sanders' devastating critique of the predominant Lutheran "Christian faith vs. Jewish works" hermeneutic. Scholars approaching Paul's letters today fall broadly into three contextual camps, with several variations within: they are Hellenistic philosophy, Roman Empire and Israel's redemption history.[80] Proponents of all three strategies for reading Paul have variously argued for the strengths of their position (and usually the weaknesses of the others).[81] No one would dispute that ancient Judaism(s) were influenced by Hellenism.[82] Certainly, Paul also lived as a Jew in a Roman cultural context, and all three of these things will have coloured the way Paul expressed his arguments. It is, however, impossible to say with any precision which aspect of Paul's socio-cultural context most affected his writings. This can be illustrated more fully by recourse to my own social context, as a black man, a Christian, and an academic. If someone were to read this thesis asking which aspect of my identity was the most appropriate filter through which to interpret it, a warped picture would surely emerge. One might, say, read the thesis with it firmly in mind that the author is a black man with all the associated cultural baggage that carries—experiences of racism or marginalization, resentment of colonialism, a tendency to understand slavery through the lens of the western trade of African peoples, and so on. It would elucidate areas of influence on my

---

80. For surveys of these trends in Pauline studies, see Wright, "Anglophone," 367–81; Taylor, *Apostle*, 51–88.

81. For Paul and Hellenistic Philosophy, see Frick, *Paul in the Grip of the Philosophers*; Malherbe, *Philosophers*, 67–78; Balch, Ferguson and Meeks, *Greeks, Romans, and Christians*; Bahnsen, "Encounter," 7–40; Boyarin, *Radical Jew*, 57–85; Downing, *Cynics, Paul and the Pauline Churches*; Engberg-Pedersen, *Paul and the Stoics*. For Paul and Empire, see Lopez, *Apostle to the Conquered*, 122–24; Elliott, "Anti-Imperial," 167–83 (indeed see the whole volume); Elliott, *Arrogance of Nations*; Judge, "Decrees of Caesar," 71–78; Carter, "Paul and the Roman Empire," 7–26. On reading Paul through redemptive-historical lenses, see Ridderbos, *When the Time Had Fully Come*, 44–60; Gaffin, "Redemption and Resurrection," 16–31; Hays, "Crucified with Christ," 231–32; Beale, *Biblical Theology*, 249–97.

82. Gilbert, "Hellenization of the Jews," 520–40.

thought and potential biases introduced into this reading of Paul, but only at the expense of other cultural influences. Similarly, if the author's words were treated as primarily the words of a Christian or a western academic, there would be unnatural emphases at key points. Of course, someone could read this project and *then* ask which of the author's own cultural influences is predominant. Similarly, reading the text of Galatians itself leads the present author to prioritize *redemptive history*, for the following reasons.

Firstly, Gal 1:4 makes clear that Paul has an age-specific soteriology.[83] Secondly, the hub of Paul's argument, that Spirit conveys the risen life of Jesus to believers, is grounded in Israel's scriptural tradition. This is seen in the Biblical citations, the various echoes of Ezekiel and Jeremiah and the argumentative presumptions regarding Abraham and his progeny. Thirdly, one aspect of Paul's argument is that Gentile followers have "fulfilled Torah" by emulating Christ's love (5:14). Fourthly, the section of the argument in Gal 4:1–7 and 4:21–31 tie together the themes of Spirit, freedom and maturity—this evidences Paul's view that rectification is prefigured by Israel's two other great freedom narratives—Exodus and restoration from exile. Fifthly, Gal 5:16ff demonstrates Paul's consistency with the prophetic vision of the Spirit as evidence of the final age.

Implications of δικαιόω Language

In what follows, a brief account will be taken of how this volume handles "justification" language in Galatians. The complexities surrounding the translation and interpretation of the δικαιόω group of Greek words are well documented within Pauline studies.[84] The following is strictly an apology for the use of the term "rectify" and its cognates to denote δικαιόω in this volume—a term most notably embraced by J. Louis Martyn.

Martyn himself is concerned to avoid the presumptions that Paul read δικαιόω as primarily forensic language and δικαιοσύνη as a moral or religious norm.[85] I share his broad concerns and sympathize with the notion that the chief subject of [Galatians] is God's making right what has gone wrong and in Paul's view the latter is known only from the former.[86]

---

83. See further Russell, "Redemptive-Historical Argumentation," 333–57.

84. See Reumann, "Justification and Justice," 26–45; Martyn, *Theological Issues*, 141–56; Seifrid, "Paul's Use of Righteousness Language," 39–75; Ziesler, *Meaning of Righteousness in Paul*.

85. Martyn, "Apocalyptic Gospel," 249.

86. Ibid; I would not insist it is the letter's "chief subject" or speculate that Paul only knew of the nature of the problem on the grounds of God's solution.

New Perspective exegetes have typically linked a forensic, juridical and imputational justification theology with Luther—though dissenting voices have challenged such reductionism[87]—and sought to undo the effects of his apparently flawed assumptions. Any attempt to put constraints on what Paul intended to convey with δικαιόω will make certain Pauline texts very awkward to interpret. Arguing, for example, that Paul's soteriology is not forensic, but participationist, may make better sense of Paul's broader thought, but ultimately compounds the problem by forcing interpreters to make hermeneutic choices Paul might not have intended. In so doing, readers may even prematurely screen out ideas of forensic acquittal, as say in Rom 5:12–21. A writer as creative as Paul could certainly employ a multiplicity of models to convey his soteriological position.[88]

The reflections on the death-life lexicon in Galatians presented here emphasize the *transformational* implications of δικαιόω in a way that accommodates how both forensic *and* participationist ideas (admittedly more the latter) might inform its meaning.

In explicating the limitations of Torah in Galatians, Paul equates its incapacity to rectify with its inability to "make alive" (Gal 3:21). As such, I treat δικαιόω as *revivification* language and as one part of a proliferation of revivification language in the letter. This thesis centralizes Paul's re-reading of scripture and reconfigured worldview resulting from his experience of the resurrected Christ. Life coming from death was, for Paul, the ultimate transformation, but the rhetoric of transformation may be meaningfully applied in juridical contexts (guilt transformed into innocence) or participationist ones (from outside Christ to in Christ). We may certainly ask which of these paradigms most profoundly influences the polemical trajectory of Galatians, but little is gained forcing a choice one way or another.

Paul describes those with faith in Christ as having been imbued with Christ's life through Spirit, putting them in correct standing before God ahead of the final judgment. Their position, or status, has been corrected so they might share the identical status of the risen Christ at the consummation (cf. 1 Cor 15:35–54). For these reasons, the present volume will not speak of justification and righteousness, but *rectification* and *right status*.[89]

---

87. As in the views of Tuomo Mannermaa and Veli-Matti Kärkkäinen—see Harink, "Setting it Right," 20–25.

88. In this work, revivification and freedom from slavery operate in tandem in Paul's presentation of rectification.

89. Right status is to be understood as "right standing before God;" right status and right standing are interchangeable. Various scholars have noted the importance of a status designation when referring to rectification and its effects. It was encouraging to see A. Andrew Das use the phrase "right status" in his commentary. See Das, *Galatians*,

Setting the Scene: Resurrection in Galatians

General Comments

This section will consider why scholars overlook the significance of resurrection in Galatians and propose that revivification is conceptually critical to the letter's argumentative thrust. I will survey scholarly comment on resurrection in Galatians and then conduct a semantic analysis of Galatians, demonstrating how revivification is a key element in the platform of Pauline thought.

The neglect of resurrection in Galatians scholarship largely stems from its singular mention of the raising of Christ. The context of Galatians does not lend itself naturally to a sustained interest in Jesus' resurrection. However, the death and resurrection of Jesus signal more than simply what happened to Jesus—they encapsulate how rectification would proceed. D. B. Bronson describes the altercation at the Antioch fellowship meal as a partial record of why the questions of individual and group identity had to be put in the great context of God's whole purpose for history.[90] The social conflict challenging the Galatians is merely a snapshot (Bronson's "partial record") of a much wider socio-religious and historical narrative, in which Jesus' resurrection is pivotal. The resurrection of Jesus stunned Israel's history, causing Paul to re-evaluate Israel's role in humanity's destiny. Galatians is a window on that re-evaluative process.

Paul's objective in Galatians was not merely to articulate a Law-independent path for Gentiles into the covenant family, but to illustrate why the external Law had no place in identifying the eschatological people of God. In Gal 6:14–15, the apostle states that the cosmos has suffered crucifixion to pave a way for new creation, and in this newly established order, ethnic distinction is irrelevant. As Hutson notes, Gal 6:15 echoes "no longer Jew or Greek" (3:28), the capstone of the letter's central theological argument.[91]

320–21. John Barclay's annotated translation of Gal 2:15–21 reflects his treatment of the language in terms of being counted worthy; see Barclay, *Paul and the Gift*, 371. For an authoritative and cogently argued challenge to the "New Perspective" centred view of reading δικαιόω language as primarily relational or associated with status in a covenant, see Irons, *The Righteousness of God*. Irons argues that the "righteouesness of God" refers to a righteous status being divinely declared as a gift, strictly in terms of the execution of judicial propriety. See further, Westerholm, *Justification Reconsidered*, 51–75. For a critique of Louis-Martyn (and my own position) which is in strong overall support of Westerholm and the translation of δικαιόω as "declare righteous," see Surburg, "Rectify or Justify?" 45–77.

90. Bronson, "Galatians and Jerusalem," 125.

91. Hutson, "Cross as Canon," 9.

Life/new creation coming from death/crucifixion is a model for the transforming activity of Jesus' resurrection in Galatians.

Philippians addresses some concerns in common with Galatians. Paul asserts that "we who worship by the Spirit, glory in Christ and do not trust in the flesh are the circumcision"—implying the *true* circumcision (Phil 3:3, NRSV). Having declared "a righteousness from God based on faith" was incomparably superior to his formerly cherished ethnic Jewish credentials, Paul continues that he wants

> . . . to know him and *the power of his resurrection* and the fellowship of his sufferings *being conformed to his death* if in some way *I might attain to the resurrection from among the dead* (Phil. 3:10–11).[92]

F. W. Beare is certainly correct in part that "the power of his resurrection" is the life-giving power of God, which he manifested in raising Christ from the dead, although "power" here is broadly synonymous with "life."[93] This transformative power is the risen life of Jesus, establishing "a righteousness of God and not of Law." That is, Paul interpreted the life with which God revivified the dead body of Jesus into a living, risen body as the same power imbuing Paul himself, transforming him from "a Pharisee in regards to the Law," to one for whom faith in Christ became the index of God's righteousness.[94] This thesis treats rectification in Galatians as a movement from death-to-life, that is, *a revivification event*.

Reasons for Marginalization of Resurrection in Galatians

For reasons to be briefly surveyed below, scholars have been largely reluctant to treat resurrection as more than a tangential theme in Galatians. Wright reasonably summarises:

> Resurrection is not a main theme in Galatians, but neither the overall argument nor the detail is comprehensible without it.[95]

Similarly Witherington states:

---

92. Cf. Eph 1:19–20.
93. Beare, *Philippians*, 122.
94. Phil 3:5, 9.
95. Wright, *Resurrection*, 219. Wright's comments in his more recent *magnum opus* on Paul suggest a possible progression. There he stresses that the Messiah's death and resurrection, the strange fulfilment of Israel's vocation and destiny, and the believer's participation in that death and resurrection forms the basis of the new reality of God's people—a people who have the same faith (pistis) as Jesus. See Wright, *Faithfulness*, 860.

> Galatians says very little about the resurrection of Jesus, but it is clear that what Jesus accomplished on the cross is very important to Paul's overall argument in this document . . .[96]

There are indeed obvious reasons for this:

1. Of the verbs associated with resurrection in Paul, ἀνίστημι appears five times, but never in Galatians; ἐγείρω appears forty-one times, but only once in Galatians. The compound verb ἐξεγείρω appears only in 1 Corinthians 6. The noun usually translated "resurrection," ἀνάστασις, appears eight times in Paul, but again, never in Galatians; the related *hapax legomenon* ἐξανάστασις is only in Phil 3:11.

2. There is more explicit resurrection theology in Romans and in the Corinthian correspondences. M. Bird correctly suggests that one of the benefits of New Perspective readings of Paul has been the increased tendency to see resurrection as integral to God's saving righteousness, yet in his study he confines his treatments to Romans 1–5, 1 Corinthians 15 and 1 Timothy 3.[97] D. Campbell in his epic assault on "justification theory" writes with reference to δικαιοῦντα in Rom 3:26 that it

> . . . denotes a divine speech act that effects some sort of release from Adamic captivity into a glorious new freedom—a saving eschatological meaning of release or liberation or deliverance *ultimately in terms of resurrection*.[98]

Campbell's attention rests largely with Romans. In J. D. Kirk's monograph, *Unlocking Romans*, he correctly notes how resurrection casts a shadow over the letter that is often longer than the particular verses that mention it explicitly; before delving into why, he invites readers to "note by way of contrast the relative paucity of references to resurrection in the otherwise quite similar Galatians."[99]

Dunn correctly observes the rhetorical impetus of Paul's emphasis on his commission by the risen and not the earthly Christ, but beyond this says only:

---

96. Witherington, *Grace in Galatia*, 76.
97. Bird, *Saving Righteousness*, 40.
98. Campbell, *Deliverance*, 672 (emphasis mine).
99. Kirk, *Unlocking*, 12.

> The fact that Paul makes no further mention of Christ's resurrection . . . is proof enough that it was part of the foundational creed, which united himself and his readers.[100]

Martyn accurately describes the resurrection as the "primal mark of God's identity" in Galatians. However, even he is content to conclude that the singular explicit reference to the resurrection in Galatians affirms that his opponents left this aspect of his gospel intact.[101]

3. Within historical treatments of the Christ event in Paul, particular pride of place goes to Jesus' death. This could reflect the importance of suffering in Paul's own career (2 Cor 11:23-28; cf. Gal 6:17) or perhaps the fact that there are more substantial Biblical precedents for suffering and dying heroic figures than dying and rising ones. Alternatively, it may be more broadly indicative of scepticism surrounding the historicity of the resurrection.

4. Furthermore, the older tendency to over assert the centrality of justification by faith in Pauline studies has pressed scholars to focus on the death aspect of the Christ event, for it is more naturally associated with justification than resurrection is (e.g., Gal 3:13; Rom 3:23-25).[102] One scholar writes of this imbalance:

> When these aspects of Pauline soteriology are emphasized at the expense of the richly multifaceted metaphorical world Paul uses to describe the work of God in the Messiah, the system is unable to deal with many of the Pauline "anomalies." . . . Rather than simply forensic and economic, we see that Paul's soteriology is cosmic, dramatic, eschatological, apocalyptic, relational and participatory.[103]

In summary, it is not difficult to comprehend the scholarly silence on resurrection in Galatians. The great Pauline treatises on resurrection (e.g., 1 Corinthians 15 or 1 Thessalonians 4-5) are predictably preoccupied with the resurrection of Jesus himself and/or the final resurrection, as are the scholarly treatments of them. In a letter like Galatians, with more obvious practical concerns, the resurrection of Jesus is marginalized. In such a fiercely polemical and seemingly urgent epistle, though, one would scarcely

---

100. Dunn, *Galatians*, 28-29.

101. Martyn, *Galatians*, 85. Paul's detractors may not have disputed the essential truth of the resurrection but if, as I suspect, Paul's reappraisal of the Law is a corollary of his resurrection theology, they would be at odds with Paul on this.

102. Rom 8:34 might imply the resurrection is more significant.

103. Liantonio, "Saved by His Life."

expect laboriously drawn out, rambling theological forays into the critical saving events of God. However, the importance of resurrection generally to Paul and the locus of the sole reference to it in Galatians should be cause to think more carefully about its relevance.

Life and Death Cognates in Galatians

Whilst Paul's traditional resurrection glossary is virtually absent from Galatians, a stock of death/crucifixion—life words are detectable, which at critical points in the argument contribute to the overall presentation of rectification.

- The noun "life (ζωή) appears once in Galatians (6:8).
- The cognate verb (ζάω) appears nine times in six verses (2:14; 2:19; 2:20 (x5); 3:11; 3:12; 5:25)—in comparison δικαιόω appears eight times in six verses; εὐαγγελίζω appears seven times in six verses; περιτέμνω appears six times in five verses; πιστεύω appears four times in the whole letter. (The respective cognates of the above verbs, however, *do* appear with greater frequency than the cognates of ζάω).
- The compound verb "to make alive" (Greek, ζῳοποιῆσαι) appears in 3:21.
- The verb "to die" (Greek, ἀποθνῄσκω) appears twice, at 2:19 and 2:21.
- The noun "dead" (Greek, νεκρός) appears in 1:1.
- The various cognates of the Greek σταυρόω ("crucify") appear four times in Galatians (2:20; 3:1; 5:24; 6:14); in 2:20, and 5:24 σταυρόω appears in a clause with ζάω.

A pervasive distribution of life-death language is also present in those Pauline texts which make more profuse reference to Jesus' resurrection. This language often combines to present aspects of Paul's ministry as revivification. This same proliferation of language further expresses aspects of believers' lives as revivification images—the new existence in which the Christian walks after metaphorically dying in baptism is depicted as new life (Rom 6:3–6); living by the Spirit and so overcoming sin is life coming from death (Rom 8:12–13); Paul can even speak of the believer's experience as a manifestation of Jesus' "risen" life because of the apostolic burden of carrying around Jesus' death (2 Cor 4:10).[104] As the next chapter will outline,

---

104. To "carry around the dying Jesus" is to suffer for the gospel in this context. See Oropeza, *Exploring Second Corinthians*, 485–86.

Galatians exhibits Jesus' resurrection as the superlative revivification act which then becomes paradigmatic for how God is rectifying humanity and creation. Romans and 2 Corinthians present Jesus' resurrection as a paradigm for the Christian walk and for Paul's ministry at particular moments, but the functionality of resurrection in Galatians may be explained as follows.

Paul's lexical choice of σταυρόω in conjunction with "life" or "new creation" language establishes an equivalence between Jesus' death and resurrection and the transformative impact of the Christ event upon Paul himself, believers in general and the world at large. Paul suffered "crucifixion" and lived to God; believers crucified the flesh and lived by virtue of Spirit; the world itself was crucified to believers and paved the way for new creation. The crucifixion and raising of Jesus was for Paul a functional template for God's transforming power—Jesus was crucified and resurrected; believers are crucified and revivified (rectification); the world is crucified and revivified (new creation). Rectification and new creation are the beginnings of resurrection in the present. Hence, though the resurrection of Jesus is only mentioned in Gal 1:1, it exerts its influence beyond this locus. The prescript of Galatians points to the rhetorical significance and paradigmatic influence of Jesus' resurrection on Paul's argument. What God had done completely to Jesus in resurrection, he initiated with believers in rectification.

The Concept of Revivification in Paul: "Life" and "Death" Cognates in Pauline Corpus

Key to Paul's lexico-semantic choices is the concept of *life*, through which Paul explains his rectification theology. We observe the following trends. There are thirty-seven occurrences of ζωή in the Pauline canon; ten are in the composite phrase 'eternal life.' If we take the twenty-seven occurrences of ζωή not in conjunction with 'eternal life', an interesting trend emerges:

- Nineteen of these twenty-seven occurrences of ζωή are in clauses where "life" is *directly* contrasted with "death" (Greek νέκρωσις, ἀποθνῄσκω, θάνατος and cognates) or "crucifixion."
- Of the eight which are not, four are from the undisputed Pauline canon.[105]

---

105. (i) Rom 5:18, where Paul contrasts "life" with "condemnation" (Greek, κατάκριμα). (ii) 1 Cor 15:19—a generic reference to existence (the hopelessness of "this life" if there is no resurrection). (iii) Phil. 2:16; 4:3; the phrases "Word of life" (2:16) and "Book of life" (4:3), which appear nowhere else in Paul.

In sum, with the exception of the composite phrase "eternal life" and the two anomalous Paulinisms in Philippians (2:16; 4:3), *the word "life" only appears twice in clauses where it is not directly contrasted with "death" in the undisputed Pauline canon.* These are (1) Rom 5:18, which itself (a) continues a line of thought from 5:17 which *does* contain a death motif and (b) contrasts δικαίωσιν ζωῆς with "condemnation" (κατάκριμα), which implies eschatological death; and (2) 1 Cor 15:19, where "life" conveys present physical existence. A comparable trend emerges in the distribution of the verbal cognates:

- There are some fifty-nine instances of the verb "to live" and cognates in Paul.
- *Thirty-four* of these are directly linked to death motifs, leaving *twenty-five* that are not.
- Of the twenty-five occurrences of "to live" not connected to a death motif, twenty-three are from the undisputed Pauline corpus.[106]
- Seven instances are participial forms merely describing something being physically alive.[107]
- Two use the euphemism "fallen asleep," which stands for death.[108]
- In Gal 3:11, 12 the verbs occur in OT quotations.
- This leaves 1 Cor 9:14; 2 Cor 13:4; Gal 2:14; 5:25; Phil 1:22; 1 Thess 3:8. The reference in 1 Cor 9:14 suggests "make a living;" the one in Gal 2:14, "living like a Gentile;" Phil 1:22 and 1 Thess 3:8 are generic references to "conducting a life" or just "being alive." 2 Corinthians 13:4 uses the verb "to live" twice—the first occurrence points to Jesus living in the power of God after his crucifixion (and uses σταυρόω). The second, (sarcastically) contrasts Paul's weakness with the divinely empowered "life" he needs to deal with the Corinthians.
- Galatians 5:25 does not employ a word for death, but is connected to a σταυρόω clause in 5:24.

Summing up, other than those places where "to live" appears either (a) in an OT citation, where Paul is quoting and not composing, or (b) in

---

106. There are five in Romans, four of which occur in OT citations—1:17; 9:26; 10:5; 14:11. The remaining one (12:1) contains the participle θυσίαν ζῶσαν ("living sacrifice"). Even here, the living nature of sacrifice contrasts the sacrificial lifestyle of believers with the Jewish sacrificial cult, which uses dead animals.

107. 1 Cor 15:45; 2 Cor 1:8; 3:3; 6:16; 1 Thess 1:9; 4:15, 17.

108. 1 Cor 7:39; 1 Thess 4:15.

a clause depicting merely a very generic expression of "existence," in the undisputed corpus *Paul always addresses the concept of "living" in conjunction with a "death" motif.*

Of course, any reference to life evokes the unspoken opposing idea of death. So Paul's statement that "to live is Christ" (Phil 1:21) may alone imply that "to die" has some other value ("not Christ?"). However, the addition of "to die is gain" demonstrates a far more deliberate conjunction between life and death. The evidence points to this being true of the broader lexical landscape of all Paul's genuine letters. The concept of life and death is of particular importance in how the apostle articulates salvation history and remedies aberrant theology and behaviour within the Pauline Jesus assemblies.

The emphasis in this analysis on the death/crucifixion-life lexicon in Galatians illuminates six distinct *revivification texts* in Galatians, which help demonstrate the centrality of resurrection to the argument of Galatians:

- Gal 1:1—The identity of God: the one raising Jesus from the dead.
- Gal 2:19-21—Paul's appropriation of his own rectification as co-crucifixion and living to God.
- Gal 3:19-21—The limitation of the Law: it lacks the capacity to make alive.
- Gal 5:24-25—Those who are "of Christ" have crucified the flesh and live by virtue of Spirit.
- Gal 6:8—Sowing to flesh yields death, sowing to Spirit yields eschatological life.
- Gal 6:14-15—The apocalyptic reconfiguration of Paul's cosmos—its crucifixion with respect to him and the concomitant establishment of a newly created order.[109]

The above texts form the core of this investigation; they bear witness to an established tradition of authors who depict great reversals or transformative experiences as life coming from death. In these instances, examples of which are outlined below, the vindication, restoration or rehabilitation of a person or community is articulated as a movement from death to life. *The critical difference for Paul is that he did not encounter an event which he articulated in terms of resurrection—Paul encountered a resurrection through which he articulated an event, namely, rectification.* In the prophetic texts, revivification images were essentially metaphorical conceptualizations, in which profound reversal dramas were likened to life coming to the dead.

---

109. We may safely assume that this is true for all believers.

That is, they understood and experienced one kind of thing in terms of another;[110] national disaster as "death" and rescue from it as "life." The situations in question had become so desperate, hopeless and overwhelming that the sufferers (God's people in various contexts) experienced two things. Firstly, a sense of emotional trauma so acute that the writers compared it to death (e.g., Job 16:16; Ps 116:3; Isa 9:2). Secondly, was the notion that remedying the disaster would involve a *volte-face* of such proportions that no amount of humanly driven military might, political *savoir faire* or municipal influence could effect it—it would be like bringing the dead to life (e.g., Ezek 37:1–14). Of course, behind these formulations was the writers' cognizance that only God's own intervention could resolve such problems.[111]

Accordingly, the revivification semantics of Galatians illustrate Paul's critical synthesis of the death-to-life event of Jesus' resurrection and the death-to-life stories of Israel's narrative history. The rest of the introductory section aims to address more broadly how deeply embedded the composite notion of death and life appears in the narration of Israel's relationship with her God. It will further suggest how the same has influenced Paul's writing; Paul appears to reckon that God's great act of resurrecting Jesus contextualized the episodes of rescue, restoration, vindication and victory in the ancient texts and traditions. As Paul relates divine action within his own ministry to realize the purposes of God, he commonly employs revivification language and imagery.

The bulk of this study will consider how this language and imagery in Galatians evidences Paul's conversance with the revivification tradition in the ancient texts and how it forms the basis of his counter-thesis regarding Gentile Torah observance. The next section begins with a selection of encounters illustrating the notion of divine action in vindication and rescue as revivification acts.

Revivification in Ancient Literature

Vindication as Resurrection

There is an established tradition of Jewish heroes for whom resurrection spelled vindication. This is how Paul most likely understood the resurrection of Jesus. This is not an exhaustive treatment, but aims only to situate Paul within a recognizable tradition of thought.

---

110. This definition of metaphor is from Lakoff and Johnson, *Metaphors*, 5.

111. Paul's recounting of the affliction he and his colleagues faced in Asia in 2 Cor 1:8–10 captures both of these ideas perfectly.

Some commentators see Deutero-Isaiah's servant vindicated through resurrection, as Barry notes of Isa 53:10:

> One can logically conclude from the context of the passage that it is because of the servant's obedience to Yahweh's will—resulting in his ultimate fulfilment of the office of servant—that he is resurrected and blessed.[112]

The Maccabean martyrs looked forward to the revivification of their bodies as vindication for their adherence to Law in the face of Hellenizing pressure:[113]

> with his blood now completely drained from him, he tore out his entrails, took them in both hands and hurled them at the crowd, calling upon the Lord of life and spirit to give them back to him again. This was the manner of his death (2 *Macc.* 14:36, NRSV).

The mother of seven sons, martyred in a single day for defying Antiochus IV, said of her heroic progeny:

> I do not know how you came into being in my womb. It was not I who gave you life and breath ... Therefore the Creator of the world ... will in his mercy give life and breath back to you again, since you now forget yourselves for the sake of his laws (2 *Macc.* 7:22–23, NRSV).

Identical sentiments accompany their resistance when Antiochus tempted the brothers to dine on pork, prohibited by Torah:

> And when he was at his last breath, [the second brother] said, "You accursed wretch, you dismiss us from this present life, but the King of the universe will raise us up to an everlasting renewal of life, because we have died for his laws." (2 *Macc.* 7:9)

Testament of Judah 25:4 reads:

> And they who have died in grief shall arise in joy ... and they who are put to death for the Lord's sake shall awake to life.[114]

Similarly, the author of the *Wisdom of Solomon* treats vindication for righteousness as resurrection:

---

112. Barry, *Resurrected Servant*, 70.
113. 2 *Macc.* 14:38.
114. Trans. R. H. Charles.

> But the souls of the righteous are in the hand of God ... In the eyes of the foolish they seemed to have died ... but they are at peace. For, though in the sight of others they were punished, their hope is full of immortality (*Wisdom of Solomon* 3:1–4, NRSV).

It seems most likely that this ideology lies behind the martyr theology of the *Assumption of Moses*:

> Let us fast for the space of three days and on the fourth let us go into a cave which is in the field, and let us die rather than transgress the commands of the Lord of Lords, the God of our fathers. For if we do this and die, our blood shall be avenged before the Lord. And then His kingdom shall appear throughout all His creation ... (*Assumption of Moses* 9:6–10:1)

Josephus describes the renewed existence of those who are willing to die for the preservation of the divine Law:

> ... but every good man has his own conscience bearing witness to himself, and by virtue of our legislator's prophetic spirit, and of the firm security God himself affords such a one; he believes that God has made this grant to those that observe these laws, even though they be obliged readily to die for them, that they shall come into being again, and at a certain revolution of things receive a better life than they had enjoyed before.[115]

Similarly, Paul envisioned God as the one who revives the dead (Gal 1:1). His manipulation of Hos 13:14b (LXX) in 1 Cor 15:55 expresses how resurrection is vindication from death.[116] Hosea 13:14b reads "from the hand of Hades I will deliver (ῥύσομαι) them and from death I will ransom (λυτρώσομαι) them; where 'death,' is your penalty? Where, 'Hades' is your thorn-sting"?[117]

Though Paul does not use ῥύομαι or λυτρόω in Galatians, the scheme of redemption from death is implicit.[118] Jesus gave himself over to rescue (ἐξαιρέω) humanity.[119] Jesus' crucifixion redeemed (ἐξαγοράζω) Israel from the curse of the Law (death).[120] Hosea 13 frames the deliverance from

---

115. Josephus, *Against Apion* 2:218.
116. Throughout book, Alfred Rahlfs edition of LXX is used.
117. Author's translation.
118. Λυτρόω only appears in Tit. 2:14 in Paul; ῥύομαι appears in Rom 7:24; 11:26; 15:31; 2 Cor 1:10 (x3); Col 1:13; 1 Thess 1:10; 2 Thess 3:2; 2 Tim 3:11; 4:17, 18.
119. Gal 1:4.
120. Gal 3:13.

Assyrian subjugation in terms of the Exodus—Israel's exile is the "death penalty" from which God will rescue her. Paul treats Jesus' resurrection as his rescue from the death penalty of crucifixion. A body of tradition linking Israel's freedom from captivity with life coming from death exists within her sacred literature—an evaluation of this, and the associated resonances with Paul, follows below.

Restoration/Deliverance as Resurrection

The above idea is present in ancient Jewish and even Greco-Roman tradition. The restoration prophecies are often "resurrection-based" declarations. The prophets also narrated freedom from national captivity as a "greater Exodus" experience—this section will end with an account of the first Exodus as a resurrection movement.

Isaiah 26:19

> Your dead shall live, their corpses shall rise. O dwellers in the dust, awake and sing for joy! (Isa 26:19, NRSV).

Most scholars posit that Isaiah 24–27 is unoriginal and cannot agree on its genre or its influence on final resurrection ideology.[121] Collins is among those arguing that Isaiah 26:19 reflects the same view espoused in Ezekiel 37—restoration, which is as miraculous as resurrection.[122] In contrast, J. F. Sawyer writes that only a Sadducee could deny it referred to the resurrection of the dead.[123] Levenson is probably correct to suggest that the debate is somewhat misleading.[124]

Either way this text illustrates deliverance as resurrection. Indeed, Paul's eschatological calendar draws upon Isa 25:8 in 1 Cor 15:54—death is swallowed up in victory.[125] Paul writes that "death is the last enemy to be destroyed" (1 Cor 15:26). Even if Isaiah had only political deliverance in view,

---

121. For a brief survey, see Skjoldal, "Isaiah 24–27," 163–7; see also Kim, *City in Isaiah 24–27*, 9–11.

122. Collins, *Daniel*, 395, cited from Levenson, *Resurrection*, 199.

123. Sawyer, "Hebrew Words," 234.

124. Levenson, *Resurrection*, 200; he cites R. Martin Achard as an example of a scholar who also sees Isa 26:19 pointing to a future resurrection of individuals.

125. Paul quotes a Hebrew form; the LXX awkwardly suggests that *death* has done the swallowing. Cf. Hos 13:14.

readers like Paul saw in his writing shadows of eschatological resurrection, nuanced though they were by the Christ event.

Isaiah 57:15–16

> This is what the highest Lord says . . . the highest Lord . . . who relieves the weak souls . . . giving patience and life to the broken-hearted. I will not take vengeance on you forever nor through all will I be angry with you, for my Spirit will go out before me and I made every breath (Isa 57:15–16, LXX).[126]

In Beale's analysis of Isa 57:15–19 as background for Gal 5:22, he observes the resurrection imagery, noting:

> The promise of resurrection is explained further in 57:16a through the affirmation that God "will not take vengeance on you forever," and he will not "be always angry with you." This prophecy is grounded in the assurance that "my Spirit will go forth from me, and I have created all breath."[127]

He notes that the crucifixion-resurrection pattern of Gal 5:24–25 may echo the "death-to-life" pattern of Isa 57:15–16.[128] The following observations press Beale's analysis further. The divine impetus to give life to the broken hearted (συντετριμμένοις τὴν καρδίαν) has connections with Gal 4:6 (which Beale points to) but more importantly for Paul's purposes, with Gal 3:21.[129] If the Law could produce eschatological life, right status would be from Law. God declares in Isa 57:16, "for my Spirit will go out before me and I made (ἐποίησα) every breath" (πνοὴν πᾶσαν). God's Spirit goes forth from him (as Ezek 36:27) and God through Spirit is author of "every breath." This validates Gal 3:21—the Law is impotent to make alive, for every life-giving breath is from the Spirit.

Psalter

"Revival" is a very common theme in the Psalms, denoting rescue from affliction. The poets typically employ ζάω or ζωοποιέω to convey their trust

---

126. Author's translation.
127. Beale, "Fruit of the Spirit," 21.
128. Ibid., 23; this reading reflects the MT more closely than the LXX.
129. Beale also correctly notes that Ps 104:30 is closer to Gal 4:6 lexically than Isa 57:16; ibid., 8.

in God's providence to deliver.[130] Below are examples, followed by a longer treatment of Psalm 142 (LXX).[131]

> So many are the terrible afflictions you have shown me and turning around you made me alive (ἐζωοποίησάς) and from the bottomless earth again you lead me up (Ps 70:20, LXX).
>
> And we will never turn aside from you, and you will make us alive (ζωώσεις) and we will call upon your name (Ps 79:18, LXX).
>
> You will not be angry with us forever or stretch out your wrath from generation to generation; you God, turning around will make us alive (ζωώσεις) . . . (Ps 84:5–6, LXX).
>
> If I might be in the midst of affliction, you will make me live (ζήσεις) . . . and your right hand saves me (Ps 137:7, LXX).

Psalm 143 has become a significant passage in the debate over πίστις Χριστοῦ and the definition of the righteousness of God in Romans in light of Käsemann's critique of Luther's imputed righteousness formula.[132] Paul cites a version of Ps 143:2 (LXX Ps 142:2) in Gal 2:16 and Rom 3:20 to demonstrate that no one is right before God.

The LXX of Ps 142:10–11 reads:

> δίδαξόν με τοῦ ποιεῖν τὸ θέλημά σου, ὅτι σὺ εἶ ὁ θεός μου, τὸ πνεῦμά σου τὸ ἀγαθὸν ὁδηγήσει με ἐν γῇ εὐθείᾳ. ἕνεκα τοῦ ὀνόματός σου, κύριε, ζήσεις με, ἐν τῇ δικαιοσύνῃ σου ἐξάξεις ἐκ θλίψεως τὴν ψυχήν μου

In Ezek 36:27, God promises to place his Spirit in the people in order that they might continue in his statutes, but prefaces this in vv. 21–23 that he does this for the sake of his name.[133] The Psalmist prays for God to make him alive for the sake of God's name (Ps 142:11).

The two stanzas of Ps 142:10–11 work in parallel as follows (a corresponding to a' and b to b')

(a) Teach me to do your will . . . because you are my *God* (142:10a-b)

(a') You will *make me alive* . . . for the sake of your name *Lord* (142:11a-b)

---

130. The Psalms are generally replete with revivification imagery, variously symbolizing national restoration, personal reawakening, and vindication. See Street, *Vine and the Son of Man*, 34–35, 41–46, 135; McCann, Jr., *Theological Introduction*, 28–30.

131. In this section, the Septuagintal enumeration of the Psalms will apply; the translations are the author's unless specified.

132. Käsemann, *NT Questions*, 168–82; see further Hays, "Psalm 143," 107–15.

133. Cf. Ezek 36:32.

(b) Your good Spirit will *lead* (ὁδηγήσει) me on the straight land (142:10c)

(b') In your righteousness you will *lead* (ἐξάξεις) my soul forth from affliction (142:11c)[134]

Though there are different words for "lead" in v. 10 and v. 11, 142:10c and 142:11c make equivalent statements—the Spirit leads the Psalmist on the straight land and, in God's righteousness, leads him out of affliction (b/b'). This "leading" is described as deliverance in Ps 142:9, using ἐξαιρέω (as in Gal 1:4). This corresponds to a "making alive" by which the Psalmist is taught to do God's will (a/a'). Paul in Gal 5:18a employs ἄγω to depict the Spirit's leading. The Psalmist's term, ἐξάγω, is common Exodus language in the OT.[135] For Paul, the Spirit's leading means one is not under Torah, for Spirit directs community ethics. For Paul, the Psalmist (and Ezekiel), part of Spirit's work is to oversee obedience to divine commands. Over and against the myriad explanations of Paul's deployment of Ps 142:2 (LXX), the present volume associates it with the common revivification tradition in Galatians and the Psalter—rectification in the former and vindication/rescue in the latter.

So when Paul cites Ps 142:2 (LXX) in Gal 2:16 to establish that rectification is Torah-independent, he makes effectively the same point he makes in Gal 5:18 and indeed at various points in Galatians—the Spirit actualises amidst the community what Law never could. The Psalmist cries out for divine intervention because he is so overwhelmed by his enemies that he is "dead" (see esp. Ps 142: 3, 7, 11, LXX). Paul's point is that faith and not works of Torah will rectify (Gal 2:16) because only faith in Christ brings forth the Spirit who makes alive, which Law cannot (3:21).

In sum, Paul's citation of Ps 142:2 (LXX) in Gal 2:16 supports his assertion that no one will be made right before God, except by divine action through the Spirit. The Psalmist describes the torment from which he craves rescue: " . . . the enemy has closely persecuted my soul; he brought my life (ζωήν μου) down to the ground; he made me sit in dark places, as those dead for an age (ὡς νεκροὺς αἰῶνος)" (Ps 142:3). He entreats God that in God's righteousness he will be revivified; this is the logic behind the polemic of Galatians. Revivification is the power by which God sets people right before him.

---

134. Various treatments of Ps 142:10 (LXX) are offered by Morales, *Spirit*, 149–50 and Wilder, *Echoes*, 130–38.

135. Exod 32:1; Deut 4:37; 9:12; Jer 31:32.

Hosea 6:2

Hosea 5 ends by foreshadowing the cause of the exile to Assyria; 5:13 sees the prophet castigate the people for appealing to the King of Assyria for help. The very appeal itself demonstrated a flagrant lack of trust in Yahweh, symbolic of Israel's wider apostasy. Assyria after all could not heal (ἰάομαι) them.

In 6:1, Hosea proclaims that God *can* heal. There are two contrasts in 6:1—snatched/will heal; beaten/will bandage up. These represent reversals, brought into full expression in the ultimate reversal image in 6:2—*resurrection*. The Hebrew describes the effects after two days as "he (God) will make us live" (יְחַיֵּנוּ—lit. "cause us to be").[136] The LXX replaces make us "live" with make us "healthy" (ὑγιάζομαι). Relating the third day activity in 6:2b, the LXX reflects the Hebrew text more faithfully:

... ἐν τῇ ἡμέρᾳ τῇ τρίτῃ ἀναστησόμεθα καὶ ζησόμεθα ἐνώπιον αὐτοῦ.[137]

In 6:3 the prophet predicts that at this time of great healing and life that "we will know and we will pursue the knowledge of the Lord."[138] Hosea 6:2–3 belongs with the tradition of freedom from captivity narratives in terms of resurrection (like Ezek 37:1–14 and Isa 26:17–19). Hosea 13:14 further depicts the release from Assyrian captivity as redemption from death. Similar resurrection ideology is found in Hos 14:8, though the LXX reads awkwardly—"they will return and they will sit under each one's shelter, *they will live* and they will be drunk with grain and they will plant flowers as a memorial of it as wine of Lebanon."[139] The planting of flowers and abundance of grain all add to the picture of new life in restoration.

Jonah

Death is often metaphorized in Jewish texts as the helplessness of drowning or being submerged and overwhelmed by water.[140] Correspondingly,

---

136. Piel imperfect of *hayah*.

137. The third day tradition is ubiquitous in the rabbinic texts and may well have influenced the early Christian confession enshrined in 1 Cor 15:4.

138. Cf. Jer 31:34.

139. "They who live under his shadow shall return" in the Hebrew text; furthermore, the Hebrew has no word for drunk in Hos 14:8.

140. Exod 14:48; cf. Isa 43:2; see esp. Pss 18:4–5; 69:1–2; cf. Ps 32:6; Rom 6:3–4.

revivification imagery is seen in Christian texts depicting the rite of baptism.[141] The words of Jonah's prayer fit the former; he sits in the bowels of the great fish and relays that "I cried out in my affliction to the Lord my God and he heard me, from the bowels of Hades you heard the shrieking of my voice."[142] Broad scholarly consensus sees Jonah's prayer as a later insertion by either the author or a redactor.[143] Nonetheless, Jonah considered his affliction equivalent to sitting in Hades (שְׁאוֹל).

In Jonah 2:7 (LXX) the author pleads κατέβην εἰς γῆν, ἧς οἱ μοχλοὶ αὐτῆς κάτοχοι αἰώνιοι, καὶ ἀναβήτω φθορὰ ζωῆς μου, κύριε ὁ θεός μου.

Jonah's entreaty is that God "brings up the corruption of his life;" the sole use of "life" in Galatians contrasts the eschatological destiny of those who sow to the Spirit with those who sow to the flesh. Those so sowing reap φθορὰ in Paul's agrarian metaphor. The synoptic tradition uses Jonah's plight to interpret the death and resurrection of Jesus.[144]

1 QH 19:10-14

The entire question of resurrection belief at Qumran is disputed. Vermes' early translations and commentaries denied that resurrection played any part in Essene eschatology.[145] Collins argued that the Teacher of Righteousness would be resurrected.[146] Jassen notes the argument of Émile Puech that the Qumran writings attest to a widespread belief in bodily resurrection.[147] For now, we may note the evidence of two Qumran texts. In the Thanksgiving Hymns, deliverance from the world and into the community is portrayed as revivification:

> For the sake of your glory; You have purified man of sin that he may be made holy for you, with no abominable uncleanness and no guilty wickedness; that he may be one [with] the children of your truth and partake of the lot of your Holy Ones; that bodies gnawed by worms may be raised from the dust (1 QH 19:10-14).[148]

---

141. Rom 6:1-7; Col 2:12; 1 Pet 3:20-22; Justin Martyr, *Dialogue with Trypho* 138:1-2.

142. Jonah 2:3 (LXX).

143. See Wolff, *Jonah*, 40; see further Alexander, "Jonah," 35-59.

144. Matt 12:39-41; 16:4; Luke 11:29-32.

145. Vermes, *Scrolls*, 56.

146. Collins, *Sceptre and the Star*, 102-12.

147. Jassen, "Religion in the Dead Sea Scrolls," 15.

148. In earlier editions of the English translations, this was formerly *1 QH* 11:19-23.

4Q521

The *Biblical Archaeology Review* published the "Messianic Apocalypse" (*4Q521*) in 1992. The following summary of details by Vermes illustrates those facets of *4Q521* pertinent to this thesis:

> The poem incorporates Ps 146:6–7 and Isa 61:1 ... As in the Gospels, healing and resurrection are linked to the idea of the Kingdom of God. Line 12 furnishes the most explicit evidence concerning the raising of the dead. Fragment 7, line 6 ... [refers] to God as "He who revives the dead of His people."[149]

Below is Vermes' translation of the key verses:

> [the hea]vens and the earth will listen to His Messiah, and none therein will stray from the commandments of the holy ones ...
>
> For the Lord will consider the pious (Hasidim) and call the righteous by name.
>
> Over the poor His spirit will hover and will renew the faithful with His power.
>
> He who liberates the captives, restores sight to the blind, straightens the b[ent] (Ps 146:7–8)
>
> For He will heal the wounded, and revive the dead and bring good news to the poor (Isa 61:1).

Firstly, the text incorporates two Biblical passages praising the God who restores Israel—Psalm 146 and Isaiah 61. *4Q521* is clearly dependent on Psalm 146, though this Psalm does not mention a Messiah.[150] More pertinently, there is resurrection imagery in both texts depicting God as reviver of the dead:

> The LORD *lifts up* (זֹקֵף) those who are bowed down ... (Ps 146:8b, NRSV).[151] They shall build up the ancient ruins, they shall *raise up* (קָם) the former devastations ... (Isa 61:4a NRSV) ... For as the earth brings forth its shoots, and as a garden causes what is sown in it to *spring up*, (יַצְמִיחַ) so the Lord GOD will cause righteousness and praise to *spring up* (יַצְמִיחַ) before all the nations (61:11).[152]

Both Biblical passages prophesy that God will heal the socially and physically marginalized in the great restoration:

---

149. Vermes, *Scrolls*, 244.
150. Collins, "Messianism and the Dead Sea Scrolls," 113.
151. Cf. Ps 145:14.
152. Same verb as Isa 44:4 above.

> The spirit of the Lord GOD is upon me ... he has sent me to bring good news to the oppressed, to bind up the brokenhearted, to proclaim liberty to the captives, and release to the prisoners ... (Isa 61:1).
>
> ... who executes justice for the oppressed; who gives food to the hungry. The LORD sets the prisoners free; the LORD opens the eyes of the blind. The LORD lifts up those who are bowed down; the LORD loves the righteous. The LORD watches over the strangers; he upholds the orphan and the widow ... (Ps 146:7–9b)

Where *4Q521* cites Isa 61:1 the author has added a description of God as the one who revives the dead. Vermes may be correct in linking this with actual resurrection, but the co-text of restoration blessings makes this unlikely. The depiction of God resonates with Gal 1:1 and the *Amidah*.

The Amidah

> You, O Lord, are mighty forever, *you revive the dead*, you have the power to save. You sustain the living with loving-kindness, you *revive the dead* with great mercy, you support the falling, heal the sick, set free the bound and keep faith with those who sleep in the dust. Who is like you, O doer of mighty acts? Who resembles you, *a king who puts to death and restores to life*, and causes salvation to flourish? And *you are certain to revive the dead*. Blessed are you, O Lord, who revives the dead.[153]

The Hebrew "revive the dead" in the *Amidah* is virtually identical to the addition made to the interpolation of Isa 61:1 in *4Q521*. Furthermore, the prayer incorporates a similar tradition of restorative blessings offered to the sick and the captives found in *4Q521*, Isaiah 61 and Psalm 146. (Commentators point to how Jesus' response to the deputation from the imprisoned John the Baptizer closely resembles *4Q521*).[154] Galatians 1:1 similarly attests to a Pauline conceptualization of God's activity as "reviver of the dead." For Paul, emphasizing freedom and revivification in Galatians, as for the composers of the *Amidah* and *4Q521*, the God of resurrection is the God who

---

153. Second Benediction, *The God of Nature*, trans. David Bivin, http://www.cbn.com/spirituallife/BibleStudyAndTheology/jewishroots/Amidah_Prayer_Bivin.aspx; Charlesworth has argued on the strength of the similarities between the *Amidah* and 4Q521 that at least some members of the Qumran community said the prayers. See Charlesworth, "Challenging the Consensus," 121.

154. Matt 11:5; Luke 7:22; see Evans, "Messianic Hopes," 25; Brooke, "Shared Intertextual Interpretations."

ends the exile and restores the fortunes of the people. It is not serendipity that the common blessing in Isaiah 61, Psalm 146, the *Amidah* and *4Q521* is freedom for captives—the principal feature of restoration characterized by OT resurrection portraits and a significant aspect of rectification in Galatians.

Paul's acquaintance with the above texts cannot be established with any precision, but the evidence seems sufficiently pervasive to suggest a common ideological matrix from which all the authors drew—that the reversal of Israel's fortunes required so complete a social, religious and political overhaul it was, symbolically, like resurrection. *Informed by this view, Paul, confronted with God's literal raising of Jesus, saw the actualization of God's life-giving restoration.* It is very likely that the prophetic portrait of Israel's freedom being concretized in Jesus' death and resurrection is what ultimately convinced Paul that Jesus was Israel's Christ. Jesus' resurrection, that is, *his rectification*, became the blueprint for the rectification of humanity and the cosmos.

Luke 15:32

Though not completely unproblematic, Wright's basic thesis regarding the parable of the lost son is correct—it retells Israel's restoration from exile.[155] The critical clause, however, comes in Luke 15:32:

εὐφρανθῆναι δὲ καὶ χαρῆναι ἔδει, ὅτι ὁ ἀδελφός σου οὗτος νεκρὸς ἦν καὶ ἔζησε, καὶ ἀπολωλὼς ἦν καὶ εὑρέθη

It was necessary to be joyful and to be happy because this brother of yours *was dead and he lived*, and having (been) lost was found.

Luke draws the ancient ideas into illuminating and ironic juxtaposition. The young runaway becomes estranged from his father and enslaved by pagan overlords and this is Israel's history in brief. Luke captures the end of the lad's exile, writing he "was dead and lived." Ironically, the merriment in the renegade son's "resurrection" foreshadows the rejoicing at Jesus' resurrection, as Luke later records (embodying Ps 15:9–11, LXX).[156]

> therefore my heart was glad, and my tongue *rejoiced*; moreover *my flesh will live* in hope. For you will not abandon my soul to Hades, or let your Holy One experience corruption. You have

---

155. Wright, *Victory*, 126–27.
156. MT, Ps 16:9–11.

made known to me the *ways of life*; you will make me full of gladness with your presence.[157]

Below is evidence from secular Greco-Roman authors that banishments from their home environments were narrated as deaths, and their restoration to the community, as "life" or "rebirth."

Secular Texts Depicting Exile and Restoration as Life and Death

Ovid

The first century BCE poet, Ovid, was exiled to Tomis when he was 50. Ovid himself said he was exiled because he wrote "amorous verses" and was an unwitting spectator of the guilt of others.[158] He described one of his poems as "a poem and a mistake"[159] and "a crime worse than murder."[160] In the two works he wrote during his banishment, *Tristia* and *Epistulae ex Ponto*, Ovid described his exile as a *death*. Sabine Grebe writes that Ovid saw his banishment as a "living death" because for Ovid exile involved a "life" in the unknown on the other side of the boundary of what was familiar and known to him. The unknown was alien to him, as unknowable as death.[161] Writing to Paulus Fabius Maximus of his life in exile Ovid wrote:

> My tears are endless, unless numbness checks them: and a lethargy like death grips my thoughts.[162]

One of the key themes in *Tristia* is the pain of having left his loved ones; he associates leaving his wife and friends with death.[163] Ovid lamented the distance that exile put between him and his wife saying

> Don't lacerate your cheeks or tear your hair, it's not now, for a first time, I'm taken from you, *mea lux*. Think that I perished when I lost my native land: that was an earlier and a deeper death.[164]

---

157. Acts 2:26–28.
158. Ovid, *Epistulae ex Ponto* 2.2. 9–14.
159. Ovid, *Tristia* 2.207.
160. Ovid, *Epistulae ex Ponto* 2.9.72.
161. Grebe, "Living Death," 492.
162. Ovid, *Epistulae ex Ponto* 1.2.26–27.
163. Grebe, "Living Death," 492.
164. Ovid, *Tristia* 3.3.56.

He frequently describes his fear of the unknown corner he was banished to as death and a place where he is susceptible to mortal dangers. Grebe further notes that one significant feature of this unknown world is one's inability to communicate because one does not speak the native language.[165] The linguistic problem Ovid faced, reinforced his image of Tomis as the unknown and unknowable world, not unlike death.[166]

Exile was the turning point in Ovid's life; at home in Rome he had been vibrant and intellectually alive, but in Tomis, as Grebe has it

> ... he became culturally and socially dead, although he remained biologically alive. Banishment signified, for Ovid, that he had crossed the boundary between life (Rome) and death (Tomis)...Rome represents safety, civilization, a warm climate, a pleasing aesthetic, and sophistication. Tomis serves as a metaphor for hostility, barbarism, an icy climate, physical ugliness, and savagery... since Rome means life for Ovid ... Tomis signifies death.[167]

It is also interesting that Ovid portrays Augustus as master over life and death:

> My life was spared, your anger stopped short of death, O Prince, how sparingly you used your powers![168]

Grebe relates that Ovid's comparison of his exile with death makes clear to the reader that Augustus could be a fatal threat to the personal security of any Roman at any time.[169]

Cicero

Plutarch tells us that Ovid's friend Cicero's boasting, disregard for propriety and excessive ambition landed him in exile. Ultimately, Plutarch writes, Cicero took jokes too far, and his increasing unpopularity resulted in exile in 58 BCE.[170] In Bruni's biography, he adds that self-praise was a factor; but

---

165. Grebe, "Living Death," 496; Ovid complains that nobody understands him (*Tristia* 5.10.37) and "there's not a single person in the population who speaks Latin—even one or two common words" (*Tristia* 5.7.53–54).

166. Ibid.

167. Ibid., 499.

168. Ovid Tristia 2:120ff, trans. A. S. Kline. http://www.poetryintranslation.com/PITBR/Latin/OvidTristiaBkTwo.htm.

169. Grebe, "Living Death," 508.

170. Plutarch, *Life of Cicero*, 143.

Bruni blames those who, alarmed at the extent of Cicero's new found power and influence, began to plot against him.[171]

In 56 BCE, Cicero returned from exile and to the restoration of his dignities and honours. He wrote of this to his friend Atticus:

> My friends' letters summon me to a triumph—a thing which, in view of the resuscitation of my reputation, I do not think I ought to neglect. Wherefore, my dear Atticus, do begin to wish it too, that I may look somewhat less foolish.[172]

Cicero imported the Greek word παλιγγενεσία, translated "resuscitation" above, to describe the restoration of all he considered lost in his exile.[173] The word is a compound of πάλιν and γένεσις which implies "born again," or "new genesis" either in the sense of (a) "return to existence," "coming back from death to life," or of (b) "renewal to a higher existence," "regeneration."[174] Though widely attested in classical literature, it appears only twice in the NT (Matt 19:28; Tit 3:5).[175]

Notably Josephus writing of the restoration from Babylon writes:

> who, when they heard the same, gave thanks also to God that he restored the land of their forefathers to them again. So they ... kept a festival, for the rebuilding and restoration (παλιγγενεσία) of their country.[176]

Epictetus

The Stoic philosopher Epictetus, himself more likely to have been personally acquainted with the ancient Jesus community than his colleague Seneca, writes:

> Let death and exile, and all other things which appear terrible be daily before your eyes, but chiefly death, and you will never entertain any abject thought, nor too eagerly covet anything.[177]

---

171. Gary Ianziti, "A Life in Politics," 53.

172. Cicero *Ad Atticum* 6:6 trans. Shuckburgh, 1908. http://www.perseus.tufts.edu/hopper/text?doc=Cic.+Att.+6.6&fromdoc=Perseus%3Atext%3A1999.02.0008.

173. Interestingly, Cicero never refers to his banishment as an exile. See Robinson, "Cicero's References," 475, 480.

174. Büchsel, "παλιγγενεσία," *TDNT*, 686.

175. It never appears in the LXX, though πάλιν γίνεσθα occurs at Job 14:14.

176. Josephus, *Ant.* 9.3.9; cf. *Ant.* 2:66 where Josephus refers to the restoration from exile and re-establishment of his people ἀνάκτησιν καὶ παλιγγενεσίαν τῆς πατρίδος.

177. Epictetus, *Enchiridion* 21.

Like most Stoic thinkers, Epictetus held that once a life held out no further potential for virtuous action, suicide was a viable option. Death itself was not such a terrible pathway, as he infers in his *Discourses*: "It is not death or pain that is to be feared, but the fear of pain or death."[178]

This makes all the more interesting the correspondence he draws between death and exile, which he also repeats in the *Discourses:* "If we were afraid not of death or exile, but of fear itself, we should have studied not to fall into what appears to us to be evil."[179]

Euripides

This excerpt is the chorus from Euripides's *The Medea*:

> O country and home, never, may I be without you, living a hopeless life, hard to pass through and painful; most pitiable of all. Let Death first lay me low and death free me from this daylight. There is no sorrow above the loss of a native land.

As Euripides captures, these sentiments seem typical of much classical Greco-Roman literature—exile is appropriately described as socio-political *death*. As some scholars suggest, it is a fate even worse than death.[180]

The Exodus as Resurrection

Though Paul never mentions Egypt, the influence of Exodus ideology and typology on his thought is difficult to overlook, and scholars have developed the theme with increasingly creative ingenuity.[181] Davies considers that Paul obviously regards the great deliverance at the Exodus and its accompaniments as the prototype of the mighty acts of God in Christ.[182]

Below are three lines of reasoning by which Paul (and his contemporary believing co-religionists) would consider the Exodus and the resurrection of Jesus as correlated events, permitting him to contextualize rectification in terms of freedom from captivity and revivification as in Galatians. There

---

178. Epictetus, *Discourses* 2.1.13.

179. Ibid., 2.16.19.

180. Gorman, "Poets, Playwrights, and the Politics of Exile," 411.

181. Wright, "Letter to the Romans," 585; Keesmaat shows how Galatians even uses the Exodus to undermine itself by linking Law with slavery—see Keesmaat, *Paul and His Story,* 224; Holland, *Contours of Pauline Theology,* 297–300.

182. Davies, *Paul and Rabbinic Judaism,* 105; Davies points to 1 Cor. 5:6–8; 10:1ff; 15:20 and 2 Cor 3:1–17 to this end.

is firstly evidence from Paul's own letters which highlight theological connections. Secondly, there are aspects of the narrative portrayal of the Exodus itself. Thirdly, as Davies above, is Paul's identification of God in terms of momentous saving act.

The Exodus in Paul's Letters

Wright has argued convincingly that the Exodus lies behind the baptism imagery of Romans 6 which is expounded as liberation of a slave.[183] This imagery is explicit in 1 Cor 10:2, when the Corinthians' rebellion is likened to the Israelites who were "baptized" in the Red Sea—1 Cor 15:54–57 also forms part of this Exodus tapestry. Here, Paul draws on two texts celebrating freedom from captivity as the subduing of death, in order to proclaim the victory of final resurrection. Paul is speaking of the defeat of death itself and not of restoration from exile; however, he draws on the conclusive declarations of two prophets speaking directly about rescue from exile, for, as will become clear, Paul saw a connection between divine acts of revivification after encountering the resurrected Messiah.

Paul's citations in 1 Cor 15:54–57 do not correspond with any known version of Isa 25:8 or Hosea 13:14 precisely—contextually, his synthesis of the texts is precisely to show that death has been defeated. It no longer has its "sting," i.e., sin, because Jesus' death has dismantled sin's stronghold. The question of death's sting is raised in the Hosea citation which employs redemption language:

> 14 ἐκ χειρὸς ᾅδου ῥύσομαι αὐτοὺς καὶ ἐκ θανάτου λυτρώσομαι αὐτούς, ποῦ ἡ δίκη σου, θάνατε; ποῦ τὸ κέντρον σου, ᾅδη; παράκλησις κέκρυπται ἀπὸ ὀφθαλμῶν μου

> From the hand of Hades I will rescue them and from death I will redeem them; death where is your penalty? Hades where is your thorn sting? Encouragement is hidden form my eyes. (Hosea 13:14; cf. Exod 6:6; 12:27; 15:13; 18:8–10).

Galatians uses the language of redemption to depict Israel's movement away from the jurisdiction of Torah. In 3:13, Christ's death redeems Israel from the Law's curse; in 4:5, Messiah redeems those "under the Law." As will be made clear, the curse of the Law is effectively equated with death. Throughout the Pauline texts an association between Law and death is manifest (Rom 7:5; 8:2; 1 Cor 15:56). Redemption from death is seen in 2 Cor 1:10, where death represents life threatening afflictions, and Rom

---

183. Wright, "New Exodus, New Inheritance," 26–35.

7:24, where death is the body ensnared by the law of sin (both texts employ ῥύομαι for "deliver"). If the Law's curse is death, then redemption from it, as in Galatians, certainly implies an association between ideas of Exodus and resurrection in the letter.

The Narrative Portrayal of the Exodus

This section outlines three aspects of *how* the portrayal of the Exodus story allows it to be read as a resurrection narrative, like the prophetic depictions of restoration from exile (e.g., Ezek 37:1–14; Hos 6:1–3). They are: Egypt as icon for death, the role of Spirit in the Exodus, and the twin portrayal of God as father and agent of revivification.

Egypt as Icon of Death

The conceptualization of Egypt as a symbolic icon for death permits the Exodus to be seen as a movement into new life. W. A. Gage observes:

> In the symbolic world of the Old Testament, Egypt represents Sheol, or the land of death and the grave. Egypt . . . is where Joseph was sold into bondage, a kind of spiritual death presented as an alternative to the physical death his brothers originally intended. He was carried down to Egypt by a caravan of Ishmaelites who were exporting gum, balm, and myrrh to meet the Egyptian requirements for their cult of the dead . . . Jacob mourned for his son Joseph, thinking him to be dead. Jacob spoke prophetically when he said that he would not see Joseph again until he himself went "down to Sheol" (Gen 37:35). As it happened, Jacob saw Joseph again when he "went down" to Egypt (Gen 46:3). The juxtaposition creates a symbolic equivalence between Egypt and Sheol, or the grave.[184]

Here we will build upon Gage's insightful observations.

THE TEN PLAGUES

The ten plagues associated with the Exodus add to the overall impression of Egypt as an arena of death. The first plague (Exod 7:14–25) involved the turning of the Nile to blood and the ensuing death of the aquatic life. In

---

184. Gage, *Milestones*, 35.

7:21a the author writes that all the fish died.[185] A recurring motif in the plague stories is the attempt of native sorcerers to recreate the signs Moses achieved through Yahweh. The narrative suggests their success with the first two plagues, but they failed to produce gnats from dust, for only Yahweh can make life from dust (Gen 2:7). Here, once more, Egypt, this place of death (represented by her failed magicians), cannot bring forth life.

In Exod 9:1–3 Yahweh commands Moses to pressurize Pharaoh to release Israel, lest he afflict Egypt's livestock with pestilence; the author describes the affliction as θάνατος μέγας σφόδρα ("an overwhelmingly great death"). In 9:4, Yahweh insists that Israel's animals would live—hence, Israel stands over and against Egypt as enduring life. Exodus 9:6 (NRSV) reads: "And on the next day the Lord did so; all the livestock of the Egyptians died, but of the livestock of the Israelites not one died."[186]

Death resulted from the plague of hail that God caused. Israel was once again divinely protected, but even Pharaoh's servants heeding God's instruction through Moses to shelter the slaves and livestock were spared. The only casualties were those Egyptians who stayed in the open field.

After the penultimate plague, the three day darkness, Pharaoh relented, permitting the people's release, but not the livestock of Israel. After Moses' insistence that the livestock were essential for the cult, Pharaoh went back on his word. His parting shot to Moses was, "Get away from me! Take care that you do not see my face again, for on the day you see my face you shall die" (Exod 10:28). The narrator has even Pharaoh himself appear as an emblem of death.

The final plague has explicit deathly overtones. The tenor is ominously set with the frank declaration that "Every firstborn in the land of Egypt shall die" (Exod 11:5). Exodus 12 outlines the stipulations for the Passover festival; in elaborating the details for the sacrificial lamb the author writes: . . . they shall take some of the blood and put it on the two doorposts and on the lintel of the houses in which they eat it (Exod 12:7). This is critical because Yahweh declares:

> . . . I will go through the land of Egypt on that night, and will strike down all the firstborn in the land of Egypt . . . "The blood shall be a sign for you on the houses where you live; and when I see the blood I will pass over you, and no plague will befall you to destroy you when I strike the land of Egypt."[187]

---

185. "Died" here is conveyed by τελευτάω, which connotes came to an end.

186. Cf. Amos 4:10.

187. Exod 12:12–13; Paul demonstrates typological importance of these texts by referring to Christ as our πάσχα in 1 Cor. 5:7.

Ancient Jewish attitudes to blood inform this reading of the Exodus. The following texts all assert that the life of a living being is in the blood: Gen 9:4; Lev 17:11, 14; Deut 12:23.[188] Consequently, readers may understand Israel being "marked" with life in this arena of death. So when the narrative moves to the flight from Egypt, *this becomes a movement from death to life—resurrection.*

The horrific effect of the final plague is summed up in Exod 12:30; ... there was a great cry in Egypt, for there was no home where there was not someone dead. The Egyptians urged the people out of the land in haste saying, "We will all be dead."[189]

Pharaoh, hearing of Israel's flight decided not to give up the cheap labour so easily and gave pursuit. The ensuing panic when the people realized they were being chased prompted them to ask "was it because there were no graves in Egypt that you have taken us away to die in the wilderness?"[190] The literary effect of this can be captured thusly: "if there's one thing Egypt has no shortage of, it is graves—we could no less easily die in a place known for death than die miserably in the desert!"[191] The association with Egypt and death is palpable in Exodus.

JEREMIAH 42

The idea reappears in Jeremiah, when the military and political leaders of Judah's diminished remnant urge him to intercede before Yahweh in view of Babylon's increasing threat (Jer 42:1-6). Ten days later (Jer 42:7) the prophet convenes a meeting of the remnant to deliver God's response (Jer 42:8-9). The divine instruction was to stay in Judah, whereby God would inspire the rebuilding of the fallen land, and to resist the urge to flee to Egypt (Jer 42:10-14).[192] The rest of the chapter (Jer 42:15-21) is the threat of disaster that will befall those who seek refuge in Egypt. Those deserters will be overtaken by the sword (42:16); the famine they are anxious about will cling to them in Egypt (42:16) and they will die there (42:16). They will die by sword, famine and plague and not escape the evils God will deliver on them in Egypt (42:17); God's anger will be poured out on those who flee to Egypt, and the people shall become "a curse, an object of horror, an imprecation and a reproach" (42:18). They will effectively be surrounded on all four sides

188. Cf. John 6:53-54.
189. Exod 12:33.
190. Exod 14:11.
191. Cf. Num 14:2; 21:5.
192. Numerous texts in Isa 30-31 make an identical point; cf. 2 Kgs 18:21.

by death. As in Exodus, Egypt is a symbol of death. Further corroboration is briefly mentioned below.

Deuteronomy 28:27

When the divine voice describes the horrors that will befall disobedient Israel, culminating in a graphic depiction of exile (Deut 28:32–68), it includes this lurid detail:

> The LORD will afflict you with the boils of Egypt, with ulcers, scurvy, and itch, of which you cannot be healed (Deut 28:27).[193]

Jeremiah 43–44

Isaiah 43:3 describes Egypt as the ransom which God will give for Israel's sake. Throughout Jer 43–44 the prophet continues to warn of the futility of turning to Egypt; Jer 43:11–13 describes how Nebuchadnezzar would raze Egypt to the ground; Jer 44:12–14 parallels 42:15–21 describing the death and destruction that will come upon the heads of those Judeans seeking shelter in Egypt (cf. 44:27). There are similar depictions of Egypt as arena of death and desolation in Ezek 29:12; 30:4, 6, 8, 11, 16.

Luke 9:30–31

Though not mentioning Egypt explicitly, Luke's transfiguration account remains pertinent for unambiguously linking the Christ event with the Exodus:

> ... καὶ ἰδοὺ ἄνδρες δύο συνελάλουν αὐτῷ, οἵτινες ἦσαν Μωϋσῆς καὶ Ἠλίας, οἳ ὀφθέντες ἐν δόξῃ ἔλεγον τὴν ἔξοδον αὐτοῦ, ἣν ἤμελλεν πληροῦν ἐν Ἰερουσαλήμ (Luke 9:30–31).

The term ἔξοδος, denoting "departure," appears in Heb 11:22 and 2 Pet 1:15 in the NT.[194] As a euphemism for death the term is found in *Wisdom* 3:2; *Wisdom* 7:5–6 reads:

---

193. Cf. Deut 28:68.
194. The 2 Peter reference is the author's recollection of the Transfiguration.

For no king has had a different beginning of existence; there is
for all one entrance into life, and one way out (ἔξοδός).[195]

This is interesting for its contrast between Exodus and entrance into *life*; for similar reasons the opening of the *Testament of Naphtali* is noteworthy:

The copy of the testament of Naphtali, which he ordained at the time of his death (ἔξοδος) in the hundred and thirtieth year of his life.[196]

Nixon writes that there can be no doubt at all that the evangelists thought the transfiguration was pregnant with Exodus symbolism.[197] Questions hover over whether Luke had Jesus' death *and* resurrection in view—given the Exodus symbolism, it is likely he did.[198]

Paul should be read within the prophetic tradition that perceived Israel hovering on the cusp of an Exodus event, grounded upon and drawing typological significance from the original one, but with more profound implications. The prophets saw the liberation from captivity in Babylon as the greater Exodus;[199] Paul saw rectification as a greater liberation from captivity. At the first Exodus, Israel was "revivified" from Egypt and the "life" which God demanded from them is captured in Torah observance (Lev 18:5). When Paul recounts his own rectification in Gal 2:19-20, it encapsulates death to Torah; the Law may have steered the newly freed Israelite captives, but it could not ultimately bring them into the life God intended.

Galatians 3:21 indicates that Law could not revivify, and thus, could not effect the new Exodus. Revivification was the work of Spirit; this can be further demonstrated by considering the Spirit's role in the Exodus.

Spirit and Exodus

A number of scholars have argued that certain Jewish writers understood the pillar of cloud that guided the Exodus community as the Spirit. W. Wilder argues persuasively, largely from Rom 8:14, that Paul saw the theophanic cloud as Spirit based on Isa 63:11-14 and Hag 2:4-5.[200] M. G. Kline connects the language of the Spirit standing amidst the people in the

---

195. NRSV translation.

196. *Testament of Naphtali* 1:1, trans. R. H. Charles. See further Philo, *Virt.* 77; Josephus, *Ant.* 4.189; Justin Martyr, *Dialogue with Trypho* 105.

197. Nixon, *Exodus*, 16.

198. For alternative positions see Marshall, *Gospel of Luke*, 384-85.

199. Isa 43:2, 16, 19; 48:21; 52:12.

200. Wilder, *Echoes*, 124-38; cf. Neh 9:12, 20.

Pentateuchal traditions with Haggai's "Spirit standing in the midst of the people" (Hag 2:5).[201] In Num 11:25, Yahweh comes down "in the cloud and places the Spirit that was upon Moses upon the seventy elders," and they prophesied—a well-documented phenomenon (1 Sam 10:6; Ezek 37:9; Joel 2:28). This further suggests a connection between Spirit and the pillar of cloud. Recall the earlier comments on the connection between the Spirit's leading in Gal 5:18 and the Spirit of the Lord in Isa 63:14. Following Wilder *et al* that Paul connects the pillar of cloud leading the people of Israel out of Egypt (Exod 13:21–22; 14:19, 24) with Spirit, it is reasonable to further suggest that Paul understood the Spirit "revivifying" the Exodus generation by bringing them out of Egypt. Similarly, Spirit brought the dead bones of Israel to life, symbolizing their liberation from Babylonian captivity, and rectifies people who have faith in Jesus by revivifying them from the dead state of enslavement to Torah or idols.

The Spirit, with respect to the pillar of cloud, performs the usual work of prophetic endowment, but the Exodus text attests to the Spirit's other great work in the biblical tradition—*creation*:

> The LORD spoke to Moses: See, I have called by name Bezalel son of Uri son of Hur, of the tribe of Judah: and I have filled him with divine spirit . . . to devise artistic designs, to *work* in gold, silver, and bronze . . . Moreover, I have appointed with him Oholiab son of Ahisamach, of the tribe of Dan . . . so that they may *make* all that I have commanded you (Exod. 31:1–6, edited, NRSV).

The italicized words above translate עָשָׂה which is frequent in the creation narratives in Genesis 1–3, corresponding to ποιέω.[202] Similar expressions are found in Exod 35:30–35; 28:1–3. The NRSV has opted for the awkward "divine Spirit" in Exod 31:3 (closer to LXX, πνεῦμα θεῖον) but the Hebrew has "Spirit of God" in Exod 31:3. Men were sought who could "devise artistic designs" (31:4) but they created through the agency of Spirit.

The creative action of Spirit is seen in Galatians by implication in 6:14–16, but we may press the pneumatological detail further. The centrality of new creation in Galatians is evidenced by the irrelevance of the circumcised/un-circumcised distinction—a new sphere of existence has been established. Comment on the last revivification text in this volume will expand this at length; for now we need only note that Gal 6:15 corresponds with Paul's community thesis statement in Gal 3:28. The first of its couplets approximates "neither circumcision nor un-circumcision is anything." Of

---

201. Kline, *Holy Spirit*, 25–26; see further Emmrich, *Pneumatological Concepts*, 77.
202. The verb in Exod. 31:4 (LXX) is ἐργάζομαι, however, not ποιέω.

the three couplets in Gal 3:28, the first two have obvious points of contact with key motifs in Galatians; the first is synonymous with 5:6a; 6:15a. The second speaks of the overriding community equality that contrasts the social inequality of ancient Greco-Roman society; it also celebrates the true paradox of Christian freedom—believers are free from the external code of Law and slavery to idols, but are enslaved to one another in the context of love (Gal 5:13–14). The male-female couplet has no obvious frame of reference in Galatians, drawing attention to the change of conjunction therein. The intertextual resonance with Gen 1:27 calls to mind the original act of creation.[203] Paul's uses of στοιχέω in Gal 5:25 and 6:16 indicate the work of Spirit. This is a way of articulating that a new act of creation is afoot.

Galatians 3:28 may be a counter thesis to a prayer ascribed to the second century CE Rabbi Yehuda ben Ilai in *Tosefta Berakhot* 6:18 that Jewish males often recited. The invocation is gratitude that God has not made them Gentiles, women or slaves, and the similarity is certainly uncanny.[204] If this is the case, it reinforces the sense of newly created community Paul was attempting to explicate. The "in Christ" community was ostensibly counter community; a new creation that dismantled the existent dominant and oppressive value systems.

In this way, Galatians bears witness to the creative action of Spirit within the wider establishment of a rectified people. Readers should recall the line in *4Q521* which states that, "over the poor his spirit will hover," a clear echo of the "hovering" Spirit of Gen 1:2.

God the "Father" in Relation to the Exodus

Every canonical Pauline epistle has a reference to God as Father in the grace section. In the introductions of both 1 and 2 Thessalonians, God is identified as Father twice.[205] Unlike Galatians, the references in the Thessalonian correspondences are distinctly innocuous. In both letters, the churches are described as in "God the Father." Galatians 1:1 describes God as "Father, the One having raised him from the dead;" the more standard "God our Father" appears in the grace in 1:3. The third of three clauses in 1:4 states that it was within the purposes of "our God and Father" that Jesus "gave himself

---

203. Despite the recent remonstrations in Uzukwu, *Unity*, 17–23.

204. The prayer may originate in prayers recited by Plato or Socrates and appears in the Babylonian Talmud, *Menahot* 43b. Kahn relays a complex tradition history possibly dating to the fifth centurty BCE. See Kahn, *Three Blessings*, 10.

205. Alexandrian Western types of text unite in supporting the shorter reading of the 1 Thess 1:1.

on behalf of our sins." The term "Father" in 1:1 and 1:4 is significant for the development of the letter. Martyn helpfully notes that Paul's identity is given in the fact God has sent him and God's identity is here given by his having raised Jesus from the dead.[206] Consider the following.

Identifying God with the deeds done on behalf of the people is a common rhetorical ploy. God is typically "the One who brought you up out of Egypt" in the Hebrew Bible (Exod 20:2; 29:46; Lev. 19:36; 25:38, 55; 26:13, 45; Num 15:41; Deut 5:6; 16:1; Judg 6:8; 1 Sam 10:18; 1 Kgs 9:9; 2 Chron 7:22; Ps 81:10; Jer 11:4; 34:13; Dan 9:15). R. Ciampa observes how references to the fatherhood of God are often in contexts linked to the Exodus or pointing to a second Exodus.[207] Kahl points to related intertextual echoes in Exod 4:22 (Moses instructing Pharaoh that Israel is God's firstborn son), Deuteronomy 32 (Moses addressing Israel as God's children who rejected their father (32:6, 18)) and Deuteronomy 27–28 (the sequence of curse, enslavement and exile that results from persistent disobedience).[208] For Paul, however, a new deliverance is afoot whose fulcrum is the death and resurrection of Jesus.

Galatians 1:1 depicts God as θεοῦ πατρὸς τοῦ ἐγείραντος αὐτὸν ἐκ νεκρῶν—not the father of Jesus or believers—but simply as "Father God." Paul's intention is to draw attention to God the Father as the Agent of resurrection. This opening shot sets up for Paul's readers the importance of God's action revivifying the dead in the argument about to unfold. References to "father" also call to mind the notion of kinship relation to God in Galatians—especially with the concept of υἱοθεσία.[209]

The next argumentatively loaded reference to the paternal God is in Gal 1:4. If 1:1 exposes the significance of resurrection for the argument by identifying God as architect of Jesus' resurrection, 1:4 summarises the narrative matrix within which this apocalyptic moment occurs. The following texts depict divine fatherhood of Israel in Exodus related contexts—Paul's commission by Jesus Christ and θεοῦ πατρὸς τοῦ ἐγείραντος αὐτὸν ἐκ νεκρῶν (Gal 1:1) should be understood within this narrative paradigm.

---

206. Martyn, *Galatians*, 85. See also Bruce, *Galatians*, 73.
207. Ciampa, *Presence and Function of Scripture*, 40.
208. Kahl, *Galatians Re-imagined*, 261.
209. See discussion in Burke, *Adopted*, 83–99.

INTRODUCTION

Texts Depicting Divine Fatherhood over Israel

Exodus 4:22–23

> Then you shall say to Pharaoh, "Thus says the LORD: Israel is my firstborn son . . . " (Exod 4:22).

There is in this text an explicit picture of God's fatherhood. A. K. Davis has argued over against Rashi and others that the firstborn son in the above text refers to the sons of Israel and not Jacob.[210] The shift from "son" (Exod 4:22) to "people" (Exod 7:16; 8:1, 20; 9:1, 13) is sufficient to persuade me that she is basically correct. God adopted those he intended to liberate.

Deuteronomy 32:5–6

> Is not he your father, who created you, who made you and established you? (Deut 32:6b).

There are textual uncertainties associated with Deut 32:5–6, but clearly the "you" is the people of Israel. Paul re-worded Deut 32:5 in Phil 2:15 so the "you" is the Philippian church. It is God the father who created (LXX, κτάομαι) the people.[211]

As Keil and Delitzsch note, the entire "song of Moses" (Deut 32:1–43), embraces Israel's unfolding history, drawing on both the ideal of the blessings conferred by the Lord upon his people and Israel's ingratitude.[212] By 32:18, Israel is accused of forgetting the Rock who "gave you birth" (יְלָדְ; γεννάω); Deut 32:15–17, with its emphasis on the period of sacrificing to demons and worshipping idols, indicates that Israel's "birth" was her liberation from Egypt. Paul writes that Isaac was born κατὰ πνεῦμα (Gal 4:29), which corresponds to being born free (to Sarah) and thus being free. Liberated Israel is divinely born Israel, for whom God becomes father. God's sons are those rectified through faith in Messiah (Gal 3:26).

Isaiah 63:7–16

> For you are our father . . . you, O LORD, are our father . . . (Isa 63:16).

---

210. Davis, "Israel's Inheritance," 80–81; cf. Herczeg, *Rashi*, 38.
211. Cf. Gen 4:1 (Eve bringing forth Cain). See Mal 2:10 for God as Father/Creator.
212. Keil and Delitzsch, *Commentary*, 985.

Isaiah 63:7–10 laments Israel's unfaithfulness and idolatry in response to the חֶסֶד of God; though uniquely, the people's rebellion is directed against the Holy Spirit.²¹³ The prophet then recalls the post-Exodus wanderings as ungrateful and self-destructive responses to God's mercies.²¹⁴ Ironically, Moses encourages the people in Exod 14:14 to keep silent, for God will fight for them; in Isa 63:10, he fought *against* them.

According to Isa 63:12, God "divided the waters to make (לַעֲשׂוֹת) an everlasting name for himself." That is, God's name derived from the Exodus—he is "the one who brought you up out of Egypt."²¹⁵ This name corresponds to Paul's divine honorific, "the one who raises the dead"—Rom 4:17, 24; 8:11; 2 Cor 1:9; Gal 1:1; for Jesus' raising was the central event of the *new* Exodus. Deutero-Isaiah's references to Holy Spirit (63:10–11) and "Spirit of the Lord" (63:14) have obvious connections with Galatians. These become particularly noteworthy in Isa 63:14, where the Spirit of the Lord who gave the people rest is also the one who "led the people" (ἤγαγες τὸν λαόν)—presumably a reference to the pillar of cloud/fire.²¹⁶ In Gal 5:18, those led by Spirit are not under Law and in 4:5, those redeemed from being under Law receive υἱοθεσία.

The reference to fatherhood comes in 63:16; Pitre links the text to the prophetic hopes for a new Exodus motion.²¹⁷ This fits well with 63:11–13, for in Isaiah the former Exodus foreshadows the second one. In the Hebrew text, God is father and Redeemer (the Greek has the imperative plea "redeem us!")

Jeremiah 31:9

The Father-son motif in Jer 31:9 describes Israel (Ephraim) as בְּכֹרִי ("my firstborn"), mirroring Exod 4:22.²¹⁸ Of course, this is also the great New Covenant chapter, where the promise of restoration begins to be expounded most fully. Both Jer 31:1 and 31:31 suggest that the Assyrian *and* Babylonian subjugations were in the prophet's consciousness; it is this very juxtaposition of key liberation moments with the Exodus that shaped Paul's thought

---

213. For "Holy Spirit" in the OT, see Isaiah 63 (x2) and Ps 51:11.

214. Isa 63:8 takes up the theme of Exod 6:7—Israel as Yahweh's people.

215. Cf. Reist, "Theological Significance," 224; Reist notes that Israel's very knowledge of God was dependent on the Exodus.

216. Cf. 1 Cor 10:1–6; Rom 8:14.

217. Pitre, "Lord's Prayer," 73–77.

218. Greek πρωτότοκος; cf. Ps 89:27–28 for Father-firstborn designation of Israel.

process.²¹⁹ Rectification was the ultimate Exodus. R. Clifford (dates aside) has captured the notion:

> There are three Exodus moments. Exodus I is the thirteenth-century B.C.E. foundational event. Exodus II is its sixth-century renewal. Exodus III is the first-century C.E. climactic renewal of Israel by Jesus . . . ²²⁰

God the Father who Raised Jesus in Galatians

To sum up, Paul's threefold reference to the fatherhood of God in the prologue of Galatians illustrates the apostle's thinking. This is corroborated by the υἱοθεσία paradigm, which explicates the true nature of Abrahamic heirship (Gal 3:26–4:7). God the father who brought you out of Egypt is God the father who raised Jesus from the dead. The parenthood of God in Gal 4:1–7 points to the following—Israel became God's son at the Exodus, but was too immature to claim full inheritance rights as sons. God gave the Law to act as overseer until Israel "grew up." Having addressed Israel directly in Gal 4:1–2, v. 3 opens with οὕτως καὶ ἡμεῖς ὅτε ἦμεν νήπιοι, ὑπὸ τὰ στοιχεῖα τοῦ κόσμου ἤμεθα δεδουλωμένοι· Jew and Gentile are both slaves, too immature to be free; *then God sent his son.*

Thus, Gal 3:13–14 and Gal 4:4–6 should be read as equivalent statements as the following demonstrates:

> Χριστὸς ἡμᾶς ἐξηγόρασεν ἐκ τῆς κατάρας τοῦ νόμου . . . ἵνα εἰς τὰ ἔθνη ἡ εὐλογία τοῦ Ἀβραὰμ γένηται ἐν Χριστῷ Ἰησοῦ, ἵνα τὴν ἐπαγγελίαν τοῦ πνεύματος λάβωμεν διὰ τῆς πίστεως (Gal 3:13–14).

> ὅτε δὲ ἦλθεν τὸ πλήρωμα τοῦ χρόνου, ἐξαπέστειλεν ὁ θεὸς τὸν υἱὸν αὐτοῦ . . . ἵνα τοὺς ὑπὸ νόμον ἐξαγοράσῃ, ἵνα τὴν υἱοθεσίαν ἀπολάβωμεν . . . ἐξαπέστειλεν ὁ θεὸς τὸ πνεῦμα τοῦ υἱοῦ αὐτοῦ εἰς τὰς καρδίας . . . (Gal 4:4–6).

The critical trajectory is this: Christ *redeemed* Israel . . . from the *Law* . . . *in order that* . . . *we might receive* . . .

The promise of Spirit is "received" in Gal 3:14; in 4:5 it is *sonship*. However, 4:6 immediately unites receiving Spirit and receiving sonship. The substantive issue is that Spirit testifies to the mature phase of Israel's sonship to God. Sonship in Galatians 3 is initially associated with Abraham, so

---

219. As Hos 11:1.
220. Clifford, "Exodus in the Christian Bible," 345.

Paul can demonstrate the centrality of faith in being in right relation to God (3:6). As Gal 3:26 implies, sons of Abraham and sons of God are effectively equivalent. So then, God the father is God who frees the slaves and brings them into maturity.

Paul, then, starts Galatians with a vital part of his argument that informs its forward movement—*God raised Jesus from the dead*; the mission of the risen Christ outlined in Gal 1:4 has probably been influenced by Exod 3:8 (LXX); God "came down" to rescue (ἐξελέσθαι) them from the hand of Egypt and to lead them out (ἐξαγαγεῖν) of that land . . .[221] Mussner writes of Gal 1:4, "dieser Äon ist als bedrohliche Macht verstanden"—an evaluation of the "age" which might just as well apply to Egypt.[222] Galatians presents the rescue mission as deliverance from slavery, a new Exodus story Paul narrates in terms of revivification, prompted by the resurrection of Jesus.

Paul sees rectification within the twin frameworks of "freedom" and "revivification." God the father raised Jesus from the dead (Gal 1:1); Israel the son is redeemed from slavery under Law and has Spirit in their hearts. The implication is manifest—those freed by God enter into kinship relation with him, and God frees them by the revivifying act of rectification.

As in Gal 3:26, if you are *all* sons of God through faith *in Christ Jesus*, then through this faith believing Jews *and* Gentiles have become 'sons' by virtue of Jesus being *the* son. God the father of Israel became God the father of Jesus and is now God the father of those in Christ through faith. God the father who freed the slaves became God the father who resurrected Jesus and is now God the father who rectifies the faithful.

Further Evidence: God the Father as Liberator in Baptism

Fatherhood and Exodus typology occur in Pauline baptism imagery. Galatians 3:27 posits baptism as the arena for appropriating the "in Christ" identity through faith. Galatians 3:26–29 is one of four baptismal metaphors in the undisputed Pauline corpus, all of which evoke Exodus ideology.

Galatians 3:26–27 and 1 Cor 12:12–13 both attest to the creation of new community by divine action. Galatians 3:28, 1 Cor 12:13 and Col 3:11 contain the refrain, "there is not Jew or Greek, slave or free." The two couplets common to all three texts point to the establishment of recalibrated social boundaries; correspondingly, a number of texts point to the Exodus as the creation of Israel as a distinct people of God: Exod 3:10; Num 22:5;

221. Exod 3:8.
222. Mussner, *Galaterbrief*, 51.

Deut 4:20; 1 Kgs 8:51; 1 Chr 17:21; Ps 80:8; Ps 114:1. For Paul, baptism, which marks the new Exodus motion, the new passing through the waters (Isa 43:2), locates someone "in Christ" or "in the body" (1 Cor 12:12–13) where new social dynamics operate and a new people is formed. For our immediate purposes is the Pauline death-burial-raising imagery in Rom 6:1–11.[223]

Romans 6:1–11 combines death/resurrection and crossing of the waters; baptism, here, represents identification with Jesus' burial. Paul is demonstrating participation in the three stage process of the Christ-event. As such, the believer participates in the crucifixion of Jesus by the "co-crucifixion of the old man" (Rom 6:5).[224] As Jesus was buried, συνετάφημεν οὖν αὐτῷ διὰ τοῦ βαπτίσματος (Rom 6:4a).[225] The raising (ἐγείρω) of Jesus from the dead corresponds to believers walking in the newness of life (Rom 6:4). The affinity between Rom 6:5 and Gal 1:1 reinforces the paradigmatic nature of God's revivifying action on the faithful—believers walk in the newness of life *just as* (ὥσπερ) Jesus was raised from the dead.[226] Jesus' resurrection is the template for the rectified life:

... καὶ θεοῦ πατρὸς τοῦ ἐγείραντος αὐτὸν ἐκ νεκρῶν (Gal 1:1)

... ἵνα ὥσπερ ἠγέρθη Χριστὸς ἐκ νεκρῶν διὰ τῆς δόξης τοῦ πατρός (Rom 6:4)

Romans 6:4 further attests God the father as the reviver of the dead and liberator from captivity. The aorist passive of ἐγείρω invokes the God of resurrection—Jesus *was raised* by the glory of *the father*. There is no word for "God" in Rom 6:4, only the designation πατήρ—in baptism Paul once more expresses that God the father who frees the slaves revivifies the dead.

Walking in the newness of life after "rising" from the tomb, the waters of baptism, recollects the experience of freedom encountered by the Israelites upon their departure from Egypt. The waters of the Red Sea became a grave for the Egyptians, "so Israel saw the Egyptians dead on the seashore."[227] The people of Israel passed through these waters of death into the newness

---

223. For a critical review of scholarly positions on the function of the death metaphor in Romans 6, see Sabou, *Between Horror and Hope*, 5–42. See also Clifton Black II, "Pauline Perspectives," 413–33.

224. Τοῦτο γινώσκοντες ὅτι ὁ παλαιὸς ἡμῶν ἄνθρωπος συνεσταυρώθη.

225. Εἰς τὸν θάνατον αὐτοῦ at the end of 6:3 should be read in conjunction with εἰς τὸν θάνατον in 6:4; we were baptized into *his* death . . . we were co-buried with him through baptism into death—the implication being *our* death.

226. Walking in newness of life may well approximate "living to God" in Pauline thought (Gal 2:19).

227. Exod 14:30b, NRSV.

of liberation.[228] One might say that in the Exodus and in baptism, those who pass through the water find life.[229]

Having explored the correlation between resurrection and Exodus, I cite Levenson to summarize:

> The Exodus has become a prototype of ultimate redemption, and historical liberation has become a partial, proleptic experience of eschatological liberation . . . that moves the *Jews not merely from slavery to freedom but quite literally from death to life as well. Beneath this last transformation lies a conviction that so long as human beings are subject to death, they are not altogether free: resurrection is the ultimate and final liberation.*[230]

In some Jewish thought, which Paul exemplifies in Galatians, God was rectifying the world by an all-embracing, re-creative act of resurrection. This act would spell freedom for all people; it was narrated through those texts describing Israel's great freedom dramas using the language of revivification and interpreted by later generations of Jewish communities. For Paul, there was a cosmic twist in the tale. Destiny no longer lay in interpreting what events *described* as resurrections said about God's plans. Rather, it lay in interpreting how the event of an *actual* resurrection reshaped the understanding of divine intervention in the history of Israel and the world. The raising of Jesus became the grid through which to comprehend the divine work of rectification. One narrative gave superlative graphic profile to this ideology—the valley of the Dry Bones.

Ezekiel 37:1–14 as Principal "Restoration as Resurrection" Text

Recourse to Ezek 37:1–14 in Ancient Jewish Literature

Many Jewish authors faced with "life and death" issues appealed to Ezek 37:1–14. The righteous mother facing the death of her seven sons comforts them with her late husband's teaching, which embodies a catena of Biblical quotes including Ezek 37:3:

> He quoted to us the proverb of Solomon, "He is a tree of life to all them that do his will." He confirmed the words of Ezekiel, "Shall these dry bones live?" For he forgot not the song that Moses

---

228. See Deut 6:20–25.
229. See earlier for water as metaphor for death and chaos.
230. Levenson, *Resurrection*, 27–28, emphasis mine.

taught, which teaches, "I will slay and I will make alive. This is your life and the blessedness of your days" (*4 Macc.* 18:16–19).

Tuell argues that the author of the canonical book of Daniel was the earliest interpreter of the "dry bones" saga on the grounds of

> ... the multiple connections between Daniel and Ezekiel (for example, compare Dan 7:9–10 with Ezek 1:4–28; or Dan 10:5 and 12:6–7 with Ezek 9:2), as well as the common image of resurrection, [which] make it most likely that Daniel is thinking here of the dry bones in the dusty valley of Ezekiel's vision.[231]

The citations from the fragmentary *Apocalypse of Peter* are clearly from Ezekiel 37. M. R. James writes, "We have not a pure and complete text of this book..."[232] A version of the *Apocalypse* is found in Ethiopic in the *Clement* literature where we read:

> For all these things come to pass on the day of decision, on the day of judgment, at the word of God, and as all things come to pass when he created the world and commanded all that is therein it and it was all done—so shall it be in the last days; for everything is possible with God, and he says in the scripture: Son of man, prophesy upon the several bones and say to the bones—bone unto bone in joints, sinews, nerves, flesh and skin and hair thereon.[233]

Evidently, a section of the *Apocalypse* exists in the second volume of the *Sibylline Oracles*, which also embodies Ezekiel 37:

> For only one is undying the Almighty himself ... then to the dead shall the heavenly give souls and breath and speech, bones fitted together, with all manner of joints, flesh and nerves and veins and skin about and hair of the head.[234]

The Qumran text *4Q Pseudo-Ezekiel* (4Q385, 386, 388, 391) is a pseudepigraphon framed as a dialogue between Ezekiel and God. Several of the extant fragments reprise portions of the Biblical Ezekiel, especially the Merkevah Vision (Ezekiel 1, 10) and the Vision of the Dry Bones.[235]

R. Suh attempted a detailed analysis of the use of Ezekiel 37 in Ephesians 2; the author of Ephesians uses the death-life language to portray the

---

231. Tuell, "True Metaphor," 470.
232. James, *Apocryphal New Testament*, 505.
233. Schneemelcher, *New Testament Apocrypha*, 627.
234. Ibid., 660.
235. Wright, "Qumran Pseudepigrapha in Early Christianity."

creation of God's people (Eph 2:1–6). The author describes Gentiles as formerly being dead (νεκρούς) in transgressions (Eph 2:1, 5); now, however, they have been made alive together (συνεζωοποίησεν) with Christ (2:5) and raised together with him (συνήγειρεν) to sit in the heavenly places (2:6). Suh observes:

Ezekiel 37:1–14
    Bringing Them to the Promised Land (vv. 12–13)
        Raising Israel from the Graves (vv. 12–13)
            Making Israel Alive (vv. 5–10)
                The Dead Bones [Israel] (vv. 1–2)

Ephesians 2:1–10
    Seating Them with Christ in the Heavenly Places in Christ (v. 6)
        Raising Them with Christ (v. 6)
            Making Them Alive with Christ (v. 5)
                Gentiles Dead in Their Sins (vv. 1, 5)[236]

There are hints the Evangelists were influenced by the life-death/resurrection portrait in Ezekiel 37. If the Talmudic tradition that Ezekiel 37 formed part of the Passover *Seder* is accurate, it supports J. Grassi's position that the curious story in Matt 27:51-53 has Ezek 37:1–14 in its narrative background.[237] Grassi observes: in Matt 27:51 there is an earthquake, (ἡ γῆ ἐσείσθη) followed by the opening of the tombs (τὰ μνημεῖα ἀνεῴχθησαν, 27:52). Likewise, in Ezek 37: 7 there is a σεισμός at the voice of prophecy. The Lord says, "I am opening your tombs" in Ezek 37:12. In Matt 27:53, Jesus goes before the dead to lead them from their tombs: it is following his resurrection that the dead rise and come into the holy city. This holy city may represent the heavenly Jerusalem (Rev 11: 2; 21: 2, 11; 22: 19). Cf. Ezek 37:12b: "I will lead you forth from your tombs and I will bring you into the land of Israel."[238]

There are possible echoes of the Ezekielian vision in the fourth Gospel. One faint resonance is in John 5:25-28; a far more convincing point

---

236. Suh, "Use of Ezekiel 37," 720–21.

237. R. Huna said in the name of R. Shesheth: On the Sabbath which falls in the intermediate days of the festival, whether Passover or Tabernacles, the passage we read from the Torah is "See, you [say to me]" and for haftarah on Passover the passage of the "dry bones," and on Tabernacles, "In that day when Gog shall come." *Babylonian Talmud, Megillah* 31a. See further, Bullock, "Ezekiel," 30.

238. Grassi, "Ezekiel 37," 163.

of contact is in John 20. Manning writes that John *alludes* to Ezekiel's dry bones prophecy twice. He argues that the language of the Son calling the dead from their tombs evokes Ezekiel's vision.²³⁹ He adds that

> John sees Ezekiel's oracle as both about the gift of life that believers in Jesus experience now and also about the final resurrection of all people. In John's second allusion to Ezekiel's oracle of the dry bones, John uses the language of breathing out the Spirit to evoke Ezekiel's interpretation of the vision (John 20:22; Ezek 37:11–14) . . . John sees Jesus as *bringing new life through the giving of the Spirit.*²⁴⁰

Evidence of Ezekiel's Influence on Paul: 2 Corinthians

Paul probably never directly cites Ezek 37:1–14 though, it does seem that he, like the writers above, in his most profound encounter with the operationalism of death and life—the resurrected Christ—was influenced by it and employed its imagery and symbolism to give impetus and semantic shape to his polemics. The writers above harnessed Ezekiel's portrayal of new life—Paul did so through the prism of Jesus' resurrection. An obvious example is how Paul describes his "ministry of reconciliation" as life coming from death in Romans 5, Romans 11, and 2 Cor 5:15–19.²⁴¹

Paul does cite Ezek 37:27 (conflating it with Lev 26:11–12) in 2 Cor 6:16. Various treatments of the complex unit 2 Cor 6:14–7:1 exist—this brief treatment is to demonstrate how reading Ezek 37 through the grid of Jesus' resurrection affected how Paul comprehended his ministry.²⁴²

In agreement with E. Hayes, ἡμεῖς γὰρ ναὸς θεοῦ ἐσμεν ζῶντος (2 Cor 6:16b), certainly seems to function as a premise statement. However, she argues that the rhetorical contrast (agreement between temple and idols) giving rise to the premise statement summarizes the other rhetorical contrasts.²⁴³ This acts as her point of departure for understanding the pericope.

---

239. Manning, *Echoes of a Prophet*, 171.

240. Ibid., emphasis mine.

241. Carol K. Stockhausen argues that the τὸ δὲ πνεῦμα ζῳοποιεῖ. of 2 Cor 3:6c is directly dependent on Ezek 37:1–14. See Stockhausen, *Moses' Veil*, 79.

242. On the complexities of this passage, see especially McCant, who observes nine terms in this short section unique to the undisputed Pauline corpus—McCant, *2 Corinthians*, 62. Fitzmyer suggests it is a Christianised interpretation of an Essene fragment later inserted. See Fitzmyer, "Qumran and the Interpolated Paragraph," 271–80; see further Hultgren, "2 Cor. 6.14–7.1 and Rev. 21.3–8," 39–56.

243. Hayes, "Influence of Ezekiel 37," 123–36.

Whilst possible, there appears to be something more immediate at the heart of the argument.

The "living God" vs. "dead idols" contrast springs from Paul's wider comprehension of ministry in terms of death and life. For Paul says this ministry is "life" to some and "death" to others (2 Cor 2:16); those who hold to Law as external reality with the hope of being rectified are *killed* and those relying on internalized Spirit are *made alive* (3:6). The thought returns in 5:12–15; Paul commends his ministry from the heart, not in any externalities—a ministry by which the faithful have shared in the death and resurrection of Christ, such that "all died" (5:14) and now "live no longer for themselves but for the one having died for them and been raised" (5:15). In chapter 6 Paul again articulates the rationale for meaningful self-commendation (2 Cor 6:3–4)—suffering for the gospel. Of this, Paul writes, "as having died and behold we live, as disciplined and not being put to death" (6:9). Paul again alludes to the Corinthians being in the hearts of both himself and his missionary entourage (6:11; cf. 3:2).[244]

The premise statement, then, explains why believers should not be yoked with unbelievers, validating the radical holiness implied by the rhetorical questions in 2 Cor 6:14–16.[245] It is because the *living* God lives among the community that the disciples cannot be associated with dead idols any more than Christ can be associated with Belial or light with darkness, etc. Paul's ministry in 2 Corinthians can be summed up as a ministry of Spirit mediated sharing in the death and life of Messiah. There is a common sharing of Spirit in the hearts (2 Cor 1:22) and so a common sharing in the New Covenant "life"—as such, Paul has the Corinthian disciples in his "heart" (3:2–3; 5:12; 6:11). The combination of Lev 26:12 and Ezek 37:27 in 2 Cor 6:16 has a dual effect. The Ezekiel text recalls how the restoration of Israel from exile and the ratification of the New Covenant (Ezek 37:26) occur in a resurrection moment (Ezek 37:1–14). Now the people "live" and God "lives" in and among the community.[246] Now that the living God lives with the people, there can be no place for dead idols.[247] The Leviticus passage brings idolatry into focus (cf. Lev 26:1).

---

244. 2 Cor 4:7–14 evidences Paul's resurrection driven ministry.

245. For the use of ναός over and against ἱερόν see Harris, *Second Epistle to the Corinthians*, 505–6; see further, Omanson and Ellington, *Paul's Second Letter*, 122.

246. Trying to sharply delineate between whether the ἐν αὐτοῖς (2 Cor 6:16b citing Ezek 37:27) refers to God in the believer or God amidst the community seems pedantic. Garland probably correctly sees the emphasis on God residing among the community and not just in "the temple" of the individual's body. See Garland, *2 Corinthians*, 338; cf. Harris, *Second Epistle to the Corinthians*, 506.

247. Cf. 1 Thess 1:9.

These ideas carry through to the opening of 2 Cor 7. The New Covenant demands a radical holiness (7:1); in incorporating this holiness code into his ministry politics, Paul has offended or wronged no one (7:2). Again, Paul can commend his ministry on the grounds of the positive effect on the community, which comes into full array in 7:3:

> πρὸς κατάκρισιν οὐ λέγω· προείρηκα γὰρ ὅτι ἐν ταῖς καρδίαις ἡμῶν ἐστε εἰς τὸ συναποθανεῖν καὶ συζῆν.
>
> I do not speak (a word of) condemnation; for I have said before that *you are in our hearts* for (us) *to die together and to live together.*

Paul's demands for holiness are in keeping with the New Covenant—Paul can say this because the Corinthians are in his heart, so he knows of their desire to live accordingly. The death-life motif could simply mean you are in our hearts "forever," pointing to Paul's enduring affection for the Corinthians, as many commentators imply. However, both the word order and the references to "hearts" elsewhere in the letter point to Paul once again talking about his ministry. The Christians at Corinth are in his heart because they have shared together in the ministry of death and life that rectifies believers before God. For Paul, corporate death evokes union with Christ (Rom 6:8; 2 Cor 5:14; Gal 2:19; cf. Col 2:20; 2 Tim 2:11). Thus, 7:3 is another reference to Paul's ministry—a ministry of death and revivification by the shared experience of Spirit. The invocation of Ezekiel 37 reiterates that Spirit has revivified dead Israel and, as such, God has made Israel his home. Now, amidst the people and in their hearts, Spirit continues to give life to the dead in Paul's ministry.

Ezekiel 36–37/Jeremiah's Influence on Galatians 4.

Various scholars have highlighted the influence of Ezekiel 36–37 and the associated New Covenant prophecy in Jeremiah 31 on Paul's thought in Galatians.[248] Here, we will present an account of the interface between Galatians and the above prophets in two ways. Firstly, attention will be drawn to the *thematic* echoes between Galatians 4 and the New Covenant prophecies. This will highlight the common narrative between Galatians and these prophets—freedom from slavery by the internalization of Spirit and renewed interaction with divine Law. Secondly, the main part of this volume will be dedicated to a discussion of the six revivification texts in Galatians.

---

248. Simeroth, "Life in the Spirit," 18–22; Rabens, "Ethics and the Spirit in Paul," 5; Fee, *Empowering Presence*, 369, 453, 812–13; Morales, *Spirit*, 107–29.

Here, the *intertextual* resonances between Galatians and Ezekiel 36–37/ Jeremiah, will demonstrate the synthesis between Spirit, revivification and internalization. Inferentially, Galatians will be shown to reflect the fulfilment of the New Covenant.[249]

Gal 4:6 and Ezek 36:26–27

καὶ δώσω ὑμῖν καρδίαν καινὴν καὶ πνεῦμα καινὸν δώσω ἐν ὑμῖν καὶ ἀφελῶ τὴν καρδίαν τὴν λιθίνην ἐκ τῆς σαρκὸς ὑμῶν καὶ δώσω ὑμῖν καρδίαν σαρκίνην. 27 καὶ τὸ πνεῦμά μου δώσω ἐν ὑμῖν καὶ ποιήσω ἵνα ἐν τοῖς δικαιώμασίν μου πορεύησθε καὶ τὰ κρίματά μου φυλάξησθε καὶ ποιήσητε (Ezek 36:26–27, LXX)

One key element of this section of Ezekiel's oracle is that Israel's renewal rests upon God's desire to protect his name (Ezek 36:22–23). Fairbairn notes Deut 9:5, 6 to this end.[250] There has been a moral and religious catastrophe resulting from Israel's idolatry, and God will re-sanctify his name by restoring Israel, endowing them with a new identity and character. Ezekiel is commanded in 36:22–28 to tell the people that a series of divine actions will create a new people.

The creation of a new people by the action of Spirit is a demonstration of divine initiative, paralleling the establishment of the community in Galatians. Galatians 4:6 testifies to the internalization of Spirit in the heart and the establishment of sonship; through Spirit God has "fathered" his eschatological people. In Harink's assessment of J. H. Yoder's interpretation of justification, he writes:

> On the judgment that the immediate result of justification is not the "saved" individual, but the ekklēsia, Yoder joins Karl Barth in testifying to the Pauline logic of the gospel, a logic in which God's reconciliation and redemption of the cosmos through Christ and the Spirit has as its first goal the creation of a new people of God, made up of Jews and Gentiles, in which the calling of Israel and the nations' unified witness to the one true God have their beginning.[251]

Both Paul and Ezekiel associate the internalization of Spirit with an end to the propensity for idolatry (Ezek 36:25; cf. Gal 4:6–8). As Levitt Kohn

---

249. For the importance of Galatians in New Covenant atonement theorizing, see Gorman, *Death of the Messiah*, 62–64.

250. Fairbairn, *Ezekiel*, 394.

251. Harink, *Paul Among the Post-Liberals*, 62.

notes, Ezekiel uses "heart" as the place of human moral response to Yahweh, as Deut 6:4–5. Elsewhere in the Deuteronomist History, the heart is where people make principled decisions.[252] If Israel could adhere to Torah's demands, worship would only be offered to Yahweh.[253] They were unable; God placed his Spirit inside them to make them responsive.[254]

Gal 4:7 and Ezek 36:27–28

The framing of Ezek 36:27–28 resonates with Galatians. After explaining that he seeks to preserve his name, God promises, "I will take you from the nations and gather you from all the countries, and bring you into your own land" (36:24, NRSV) ... Then you shall live in the land that I gave to your ancestors (36:28). The prophet connects the internalization of God's Spirit with the concept of freedom and restoration from exile. Paul articulates that the Spirit of God's Son in the hearts affirms the fatherhood of God in believers, *so that you are no longer a slave* (Gal 4:7a).

Observe then:

MOTIF	EZEKIEL	GALATIANS
Freedom	I will take you from the nations ... and bring you into your own land (36:24).	So you are no longer a slave but a son ... (4:7)
Spirit	I will put my spirit within you ... (36:27)	God has sent the Spirit of his Son ... (4:6)
Heart	A new heart I will give you ... (36:26)	into our hearts ... (4:6)
Relation to God	... you shall be my people, and I will be your God (36:28)	... crying, "Abba! Father! (4:6)
Heirs	Then you shall live in the land that I gave to your fathers ... (36:28)	... and if a child then also an heir (4:7)

The Spirit's liberating work is also seen in Rom 7:6; 8:2; 2 Cor 3:17. Ezekiel prophesies the New Covenant blessings in the context of Judah's physical freedom from exile (Ezek 36:24) in which the Law becomes inner

---

252. Kohn, *New Heart*, 93; cf. Deut 30:2, 14; Josh 24:23; 1 Kgs 8:48.
253. Thielman, *From Plight to Solution*, 36.
254. See also Zimmerli, *Ezekiel 2*, 248.

reality (36:26–27). For Paul, this pneumatological internalization of God's Law, creates a freedom that becomes the basis for an ethic of love (Gal 4:4–7; 5:13–14). Freedom is an aspect of the basis of Christian *spirituality* in Galatians.[255] Galatians 4:21–31, despite its complex symbolism, further exhibits the critical narrative connecting the Ezekielian New Covenant prophecy and its fulfilment in the Pauline Jesus communities—Spirit brings into being (Gal 4:29) the people of God (4:28), who have been freed from slavery (4:26, 30–31) and now exist in a renewed proximity to Torah (4:21–25).

Although Jeremiah did not mention Spirit in his New Covenant prophecy, and Paul does not mention Law in Gal 4:6, a connection is implied. Block demonstrates how the Hebrew of Ezek 36:27–28 and Jer 31:33 tallies linguistically. The LXX also tallies:

Ezekiel 36:27–28 (LXX)	Jeremiah 31:33 (LXX)
καὶ τὸ πνεῦμά μου δώσω	δώσω νόμους μου
ἐν ὑμῖν	εἰς τὴν διάνοιαν αὐτῶν καὶ ἐπὶ καρδίας
καὶ ἔσεσθέ μοι εἰς λαόν	καὶ αὐτοὶ ἔσονταί μοι εἰς λαόν
κἀγὼ ἔσομαι ὑμῖν εἰς θεόν	καὶ ἔσομαι αὐτοῖς εἰς θεόν

Block correctly concludes that at these points they are describing the same event. What Jeremiah attributes to the infusion of the divine Torah, Ezekiel ascribes to the infusion of the רוּחַ.[256] Woodhouse is also surely correct in his linkage of Ezek 36:27 and Jer 31:31–34; he notes that there is little obvious difference between God writing his Law on the heart, and placing his (speaking) breath within.[257]

Ezekiel's employment of key Jeremianic ideas is important for the understanding of restoration eschatology presented in this volume because he frames the divine initiative of internalization in terms of *Spirit*. In his study of individualism in Jeremiah and Ezekiel, M. H. Oh acutely observes:

> The similarities between the prophets are . . . Jeremiah and Ezekiel sought the source of sin in the hard heart of each individual . . . They also emphasized true heart repentance accomplished

---

255. Wesley Institute, "Spirituality as Eschatology: The Rhetoric of the Spirit in Galatians," http://webjournals.ac.edu.au/journals/aps/issue-1/spirituality-as-eschatology-the-rhetoric-of-the-sp/.

256. Block, "Prophet of the Spirit," 39; for thematic intertexts regarding the new covenant between the two prophets, see Zimmerli, *Ezekiel 25–48*, 248–52.

257. Woodhouse, "'Spirit' in the Book of Ezekiel," 17; Woodhouse sees no radical difference in the natural breath of life given to all things and the Spirit of God in Ezekiel's usage. See further Robson, *Word and Spirit*, 79–93.

by a radical change of the heart ... They argued the principle of individual responsibility ... .They promised the restoration of the law which will be accomplished by God's making the New Covenant with his people.[258]

This common idea of internalization in Jeremiah and Ezekiel—of Law in the former and Spirit in the latter—finds completion when the Spirit enters the heart in Gal 4:6. Jesus effects redemption from situation under the Law in Gal 4:4-5 and Spirit enters the hearts of the redeemed. Furthermore, the Spirit led are *not under Law* (Gal 5:18) but can resist indulgence (Gal 5:16-17).[259] The internal presence of Spirit instigates the moral conduct that the Law demands, evidenced by the fruit of the Spirit (Gal 5:22-23).

Gal 4:4-7 and Jer 31:33

Neither the prophetic oracles themselves nor Paul's harnessing of them suggest that the covenant is new in that it conveys anything unknown to Israel's sacred tradition. Jeremiah declares:

> ὅτι αὕτη ἡ διαθήκη, ἣν διαθήσομαι τῷ οἴκῳ Ισραηλ μετὰ τὰς ἡμέρας ἐκείνας, φησὶν κύριος Διδοὺς δώσω νόμους μου εἰς τὴν διάνοιαν αὐτῶν καὶ ἐπὶ καρδίας αὐτῶν γράψω αὐτούς, καὶ ἔσομαι αὐτοῖς εἰς θεόν, καὶ αὐτοὶ ἔσονταί μοι εἰς λαόν (Jer 31:33).

In Jer 31:31, God declares that he will cut a new covenant, contrasted with the Sinai covenant in v. 32 (cf. Exod 19:1-24:11). The emphatic statement of v. 33 sets the agenda—αὕτη ἡ διαθήκη (this is the covenant).[260] Following this introductory clause, Jeremiah outlines the internalization of God's Laws, suggesting that the newness of the covenant is a *renewed engagement* with Torah.

Paul sets the eschatological agenda in Gal 4:4—"when the fullness of time came."[261] Jeremiah says that the giving of God's Laws in the minds of his people and the inscription of the Laws in their hearts will happen "after those days." Paul relays that God's Son came to redeem those under the Law *in order that* they might become sons of God (Gal 4:5). For Paul, the internalization of the Spirit coincides with Israel's redemption from Torah's jurisdiction and the attendant inclusion into kinship with God. Earlier in Jeremiah's oracle, God condemns the faithlessness of Israel as an

---

258. Oh, "Individualism."
259. For the significance of "under the Law," see Belleville, "Under Law," 54.
260. Verb must be supplied.
261. See discussion in Martyn, *Galatians*, 389.

untrustworthy wife and extends the indictment to Judah as Israel's sister, foolishly not learning from her sibling's fate.²⁶² This is followed by a plea for repentance whereby "in those days" Jerusalem will be called "the throne of the Lord" and the nations will gather to it.²⁶³ Then, with 31:31 in view (cf. 31:27) Yahweh speaks of an inheritance, promised to the houses of Israel and Judah.²⁶⁴ We read the following in Jer 31:20 (LXX)

> Ephraim is a beloved son to me, a child I delight in, because my words are in him, his memory I will remember . . . (cf. 3:19).

Paul depicts the peoplehood of the community in terms of kinship relation to God. In Jer 31:9 the divine voice relays "for I have become a father to Israel, and Ephraim is my firstborn (NRSV)."

When we read Paul's assertions regarding Law and sonship in Gal 4:5–7, readers should observe three related ideals. (1) Paul treats Israel's discharge from Torah's dominion to be the moment of Israel's eschatological sonship relation to God. (2) Simultaneously, the Spirit of Jesus enters the hearts signifying this sonship; Israel's release from Torah and the instantiation of sonship corresponds to the internalization of the Law and resultant becoming the people of God in Jeremiah. (3) Sonship implies freedom, a motif that reaches full bloom in 4:21–5:1. Once this sonship is established, "you are no longer a slave but a son" (Gal 4:7). As a son, the believer is an heir through God—Gal 4:7; cf. Jer 3:19; 31:33.²⁶⁵

Paul never says that the *Law* will be in the hearts of the people in Galatians; nonetheless, "led by the Spirit," the people will not complete the desires of the flesh (5:16) and are not under Law (5:18). The phrase ὑπὸ νόμον appears ten times in the undisputed Pauline corpus—Rom 6:14, 15; 1 Cor 9:20 (x3); Gal 3:23; 4:4, 5, 21; 5:18. The meaning is consistent; note the only other occurrence of "led by Spirit" in Paul is Rom 8:14, where those so led are sons of God. This appears to directly correspond to Gal 4:4–5 where those redeemed from "under Law" receive υἱοθεσία.²⁶⁶

The term ὑπὸ νόμον denotes existence in submission to Law in the age before Spirit. In Galatians, moving from Spirit-led to being under Law is

---

262. Jer 3:6–10.

263. Jer 3:17.

264. Jer 3:18.

265. Philip argues that Paul's letters emphasise the presence and action of the Spirit at the beginning of all Christian "conversions," citing Gal 4:4–7 amidst a number of other Pauline texts to this end. He particularly asserts that the Damascus Christophany included an experience of the Spirit. See Philip, *Origins of Pauline Pneumatology*, 166–203.

266. Note later comments on T. A. Wilson's reading of ὑπὸ νόμον.

manifestly retrograde. To be under the Law in the age of Law, in the context of Galatians, is to be confined (φρουρέω) until the revelation of faith (3:23), the origin of Spirit (3:2–5). It is a place Israel must be redeemed from by *the* son of God, in order to become *sons of God* by the internalization of Spirit (4:5–6). The evidence points to Paul's comprehension of being situated "under Law," to contrast the notion of Law in the mind and on the heart, for, to be under Law is to obey Law as *external code*. As Ezek 36:26–27 foretells, faithful obedience to the divine commands ultimately results from the internalization of God's Spirit.

The Spirit-led will be empowered to resist carnal human desire (σάρξ) without recourse to the external Law. Therefore, Gal 4:5–6 should be understood as a fulfilment of Jeremiah's prophecy of "Law written on hearts."

Gal 4:8 and Jer 5:7

In Jeremiah 5 the prophet portrays the sorry state of moral decay in Jerusalem and obduracy of the people towards God despite his efforts to make their failures manifest. Twice they are charged with their laxity regarding "knowing the way of God" (5:4–5); they incur the punishment exacted upon them through Babylon (5:6). Then we read in Jer 5:7:

> Ποίᾳ τούτων ἴλεως γένωμαί σοι; οἱ υἱοί σου ἐγκατέλιπόν με καὶ ὤμνυον ἐν τοῖς οὐκ οὖσιν θεοῖς . . . (Jer 5:7, LXX).
>
> Why should I pardon you for this? Your sons have forsaken me and have sworn by things *which are not gods*.

Paul in describing the Gentiles' pre-Christian experience at the beginning of Gal 4:8 writes that they too had not known God (οὐκ εἰδότες θεὸν). He adds that they also were enslaved by those things not being gods, using a virtually identical phrase to the one Jeremiah uses: ἐδουλεύσατε τοῖς φύσει μὴ οὖσιν θεοῖς (Gal 4:8b).[267]

The things which are not gods are the στοιχεῖα τοῦ κόσμου (4:3; cf. 4:8), though only very general consensus exists concerning them. Arnold argues that they are evil spirits equivalent to the "principalities and powers" Paul speaks about elsewhere.[268] Bundrick (along with Lightfoot and Burton in their own nuanced ways) suggests they are the elementary religious teachings all people had, which Jew and Gentile were enslaved to before experiencing freedom through faith in Christ.[269] De Boer helpfully refers

---

267. The key addition to Gal 4:8b is φύσει.
268. Arnold, "Returning to the Domain," 55–76.
269. Bundrick, "Ta Stoicheia Tou Kosmou," 353–64; he believes the cosmological

to the work of Blinzler, Schweizer and Rusam, who persuasively argue that by far the commonest meaning of στοιχεῖα τοῦ κόσμου in Paul's time was fire, earth, air and water.[270] Context must dictate how the term functions for Paul, however, who in the present text can hardly be concerned with the composition of the physical universe. Considering the clear context of idolatry, in which Paul equates the στοιχεῖα with the deities of the Galatian Gentiles' former religion, and Paul's assertion that the Gentiles verged on being re-enslaved by them, the position taken here is that the στοιχεῖα are *any enslaving powers or forces to which people give their allegiance*. This would seem to be corroborated by Gal 4:3, where Paul suggests that the Jews were once enslaved under (ὑπὸ) the στοιχεῖα τοῦ κόσμου. In light of 4:5 where Jews are said to be redeemed from under (ὑπὸ) *Law*, the στοιχεῖα controversially, albeit with contextual appropriateness, include Torah. The power with which the στοιχεῖα prevent their slaves being in right relation to God is the critical issue for Paul—he certainly did not accept the existential reality of idols.

Gal 4:9 and Jer 31:34

One New Covenant blessing is the knowledge of the true God, which fits a people with a past marred by idolatry. The prophet writes:

> καὶ οὐ μὴ διδάξωσιν ἕκαστος τὸν πολίτην αὐτοῦ καὶ ἕκαστος τὸν ἀδελφὸν αὐτοῦ λέγων Γνῶθι τὸν κύριον, ὅτι πάντες εἰδήσουσίν με ἀπὸ μικροῦ αὐτῶν καὶ ἕως μεγάλου αὐτῶν, ὅτι ἵλεως ἔσομαι ταῖς ἀδικίαις αὐτῶν καὶ τῶν ἁμαρτιῶν αὐτῶν οὐ μὴ μνησθῶ ἔτι
> (Jer 31:34, LXX)

The Bible is replete with passages emphasizing the centrality of "knowing God" (Prov 9:10; Isa 11:9; cf. Hab 2:14; Jer 9:24; 22:16; 24:7; Hos 6:6). Significantly, the refrain "they will know that I am the Lord" occurs in Exodus to depict the conclusion to be drawn by those Egyptians observing Yahweh's mighty acts (Exod 7:5; 14:4, 18; 29:46). Ezekiel incorporates this refrain to describe the impact of God's actions upon Judah's oppressors and Judah herself (Ezek 6:10, 14; 12:15; 24:7; 25:11; 26:6).[271] Both Israel and

---

views of the phrase ill fit the context of Gal 3–4; for excellent general surveys see Calvert Koyzis, *Monotheism*, 104–10; Schweizer, "Slaves of the Elements," 455–68.

270. De Boer, *Galatians*, 253; De Boer makes the very plausible suggestion that the Galatian Gentiles used to worship the four elements of the physical universe; ibid., 253–56.

271. The repeated phrase "you will know that I am the Lord" appears in Exod 6:7; 7:17; 10:2; etc.; it is then drawn into Ezek 6:7, 13; 7:4; 11:10, 12; etc.).

the nations are hauled over the coals for wilful ignorance of God (Ps 79:6; 95:10; Judg 2:10; Jer 2:8; 9:6; 10:25; Hos 4:1; Mic 4:12). The plethora of texts referring to the knowledge of God covers a broad epistemological field; it involved experience, recognising him because of his deeds and acknowledging him in praise and thanksgiving.

As in the previous intertext, Paul depicts the pre-Christian Galatian Gentiles as lacking knowledge of God and being enslaved by "non-gods." Verse 9 serves as a reiterative and rhetorical question; how could these believers wish to be re-enslaved by any element belonging to the former age—even the Law?

> 8 Ἀλλὰ τότε μὲν οὐκ εἰδότες θεὸν ἐδουλεύσατε τοῖς φύσει μὴ οὖσιν θεοῖς· 9 νῦν δὲ γνόντες θεόν, μᾶλλον δὲ γνωσθέντες ὑπὸ θεοῦ, πῶς ἐπιστρέφετε πάλιν ἐπὶ τὰ ἀσθενῆ καὶ πτωχὰ στοιχεῖα οἷς πάλιν ἄνωθεν δουλεύειν θέλετε; (Gal 4:8–9).

By couching Gal 4:1–7 within the historical framework of Israel's Exodus moments, Paul lays the groundwork for depicting right status as *freedom*. His interchange of personal pronouns reveals a common predicament—slavery. There were different slave-masters—Law and idols; and a common solution—Spirit.[272] The experience of the Spirit evidenced Israel's maturity, when she could exercise the inheritance rights held back during her infancy (νήπιός).[273] Hence, Israel's coming of age and the actualization of Gentile sonship are expressions of the one eschatological moment—the advent of God's son in the fullness of time.

Now that the Galatian Gentiles had experienced the Spirit who mediates the risen life of Jesus to believers, how could they wish to submit to something unable to mediate life and render them free? Indeed, Paul commonly aligns ignorance of God with the propensity to sin, a feature Jeremiah's oracle shares.[274] In Romans 1, the ignorance of God was the precursor to idolatry.[275]

Structurally, Jer 31:34 is arranged around two explanatory ὅτι clauses explaining why people will not need to be taught to know God:

καὶ οὐ μὴ διδάξωσιν ἕκαστος τὸν πολίτην αὐτοῦ καὶ ἕκαστος τὸν ἀδελφὸν αὐτοῦ λέγων Γνῶθι τὸν κύριον (a)

ὅτι πάντες εἰδήσουσίν με ἀπὸ μικροῦ αὐτῶν καὶ ἕως μεγάλου αὐτῶν (b)

---

272. Spirit is articulated in relation to Jesus in the context of sonship (Gal 4:6; Rom 8:15).

273. Cf. Hos 11:1

274. Rom 1:21, 28; 1 Cor 1:21; 1 Thess 4:5; cf. Tit 1:16.

275. Rom 1:21–32.

ὅτι ἵλεως ἔσομαι ταῖς ἀδικίαις αὐτῶν καὶ τῶν ἁμαρτιῶν αὐτῶν οὐ μὴ μνησθῶ ἔτι (c)

Clause (a)—people will not require instruction to know God

Clause (b)—initial explanation of clause (a)—because all from the greatest to the smallest will know God

Clause (c)—initial explanation of clause (b) which is consequently expansive explanation for clause (a). *All* will know God because the inauguration of the New Covenant will mark a divine outpouring of grace by which God forgets Israel's sin.

No one will need to teach another to "come to know God" because by *divine* initiative all obstacles to knowing God are removed. All people will be acquainted with the true God and not confuse him with an idol. The context of the previous intertext in Jer 5:7 is idolatry, worded with respect to the knowledge of God. Those in Israel unacquainted with the truth "have not *known* the way of the Lord" (Jer 5:4) contrasting those who have *known* the way of the Lord in 5:5. They swear by "no gods" in Jer 5:7. Correspondingly, it is the rectification of those who could not formerly tell God from an idol who know and are known by God in Gal 4:8–9.

The contrast, "know God and be known by him" in Gal 4:8–9, which, interestingly employs both οἶδα and γινώσκω like the Jeremiah text, reflects the divine causation/human effect of the New Covenant knowledge of God. Though the knowledge of God is attested in Paul, the idea of being known *by* him is less common.[276] The twinning of the expressions is only in Gal 4:9, where it points to the completeness of the knowledge of God, which makes plain sense in Galatians. The Galatian Gentiles have a complete knowledge of God through Spirit, which does not require augmentation by Torah. God has accepted them based on faith in Messiah—they are not somehow more accepted by being circumcised.

It is apparent that the twinned concept of knowing God and being known by him is Paul's embodiment of the divine declaration of the future New Covenant relationship—"I will be their God, and they will be My people" (Jer 31:33).[277] In both the prophetic declaration and Gal 4:9, the essence is the cessation of idolatry. God will be Israel's god and not an idol, and they will belong to him only (Ezekiel/Jeremiah). Knowing God is the rejection of idols and being known by him is effectively being accepted by him (Gal

---

276. 1 Cor 8:3; 2 Cor 5:11; the concept of "knowledge" in general is far more central to the issues highlighted in the Corinthian assemblies.

277. Cf. Jer 24:7; 32:38; Ezek 34:24; 37:23, 27; Zech 8:8.

4:8–9). In Paul's thinking, rectification by faith in Christ fully actualizes the New Covenant relationship with God.

Furthermore, faced with the dilemma in Galatia, Paul likely envisioned Jews and Gentiles as the "greatest" and "least" of people who would possess knowledge of God. As Potter notes, Jeremiah predicts that elitism will now cease—no one will teach it, no one will be able, by his superior expertise, to use it to his own advantage, no one will be able to claim mitigation through ignorance.[278] The phrase "from the least to the greatest" occurs six times in Jeremiah implying inclusion. Even if Paul did not specifically identify the greatest and least as Jew and Gentile respectively, the warnings against empty glorying and provocation in Gal 5:26 and the injunctions regarding boasting in Gal 6:13–14, imply that elitism was one concern instigated by the problems in Galatia.

Gal 4:6–9 and Ezek 37:6

In Ezek 37:6, the prophet draws together the life-giving power of God's Spirit and the consequent knowledge that God is the Lord. Ezekiel writes: δώσω πνεῦμά μου εἰς ὑμᾶς, καὶ ζήσεσθε, καὶ γνώσεσθε ὅτι ἐγώ εἰμι κύριος (Ezek 37:6b). "You will live" denotes "you will be free" and thus, you will know that "I am the Lord," for true freedom derives only from the true Lord—not an idol. In Gal 4:6–7, the Spirit evidences the end of slavery and, consequently, the presence and action of the true God; Gal 4:8–9 testifies to the complete knowledge of God and freedom from idols. This is the Pauline vision of life from death as freedom from slavery.

The revivification texts in Galatians resonate with Deuteronomy 30, Ezek 36:22–28; 37:1–14 as follows. (1) The association of Spirit and "Life" is seen in Gal 2:19–3:5; 3:10–14; 5:25; 6:8 and Ezek 37:5–6, 9, 10, 14. (2) The juxtaposition of Spirit and freedom is seen in Gal 4:4–7, 28–31 and Ezek 36:27–28; 37:12, 14. (3) The internalization of Spirit in the heart and associated renewed engagement with divine commands is seen in Gal 4:4–6; 5:16–23 and Ezek 36:26–28. (4) Deuteronomy 27–30 contains the exile/death-restoration/life fabric in embryonic form, which the exilic prophets experienced and narrated as present realities. Galatians points to Paul's eschatological interpretation of these realities. (5) Galatians 4:21–31 and Ezek 37:1–14 are both "freedom from slavery" narratives in terms of Spirit-instigated new life. These connections suggest that the understanding of exile-restoration as death-life embedded in Deuteronomy 27–30 and Ezekiel 36–37 have influenced Galatians.

278. Potter, "New Covenant in Jeremiah," 353.

Summary of Introductory Issues

Galatians' scholarship has slighted the soteriological significance of "life" (ζάω and cognates) in the letter. Though scholarly comment on the impact of prophetic restoration eschatology on Galatians is well documented, the significance of resurrection imagery therein is under-investigated. An examination of the "life/death" motifs in Galatians demonstrates why a reconsideration of the subject is warranted. Several Jewish and Greco-Roman texts employ revivification imagery to depict freedom from exile; the revivification texts analyzed in the present volume suggest that Paul belongs within this tradition. The resonances between Ezekiel 36–37/Jeremiah (mainly Jeremiah 31) and Galatians 4 evidence a significant interface to this end—the work of Spirit in liberation from bondage and in provoking submission to divine instruction.

2

Revivification Text One

Galatians 1:1–5: Resurrection as Paradigm
in Galatians

With the necessary preamble and introductory details in place, this first section of the argument proper seeks to establish that the principal purpose of Gal 1:1–5 is not to defend the authenticity of Paul's apostleship, though his wording helps to that end. He attends directly to questions regarding the legitimacy of his apostleship later in chapter one. It is argued here that *the prescript of Galatians centralizes the risen Messiah to contextualize the rectification as revivification argument.*

Scholarly Comment on Gal 1:1–5

The magnitude of the concept of "life" to Paul's argument and to the wider soteriological narrative against which it is set becomes increasingly apparent as the letter unfolds. Methodologically, the argument presented here will analyze the structure of the constituent units of Gal 1:1–5 to highlight the incongruence in traditional interpretations of its purpose. Attention will be drawn to the unique features of the prologue of Galatians to show that, quite apart from mere opening greetings, the beginning of this epistle introduces the argument. To buttress this interpretation, the structural and ideological similarities in the prologue of the thematically proximal letter to the Romans will be briefly examined. Throughout this project, Romans will serve as a Pauline text post-dating Galatians and dealing with very similar material in a non-polemical fashion. As such, this book will consider the comparable formulations in Romans in corroborative fashion, but reserve comment on the nature of the development of the common ideas, which is a much more complex issue reaching beyond the scope of this volume.

Many have ventured to demonstrate how the introduction to Galatians is paradigmatic for the broader interpretation of the letter. B. Gaventa pointed out that the introduction of Galatians has often set the agenda for Galatians 1–2 to be seen primarily as a defence of Paul's apostleship, divorcing it from the rest of his theological argument.[1] Her analysis reveals that Galatians 1–2 cannot be confined to the category of apologetic, contra Betz.[2] Yet she largely overlooked the paradigmatic nature of the resurrection reference.

P. Koptak adopted the literary rhetorical method of Kenneth Burke to analyze the importance of the autobiographical sections of Galatians. He employed Burke's theory of *identification*, which stipulates that people attempt to overcome human division by establishing common ground. He concluded that, for Paul, pleasing God over humans (Gal 1:10) corresponded to embracing the gospel of Christ over/against a human gospel (1:11–12). Koptak shows that the gospel formed a community that remained intact as long as its members shared the pursuit of pleasing God based on the revealed, circumcision-free gospel. Any attempt to adopt circumcision was a people-pleasing move that segregates rather than unites.[3]

In 1994, J. Vos criticised the various methods of reconstructing the charges to which Paul was responding in Galatians. He particularly railed against the charge of Paul's defending his apostleship to the Jerusalem leadership.[4] Rather, he argues that Galatians 1–2 can be understood completely as a response to the one charge that *can* be explicitly determined from the text, namely, Paul's alleged failure to demand Gentile submission to Torah.

For Vos the prescript is solely to establish Paul's authority—he was not speaking independently, but as God's envoy. The twofold *correctio* οὐκ ἀπ' ἀνθρώπων οὐδὲ δι' ἀνθρώπου underlines this claim to authority and accentuates the positive part of the statement ἀλλὰ διὰ Ἰησοῦ Χριστοῦ καὶ θεοῦ πατρός.[5] Whilst Vos correctly infers that concocting further charges is unnecessary, the argument seems overstated; we cannot know that Paul's opponents only had one complaint against him. Furthermore, although Galatians 1–2 are certainly integral elements of the defence of Paul's Law-

---

1. Gaventa, "Galatians 1 and 2," 312. Cf. Berchman, "Galatians 1:1–5," 60–72. Berchman sees forensic rhetoric in Gal 1:1–2, deliberative rhetoric in Gal 1:3–4 and epideictic rhetoric in Gal 1:5.

2. Gaventa, "Galatians 1 and 2," 326.

3. Koptak, "Rhetorical Identification," 97–113.

4. Vos, "Paul's Argumentation," 2.

5. Ibid., 3.

independent gospel, Vos considers the introductory formula commonplace enough not to require more of it than Paul's other introductory formulae. He neglects the uniqueness of the designation of God as "the one having raised Jesus from the dead" in a Pauline prescript.

In D. Cook's innovative reading of the prologue of Galatians, there is a much more able attempt at acknowledging the significance of Jesus' resurrection. Despite the thoroughness of what is a brief paper, Cook's broader thesis is to establish how the battle for Galatia is a one of competing eschatologies, one component of which is the centrality of Jesus' resurrection.[6] The centrality of resurrection to the actual polemics is not afforded significant profile.

Closer to my position is R. A. Bryant, whose monograph merges rhetorical and epistolary criticism to analyze Gal 1:1–5. Thus, Bryant identifies a number of "rhetorical cords" in the prescript that resurface throughout the letter. Bryant rightly draws attention to the uniqueness of what he calls the "remarkable beginning" of Galatians.[7]

The first of these rhetorical cords is the risen Christ. Bryant contends that Gal 1:1 is foundational to several key points in Galatians, a view the present volume also embraces. He can argue this because he reads resurrection language as wholly apocalyptic.[8] As such, Bryant can argue for the importance of Christ's resurrection where it is not mentioned, through a consideration of apocalyptic ideology. Examples include Paul's use of the ἀποκάλυπ- cognates in 1:11—2:10, the dawn of the new age (3:6—4:7), the flesh/Spirit dualism (5:13—6:10), and the language of new creation (6:11–18).

As much as the argument of this book has in common with Bryant, his explanation of the risen Christ as rhetorical cord is ultimately unconvincing.[9] It is simply not grounded in actual resurrection ideology—rather, having declared that resurrection is thoroughly apocalyptic, he then relies on the use of ἀποκαλύπτω. This is another argument that does not get past the singular explicit resurrection reference in Galatians with any conviction, consequently offering no ultimately compelling reason why the resurrection should set the agenda for the epistle.

It may appear that my approach only differs from Bryant insofar as it relates resurrection to death and life rather than "apocalyptic." However,

6. Cook, "Prescript as Program," 515.
7. Bryant, *Crucified Christ*, 111.
8. Ibid., 143.
9. See the critique by M. S. Harmon of Wheaton College, http://www.bookreviews.org/pdf/1830_4226.pdf.

"apocalyptic" is a *category*, which may embody a whole host of ideas (e.g., the world divided into ages) unrelated to resurrection. To simply assert that resurrection is one of them and proceed on this basis bypasses the *actual* presence of resurrection in the letter. My contention is not simply that resurrection is related to death and life categorically, but *conceptually*. Resurrection *is* life being given to the dead, as the death/life lexicon in Paul broadly demonstrates (Rom 4:17; 6:4; 14:9; 1 Cor 15:45). To consider how death and life as joint concepts function in the letter is to consider resurrection *directly*.

Others make tangential reference to the significance of resurrection in Gal 1:1. T. Gallant writes in his 2006 article that Paul's mention of the resurrection in Gal 1:1 hints at something paradigmatic.[10] Others offer plausible possible reasons why Paul would even mention the resurrection at all.[11] Voluminous literature expands upon the uncharacteristically harsh and defensive tenor of Paul's opening comments in Galatians. A more seldom explored emphasis is outlined below—the paradigmatic influence of God the father raising Jesus from the dead for the letter as a whole.[12]

This re-reading of the structural details of the prescript will make the overall reading of it markedly different from most scholarly treatments. Though due caution is given to Barclay's warning about mirror reading, some of it is inevitable;[13] by so doing, scholars quite correctly suggest that Paul's opponents' argumentative strategy included undermining his apostolic credentials. They may have insisted on his need to remain subordinate to the Jerusalem leaders or exploited his disconnectedness from them to explain the incompleteness of his message.

Though the first clause of Gal 1:1 goes some way towards answering these charges, if this is the *principal* objective of the prescript then Paul has expressed himself in awkward fashion. Neither the description of God as "raiser" nor any part of 1:4 say anything regarding the legitimacy of Paul's apostleship. A rigid focus on Paul's defensiveness unceremoniously drowns out the resurrection motif.

---

10. Tim Gallant, "What Saint Paul Should Have Said," http://www.biblicalstudies-center.org/interpretation/shouldhave.htm.

11. Garlington, *Exposition of Galatians*, 46–48; Burton, *Galatians*, 7.

12. See Gaffin, *Resurrection and Redemption*, 62–66.

13. Barclay, "Mirror-Reading," 73–93.

Co-textual Analysis: Gal 1:1 in Relation to 1:2–4

Structural Detail of Gal 1:1

Looking at its constituent units, observe:

> Paul, an apostle . . . is:
>
> οὐκ ἀπ' ἀνθρώπων—not from men: ἀπό plus the noun ἄνθρωπος in the genitive plural is a generic reference to the leadership of a Jesus community—so Paul was not commissioned by any given "church." He continues:
>
> οὐδὲ δι' ἀνθρώπου—nor through a man: διά plus the noun in the genitive singular is a reference to any specific leader—so Paul was not commissioned by, say, Peter or James.

However, the rest of the clause raises issues that radically shift the focus of the verse and resultantly the pericope:

> ἀλλὰ διὰ Ἰησοῦ Χριστοῦ καὶ θεοῦ πατρὸς τοῦ ἐγείραντος αὐτὸν ἐκ νεκρῶν.

Firstly, there is the glaringly inharmonious resurrection clause; secondly, the order of names seems awkward—in Paul's typical bipartite references to God and Jesus together, Jesus' name appears second.[14] Moreover, God is notably identified with respect to Jesus. Thirdly, how can Paul argue that he was not commissioned through *a man*, but through *Jesus Christ*? The following explains the position taken here.

The strong adversative ἀλλά seems to be an explicit attempt to ascribe divine status to Jesus, but divinity of itself is scarcely reason for Paul to say he was not commissioned through a man—*unless Paul wanted to place the emphasis on the risen status of his commissioner*. Resurrected status could certainly imply Jesus was more than a man (cf. 1 Cor 15:39–45).[15]

The clause identifying God as the Architect of Jesus' resurrected status is connected to Jesus' name with the conjunction καὶ; but, Paul is clearly not suggesting two separate commissions—one by Jesus and one by God. Rather, Paul is identifying God as "the God of resurrection" in much the same way as the prophets identified God as "the One who brought you up out of Egypt," as per the earlier discussion. This is Paul's attempt to depict

---

14. R. Longenecker, *Galatians*, 4.

15. Churchill argues that this clause distinguishes the roles and identity of God and Jesus Christ whilst showing they share a bond that "supersedes Jesus' very humanity." See Churchill, *Divine Initiative*, 107.

God in terms of a pivotal act. Similar designations are found in Rom 4:24; 8:11; 2 Cor 1:9; 4:14; but in no other Pauline prescript. The following two lines of evidence substantiate this overall position.

Evidence of Emphasis on Risen Christ in Gal 1:12

Assuming that Gal 1:12 and 1:16 refer to the Damascus christophany, they accentuate this emphasis on the resurrected Christ. In 1:12, Paul effectively writes of his *preaching* what he writes in 1:1 concerning his *apostleship*. Of Paul's gospel we read—οὐδὲ γὰρ ἐγὼ παρὰ ἀνθρώπου παρέλαβον αὐτὸ οὔτε ἐδιδάχθην (Gal 1:12a). Instead, (again the strong adversative ἀλλά) he received the gospel δι' ἀποκαλύψεως Ἰησοῦ Χριστοῦ (through a revelation of Jesus Christ—again signifying the risen Christ). Paul writes concerning both his commission (1:1) and the substance of his gospel (1:12)[16] that they were:

" . . . not (οὐδὲ) . . . from a man (ἄνθρωπος) . . . but (ἀλλὰ) . . . through (διὰ) . . . Jesus Christ."

Whilst space prevents exhaustive comment on the Damascus Christophany, it seems this event prompted Paul to completely rethink his inherited salvation agenda and construct a Gentile message with a radical reappraisal of Torah. As such, what follows is a brief elaboration on how the minimal details of the Damascus encounter in 1:13–17 broaden the focus of the risen Christ in the opening lines of Galatians.

We may surmise from Gal 1:13–17 that Paul experienced the risen Jesus and that a Law-independent Gentile gospel resulted, but how are these two eventualities linked? Why did this unforeseen encounter with a resurrected Messiah lead to the preaching of a Law-independent gospel?

What the apostle does not do is recite something he was told—he does *not* say the risen Christ told him to preach that the Law had run its course or that it had no jurisdiction over non-Jews, though this might be implied.[17] Rather, he writes:

Οὐδὲ γὰρ ἐγὼ παρὰ ἀνθρώπου παρέλαβον αὐτὸ

For neither (did) I from a man receive it, (Gal 1:12a)

---

16. I think the genitive Ἰησοῦ Χριστοῦ should be read objectively—it was Jesus who was revealed rather than doing the revealing on the grounds that God is the subject of ἀποκαλύπτω in 1:16.

17. The scant and conflicting details in the three Lucan accounts of the encounter (Acts 9:3–9; 22:6–11; 26:12–21) say nothing of the substance of the message Paul was instructed to disseminate.

> ... οὔτε ἐδιδάχθην, ἀλλὰ δι'
>
> ... nor was I taught, but through (Gal 1:12b)
>
> ... ἀποκαλύψεως Ἰησοῦ Χριστοῦ.
>
> ... a revelation of Jesus Christ (Gal 1:12c).[18]

Observe, firstly, there are no qualifying verbs in 1:12c. The gospel Paul proclaimed was neither *received* from men (1:12a) nor *taught* to Paul (1:12b), but through a revelation of Jesus Christ. Readers may supply qualifiers—perhaps Paul neither received nor was taught the gospel by *a man*, but *did* receive it and *was* taught it by the risen Christ. However, ἀποκαλύψεως Ἰησοῦ Χριστοῦ is given some qualification in 1:16—it was ἐν ἐμοί, ἵνα εὐαγγελίζωμαι αὐτὸν ἐν τοῖς ἔθνεσιν. The dative ἐμοί would be sufficient if Jesus revealed the gospel *to* Paul. The pronoun ἐν is redundant unless something else is implied, namely an interiorized component to this revelation.[19] A few words regarding the encounter seem appropriate at this juncture.

Scholars differ regarding what happened to Paul on the Damascus path; K. Stendahl is adamant that Paul was not "converted" in any sense, but *called* like Israel's prophets.[20] R. Peace suggests Damascus awakened Paul to the fact that the God who revealed Jesus to him was the same God he served as a Pharisee. He writes:

> The coming of Jesus fulfils the old covenant and creates a new covenant. But it is still the same God at work. Paul has not joined a new religious movement or altered all his ideas about God.[21]

Alternatively, Alan Segal stresses that Paul was indeed a convert, having jettisoned some and maintained other aspects of his former life. In Segal's opinion, Paul was a Pharisaic Jew who converted to a new apocalyptic, Jewish sect and then lived in a Hellenistic Gentile Christian community as a Jew among Gentiles.[22] J. M. Everts treads most safely noting simply that

---

18. Gal 1:12.

19. See Bruce, *Galatians*, 93; for a summary of possibilities see Arichea and Nida, *Galatians: A Translator's Handbook*, 22. Schmisek's insistence that there was no physical component to the vision over-extrapolates the evidence. See Schmisek, "Paul's Vision," 82. The assertions of commentators like Lightfoot that the ἐν ἐμοί denotes something preached *through* Paul *to* others, whilst by no means implausible, does not really address the linguistic anomaly. See Lightfoot, *Galatians*, 83.

20. Stendahl, *Paul among Jews and Gentiles*, 7–23. Both Paul and Jeremiah were "set apart from the womb of their mother"—see Jer 1:5; Gal 1:15.

21. Peace, *Conversion in the New Testament*, 82.

22. Segal, *Paul the Convert*, 6–7.

no single term seems able to describe the complexities of Paul's Damascus Road experience.[23] Needless to say, the complexities of attempting to categorize the Damascus Road experience are manifold.[24] Galatians 1:12 would seem to point to Paul having interpreted the event himself, though we cannot know whether it confirmed prior knowledge Paul had about Jesus or if through the event itself Paul attained this awareness. So to the qualification of Gal 1:16.

Evidence of Emphasis on Risen Christ in Gal 1:16

According to 1:12, the *gospel* came through a revelation of Jesus Christ. In 1:16, *Jesus himself* is revealed "in" Paul.[25] These two statements point to one revelatory moment—*the unveiling of the risen Jesus was the unveiling of the gospel*. Bruce correctly renders the awkward genitive clause "revelation of Jesus Christ" in 1:12, noting:

> That Ἰησοῦ Χριστοῦ here is an objective genitive is rendered most probable by the wording of vv. 15f.: God "was pleased to reveal his Son in me" . . . it was Jesus Christ who was revealed, and in that revelation Paul received his gospel . . . *The gospel and the risen Christ were inseparable; both were revealed to Paul in the same moment.*[26]

Galatians 1:16 suggests the experience was internal and simultaneously the impetus for Paul's Gentile gospel. We need not, however, conclusively classify the nature of the experience beyond Paul's own comments, for Paul has provided the essential commentary. In 2:19–20, he narrates a "death to Law in order to live to God," which is qualified as "co-crucifixion with Christ and life energized by faith in Christ." The revelation of the crucified and now resurrected Christ and his gospel "in Paul" prompted the apostle to compose a narrative of personal crucifixion and revivification to account for his rectification. The experience of the resurrected Christ reconfigured Paul's comprehension of Torah and reconfigured him personally as well. Paul had died to the Law (2:19) and lived by faith in God's son. Just as Jesus' transformation was effected by death and life, so Paul was transformed by dying to that which had identified him, so he might be identified by faith in

---

23. Everts, "Conversion and Call of Paul," 162.

24. E.g., Newman, "Transforming Images of Paul," 73; cf. Segal, *Paul the Convert*, 105–10.

25. The referent of αὐτὸ in 1:12 is τὸ εὐαγγέλιον τὸ εὐαγγελισθὲν in 1:11.

26. Bruce, *Galatians*, 89 (emphasis mine); cf. R. Longenecker, *Galatians*, 23–24.

Messiah. *So then, resurrection had been revealed in Paul—the internal revelation of Messiah's death-to-life transformation prompted Paul to communicate his own transformation in Christ as "death . . . in order to live"* (Gal 2:19). If this change was a matter of death and revivification by eschatologically participating in the Christ event, as Paul conveys, then clearly it did not necessitate recourse to Torah, and to demand such recourse of Gentiles was thus doubly futile, for they were never its intended recipients.

Resultantly, two things should be manifest; firstly, far from a marginal actor, the risen Christ takes centre stage in the drama of Galatians. Secondly, the identification of God as "raiser of the dead" becomes the linchpin for understanding the letter of Galatians. God had revivified the dead Jesus (Gal 1:1), the Paul who had died to Torah (2:19), the believers who had crucified the flesh (5:24–25) and the crucified, created order (6:14–16). This act of raising the dead was never the Law's role (3:21b). Galatians argues how and why rectification is revivification—an act the Law could never perform. As such, no Gentile needed to be bound to it, contra Paul's opponents. The paradigmatic opening of Galatians effectively rehearses:

Paul, an apostle not commissioned by any church or person, but rather by the resurrected Christ, raised from the dead by the God of Resurrection.

Structural Detail of Gal 1:2–4

The grace in Gal 1:2–3 is qualified in 1:4 with a startling effect, which further accentuates the prominence of the resurrection for Paul's counter-thesis in Galatians. In every canonical Pauline text, the grace section of the opening has a phrase approximate to χάρις ὑμῖν καὶ εἰρήνη ἀπὸ θεοῦ πατρὸς ἡμῶν καὶ κυρίου Ἰησοῦ Χριστοῦ with only minor syntactical elaborations differentiating between them.[27] These stanzas appear in what are implied present tenses (there are no verbs), suggesting the grace is extended from God and the *risen* Jesus in each instance. However, *only* in Galatians is the grace section elaborated with supplementary detail about Jesus' messianic identity. The embellishments are as follows:

. . . τοῦ δόντος ἑαυτὸν ὑπὲρ τῶν ἁμαρτιῶν ἡμῶν, (1:4a)

. . . ὅπως ἐξέληται ἡμᾶς ἐκ τοῦ αἰῶνος τοῦ ἐνεστῶτος πονηροῦ (1:4b)

. . . κατὰ τὸ θέλημα τοῦ θεοῦ καὶ πατρὸς ἡμῶν, (1:4c).

---

27. The pastorals epistles add ἔλεος to the grace.

After the extended grace from the implied risen Christ, Christ is then qualified in the aorist active participial clause of 1:4a as "the one having given himself on behalf of our sins."[28] This must refer then to the *earthly* Christ, suggesting that it is ostensibly the *risen* Christ who "rescues us from the age of the present evil." It may be axiomatic that the earthly Christ died for our sins and then was raised, as 1 Cor 15:3-4; but, of course, 1 Corinthians 15 is a passage *specifically* about resurrection. Hence, the detail in the prologue of Galatians places unique emphasis on this aspect of Jesus' redemptive activity. An analogous and more pointed phrase is Rom 4:25: ὃς παρεδόθη διὰ τὰ παραπτώματα ἡμῶν καὶ ἠγέρθη διὰ τὴν δικαίωσιν ἡμῶν.

Juxtaposing Gal 1:4 and Rom 4:25 noteworthily suggests a broad equivalence; Jesus was given (παρεδόθη) in Rom 4:25, but gave himself (τοῦ δόντος ἑαυτὸν) in Gal 1:4. "Because of our transgressions" is consistent with "on behalf of our sins"; rectification (δικαίωσιν) language in Galatians as in Romans is central to the fabric of soteriological expression (e.g., Rom 3:24; Gal 3:11-13).

The broader Pauline witness treats the *risen* Christ as the agent of rescue, deliverance and salvation. Rom 5:10 implies that Jesus' death reconciles, but his *life* saves; Rom 10:9 instructs that faith in *the risen* Christ leads to salvation (cf. Col 2:12). In 1 Thess 1:10, Paul encourages the Gentiles to await God's son *from Heaven*, the one *raised from the dead* who *delivers* us from the coming wrath—this, of course, paves the way for the eschatological portrait in 1 Thess 4:14-17 where the risen Christ finally gathers all those in Christ. Paul's description of the resurrected Christ as first-fruits in 1 Cor 15:20, 23 recalls the cultic significance of the Mosaic offerings; on the one hand, the first-fruits represented the total harvest or flock, pointing to the thanksgiving of the people for the everything God has given (Deut 26:1-10). On the other, they denoted an organic unity between the offered part and the whole. For Paul, Christ is the initial portion of the resurrection harvest of believers.[29] Paul even spoke of his own "deliverance" from persecution in his ministry as "resurrection" (2 Cor 1:9-10). Jesus' self-giving *and* resurrection then, are to be understood as "according to the will of our God and father" (Gal 1:4).

In Paul's autobiography of rectification in 2:19-20, there is prominent revivification imagery, so we understand that not only did the deliverer go from death to life, *but that is how he delivered others.* Below is an outline of how Gal 2:19-20 demonstrates the paradigmatic trajectory of the

---

28 Δόντος is the aorist active participle of δίδωμι; NRSV, NIV and NASB all simply have '"gave" himself.

29 See Gaffin, *Resurrection*, 34-35.

prescript—the corroborative comments on Gal 2:21 and the structurally/soteriologically related comment in 3:21b are to reinforce the point further.

Paul's Rectification: Gal 2:19–20 in Light of the Prescript

θεοῦ πατρὸς τοῦ ἐγείραντος αὐτὸν ἐκ νεκρῶν (Gal 1:1b)

τοῦ δόντος ἑαυτὸν ὑπὲρ τῶν ἁμαρτιῶν ἡμῶν, (Gal 1:4a)

ὅπως ἐξέληται ἡμᾶς ἐκ τοῦ αἰῶνος τοῦ ἐνεστῶτος πονηροῦ (Gal 1:4b)

κατὰ τὸ θέλημα τοῦ θεοῦ καὶ πατρὸς ἡμῶν (Gal 1:4c)

ἐγὼ γὰρ διὰ νόμου νόμῳ ἀπέθανον, ἵνα θεῷ ζήσω. Χριστῷ συνεσταύρωμαι· (Gal 2:19)

ζῶ δὲ οὐκέτι ἐγώ, ζῇ δὲ ἐν ἐμοὶ Χριστός· ὃ δὲ νῦν ζῶ ἐν σαρκί, ἐν πίστει ζῶ τῇ τοῦ υἱοῦ τοῦ θεοῦ τοῦ ἀγαπήσαντός με καὶ παραδόντος ἑαυτὸν ὑπὲρ ἐμοῦ (Gal 2:20)

εἰ γὰρ διὰ νόμου δικαιοσύνη, ἄρα Χριστὸς δωρεὰν ἀπέθανεν (Gal 2:21b).

εἰ γὰρ ἐδόθη νόμος ὁ δυνάμενος ζῳοποιῆσαι, ὄντως ἐκ νόμου ἂν ἦν ἡ δικαιοσύνη· (Gal 3:21b).

The programmatic nature of the prescript for the forward direction of the argument of Galatians may be explained with reference to the above as follows:

1. *Gal 1:1 & Gal 2:19.* God raised (ἐγείρω) Jesus from the dead (νεκρῶν); correspondingly, Paul "died" (ἀποθνήσκω) in order that he might live (ζάω). The death that Paul died was "co-crucifixion" (συσταυρόω) with Christ leading to new life—Paul identified his transformation with the Christ event.

2. *Gal 1:4a & Gal 2:20.* Jesus is, "the one having given himself over on behalf of our sins to rescue us from the present age of evil;" Paul employs a similar construction to articulate how Jesus rescued him in particular. There are two key differences—παραδίδωμι in 2:20 replaces δίδωμι in 1:4;[30] Jesus' self-giving in 1:4 is "on behalf of our sins," but "on behalf of me" in 2:20.

---

30. Note again use of παραδίδωμι in Rom 4:25.

3. *Gal 2:21b & Gal 3:21b*. In both these texts, Paul employs a conditional formula concerning Law (εἰ γὰρ . . . . νόμος . . . δικαιοσύνη). As such, Paul asserts that (1) Christ did not die needlessly for *right status is not through Law* (2:21) (2) *Right status is not through Law* because it lacks the power to revivify (3:21). Galatians 2:21 implies that Christ's death was integral to how people attain right status. This thought continues in 3:1, for the Galatians were (clearly) cognizant of Jesus' death.[31] Here, Paul launches into the first of two driving questions in the letter (cf. 3:19). Was the Galatians' possession by the Spirit the result of faith or legal observance? The introduction of Abraham in 3:6 makes the entire enquiry of 3:2–5 academic—the origin of Spirit is faith. Galatians 3:21 adds a complementary line of reasoning. The reason right status is not from Law is its incapacity to make alive. The argument seems to be this: Christ's death was necessary because the Law could not bring forth the Spirit who makes alive; the Spirit is received by virtue of faith in Christ. Thus, Paul writes in 3:13–14 that the crucifixion of Christ secured the coming of the promised Spirit, received through faith. These correspondences between the prescript of Galatians and Paul's autobiography of rectification in 2:19–20 illuminate the following: the God of resurrection raised Jesus from the dead; the risen Christ delivers people from the present age by his risen life through the agency of Spirit. The Law did not have this life-giving, Spirit-giving power. A seemingly incongruous resurrection image is also detectable in the prescript of Romans, to which we will now turn our attention.

Further Evidence: The Prescript of Romans

The table below illustrates in simple fashion the connections between the openings of the two Pauline epistles.

---

31. The Galatian Gentiles' acquaintance with Jesus' crucifixion is largely governed by how translators deal with προγράφω in 3:1. It simply denotes "written before" in Rom 15:4; some like Hays argue that in Gal 3:1 it points to Christ's crucifixion being prophetically enshrined in the scriptures. See Hays, "Galatians," 250–51.

Motif	Romans	Galatians
Elaboration of Paul's identity	Slave, apostle (1:1)	Apostle (1:1)
Paul's prophetic call	Separated for gospel of God (1:1)	Sent through Christ, not men (1:1)
Elaboration of God's identity	Announced gospel through prophets (1:2)	Raised Jesus from dead (1:1)
Elaboration of Jesus' identity	Son of David according to flesh, son of God according to spirit by resurrection (1:3–4)	Lord who gave himself for sins to rescue us from evil age (1:4)

Romans and Galatians have approximately the same related issues in scope—rectification, Abraham, circumcision, Jewish versus Gentile ethnicity, faith and Spirit. These issues point to fundamental elements of Paul's vision of the eschatological people of God. For example, Günther Juncker, in examining Rom 4; 9:13–17 and Gal 4:21–31 to demonstrate an underlying hermeneutical consistency to Paul's typological use of the patriarchs, writes that:

> ... the identity of the people of God ... reduces to a question of paternity. Who are the children and heirs of Abraham and of the blessings and promises of Scripture? In answering this question, Paul consistently spiritualizes descent from Abraham.[32]

Having cited a number of close connections between Galatians and Romans, Bruce writes of the common themes that:

> All this comes to expression in Galatians in a situation of anxiety, indignation and conflict; in Romans it is expounded more dispassionately and in a more logical sequence.[33]

Nonetheless, the congruity between the openings of the two letters receives minimal scholarly attention. J. R. D. Kirk suggests that Rom 1:4 is somewhat marginalized because of its widely proclaimed origin as hymnic material.[34] According to the prescript of Romans, Jesus has come from (γενομένου) the seed of David according to flesh, but by parallel token, from God according to Spirit. The critical section of the opening of Romans for our purposes is below—Jesus is:

---

32. Juncker, "Children of Promise," 131–60 (esp. 158).
33. Bruce, "Galatian Problems 4," 255.
34. Kirk, "Appointed Son(s)," 242.

τοῦ γενομένου (a)

    ἐκ σπέρματος Δαυὶδ (b)

        κατὰ σάρκα, (c)

τοῦ ὁρισθέντος (a')

    υἱοῦ θεοῦ ἐν δυνάμει (b')

        κατὰ πνεῦμα ἁγιωσύνης (c')

ἐξ ἀναστάσεως νεκρῶν . . . . (Rom 1:3–4a)

The simple structure (a-a'; b-b'; c-c') evidences the two aspects of Jesus' messianic identity; (a-a') relates to Jesus' origin. The contrast is between γίνομαι and ὁρίζω; the former verb refers to biological ancestry. The latter is defined as "separating entities so as to establish a boundary" and later derived the sense, "to define ideas or concepts" and, of people, "to declare to be something"—here it implies that Jesus was "marked off from everyone else."[35] According to genealogical descent, Jesus was "from the seed of David;" yet he was marked off as "Son of God in power" (b-b').[36] His Davidic connection was according to flesh; his sonship to God in power was predicated on the action of the Spirit (c-c'). The resurrection image hangs awkwardly at the end, further qualifying Jesus' marking off as God's son in power by the Spirit. We observe the following.

Firstly, like Galatians, the resurrection image in the prescript initially ill fits the rest of the pericope. Secondly, the prescript testifies to the Spirit's role in marking out sons for God. Kirk's observation is interesting that the verb προορίζω in Rom 8:29, using the same root ὁρίζω as 1:4, depicts what God does to believers "beforehand."[37] Though it is not immediately clear what Paul means in saying Jesus was marked out as Son of God in power *according to* a Spirit of holiness *from* a resurrection of the dead, we may speculate intelligently on the basis of related texts.[38] Romans 8:11 reads: "but if the Spirit of the one having raised Jesus from the dead [i.e., the Spirit of God] is housed in you, the one having raised the Christ from the dead [that is, *God*] will *also* (καί) make your mortal bodies live [because the Spirit makes alive (ζῳοποιέω)] through the in-housing of his Spirit in you." The implication

---

35. Arndt et al., *A Greek-English Lexicon*, 723 (BAGD hereafter).
36. Isa 11:1, 10; Jer 23:5–6; Ezek 34:23–24.
37. Kirk, "Appointed Son(s)," 242.
38. The phrase ἐν δυνάμει may modify ὁρισθέντος (powerfully marked out) or υἱοῦ θεοῦ (Son of God in power). The latter seems more likely; cf. 2 Cor. 13:4. The meaning of "spirit of holiness" is disputed; those (like myself) equating it with "Holy Spirit," acknowledge a complex connection between Spirit and resurrection.

is that if someone is possessed by Spirit, God extends to them the "life" of the risen Christ. The believer is not resurrected, but made alive—so we may infer that when someone is made alive by virtue of Spirit, they attain sonship to God.

The rhetorical impetus of the prescript of Galatians lies in isolating the role of the risen Jesus as commissioner of Paul and deliverer of humanity. It is not happenstance that in Galatians and Romans, concerned as they are with the identity of God's eschatological people, ideas of resurrection and sonship are interwoven in such theologically elaborate fashion.

In Gal 4:6, the Spirit of God's son in the hearts of believers cries out "Abba Father." Just as rectification is predicated upon Jesus' resurrection, the sonship of believers is a derivative of the unique sonship of Jesus to God. This explains the use of "Spirit of his son" in Gal 4:6 for Spirit. It is because (ὅτι) you are sons, Paul writes, that God sent the Spirit of his son into believers' hearts, as if to ratify that believers are *sons* because Christ is *the* Son.[39] As previously argued, the threefold use of "father" in Gal 1:1–4 (in which God is implied as both the father of believers and of Jesus) introduces the importance of sonship. The making alive of believers ratifies their status as sons just as the resurrection of Jesus marked his status as Son.

Summary: Gal 1:1—Risen Christ, Revivified Believers

The structural details and idiosyncratic etiquette of Gal 1:1–5 suggest that the argument proper begins here. Paul purposes to identify God as the God of Resurrection much like the prophets who styled him "the God who led you out of Egypt." As the argument of the letter unfolds, a number of restoration and new Exodus motifs emerge. Paul treats the crucifixion and resurrection of Jesus as the central event of this "new Exodus." After challenging the Galatians for being so easily swayed (Gal 1:6–10), Paul relays how he received the revelation of Jesus' gospel. According to 1:12, the gospel came through a revelation of Jesus Christ. In 1:16, Jesus himself is revealed in Paul. These two statements point to the simultaneous unveiling of Jesus *and* the gospel. The resurrection of Jesus had been "revealed in Paul"—the internal revelation of Messiah's death-to-life transformation prompted Paul to communicate his own transformation in Christ as "death . . . in order to

---

39. One need not press the chronology of sonship and Spirit possession on the strength of the word "because"; Betz warns against trying to answer quandaries such as these by the importation of "dogmatic and philosophical categories." See Betz, *Galatians*, 209–10. Bruce writes that their instatement as sons and their receiving the Spirit appear to be simultaneous. See Bruce, *Galatians*, 198.

live" (Gal 2:19). Resurrection was how God acted to vindicate Jesus, and became a paradigm for how he now planned to rectify humankind.

The rest of Galatians, then, hinges upon Paul's account of rectification as immersion in the Christ event—death by co-crucifixion with Christ and Spirit initiated "life." The objective of the polemic becomes clear in two key questions the apostle asks. If rectification is revivification at the instigation of Spirit, how does one receive the Spirit—from faith in Christ or legal observance (3:2)? If we grant that Spirit comes through faith, then why did God give the Law (3:19)? Paul answers these quandaries in terms of death and life to counter his opponents.

The occurrences of death/crucifixion-life in Galatians represent milestones in the letter, where Paul evokes the revivification imagery associated with the accounts of restoration from Israel's redemptive-historical narrative. The resurrection of Jesus was for Paul the supreme act of God and the interpretive grid through which he now understood the prophetic symbols of life coming from death.

The resurrection of Jesus is paradigmatic for Paul's presentation of rectification; it is the conceptualization of "life" and "Spirit" that gives the paradigm its functional impetus.[40] God raised Jesus from death; Jesus set about the cosmic deliverance of humanity by imparting his life through Spirit to those dead because of sin.

This presentation treats life and death as interpretive keys for Galatians. Marshall observes (in connection with Rom 4:25) that the resurrection "representatively justified" Jesus so that those baptized into his death (Rom 6:3–4) may also share in his new life.[41] The concept of the "rectification of Jesus" may seem misplaced. Whilst it is broadly accepted that the resurrection of Jesus was divine vindication of his gospel, it is more difficult to imagine Paul articulating that Jesus attained "right status" before God, as if, in Paul's mind, he ever lacked it. However, Paul does argue for the superiority of his apostolic commissioning on the grounds it originated from the *risen* Christ. It is evident from Rom 1:3–4 that Jesus was genetically affiliated to David according to flesh, but by resurrection according to Spirit was affiliated to God.

It seems correct then, within Galatians, that the resurrected Jesus is a type for the rectified believer. In his resurrection, Jesus enters the "life" which, through Spirit, he will make available to all on the grounds of faith. The next stage of the argument is to demonstrate how this premise unfolds in the revivification imagery of Galatians.

---

40. The implicit assumption is that Christ is present in believers through the Spirit. See Tolmie, "Spirituality," 176. Cf. Gal 2:20.

41. Marshall, *Aspects of the Atonement*, 97.

3

Revivification Text Two

Galatians 2:19–20: Paul's Autobiography
of Rectification.

The remaining chapters will consider how the revivification texts propel the argument of Galatians. Methodologically, the rubric of the case presented here can be summarized as how the death-life language in Galatians establishes a "narrative of revivification," which lies behind the text of the letter. This revivification lexicon will be examined to determine its functionality within its co-textual framework to suggest how it advances the argument of the letter at large (context). Rounding off the examination of each revivification text, is a review of the intertextual echoes connecting the argument to the wider redemptive-historical narrative, of which Paul considered the Christ event the cardinal moment.

Like an increasing number of interpretations of Paul, this book aims to give due attention to the narrative component of non-narrative texts. R. Hays, in the words of B. Longenecker, put the issue of narrative contours explicitly on the agenda of Pauline study and in so doing highlighted that the Jesus story lay underneath the text, "undergirding it, supporting it, animating it, and giving it coherence, while also constraining its discursive options."[1] For Hays, it is the underlying Jesus story in which the units of Paul's letters are anchored; my approach to Galatians treats the resurrection aspect of that story as of foremost importance. Of course, Paul is not telling a story in Galatians—he pens a letter to confront a problem with potentially destructive social implications. However, at key moments in the letter, Paul's rebuttals and explanations employ resurrection based language to elucidate the connection between the issues on the ground in the churches and the

1. Longenecker, "Narrative Interest," 6.

divine action in Christ to rectify humanity. In view of this, our examination will draw attention to the co-textual material to determine how the revivification units function; cumulatively a theological picture of life-giving emerges which explains why it is superfluous to demand legal observance of Gentiles.

Context: Opening Comments/Significance of Unit Gal 2:15–21

There is a consensus that Gal 2:15–21 is a response to the public debacle in Antioch involving Peter and other Jewish disciples when colleagues of James from Jerusalem arrived there.[2] Betz notably disagrees, rather seeing the pericope as part of the *propositio* section of Galatians.[3]

The significance of the unit, however, cannot be over-estimated. Several key terms are introduced here—δικαιόω, ἔργον, νόμος, ἐκ πίστεως Χριστοῦ, and ζάω. Commentators on Galatians routinely see a theological core to Paul's polemic in these verses. As Moo notes, most scholars appropriately recognize that 2:15–21 is a transitional paragraph. Paul continues, to some degree, his "speech" at Antioch (2:11–14); but he clearly has the Galatians in view, and more so as the speech progresses.[4] The unit forms a conclusive set of proposals outlining in rudimentary form Paul's major contention—works of the Law do not rectify someone before God. Seifrid rightly refers to it as a preview to the thoughts about to develop.[5] The com-

---

2. There is not unanimity on where the "reply" to Peter ends. Esler follows Betz in saying that Paul's address to Peter ends at 2:14—Esler, *Galatians*, 139–40. R. Longenecker also sees 2:15–21 as part of the *propositio* and regards Galatians 1–2 as an apologetic letter even if the entire epistle cannot be so classified—R. Longenecker, *Galatians*, 81–82. Guthrie writes that with 2:15, Paul leaves his historical comments and passes on to a theological discussion of the main principles lying behind the incidents just mentioned although he still mentally addresses Peter and his fellow Christian Jews—see Guthrie, *Galatians*, 89. Dunn reads vv. 14–21 as all addressed to Peter, as does Schreiner, who lists four reasons for so doing: the fact that 2:15 is not clearly set off from 2:11–14; the first person plural pronouns in 2:15–17 naturally referring to Jewish Christians; v. 17 possibly reflecting the charge against Peter; 3:1 commencing a new subject addressing the Galatians directly. I would largely agree, though I would advise caution about the break between 2:21 and 3:1—it is not so much a new subject that is being addressed, as it is a new aspect of the same subject, the place of Torah. See Dunn, *Galatians*, 131–33; see Schreiner, *Galatians*, 150. Fung takes a similar view with regards to the structure, but adds that with regards to content it should be understood as the first part of Paul's "doctrinal argument"—Fung, *Epistle to the Galatians*, 112.

3. Betz, *Galatians*, 113–14.

4. Moo, "Justification in Galatians," 164. See further Betz, *Galatians*, 114.

5. Seifrid, "Paul, Luther, and Justification," 215.

ments of two further scholars are particularly pertinent for how the argument in this book proceeds. Williams observes:

> To ask whether 2:15–21 is a continuation of Paul's response to Cephas in Antioch or a statement formulated especially for the Galatians is . . . a false alternative. The passage is certainly aimed at the Galatians, and yet nothing in the text signals any break between 2:14 and 2:15 . . . .although the phrase can . . . include other Christian Jews as well, "We ourselves . . . Jews by birth" refers most naturally to Paul and Cephas.[6]

Williams' disclaimer is significant within the approach of autobiography as polemic that Paul adopts and for the methodological approach of this thesis.

Kenneth Grayston comments on the "decisive encounter" at Antioch, which prompted the question of Jew/Gentile coexistence within the assembly and the reasonableness of Gentiles Judaizing to that end. He writes:

> It is in that context . . . that the question of "justification" arises in Paul's epistles. The "justification" group of words has minimal significance unless the relations between Jews and Gentiles are of central importance, as it is in Galatians and Romans . . . Paul argues thus: "If I, a Jew and not a Gentile sinner [meant ironically], cannot be acceptable to God by acting as required by Torah, how much less can Gentiles be acceptable to God, by performance of Torah."[7]

Grayston's observations correctly contextualize rectification.[8] Rectification will be shown to operate as a revivifying moment by which believers are imbued with the resurrected life of Jesus, through Spirit, who possesses them on the grounds of faith in Jesus. To extend Grayston's very acute observations, the rectified life given by Messiah embodies an inclusive community ethic. This most closely relates to what Paul calls the "truth of the gospel." Though the Torah never prohibits Jews and Gentiles eating together, Jews clearly took food customs seriously enough to not impose or be imposed upon by foreign eating practices.[9] Even Gentile writers were

---

6. Williams, *Galatians*, 61.

7. Grayston, *Dying We Live*, 71.

8. See Westerholm, "Justification by Faith is the Answer," 207.

9. *Joseph and Aseneth* 7:1; 8:5; 12:5; Josephus seemed reluctant to engage in fellowship with any non-Jewish lifestyle, e.g., *Against Apion* 2.258; cf. *Jubilees* 22:16; 3 *Macc.* 3:3–4.

aware that traditionally Jews and Gentiles ate at separate tables.[10] Rectification language grew in part out of the need to articulate whom and what the eschatological people of God were—how accepted norms were overridden by a gospel given to bring forth God's family. Davies notes how Galatians and Romans have a justification discourse immediately followed by discussion of who and what constitutes God's people.[11] In what follows, we will observe how Paul's argument tells this very story.

Galatians 1:13–20; 2:1–9; 2:11–14—Three Connected Narratives Concluded by 2:15–21

A series of recurring ideas and lexical motifs imply that there are three inter-connected narratives, whose conclusion is Gal 2:15–21. Individually and cumulatively, these narratives demonstrate how an incorrect understanding of the Law ultimately violates the truth of the gospel. The three narratives are: (i) Paul's campaign of terror against the Jesus movement (Gal 1:13–20); (ii) the attempt of "false brothers" to impose circumcision on Paul's Greek co-missionary Titus (Gal 2:1–9); (iii) Peter's retreat from the mixed meal table at Antioch (Gal 2:11–14). The connections are as follows:

James/Cephas

James and Cephas appear in Gal 1:18–19; 2:9; 2:11–12. Paul describes himself in abjectly negative terms in Gal 1:13–14, but his treatment of both Cephas and James in 1:18–19 is comparatively sympathetic. Cephas sits with Paul for fifteen days and James is affectionately referred to as "the Lord's brother."[12] The contrast in the next two units could not be more striking. In 2:6 Paul is ambivalent towards the status of "those seeming to be something," including Cephas and James; this is confirmed in 2:9.

By 2:11, Cephas "stands condemned;" in 2:12b he "fears the circumcision;" in 2:13 the other Jews joined Cephas in *his* hypocrisy, resulting in Paul's public dressing down of Cephas (2:14b). The troublemakers were "men from James"—though the designation is somewhat ambiguous, Paul's

---

10. E.g., Philostratus, *Vita Apollonii* 5:33; Tacitus, *History* 5.5; Diodorus of Siculus, *Bibliotheca Historia* 34:1:2.

11. Davies, "Paul: From the Jewish Point of View," 716.

12. This could just be to clarify which James was in question.

reasons for naming James must be to highlight the conflict between Jerusalem's ideas of inter-ethnic fellowship and his own.[13]

The essential issue here is once more a question of autobiography as polemic. Paul once had formidable public status—advancing in Judaism beyond many, being more extremely zealous for his ancestral traditions (1:14). Yet he unwittingly worked against God.[14] In Galatians 2, Paul is dismissive of the implied status of Peter and James—pillars in each other's eyes but not before God.[15] Furthermore, James managed to exert his influence upon the Gentiles even in absentia, but in a fashion that worked against the truth of the gospel. Paul writes as one aware of his own former lofty status and misplaced zeal, which he now sees at work in Peter and James' hindrance of God's work of unifying Jew and Gentile.

Jewish Persecution of the Church

This motif is present in 1:13; 2:4; 2:12b. Clearly, in Paul's history there was a time he terrorised the Jesus movement. Commentators speculate as to why, though their ruminations revolve typically around Torah.[16] In my own view, Paul's anti-Jesus movement campaign was *zeal* for the Law.[17] Like Jacques Dupont, I agree with Martin Dibelius that understanding Paul's Damascus road encounter requires us to comprehend why he persecuted the Jesus movement.[18] This "zeal" implies a relentless commitment to the Law as suggested in the following texts. Jehu declared, "Come with me, and see my zeal

---

13. Translations which claim that these men were "sent" by James make a very significant interpretive decision and probably say more than they need to. If we assume that 2:1–10 is Paul's account of the Jerusalem council in Acts 15 and that Luke's information is accurate, then James did *not* send the men though he knew of their actions—see Acts 15:24.

14. Cf. 1 Tim 1:13.

15. For God, literally, "does not receive the face of a man" (Gal 2:6b).

16. Nanos argues that Paul was angered by the church's compromises on Torah to accommodate Gentiles in the covenant. See Nanos, "Paul and Judaism," 144–46; Donaldson sees Christ and Torah as "mutually exclusive ways of defining membership in the people of God—Christ and Torah are rival boundary markers for the community of the righteous" in Donaldson, *Paul and the Gentiles*, 284–85; some suggest that Paul feared Imperial anti-Jesus movement sentiment negatively impacting the synagogue. Others posit simple jealousy at the missionary successes the church enjoyed—if Paul did indeed exercise some kind of ministry of circumcision to Gentiles before his association with the movement (as 5:11 may indicate), he may have been envious—especially if his efforts bore little fruit.

17. Some of my observations on "zeal" are inspired by the account of the salient issues in Dupont, "Conversion of Paul," 176–94.

18. Ibid., 182.

for the Lord" before he slaughtered members of Ahab's family (2 Kgs 10:16); when Mattathias witnessed a Jew sacrifice on the altar of Antiochus IV, the author of 1 Maccabees relays that:

> he burned with *zeal* and his heart was stirred ... 26 Thus he burned with *zeal* for the law, just as Phinehas did against Zimri son of Salu. 27 Then Mattathias cried out in the town with a loud voice, saying: "Let everyone who is *zealous* for the law and supports the covenant come out with me!"[19]

This Phineas impaled a Jewish man and his Midianite lover with a javelin; of this, the divine voice announces:

> Phinehas ... has turned back my wrath from the Israelites by manifesting such *zeal* among them on my behalf that in my jealousy I did not consume the Israelites ... 13 It shall be for him and for his descendants after him a covenant of perpetual priesthood, because he was *zealous* for his God, and made atonement for the Israelites'. (Num 25:11–13)[20]

Similar sentiments are in Ps 69:9 (which the fourth Gospel applies to Jesus' zeal); Ps 119:53; *Judith* 9:4. Paul in his fervour for Torah saw in the Jesus movement a potentially dangerous compromise. It may well have been the notion of a crucified Messiah that inspired Paul's enthusiastic campaign of harassment.[21] Certainly he saw fit to radically revise the understanding of Deut 21:23 in his argument (Gal 3:13).

Paul relays aspects of his former way of life in Gal 1:13; he continues in 2:4 describing how certain Jewish Christians tried to force Titus to be circumcised.[22] In the Antioch section, Paul describes how certain Jewish believers "from James" then came and pressurized Gentile believers by inciting several Jewish believers to withdraw from them. Paul had been "excessively persecuting the church of God and was destroying it" because of his zeal for Torah; he now witnessed this same misplaced zeal in the pseudo-brothers and the men from James—Paul saw in both these groups of Jews a mirror of his former self. The "former" Paul, the false brothers, the men from James,

---

19. 1 *Macc.* 2:24–27 (NRSV).

20. Cf. Phil 3:2–7.

21. 2 *Macc.* 6:13 and *1QS* 9:22 suggest there was a piety in vehemently rooting out apostasy in the final eschatological days.

22. Harrison notes that Josephus demonstrates that by 66 CE there was a concerted move on the part of some Galilean revolutionaries to link Jewish nationalism to the forcible circumcision of Gentiles (*Life* 112–13). Harrison suggests the false brethren of Gal 2:4 may have been animated by a similar zeal. Harrison, "Why did Josephus and Paul Refuse to Circumcise?" 148.

Peter and the other Jews who followed him marginalized Christians by their misdirected fervour.

Peter, by Paul's own assertion, knew the demands and limitations of Torah; his aloofness stemmed from the intimidation he felt from the circumcision party (2:12). Nonetheless, Paul's accusation was that Peter was not walking in line with τὴν ἀλήθειαν τοῦ εὐαγγελίου; Paul wrote that this would be jeopardised had he capitulated to the ψευδαδέλφοι in 2:4–5, demonstrating that he read the situations the same way. Sumney seems correct, however, insofar as the contingent from James would probably not have insisted on Gentile circumcision. Rather, the main contention Paul had was the nature of "in Christ" identity. The question surrounded the *primary* identity of believers (see later on 5:24–25)—were Jewish believers "Jews in Christ" or "Jesus believers" who just happened to be Jewish? Sumney states:

> Separation at the table embodied an understanding of their primary identity that made Christ-believing (or better, being in Christ) secondary to their identity as Jews . . . It is subordinating belief in Christ or membership "in Christ" to membership in the Mosaic covenant that Paul will not accept.[23]

However, these men and those who shared their views would have maintained that some separation between Jew and Gentile believers was warranted.[24]

Truth

Following the references to "the truth of the gospel" (2:5, 14), the concept of "truth" is notably raised again in 4:16; 5:7. *Codex Ephraemi, Claromontanus, Regius* and several miniscules add τῇ ἀληθείᾳ μὴ πείθεσθαι from 5:7 to 3:1 (O foolish Galatians, who bewitched you *not to obey the truth* . . .)?[25] H. S. Choi argues:

> the truth of the gospel seems to be represented and summarised in the six antitheses in 5.2–6 because the antitheses encapsulate the substance of Paul's theological convictions and arguments

---

23. Sumney, "Paul and the Christ-Believing Jews," 69.

24. Schnelle writes that the James people were insisting that Peter and the other Jewish Christians maintain their separation from (ritually unclean) Gentile Christians. See Schnelle, *Apostle Paul*, 135.

25. Metzger, *Textual Commentary*, 524.

and crystallize Paul's view of circumcision, Christ, the law, the Spirit, grace, Christ's faithfulness, and justification.[26]

Given the full uses of the phrase in 2:5 and 2:14 in close contextual proximity, it makes sense to begin there, though Choi is correct to approach the term as more all-encompassing. In both 2:5 and 2:14, Paul is exposing error, or even lies—(hence "pseudo" brothers in 2:1–5). The truth of the gospel, contextually, must contrast the falsehood of ἕτερον εὐαγγέλιον of 1:6. It is a pseudo-gospel that divides; in Gal 1:20, Paul makes the emphatic declaration, ἃ δὲ γράφω ὑμῖν, ἰδοὺ ἐνώπιον τοῦ θεοῦ ὅτι οὐ ψεύδομαι.[27] Paul does not lie (ψεύδομαι) as the false brothers (ψευδαδέλφους) of 2:4. Thus, a motif of truth exists in all three sections—though indirectly in the first section.

Paul described the truth of the gospel as something Peter failed to "walk in accordance with" (ὀρθοποδέω),[28] and something jeopardised if Titus was coerced into circumcision. Interestingly, De Boer suggests related but different definitions of the phrase in 2:5 from 2:14. In the context of 2:1–5, he thinks the initial use of the phrase denotes freedom from the imposition of the Law.[29] In 2:14 it stands contextually for "God's unconditional grace in Christ for all who believe" which is concretely freedom from the imposition of the Law.[30] Burton suggests it refers to the truth *contained* in the gospel.[31] Yet the phrase can be scrutinized with closer precision.

Contextually, it is related to *the oneness of the eschatological community*. Peter was clearly not walking in this truth, for his behaviour in Antioch established an ethnic hierarchy within the community. If Titus was circumcised, people might infer that faith in Christ needed supplementing with Jewish ethnicity for right status. It seems most likely that ἡ ἀλήθεια τοῦ εὐαγγελίου denotes *the inconsequence of ethnic categorisation for those in Christ*, which is reinforced by the uses of "truth" in 4:16 and 5:7.

In 4:13–15 Paul recounts how the Galatian Gentiles treated him sympathetically during an illness—but had Paul become their enemy telling them the truth about the community (4:16)? For he then describes the *zeal* of the agitators which is not good (4:17a)—rather, "they want to shut you out *in order that you might be zealous for them*." Deep down, Paul suggests, the agitators want you as Gentiles to know of your inferiority to them as

---

26. Choi, "Truth of the Gospel," 229.
27. See Dunn, *Galatians*, 77–78.
28. Literally "walk rightly"—a compound of ὀρθός and πούς.
29. De Boer, *Galatians*, 114.
30. Ibid., 136.
31. Burton, *Galatians*, 86.

Law observers, and consequently for your need to fully Judaize in order to be acceptable to God.[32]

This understanding is more explicit in 5:7 for it follows Paul's denunciation of circumcision *and* uncircumcision as identifying markers of God's people. Neither presence nor absence of a foreskin marks God's people, only the presence of faith working in love. In 5:7 Paul asks, "Who hindered you from obeying the truth?" Truth, here, is the irrelevance of the circumcised/uncircumcised distinction. Galatians 5:8 reiterates that it is not God's design for Gentiles to embrace Torah. Such persuasion is coming from an anonymous ringleader (5:10) who is influencing many (5:9). The Gentiles should be obeying the truth—the gospel, which births one unified community—and not obeying Torah.

Colossians 1:5 and Eph 1:13 employ the phrase. Both texts are thanksgiving prayers for the faith of the believers, and for how this earthly thanksgiving foreshadows the heavenly celebration of eschatological inheritance.[33] The association of the (word of) truth of the gospel with a people united in their faith in Christ is hermeneutically close to that of Galatians.

Compulsion to Judaize.

This reading of "the truth of the gospel" is consistent with the use of ἀναγκάζω in 2:3 and 2:14. The compulsion to be circumcised in 2:3 is equivalent to the compulsion to Judaize in 2:14. The verb appears again in 6:12 to depict the agitators' designs on Gentile circumcision. The lexical correlation of ἀναγκάζω in 2:14 and 6:12 suggests Peter's actions at the Antiochene fellowship dinner mirrored the same gross misjudgement as the troublemakers pressurizing Gentiles in Galatia to Judaize.[34]

Of course, the pre-Damascus Paul himself was applying violent pressure on the church, though he does not use ἀναγκάζω in Galatians to describe it. Luke employs the verb in relation to Paul in Acts 26:11.

---

32. Hence, the triple use of ζηλόω in 4:17–18; cf. 1:14.

33. Eph 1:15–16 probably depends on Col 1:4–5.

34. P. Richardson argues that Peter was only adopting the Pauline technique of adaptability in this circumstance—"becoming weak to the weak." See Richardson, "Pauline Inconsistency," 348.

Co-Text: Gal 2:15–21 as Riposte to Events of Gal 1:13–20; 2:1–9; 2:11–14

The three incidents Paul narrates contextualize the problems in Galatia. Paul's former zealous intimidation of the church, the pseudo-brothers' attempt to circumcise Titus and Peter's aloofness at Antioch all evidenced pressure applied to believers based on a misplaced zeal for Torah. The agitators in the Galatian Jesus communities were similarly zealous (Gal 4:17) and guilty of the same crime. They too pressurized Gentiles to embrace the Jewish Law. They saw the Law as the grid through which one understood and embraced Messiah—Paul saw Messiah as the grid through which one understood and embraced Torah. This is the background for reading 2:15–21 and specifically the revivification text at 2:19–20, which is our primary concern here.

The section begins with the rhetorically potent device of assumed shared knowledge. Peter's assumed cognizance that the Law could not rectify strengthened Paul's position. "*We*, Jews by nature", the apostle begins (2:15), have Torah as the index of our self-identity and the religious context for our social praxis. Φύσει is best rendered "by nature."[35] Paul says in 2:15 that he is a Jew because Torah defines him. When read with 2:16a, we understand nothing he has done by virtue of his "Jewishness" rectifies him—and Peter knew it also. Neither Paul nor Peter was a *Gentile sinner*; we read in *Jubilees* 23:23–24:

> And He will wake up against them the *sinners of the Gentiles*, who have neither mercy nor compassion . . . for they are more wicked and strong to do evil than all the children of men . . . In those days they shall cry aloud, and call and pray that they may be saved from the hand of *the sinners, the Gentiles*; but none shall be saved.[36]

The Gentiles are sinners because their nature, that is, their mode of life, is not governed by the divine morality of Torah.[37] Those who were brought up to be Torah-observant are acquainted with God's designs, unlike the

---

35. "By nature" is to be preferred to "by birth" for the following reasons: Gal 2:14 employs the adverb ἐθνικῶς and the verb Ἰουδαΐζειν—Peter, a Jew, can live as a Gentile; Gentiles who became proselytes are said to "Judaize," that is, live like Jews by nature. Paul's other uses of φύσει point to "by nature;" in Rom 2:14 and Gal 4:8, φύσις is unintelligible as "by birth;" rather it denotes 'by virtue of what something happens to be' or that which is modal because of habit.

36. See also 1 *Macc.* 2:44; *Psalms of Solomon* 1:1; 2:1.

37. 1 Thess 4:3–5.

morally unruly Gentiles—and even then, Paul and Peter know that without faith in Christ no one is rectified.

The issues raised by 2:16 are abundant and convoluted, and the literature devoted to untangling them voluminous.[38] Any attempt in this thesis to address them is limited by this thesis' objectives. Perhaps the two most awkward debates in this text surround the correct interpretation of ἔργα νόμου and πίστις Χριστοῦ, which from 2:16 seem to form the battle terrain between Paul and his interlocutors. For he writes that the former does not put someone in right status before God but the latter does.

For J. D. G. Dunn, ἔργα νόμου are those ethnically exclusivist aspects of Torah, which amount to boundary lines between Jew and Gentile.[39] He appealed to the Qumran text *Miqsat Ma'ase Ha-Torah* (*4QMMT*) to validate his position.[40] Many who have been unpersuaded by Dunn have argued against restricting ἔργα νόμου to specific covenant badges and suggest that the more natural reading is the praxis of all Torah's demands.[41] Others have taken sharp issue with his use of *4QMMT*.[42]

Luther, for whom rectification without Law was the foundational article of the church's doctrine, included within the works of Law the whole Law—judicial, ceremonial and moral.[43] Reacting against the Catholic bishopric (and effectively treating Jewish Christians in Galatians like the echelons of Catholic hierarchy), works were for Luther any human striving that denied divine grace.[44] J. B. Tyson is typical of those scholars who disagree with the Lutheran stance; for Tyson, ἔργα νόμου and νόμος are interchangeable in Galatians and with both Paul is designating a set of conditions associated with nomistic service.[45] Without probing the issue beyond present requirements, it suffices to say that on the grounds of Gal 3:21, Tyson seems basically correct. Nonetheless, in Galatians specifically,

---

38. See the excellent discussion in Sanders, *Apostle's Life*, 505–15; see further the equally weighty analysis in Oakes, *Galatians*, 80–91.

39. Dunn, *Galatians*, 136–37; in the 1982 *Manson Memorial Lecture*, Dunn stated these works of Law "are rather seen as badges: they are simply what membership of the covenant people involves, what marks out the Jews as God's people . . ."

40. Dunn, "*4QMMT* and Galatians," 151; for a balanced reaction to Dunn see Abegg, "*4QMMT* C 27, 31 and '"Works Righteousness,"' 139–47.

41. E.g., Cranfield, "'Works of the Law,'" 91–92. Cranfield concedes that Dunn's argument fits Galatians more closely than Romans but argues that this can be explained by the contextual matrix of the former.

42. E.g., Fitzmyer, *Romans*, 338.

43. Luther, *Galatians*, 49.

44. Ibid., 50.

45. Tyson, "Works," 429–30; see further Schreiner, "Works of the Law," 975–79.

the pressure to adhere to Torah does make ἔργα νόμου ethnically exclusivist in the sense Dunn suggests.

To this end, "faith" functions in contrast to works of Law in Galatians. Having introduced ἐξ ἔργων νόμου into the argument and contrasted it with ἐκ πίστεως Χριστοῦ, Galatians 3 sharpens the focus of the opposition—in 3:9–10, οἱ ἐκ πίστεως are juxtaposed against Ὅσοι (γὰρ) ἐξ ἔργων νόμου; the former are sons of Abraham and heirs of the blessing of Abraham and the latter incur the curse of the Law. The reasoning seems clear.

Galatians 3:6 suggests God entered into relationship with Abraham on the grounds of faith and Paul treats this as paradigmatic for believers—the only requirement for right covenant status is faith. Indeed, God accepted Abraham's faith as a kinship bond. With the advent of Messiah, God actualizes faith in Messiah as a kinship bond—as sonship (υἱοθεσία).[46] (For obvious reasons, Paul does not call Abraham God's son in the context of 3:6). The divine actualization of faith as υἱοθεσία occurs irrespective of ethnic distinction. For Paul, this process of becoming the child of God entails going from death to life—this truth he will expand personally in 2:19–20 (and sketch more fully in relation to Abraham in Rom 4:16–25).

Paul declares, then, that rectification is διὰ πίστεως Ἰησοῦ Χριστοῦ, a troublesome phrase about which fierce debate persists. The degree to which the term polarizes interpreters is perfectly exemplified by Francis Watson and Douglas Campbell. Both *agree* that Paul's employment of Hab. 2:4 is the interpretive key to unlocking the functionality of πίστις in Galatians; they then completely *disagree* about what lies behind the door.[47]

Historically, the genitive πίστις Ἰησοῦ Χριστοῦ has been interpreted objectively as "faith in Christ." R. Hays fuelled a furious wrangling as to whether this abstruse genitive phrase might be read subjectively as "the *faithfulness of* Christ." M. Hooker rightly notes that grammatical analysis alone will not break the scholarly deadlock, for grammatically both readings are possible.[48] D. Hunn (also correctly) suspects that though scholars have continued to offer grammatical arguments, theology more than grammar

---

46. As Gal 3:9.

47. Campbell reads "the righteous one" as a prophecy of Messiah himself, whereas Watson sees it as a reference to believers. Their agreement lies in seeing Hab. 2:4 as the origin of ἐκ πίστεως—Campbell opts for a Christological reading, Watson an anthropological one. As such, Campbell insists on the *subjective* reading of πίστεως Ἰησοῦ Χριστοῦ, whereas Watson on the objective rendering. See Watson, "By Faith of Christ," 147–63. See also Campbell, "*Crux Interpretum*," 265–85.

48. Hooker, "ΠΙΣΤΙΣ ΧΡΙΣΤΟΥ," 321.

has driven the debate from the start.⁴⁹ Accordingly, Hays himself says the debated phrase

> ... may be understood as a reference to the faithfulness of "the one man Jesus Christ" whose act of obedient self-giving on the cross became the means by which 'the promise' of God was fulfilled.⁵⁰

Proponents of the subjective genitive view often are keen to protect the Christ-initiative of rectification, so right status is not misunderstood as something prompted by human effort. As to its correctness—both theologically and grammatically—the polarisation feels overblown. S. K. Williams suggests a more neutral resolution, translating the phrase "Christ faith," a way of depicting how πίστις Χριστοῦ

> ... bears a sense different from either faith in Christ or faith of Christ. Pistis Christou is that faith which is characteristic of believers because they are "in Christ." It identifies those who are in Christ because it is ... the same absolute trust and unwavering obedience that Jesus actualized and exemplified.⁵¹

The claim of the present volume that God actualizes faith as sonship evidences a preference for an objective reading of πίστις Χριστοῦ, for it is God's reckoning of the believer's faith (not Jesus') that is critical. Nonetheless, as per Williams' reckoning, the phrase should be understood with a more sophisticated hermeneutical nuance. For the believers' faith is in Christ's faithful death and resurrection in accordance with the divine plan. There are numerous sources where the discussion can be followed up.⁵²

If Paul is wrong about the place of Torah and defends his stance by appealing to the common "Christ-faith," one might argue that Paul and his supporters have rendered themselves sinners and Christ a minister of sin (2:17). Paul insists that such a charge is outlandish. Rather, having preached to the Galatian Gentiles the correct place of the Law, had he not challenged Peter he would be rebuilding the walls of separation he tore down—and *that* would make him a sinner (2:18).

The γὰρ at the head of 2:19 denotes the corroborative capacity of verses 19–20 for the stance on the Law Paul has thus far presented. To bind

---

49. Hunn, "ΠΙΣΤΙΣ ΧΡΙΣΤΟΥ in Galatians 2:16," 23.
50. Hays, *Faith of Jesus Christ*, 161.
51. Williams, *Galatians*, 69.
52. Lee, "Against Richard B. Hays," 51–80; Pollard, "'Faith of Christ,'" 213–28; for an early church stance on Jesus' faith see Wallis, *Faith of Jesus Christ*; Easter, "Pistis Christou Debate," 33–47; Choi, "PISTIS in Galatians 3:5–6," 467–90.

Gentiles to the Law would be retrograde, *for* it is by practicing the Law Paul knew to look *beyond the Law* for rectification—it was *through* the Law Paul died to Law. In this way, the Law acted as pedagogue to lead Paul to Christ from whom came right standing before God—see later on Gal 3:19–25. With this in mind, we move to how the life-death contrast concludes Paul's corrective to the Galatians via Peter.

Paul writes "I died . . . in order to live"—*this is a revivification framework*. He "died" with respect to one thing (Law) in order that he might experience new life within another sphere. The claim that the "I" is dead implies a new "I" lives—in this sense rectification was identity transforming for Paul. "Identity" here means no more than the answer to the question "who am I?" K. Snodgrass defined identity as that sense of being and self-understanding that frames our actions, communicates to others who we are, and sets the agenda for our acts.[53] Paul's self-understanding, with respect to Torah, was dead. He could no longer articulate his relation to God by recourse to Torah in the age of Messiah. As De Boer writes concerning Paul, the nomistically determined "I" was destroyed in the crucifixion of Christ.[54] At this juncture Paul could consider himself in Christ and, as he later penned, "if anyone is in Christ, new creation."[55]

As should already be becoming clear, the notion of *live* in this context, and functionally throughout Galatians according to the reading posed here, refers to the ontology of identity (see later on Gal 5:24–25). Paul did not die to the Law in order to "do things" for God as "live for" might otherwise initially imply. It is, of course, reasonable to posit a practical component to Paul's identity transformation, commensurate with his renewed vision and direction—a component that is captured by and contained within, albeit secondarily, the semantic range of ζάω. We will in succinct fashion examine some of these practicalities momentarily. The "life" Paul speaks of is an animating energy—we shall return to this after a short explanatory digression.

Some debate surrounds to whom Paul's dictum of the "crucified ego" applies. Some propose that it applies uniquely to Paul.[56] Others suggest it is typical of Jewish Christians.[57] Some would argue Paul's autobiographical narrative applies to all believers.[58] T. Soding, for whom Gal 2:19 is "Der

---

53. Snodgrass, "Hermeneutics of Identity," 9.
54. De Boer, *Galatians*, 160–61.
55. 2 Cor 5:17.
56. Grayston, *Dying We Live*, 73.
57. McKnight, "Ego and 'I'," 279.
58. Callan, *Dying and Rising*, 92.

positive Nachweis," writes, "Das Ich des Glaubenden ist durch die Liebe Jesu Christi geprägt, ein für allemal; Paulus ist ein Beispiel."[59]

We can probe this by asking how the death and life imagery here coheres. Paul's death to Law must be read in conjunction with what Paul says of the role of the Law in 3:22–25. For, as Ziesler observes, Law in this pericope represents an alternative to God's designs rather than his power or regime.[60] Once boxed in under sin by the Law, Paul was trained by Law of his need for another rescuer. As R. Longenecker quite accurately opines, the Law's purpose was to work itself out of a job and point us beyond itself to a fuller relationship with God.[61] For Paul, Jews who did not believe in Jesus remained "dead," enslaved to a Law that accentuates awareness of sin, but is powerless to redeem anyone from it.[62] For doing the Law in the pre-Messianic age teaches the practitioner of the Law's limitations (cf. Rom 3:20b; 5:13)—hence, it was *through* Law Paul died. Paul died *to* the Law in that he acknowledged the decisive eschatological moment—the end of Torah's critical role in Israel's history (3:24–25; cf. Rom 10:4). Messiah was the key to rectification, for faith in him brought forth Spirit. As such, 2:19–20 should be seen as paradigmatic for all ethnic Israel—Israel must die to Law and find its identity in Christ to live to God. With this slight digression over, we may return to a fuller exposition of "live" in the context of Gal 2:19–20 by considering other uses of "live to God."

In a number of texts, "life to God" refers to *actual* resurrection. In Rom 6:10 Paul writes of Jesus that ὃ γὰρ ἀπέθανεν, τῇ ἁμαρτίᾳ ἀπέθανεν ἐφάπαξ· ὃ δὲ ζῇ, ζῇ τῷ θεῷ. The Lucan Jesus in his rebuttal to the Sadducees' question concerning marriage at the resurrection writes of the patriarchs: θεὸς δὲ οὐκ ἔστιν νεκρῶν ἀλλὰ ζώντων, πάντες γὰρ αὐτῷ ζῶσιν.[63] The author of 4 Maccabees in describing how the pious approach martyrdom writes:

> ἀλλ᾽ ὅσοι τῆς εὐσεβείας προνοοῦσιν ἐξ ὅλης καρδίας, οὗτοι μόνοι δύνανται κρατεῖν τῶν τῆς σαρκὸς παθῶν πιστεύοντες ὅτι θεῷ οὐκ ἀποθνήσκουσιν, ὥσπερ οὐδὲ οἱ πατριάρχαι ἡμῶν Αβρααμ καὶ Ισαακ καὶ Ιακωβ, ἀλλὰ ζῶσιν τῷ θεῷ (4 Macc. 7: 18–19).

The same author later writes of the God-fearing mother, who encourages her seven children to face martyrdom rather than break a divine command, something similar:

---

59. Soding, *Die Freiheit des Glaubens*, www.rub.de/nt, 34.
60. John A. Ziesler, *Galatians*, 29.
61. R. Longenecker, *Galatians*, 91.
62. As Rom 7:7–11 implies.
63. Luke 20:38—the key term is "live to Him," where the referent is God.

ἔτι δὲ καὶ ταῦτα εἰδότες ὅτι οἱ διὰ τὸν θεὸν ἀποθνήσκοντες ζῶσιν τῷ θεῷ ὥσπερ Αβρααμ καὶ Ισαακ καὶ Ιακωβ καὶ πάντες οἱ πατριάρχαι (*4 Macc.* 16:25).

The phrase appears frequently throughout the Visions, Mandates and Similitudes of the *Shepherd of Hermas,* in which believers awaiting the Parousia are told that if they keep the commands and abstain from wickedness they will "live to God."

In the texts from *4 Maccabees,* "living to God" seems to reflect eschatological resurrection as the destiny of those literally dying in order to keep the Law. Luke 20:37-38 seems to point in a similar direction. Again, the directives of *Hermas* suggest some manner of risen life resulting from adherence to Law. Paul may have had resurrection on the horizon, but in the immediate term, he has died and only lives because *he is animated by the risen Christ.* In the context of Galatians, "life to God" has begun; employing a phrase that Jewish and Christian writers utilised to depict resurrection reaffirms that Paul saw rectification and resurrection as connected.

Life to God is the destiny of all those with faith; McKnight's notion that somehow Gentiles must die to Law is comprehensible, but needlessly involved, demanding a generic interpretation of Law.[64] Gentiles must be rectified, "crucifying the flesh" and being made alive by Spirit (5:24-25). For now we may note that the section following Paul's rectification autobiography (Gal 2:21-3:5) indicates faith and not Law is the origin of Spirit. Paul declares that those of Christ, having crucified the flesh, now live by virtue of Spirit. *Living to God is life initialised by Spirit, who revivifies those co-crucified with Christ.*

We may now briefly explore the practical component of *life* mentioned previously. Galatians 5:25, which signals the "life" that follows "crucifixion" in a Gentile context, denotes that one must "order their steps" (στοιχέω) in a fashion consistent with Spirit. This ethical element of living to God is seen in Rom 6:10-11. Paul states that the risen Christ lives to God and instructs believers to count themselves ζῶντας (δὲ) τῷ θεῷ ἐν Χριστῷ Ἰησοῦ and correspondingly νεκροὺς μὲν τῇ ἁμαρτίᾳ. This is reinforced in Rom 6:17 (cf. Rom 8:13; 14:7-8). Beyond the ethical parameters of life to God, *sharing in the risen life for Paul pointed to how he conducted a ministry.* I have alluded to this in 2 Corinthians; this is a ministry in which divine rescue from opposition was an act of resurrection by the God of resurrection (2 Cor 1:8-10). This ministry can "smell" like death or life (2 Cor 2:15-16), for the Spirit is making people alive (2 Cor 3:6); his opponents' ministry is accordingly a ministry of death (2 Cor 3:7). Death works in Paul so life works in

---

64. McKnight, "Ego and 'I,'" 279.

the believers (2 Cor 4:10–12), who are in Paul's heart such that they die and live together (2 Cor 7:3). Paul's gospel aimed to turn Gentiles from dead idols to the *living* God and await the one God raised from death (1 Thess 1:9–10). Paul's ministry to the Gentiles also aimed to provoke jealousy in Israel, whose eventual reception of the message was *life from the dead* (Rom 11:14–15). Paul's Messiah was a "life-giving Spirit" (1 Cor 15:45); the Pauline devotee who penned 2 Timothy described the gospel as the means by which life and incorruptibility would bear upon believers (2 Tim 1:8–10). In Galatians, where Paul addresses a specific church conflict, the "life" language is confined to his articulation of rectification.

Galatians 2:19 pushes the theme of rectification—*it embodies co-crucifixion with Christ.*[65] This is the quintessential expression of participationist soteriology in Galatians. In the clause, the verb is in the perfect passive (συνεσταύρωμαι). Paul *has been* co-crucified; God is the one who put Paul on Jesus' cross, immersing him in the experience of Christ. So, Paul narrates his rectification as identification with the Christ event—Paul's death to Law and revivification mirrored the death and resurrection of Jesus.

The place of the Spirit in this transformative process is evident if readers see the argument run naturally beyond the chapter division, zeroing in on the language of crucifixion and death, to set the stage for the critical question in 3:2. Paul's *death* to Law is qualified as *co-crucifixion* with Christ (2:19); Jesus is the one who loved Paul and *gave himself over* on Paul's behalf (2:20); if right status is through Law then Christ *died* needlessly (2:21); Jesus was publicly portrayed as *crucified* before the eyes of the Galatians believers (3:1).

The lexical correlation between 2:21b and 3:21b (see earlier) exhibits Paul's train of thought as the hub of his argument sharpens in focus:

εἰ γὰρ διὰ νόμου δικαιοσύνη, ἄρα Χριστὸς δωρεὰν ἀπέθανεν (Gal 2:21b).

---

65. The Greek text has Χριστῷ συνεσταύρωμαι· at the end of 2:19. Brondos has been a voice deeply critical of the central participationist idea of mystical union with Christ espoused by Deissmann and Schweitzer and persisting in various guises in the work of Robert Tannehill, E. P. Sanders, Morna Hooker, James Dunn, N. T. Wright, and Richard Hays. Brondos points out a number of both theological and historical problems with these ideas, but essentially he militates against what he sees as a decentralising of the historical crucifixion and resurrection of Jesus for some sort of ever present cosmic 'event', which is somehow not unique to Christ but true of all his followers as well. Gorman is surely correct that Brondos's claim of a non-ontological, totally future transformation process simply does not do justice to the texts. See Brondos, *Paul on the Cross*; cf. Gorman, *Inhabiting*, 92.

εἰ γὰρ ἐδόθη νόμος ὁ δυνάμενος ζῳοποιῆσαι, ὄντως ἐκ νόμου ἂν ἦν ἡ δικαιοσύνη· (Gal 3:21b).

One point is in view—right status does not come through Law. Galatians 2:21 introduces the question of Jesus' crucifixion that then becomes the subject of 3:1, with the question of 3:2 rhetorically answering why the crucifixion was imperative.

The one thing Paul wished to learn from the Galatian Gentiles was the origin of their possession by Spirit. Was it the works of Law or the hearing of faith? The inference from the pericope is clear—the death of Christ was not needless (2:21) because it is by faith in the crucified and risen Christ that believers receive Spirit and, therefore, right status. We note that the rhetorical interrogation of 3:2–5 queries the origin of Spirit—was it ἐξ ἀκοῆς πίστεως or ἐξ ἔργων νόμου? The questioning is strategic, for ἐξ ἔργων νόμου has been introduced into the letter in 2:16, in an emphatic, threefold repudiation of his opponents' alleged thesis—namely, that works of Law *can* rectify. It is clear that Paul intends his audience to infer that the hearing of faith is the origin of Spirit in 3:2–5—a position proved beyond any reasonable doubt by the example of Abraham in 3:6, whose own hearing of faith in God was reckoned as δικαιοσύνη. That neither rectification nor Spirit is derived from works of Law in Paul's synthesis in Galatians is critical; the idea reemerges in that Ὅσοι γὰρ ἐξ ἔργων νόμου εἰσίν are under the curse of the Law in 3:10. The flow of reasoning is as follows:

Gal 2:16—Paul vehemently disavows works of Law as a means of rectification.

Gal 2:19—Paul describes his rectification as revivification. There are four references to death/crucifixion in 2:19–21 (ἀπέθανον and συνεσταύρωμαι in 2:19; παραδόντος in 2:20; ἀπέθανεν in 2:21). There are also five occurrences of ζάω in 2:19–20 alone. The death/crucifixion—life contrasts indicate that: Paul *died* in order to *live* to God; he was *co-crucified* with Christ and no longer *lives* but Christ *lives* in him; that which Paul *lives*, he *lives* by faith in the Christ that *gave himself over* in love for Paul's sake; Christ did not *die* needlessly.

Gal 3:1—Christ's necessary death was known to the Galatian Gentiles.

Gal 3:2–5—The hearing of faith is the origin of Spirit and not works of Law (cf. 3:6).

Paul's proposition is that works of the Law are inept for rectification because they are not the origin of Spirit. The apostle died and was revivified, living to God, because faith instigates Spirit who is the agent of revivification—*the one who mediates the risen life of Jesus into the faithful*. The Law cannot revivify (ζωοποιέω), so carrying out its dictates could never lead to right status before God.⁶⁶

The precise sequence of rectification, even with the above in mind, is not easy to unstitch, for Paul seems to move easily between Jesus (e.g., Gal 2:20) and Spirit (Gal 5:25) as the enlivening power of rectification. Furthermore, 1 Cor 15:45, in suggesting that Jesus *became a life-giving Spirit*, makes such a direct association between Jesus and Spirit as source of life that it is possible Paul saw no meaningful distinction.⁶⁷ Similarly, Rom 8:10 outlines that "if *Christ* is in you, the body indeed is dead because of sin, but the *Spirit is life* because of righteousness."⁶⁸ Paul's verb of choice for revivification is ζωοποιέω; he variously ascribes the action to God (Rom 4:17), Jesus (1 Cor 15:22, 45), and Spirit (Rom 8:11; 2 Cor 3:6). With the above in mind, the following most coherently explicates the sequence.⁶⁹

The risen Christ is a life-giving and life sustaining entity. Spirit is the agent that conveys this life into people—a process initiated by faith in Christ. It is Paul's broad testimony that *God* raised Jesus from the dead (Rom 4:24; 10:9; 1 Cor 15:15; Gal 1:1; 1 Thess 1:10). There may be an implication that Spirit was the agent of even of Jesus' raising (Rom 8:11?), though Paul never states as much in explicit fashion.⁷⁰ As suggested, Paul readily affords all partners in the Godhead the ability to make alive, so whilst it may not be prudent to say more than rectification is a *divine* act, Galatians offers some pointers as to what Paul believed to be happening and to the connection between rectification and regeneration.

The hearing of faith initiates Spirit possession and, thus, right status before God, as Abraham experienced (Gal 3:6). Abraham believed what God promised (Gen 15:6); the language of promise does not feature in Genesis in relation to Abraham, but the language of *blessing* certainly does (Gen 12:3; 18:18; 22:17–18). Galatians 3:14 pivotally equates the blessing of Abraham with the promise of Spirit, which are received *through faith*. The Galatian Gentiles had put their faith in Christ and received the Spirit just as (καθώς) Abraham had put his faith in God and received right status. Clearly, in Paul's harnessing of the Abraham texts in Galatians, *to attain right status*

---

66. Gal 3:21.

67. Cf. 2 Cor 3:17–18 for the equation of Jesus and Spirit.

68. This is coupled with the preceding verse, where believers are not ἐν σαρκὶ ἀλλὰ ἐν πνεύματι, because the Spirit of God lives ἐν ὑμῖν; and if someone does not have πνεῦμα Χριστοῦ they are not his.

69. For Christ as "our life," see Col 3:4.

70. Gaffin, *Resurrection*, 66; Gaffin considers Jesus' raising by Spirit as a "clear presupposition" of Paul. For a similar position see Dabney, "Justified by the Spirit," 46–69. Note the objections of Fee, *Empowering Presence*, 808–11.

before God and to receive the Spirit occurred in one eschatological moment. In Galatians, Spirit is the active agent in making believers alive (5:25; 6:8). The various corollaries of this can be seen in how Spirit functions in the letter.

Firstly, the Spirit in the hearts of believers acknowledges their sonship to God (4:6). Sonship to God is concomitant with freedom from slavery—to the Law for Jews (4:5, 7) and idolatry for Gentiles (4:7–9), which is consistent with 4:21–31. That is, *the right status of humanity is to be a son of God and free from any master but God*. In the present age, this is what it means to "live" (cf. Rom 8:2).

Secondly, to understand the Spirit as the agent of revivification sets Spirit in opposition to Law, for Paul quite explicitly states that the Law is not an agent of revivification (Gal 3:21). This oppositional relationship is also present in Paul's dictum that if you are led by the Spirit, you are not under Law (5:18).

Thirdly, is Spirit's antithetical relationship with "flesh." This dichotomy will be examined in due course in the consideration of Gal 5:24–25. For now, we may note simply that in Galatians, Law belongs to the realm of flesh; Gal 5:16–25 outlines how once made alive by Spirit, believers are guided ethically by Spirit and not adherence to Torah.

To summarize, raising the issue of the origin of Spirit in 3:1–5 immediately following Paul's depiction of his own rectification experience makes a clear and important point. For Paul, living to God meant being alive because of the risen life of Jesus enlivened him to do so. The Spirit made this alignment of the risen Christ and Paul's flesh possible, and the Spirit's presence in the believer was initiated by faith in Christ.

Intertextual Resonances: Galatians 2:19–20 and Ezekiel 37

It was suggested above that the kernel of Paul's missionary ideology, a gospel that brings life to the dead, though more prominent in 2 Corinthians and Romans, is detectable in Galatians. The following intertextual section presents an apology for Ezekiel's influence on Gal 2:19–20 to illustrate this norm in Galatians.

Block outlines the prominence of "death" vocabulary in Ezekiel, suggesting death's shadow hangs like a cloud over the inhabitants of Jerusalem and Judah.[71] This vocabulary thins substantially in the restoration visions. One of the key functions of "death" in Ezekiel is to symbolize the reprimand for unfaithfulness to God. The hideous spectacle of the field of corpses in

---

71. Block, "Beyond the Grave," 116; he notes that the common Semitic root *mwt* occurs fifty-one times in Ezekiel.

Ezekiel 37, presumably ravaged by scavengers, points to the effect of divine curse, especially considering the austerity Torah assigns to burial protocol (Gen 23:6–19; Deut 21:23; 28:26; Ps 79:2; Josephus *Contra Apionem* 2:29–30). This calamitous picture of death is the Deuteronomic curse of exile. However, most prominently for Ezekiel, the future indicative "will live" denotes the outcome of obedience to God. The multiple occurrences of "will live" in Ezekiel 18 and 33 make "life as the reward for repentance" the theme of these chapters. Speaking of Ezekiel 18, Tuell writes that the prophet composed a sermon dealing quite literally with matters of life and death.[72] In Strine's critique of the over-theocentric approach to exegesis of Ezekiel by scholars building on Paul Joyce's work, he analyzes chapters 14, 20, 18 and 33 to stress the importance of repentance in the community God will restore.[73] For Strine, these chapters rest upon the exiles' call to repent, identifying themselves as the people of YHWH. As such, they appropriate the role of the second generation of the Exodus.[74] He writes that

> ... the message of Ezekiel 18 is that the exiles are in a transitory period between *life and death* and must choose the generation with which they will identify: if they deny ... their culpability for the Exile ... they will choose solidarity with the first Exodus generation who forfeited the opportunity to inhabit the land by doubting YHWH. Death shall come ... If they accept the rebuke ... and turn from ... idolatry (cf. 20:1–31), they will equate themselves with ... the faithful second generation of the Exodus who persevered and inhabited the land; life awaits.[75]

Divine initiative and human response are necessary for pursuing the life of God, a life which has existential, eschatological and practical dimensions. C. G. Rata does not exaggerate when he writes:

> The Old Testament is preoccupied with life ... "to live" is found approximately 800 times in the OT. Life is an "all-encompassing concept" usually centred on the God of Israel, the "living" God.[76]

We now turn to Gal 2:19–20; in the discussion of revivification text one, the internal revelation of the risen Jesus in Paul was equated with the simultaneous revelation of the gospel Paul proclaimed to the non-Jews (Gal

---

72. Tuell, *Ezekiel*, 107.
73. See Joyce, *Divine Initiative*, 89–105.
74. Casey Strine, "Role of Repentance in the Book of Ezekiel," 19.
75. Ibid 12–13, emphasis mine.
76. Rata, "Reflections on Life and Death," 8; see also Knibb, "Life and Death," 395–407.

1:12, 16). God raised Jesus from the dead (Gal 1:1) and Paul experienced this death-to-life transformation within, reasoning like many of his contemporaries that resurrection spelled vindication (e.g., 1 Cor 15:43). The articulation of his own transformation in terms of co-crucifixion with Christ and life to God make a clear statement—*God had effected in Paul, by virtue of Paul's faith, what he had effected in Jesus.* Paul was conscious of the life that was in him through divine intervention, a consciousness prompted by his experience of the life that was in Jesus through divine intervention.

Immediately tailing Paul's autobiographical recital is a discourse pointing to a deeper connective thread—the questions surrounding the origins of Spirit (3:1–5), the dynamics of sonship to Abraham (3:6–9), the relationship between the blessing of life and the curse of death (3:10–13) and the qualification of the blessing of Abraham as the promise of Spirit (3:14) all point to a narrative that Paul and Ezekiel share. In Paul's portrayal of rectification, as in Ezekiel's restoration narrative:

a. People are in a state of "death."
b. This death is the curse incurred as punishment for sin, so . . .
c. God intervenes . . .
d. through his Spirit.
e. The Spirit revivifies the dead . . .
f. birthing a new community . . .
g. who engage with God's Law(s) in an unprecedented way.

Those dry bones given "life" in the Valley were the repentant exiles. Those given life in Paul's context were those "rectified" by faith in Messiah. In his own experience, Paul "died in order to live" (Gal 2:19) and "no longer lives but has internalized the risen life of Christ" (2:20)—Galatians 3 clarifies that this is the work of Spirit. Paul acknowledges the pragmatic answer to Ezekiel's question in Ezek 37:3; these bones can only live if God intervenes and imparts life, which the Law could not (Gal 3:21b). Paul is cognizant that Jesus' crucifixion, an indispensable requisite of right status (2:21), was on behalf of his sin (1:4; cf. 2:20). The prophet Ezekiel was equally aware that the "death" of exile was a consequence of Israel's sin (Ezek 36:17–19). Co-crucifixion with Christ, in Paul's thinking, was for the nullification of sin (Gal 2:19; cf. καταργέω in Rom 6:6). The outcome of co-crucifixion was life—rectification now and salvation in the final age (Gal 2:19 has "life to God;" cf. Rom 6:4–8; Col 3:3–4; 1 Thess 5:10; 2 Tim 2:11). *In both Paul and Ezekiel, people's sin led to death, which could only be reversed by the life that comes from Spirit*. Paul is simultaneously dead to Law and alive to God. The restored community will only respond positively to the Law because of the Spirit's presence (Ezek 36:27; 37:24).

Excursus: Ἐν Χριστῷ

Before summing up, it is crucial to add at least some minimal commentary to contextualize my numerous references above to the term ἐν Χριστῷ, so frequent in Paul, significant in Galatians, and, as will become transparent, intimately bound with the wider revivification framework at the heart of this thesis.

There is no consensus on how readers are to interpret ἐν Χριστῷ. Though some manner of incorporative image has been dominant, scholars have trodden cautiously around any attempt to define it conclusively.[77] Other scholars have provided helpful summaries of the range of meanings Paul affords the term.[78] Some recent work, though, has challenged the notion of incorporation into Christ popularized by Schweitzer and later by E. P. Sanders and others. M. Novenson has suggested that ἐν Χριστῷ should be read with a conventional, figurative use of the locative ἐν with the dative, denoting "by means of" or "through the agency of," without any suggestion of mystical union.[79]

The term's semantic range, which comes to the fore especially when compared to terms like "with Christ," is reason enough in my mind to jettison the hunt for hermeneutic precision.[80] Meaning will only stem from a case-by-case analysis of Paul's employment of ἐν Χριστῷ. Wedderburn, Novenson and others have correctly broadened scholarly horizons, but two objections to their proposals seem appropriate. Firstly, their readings rarely necessitate mutual exclusivity with ἐν Χριστῷ as an eschatological, spatial metaphor. Secondly, their rendering of the term makes best sense (as Wedderburn himself acknowledges) in the context of some divine activity, that is, "where God or his agents do something to people 'in Christ' or something is done to them (a 'divine passive') 'in Christ.'"[81] Consequently, Wedderburn

---

77. Barrett, "New Testament Eschatology," 149.

78. Parsons has compiled a list based on the work of Best, *One Body in Christ*, 1–7. See Parsons, "'In Christ' in Paul," 27–28.

79. Novenson, *Christ among the Messiahs*, 126. In this, he is in overall agreement with Wedderburn, "Observations," 83–97.

80. For the "with Christ-in Christ" comparison, see Harvey, "'With Christ' Motif," 329–32.

81. Wedderburn, "Observations," 89.

omits *most* of the "in Christ" texts from Galatians as exemplary of his approach. Most notable in this respect are Gal 5:6; 6:15—it can scarcely be "by means of Christ" that neither circumcision nor uncircumcision have strength.

For those who would rule out the spatial reading of "in Christ," the ramifications are seen most clearly in the assessment of Israel's ongoing role in God's salvific activity, (essentially, the question of whether Israel's destiny is resolved "in Christ"). Paul's most thorough treatment of the question is in the convoluted section Romans 9–11. His assertion in Rom 11:26 that "all Israel will be saved," is, for socio-political and theological reasons, a hermeneutical minefield, provoking extensive, divergent scholarly comment beyond the present scope. Zoccali has fairly recently argued that πᾶς Ἰσραὴλ refers to the complete number of elect from the historical/empirical nation, having outlined the problems he sees with alternative readings.[82] His refusal to understand καὶ οὕτως modally, however, seems to be a flaw, for it obscures the way in which Rom 11:25 sets up the conclusion of 11:26.[83] If ἐν Χριστῷ is to be understood in spatial-eschatological terms, and Israel's future is fulfilled "in Christ," then it would make sense that "all Israel" embodies Gentiles.

A spatial-eschatological interpretation of ἐν Χριστῷ fits the reading of Galatians presented here. For neither the marks of Jewish ethnicity nor their absence holds any water. Jews, represented by Paul himself in Gal 2:19–20, and Gentiles (Gal 5:24–25) suffer crucifixion which paves the way for life. Paul's controversial reassessment of Judaism and Jewish scripture has been instigated by his encounter with the resurrected Jesus; only an apocalyptic episode of this magnitude would prompt an observant Jew to proclaim that he had to die to the Law through the Law itself, so that he might live to God—a declaration which would disgust most ancient Jews.

With the above in mind, and in view of my reticence for over specificity in interpreting ἐν Χριστῷ, it seems rational to interpret the seven uses of the term in Galatians, (1:22; 2:4; 2:17; 3:14, 26, 28; 5:6—and I suspect more widely in Paul) approximately as "in the realm/sphere of the risen Christ." Such a reading allows for the term as generic shorthand for believers (as Gal 1:22, where ταῖς ἐκκλησίαις τῆς Ἰουδαίας ταῖς ἐν Χριστῷ is probably Paul's way of saying "those assemblies of Jews in the Jewish heartland who believe that Jesus is Messiah," over and against the non-believing Jewish

---

82. Zoccali, "And So All Israel," 289–93.

83. It is also very difficult to overlook the earlier assertion that not all those of Israel are Israel (Rom 9:6b). For more on this complex issue of Romans 9–11, see Horne, "And Thus All Israel," 329–34; Munck, *Christ & Israel*; Vanlaningham, "Romans 11:25–27," 141–74; Dahl, "Future of Israel," 137–58.

communities of Judea). More importantly, however, it meaningfully depicts how in Galatians rectification is revivification, by which one takes on the *identity* of the end-time people of God. A couple of examples from Galatians should suffice.

The rhetorical question of Gal 2:17 asks whether those ζητοῦντες δικαιωθῆναι ἐν Χριστῷ are sinners who negatively implicate Christ by their "sin." This is part of Paul's refutation of Peter's hypocrisy at the Antioch showdown, which opened up the issue of fellowship dynamics in ethnically mixed believing communities. As such, Paul is asking if believers make Christ a sinner by *seeking to be the people of God through sharing in the risen life of Jesus*; the answer, naturally, is "no way!" The sinner is the one who does not acknowledge the role of Torah in light of Messiah (2:18); logically, what follows is Paul's account of how Messiah has allowed him to truly comprehend the Law's vocation, and how he consequently articulates his own identity in terms of sharing in the resurrected life of Jesus (2:19–20).

An explicit identity declaration is made in Gal 3:26, where Paul writes Πάντες γὰρ υἱοὶ θεοῦ ἐστε διὰ τῆς πίστεως ἐν Χριστῷ Ἰησοῦ. This clause is interesting both for its use of ἐν Χριστῷ with respect to faith, and not the πίστεως Χριστοῦ of 2:16, and the definite article with "faith." Employing the same rendition of "in Christ," observe the following.

Galatians 3:26–29, which brings the Abraham section of the argument full circle, identifying "those of Christ" with Abraham's seed, has a clearly Christological emphasis, a focus made blatant by the fivefold repetition of Χριστός in three verses. The references to Χριστός in 3:27–29 all make a pronouncement of the believers' identity in relation to Christ in a way that deliberately portrays the socio-ethnically diverse community in a supra socio-ethnic unity; as many as have been baptized into Christ have been *clothed with Christ*; Jew and Gentile are *one in Christ*; *those of Christ* are the seed of Abraham. As such, it makes sense to read 3:26 as, "for you are all sons of God in Christ Jesus through the faith." That is, irrespective of external socio-ethnic definition, you are all God's people in the sphere of the resurrected Messiah, by whose life you now live by the Spirit you received through faith.

Summary: Gal 2:19–20—Christ Lives in Me.

Paul narrates three past traumas to contextualize the galling blunder of his opponents in Galatia and all three evidenced a common flaw. This was Paul's way of saying to the Galatian Gentiles of their predicament, "I've seen this happen before and it will end disastrously." If the Law's role is not understood to terminate with Messiah's advent, it will be erroneously treated as the *primary index of the identity of God's people*. Those guilty of this error adopt a misguided superiority resulting in pressure—violent, and/or exclusivist—being applied to a subjugated minority. If people comprehend the Law as a roadmap to faith in the Messiah, the Spirit assumes the role of primary identity-indicator of God's people. For Spirit, in making believers alive, makes them freed sons of God.

Paul concluded his account of these three events with a challenge levelled at Peter. As he and Peter were aware, right status did not arise from submission to the works of Torah, but faith in Christ. To reinstate the authority of the Law would actually be to work against the Law. Having been co-crucified with Christ, Christ now lives in Paul (2:20). That Paul may speak of Christ's crucifixion and follow this statement up with "Christ lives" demonstrates the immediacy of the risen Christ in Paul's reckoning of his own rectification. The risen Christ lives in Paul. The former Paul no longer lives—the newly created apostle has new life flowing through him, and this new life is the resurrected Messiah.

The first substantive occurrence of ζάω appears in Gal 2:19.[84] Indeed, it appears five times in Gal 2:19–20 alone, signaling the key idea in Paul's personal story of being rectified before God, which will permeate the entire argument; he is dead, dead to Law and now only lives because he is energized by the risen life of Messiah. As he will go on to show in the section 3:1–14, this risen life is mediated by Spirit. This will be expanded in the next chapter; for now, we may surmise the trajectory of thought stemming from this second revivification text by highlighting the quite deliberate illogicality Paul introduces in the clauses of Gal 2:20:

> ζῶ δὲ οὐκέτι ἐγώ [Gal 2:20a]
>
> ζῇ δὲ ἐν ἐμοὶ Χριστός· [Gal 2:20b]
>
> ὃ δὲ νῦν ζῶ ἐν σαρκί, ἐν πίστει ζῶ τῇ τοῦ υἱοῦ τοῦ θεοῦ τοῦ ἀγαπήσαντός με καὶ παραδόντος ἑαυτὸν ὑπὲρ ἐμοῦ. [Gal 2:20c]

Having pronounced himself dead by co-crucifixion with Christ in v. 19, Paul quite rightly follows up with the opening statement of v. 20—*I no longer live*. However, by 2:20c, it appears Paul is alive again, writing as he does: "and that which I now *live* in flesh, I *live* by faith in the son of God." Paul's self-comprehension is that he has indeed been reanimated by an unprecedented potency, explicated by the adjoining phrase in 2:20b—Christ *lives*

---

84. It appears in 2:14 to denote simply that Peter "lived" like a gentile, that is, ate with non-Jews, before James's associates turned up in Antioch.

in me. This power is, in Paul's theologizing, the divine power of resurrection which believers share in (2 Cor 13:4; cf. Rom 8:11; 1 Cor 6:14; Phil 1:21; 3:9–11). Undoubtedly Paul ascribes soteriological value to Christ's risen life (e.g., Rom 5:10). Furthermore, at the heart of Paul's Adamic Christology in Romans 5, is the consciousness that Jesus' righteous act (δικαιώματος) of obedience, negating Adam's indiscretion (παραπτώματος), produced for all a "rectification of life" (δικαίωσιν ζωῆς).[85] In Romans 5, life has put right what death blighted. The internalization of Christ is the basis of rectification, by which the Spirit is life, despite the body being in the necrosis of sin (Rom 8:10).

The interplay of death-life language in Gal 2:19–21 leads seamlessly into the discussion of Spirit in 3:2–5, for Spirit conveys the risen life of Messiah into those with faith. *This very chronicle of God imparting life to the dead by the agency of Spirit is the story of Ezek 37:1–14.* Moreover, the Ezekielian Spirit is given to effect obedience to God's laws and commands in his people (Ezek 36:27). Paul is aware that God sent Jesus because of human sin (Gal 1:4; 2:20) and faith in Jesus brought forth Spirit (3:2–5). Ezekiel knew that Judah's sin led to the exile (Ezek 36:17–19) and that God's giving of Spirit was the remedy (Ezek 36:26–27). *In the case of Ezekiel and Paul, the intentions of God, crystallized in his Law, could only be realized through Spirit.*

Paul's theologizing raises predictable questions that Paul answers by recourse to the language of life and death. The most pressing of these was articulating the true purpose of the Law. The material encapsulated between 2:21 and 3:21 provides the basis of his answer—Gal 3:22–25 attempts a direct answer.

In Gal 2:19–21, Paul introduces the fulcrum of his soteriological vision, which appropriately punctuates his epistles, most notably Romans and 2 Corinthians, as he narrates his apostolic vocation within the divine economy of salvation. Human sin has so marred the created order, that it is dead. God has acted to reverse the damage by bringing life and freedom to the dead through his Spirit. This narrative is captured in Ezek 36:1—37:14 and has shaped Paul's depiction of rectification.

---

85. Rom 5:18.

4

Revivification Text Three

Galatians 3:21: The Law Cannot Generate Life

Context: Life as Headline for Restoration Blessing

The significance of Gal 3:21 within the argument of Galatians is critical, not least of all because the section Gal 3:19–25 addresses the crucial question of why God gave the Law. Before outlining what the Law *was* apt to do, Paul writes emphatically what it was *not* apt to do.[1]

This chapter will argue that *life* is the heart of the blessing of Abraham. It is the risen life of Jesus that Spirit conveys to believers; when Paul harnesses Habakkuk's prophecy, that from faith the righteous will *live*, it is to the risen life of Jesus that Paul believes Habakkuk points. To appreciate the scope of Paul's thought process a brief case for Paul's Deuteronomist view of Israel's history will be outlined. Finally, in this section, a juxtaposition of Gal 3:22–25 with Gal 2:19–20 will help ascertain how Paul computed the correct understanding of the Law within God's economy.

Co-Text: Gal 3:10–14

We have already established how Gal 3:6 connects Abraham's experience with Paul's reasoning in Galatians—Abraham entered into right status with God without recourse to Law. Not until 3:14 is an explicit link made between Abraham and Spirit, though the link is clearly implied in how 3:6 follows

---

1. For an excellent summary of the diverse reasons offered for why the Law cannot save see Sloan, "Paul and the Law," 35–60, esp. 42–50.

on from 3:2-5; faith is the origin of Spirit *and* the grounds of Abraham's right relation to God. The notion that Spirit is not attained ἐξ ἔργων νόμου from 3:2-5 carries through to 3:6-9 where the phrase clearly contrasts οἱ ἐκ πίστεως. This contrast allows us to identify the "cursed" party of 3:10, about which there is no end of dispute.[2] We need only note here that Paul clearly intends a co-textual contrast with οἱ ἐκ πίστεως (3:7, 9).

In Gal 3:6-9, we learn that God accepted Abraham's faith as right status (Gal 3:6/Gen 15:6). Thus, "those of faith" in 3:7 are those who have received the Spirit on the grounds of faith—they are related to Abraham through the same trait by which Abraham himself related to God. In view of 3:6, γινώσκετε ἄρα, introducing 3:7, best functions as an imperative followed by a consequential particle, so 3:7 conclusively completes 3:6—*because* God actualized Abraham's faith as righteousness, readers should know that the *sons of Abraham* are analogously ἐκ πίστεως.

This is the gospel that the scripture "afore-preached" to Abraham (3:8), which blesses Gentiles with him (3:9). Gentiles become sons and heirs of Abraham in a family whose shared "gene" is faith. Galatians 3:6-9 also suggests that sonship to Abraham and right status with God are equivalent ideas (as 3:26, 29)—δικαιοσύνη (right status) is to be in filial relation to God. With this in mind, ἐξ ἔργων νόμου is perhaps most cogently (contextually) read as those "whose identity is grounded in Law." This makes reasonable sense of 3:1-14; those whose identity is grounded in Law do not receive the Spirit (3:2-5) and are, therefore, not true sons of Abraham (3:6-9). Abraham's identity was established on the grounds of faith in the period before the nationalising influence of the Law. I have argued elsewhere that Abraham was consequently "ethnically ambiguous," though texts like *Sirach* 44:19 spoke of him as a Law keeper. Abraham is often the protagonist in ancient literature that extends the olive branch to Gentiles because of his indefinite ethnic identity. For example, *Artapanus, Pseudo-Eupolemus* and *Josephus* all depict Abraham instructing Gentiles in astrology, an anathema in scripture, in an attempt to make Judaism more appealing to Gentiles.[3] So

---

2. Tolmie opts for the standard "those who rely on the works of the Law;" see Tolmie, *Persuading the Galatians*, 115; others see a more direct association with the predication of identity, so Dunn: "those whose identity was grounded on works of the law, whose relationship with God was characterized and determined by works of the law, in contrast to those characterized by faith;" see Dunn, *Galatians*, 171. J. Louis Martyn accurately has "those whose identity is derived from observance of the Law" (*Galatians*, 307). Bruce reads (literally) "those who are of the works of the Law," which has merits also—Bruce, "Curse of the Law," 27-8. Bruce's interpretation is virtually identical to Tolmie, however. For a detailed discussion of this issue and the difficult interpretation of the 3:10, see Bonneau, "Logic of Paul's Argument," 60-80.

3. *Praeparatio Evangelica* 9:8, 17-18; *Ant.* 1.165-68.

then, the sons of Abraham are those whose identity *is grounded* in faith, and, therefore, have received Spirit. Those whose identity is grounded in Law have not received the Spirit and are under the curse of the Law, for Israel was commanded to *do* the Law (ποιῆσαι αὐτά) and not be identified as God's eschatological people by it.

In order to do justice to the pericope, Gal 3:10-14, the aforementioned connections between Deuteronomy and the narrative thought world Paul is attempting to evoke require limited exposition. Having established this context, the non-necessity of Gentile circumcision will become a clear corollary of Paul's rectification as revivification argument.

The Deuteronomic Context of Galatians—A Survey

James M. Scott acknowledges the influential work of Odil H. Steck, who argues that for Palestinian Judaism c. 200 BCE–100 CE the Deuteronomic view of Israel's history permeated most extant literature and covered the whole history of Israel from initial election to ultimate salvation.[4] Following Steck, Scott outlines six elements of the Deuteronomistic scheme of Israel's history:

(1) Israel's whole history has been one of disobedience. (2) God constantly sent prophets to inspire Israel's repentance. (3) Nevertheless, Israel rejected the message of the prophets and treated them violently.[5] (4) Therefore, God was angry with Israel and exiled them. (5) During the exile, Israel still has the opportunity to repent; (6) if Israel repents, God will restore them to the covenant blessings, including the possession of the land.[6]

Scholarly investigation into Paul's reliance on the book of Deuteronomy itself affirms his basic adoption of this view of history. Hays's appropriation of how Deuteronomy 32 (the Song of Moses) contains the salvation-historical scheme of Romans ably demonstrates Paul's dependence on Deuteronomy.[7] To this end, Hays reads in Romans (and to a degree Galatians) a scheme of God's election of a people, the people's rebellion, the ensuing divine judgment of the people and the eventual divine rescue.[8] Hays's work, like few others, highlights the poetic and creative techniques by which Paul harnesses the Bible to illuminate his arguments, bringing Scripture and gospel

---

4. Scott, "Deuteronomic Tradition," 647, citing Steck, *Israel und das gewaltsame Geschick der Propheten*, 189.

5. Mark 12:1-5.

6. Scott, "Deuteronomic Tradition," 647-50.

7. Hays, *Echoes*, 164.

8. See Scott's critique in Scott, "Deuteronomic Tradition," 647.

into a mutually interpretive relation.⁹ As Lincicum states, Paul's quotations and allusions often form only the tip of a sprawling narrative iceberg.¹⁰ F. Watson also acknowledges Paul's manipulation of the Song of Moses; for Watson, it predicts the limitations and ultimate failure of the law, the later inclusion of the Gentiles and God's action in Israel's salvation. In this way, it foreshadows the victory over the curse of the law.¹¹

The work of Lincicum, Stanley and Hays has been ground-breaking in illuminating Paul's intertextual reflections.¹² Here, we are confined only to those aspects of Paul's theological reflections on Deuteronomy evident from Galatians itself. The impact of Deuteronomy on Second Temple Jewish literature is apparent from the diverse ways it was harnessed. As Crawford observes in her appraisal of the Deuteronomy text tradition in liturgical texts from Qumran, the chief observation regarding the reading of Deuteronomy in the Second Temple period is that it is expansionistic.¹³ With the above in mind, we now turn to specific evidence for the Deuteronomic framing of Gal 3:10–14 and its implications for foregrounding life and death throughout Galatians.

Life as Blessing and Death as Curse

Evidence: Galatians 3:9–14

Firstly, it is clear from the condensation of the *life and blessing/curse language* in Gal 3:10–14 that Paul has been ruminating on Deuteronomy 27–30. Verse 11 contains the Habakkuk citation with the future indicative ζήσεται ("will live"); verse 12 contains the citation from Leviticus with the same verb "will live." These verses are flanked by Gal 3:10 and Gal 3:13, which both quote scriptures speaking directly of curse.

Secondly, both 3:9 and 3:14 speak of the blessing of Abraham coming to the nations; Paul apparently regards the blessings of Deuteronomy and

---

9. Hays, *Echoes*, 176.

10. Lincicum, "Paul's Engagement with Deuteronomy," 44. His critique of Hays is well noted especially in light of J. Ross Wagner's investigation in Paul's use of Isaiah, particularly the question of how the OT was read in the first century. Lincicum's eminently accessible sweep of history of research in Paul-Deuteronomy studies has been a useful starting point in this thesis. See also Wagner, *Heralds of the Good News*, 20–39.

11. Watson, *Hermeneutics*, 440–44.

12. Lincicum, "Paul and the Testimonia," 297–308. See esp. note 38—the quote from Stanley, *Paul and the Language of Scripture*, 73–79.

13. Crawford, "Reading Deuteronomy," 128.

the blessing of Abraham as synonymous or, at least, very closely related. This is confirmed by the γὰρ at the head of 3:10 outlining an inferential connection to 3:9. In other words, Paul contrasts the Deuteronomic curse of the Law not with the blessing of the *Law*, but the blessing of *Abraham*—we shall return to this in due course.

Thirdly, a number of Biblical and Post-Biblical texts suggest that the Deuteronomic view of Israelite history was a prevalent if not predominant outlook—texts suggesting that Israel was calloused and rebellious, flouting the Law and invoking divine wrath. A couple of examples should suffice:

> We have disobeyed him [the Lord], and have not heeded the voice of the Lord our God, to walk in the statutes of the Lord that he set before us . . . .From the time when the Lord brought our ancestors out of the land of Egypt . . . we have been disobedient to the Lord our God and we have been negligent, in not heeding his voice (*Baruch* 1:18–19, NRSV).

Nehemiah records of God's people that

> they are disobedient, and rebel against you, and cast your law behind their back, and your prophets they have slain, who testified against them, to bring them back to you, and they commit greatly hateful deeds (Neh. 9:26, NRSV).[14]

The entire question of a Deuteronomist redactor behind the texts outlining Israel's history, first proposed by M. Noth, has been subject to numerous redactions and revisions.[15] R. D. Nelson writes that, other than very general agreement that some textual redaction occurred based on theological perspectives characteristic of Deuteronomy

> I suspect we would find little agreement on much of anything else, except that the title "Deuteronomistic History" . . . provides handy and wonderfully elastic shorthand phrases that mask a multitude of problems . . .[16]

From Galatians, we may surmise that Paul adjudged the curse of exile to have come upon Israel and to have persisted beyond the historical restorations from exile by two statements he makes. The apostle declares that "as many as *are* of the works of the Law *are* under a curse" (Gal 3:10) and "*Christ* redeemed *us* from the curse of the Law" (Gal 3:13). The present indicative active tense of the verbs 'to be' in 3:10 point to a current state of

---

14. See Scott, "Deuteronomic Tradition," 647.
15. See O'Brien, "Deuteronomistic History," 14.
16. Nelson, "Response to Thomas Römer."

affairs and acknowledging *Jesus* as the "curse-breaker" for "us" only makes sense if Paul believed (a) the curse had dawned and (b) it was an enduring state of affairs up to Messiah's advent.

Evidence: Influence of Deuteronomy 30 & 32

The critical connections already alluded to are found in the condensation of life-death/blessing-curse language at the heart of the (so-called) scriptural section of the argument of Galatians, but also in how exile and restoration are portrayed with revivification images. In the same fashion, Paul casts his presentation of rectification by faith within the revivification texts highlighted in this thesis.

Observe:

> And it shall be when all these things have come on you, the *blessing and the curse which I have set before you* among all the nations where the LORD your God shall banish you, you shall bring these things back to your heart (Deut. 30:1).

> Behold, *I have set before you* today *life and good and death* and evil . . . (Deut. 30:15).

> I call Heaven and earth to witness against you today that *I have set before you life and death, the blessing and the curse*. Therefore, choose life, that you may live, you and your seed (Deut. 30:19).

The italicized recurrent phrase, "I have set before you today" above, is virtually identical in the Greek, δέδωκα πρὸ προσώπου σου, and is not found elsewhere in Deuteronomy.[17] The author of Deuteronomy himself casts blessing and curse, (which contextually was prospering in the land versus being exiled from it), in terms of life and death. L. L. Bronner suggests that the word order of the similar motif in Deut 32:39—the death element preceding the life element—marks it as an OT resurrection motif.[18] The semantic detail is, however, more compelling than the syntactical given the depiction of blessing and curse as life and death:

---

17. The only difference is the second person plural form ὑμῶν in v. 19 replaces the σου of vv. 1, 15.

18. Bronner, "Resurrection Motif," 11. She notes *Sanhedrin* 91b where rabbis employed the life-death motif in Deut 32:39 to strengthen their position that resurrection had its roots in Torah.

> ἴδετε ἴδετε ὅτι ἐγώ εἰμι, καὶ οὐκ ἔστιν θεὸς πλὴν ἐμοῦ, ἐγὼ ἀποκτενῶ καὶ ζῆν ποιήσω, πατάξω κἀγὼ ἰάσομαι, καὶ οὐκ ἔστιν ὃς ἐξελεῖται ἐκ τῶν χειρῶν μου
>
> Behold, behold that I am, and there is not a god except me; *I will kill and I will make alive,* I will beat and I will heal, and there is none who will take out of my hand (Deut. 32:29, LXX).

Paul never mentions exile, but the life-death/blessing-curse language in Galatians make fairly clear what Paul is suggesting in Galatians—*the curse of the Law is ultimately death, not exile, and the blessing is life, the risen life in which those rectified by faith in Jesus, share.* On the curse of the Law as death, R. J. Morales is correct.[19]

A number of theories have been proposed as to how Paul intends this to be understood.[20] If indeed Paul has been influenced by the Deuteronomist view and reads the curse of the Law in terms of death, then the following makes sense of Paul's train of thought. Performing Torah hoping it would set one in right status with God, which it was incapable of achieving, would render someone estranged from God. An English expression depicts the impossible as "trying to get blood out of a stone"—imagine for a moment someone needed blood for a life-saving transfusion and surgeons attempted to *literally* extract it from a stone. They would be guaranteeing the patient's death. This is analogous to trying to "extract" eschatological life from the Law—this is why the Law's curse in Gal 3:10 remains on those whose identity is grounded in Law, for the Law cannot make alive (Gal 3:21). So to the question why; why, with Deuteronomy in the background, did Paul judge the Law inept to revivify?

Deuteronomy 27–30 makes clear that there will be blessing and prosperity for obedience and curse and disaster for non-compliance to Yahweh. Deut 28:49–68 paints a grotesque portrait of how exile will befall an insubordinate people, effectively recreating their subjugation in Egypt (Deut 28:27, 60, 68). Obedience to the divine commands is tied to Israel becoming a people of God (Deut 27:9; 28:9; 29:13). That is, obedience to the Law's requirements would mark Israel out as a people who did not worship the idols of the polytheists. They would be known as those who feared and served the God who miraculously rescued them from Egypt.

Throughout Deuteronomy, the divine rescue from Egypt is a recurring theme (Deut 1:30–31; 4:20, 37, 45; 5:6, 15; 6:12, 20–25; 7:8; 8:11–14; 9:7–12, 26; 11:10; 13:5, 10; 15:15; 16:1, 3, 6, 12; 20:1; 24:18; 26:8; 29:2, 25)—this

---

19. Morales, *Spirit*, 86–96; Wright, *Faithfulness*, 864–68.
20. Bonneau, "Logic of Paul's Argument," 60–62.

divine act singled Yahweh out from idols. Unsurprisingly, then, refraining from the urge to worship the deities of the Gentiles is another recurrent motif in Deuteronomy—Deut 5:7; 6:14–15; 7:4; 8:19; 11:16, 28; 13:2–7, 13; 17:3; 18:20; 28:14, 36, 64; 29:26; 30:17; 31:18, 20. The Exodus identified God as the God of Israel and Israel as his people (e.g., Deut 4:32–39; 20:1). The author of Deuteronomy outlined specifically that failure to hold to the commands of God laid and cultivated the soil from which idolatry grew—another point that the author labours—Deut 4:1–4, 12–19; chapter 6 in its entirety; 7:1–12; 8:11–20; 11:13–16; 13:1–8; 27:10–15; 28:13–15. The penalty for failing to keep the commands was exile—estrangement from God, a breaking of covenant faith with the one who brought them out of Egypt, established them as a people and declared himself their God.

However, the writer of Deuteronomy routinely articulates the people's failure as inevitable (e.g., Deut 4:26–28; 30:1–6; 31:29); they were seemingly doomed to become the subordinates of pagans, worship strange deities and languish in geographical and, moreover, ideological abandonment from Yahweh, until he acted to restore their fortunes. With these Deuteronomic ideas in view, we approach how Paul comprehended the salient issues as expressed through Galatians.

Israel was presented with a choice—obedience to the commands of Yahweh by which they would *live* and disobedience by which they would *die*. On their horizon lay life and blessing, or curse and death. Doing the Law spelled sustenance for the people; the nations would know Israel's god was the God of the Exodus and Israel could register this by not worshipping the nations' deities. This sustenance is the *life* of the Law. The understanding of *live* that the writer of Deuteronomy adopts here seems consistent with Lev 18:5—both in its own context and in Paul's employment of it (Gal 3:12). For example, we read in Deuteronomy:

> So now, Israel, give heed to the statutes and ordinances that I am teaching you to observe, so that you may *live* to enter and occupy the land that the LORD, the God of your ancestors, is giving you. (Deut 4:1, NRSV).

> You must follow exactly the path that the LORD your God has commanded you, so that you may *live*, and that it may go well with you, and that you may *live* long in the land that you are to possess. (Deut 5:33, NRSV).[21]

The tone changes in the reference to "live" in Deut 30:6 when God's intervention in the people's hearts reverses the disaster of exile. Israel's

---

21. Cf. Deut 8:1; 11:31; 12:10, 29; 13:12; 16:20; 26:1.

prophets narrated the ugly truth—*Israel chose death and the curse of exile and estrangement from God befell Israel. Paul raises the inevitable—why did God give the Law (Gal 3:19a)?* He gave it to Israel so that they might understand their sinful and idolatrous actions were transgressions (Gal 3:19b). If they obeyed the Law, they would *live* in the land God gave them in peace and security. They did *not* obey—they broke faith with God and "died." The nation's relationship with God was in tatters, and only divine action could repair it. That is, only God could make the people alive again—"doing" the Law, whilst in this state of death, could not revivify the people (Gal 3:21b). Through Law one could "live" in the Lev 18:5 (Deut 4:1; 5:33) sense of the word—*but now that the people were dead in the curse of estrangement from God, observing the Law could not make them alive* (ζωοποιέω) *again, ending the exile and restoring the relationship.*[22]

As per the Deuteronomic warnings, if they chose to obey again, God would restore them to and sustain them within the "life" promised within the covenant stipulations (e.g., Deut 30:1–5)—that is, the life depicted by Lev 18:5. However, in order to finally break the curse, to end the cycle of idolatry and exile required the people to be brought to life by divine intervention, in a way obeying Torah could never achieve.[23] This life, quite beyond the provisions of the Mosaic covenant, was a divine act by which the very inclination to be disobedient and, thus, overwhelmed by their own transgressions would be undermined. By this act, crystallized by Jeremiah and Ezekiel, God's people would experience an unprecedented proclivity to submit to his commands because of two related outcomes. The first is the heart reformation which God himself will orchestrate (Deut 30:6; Jer 31:33), which Paul interprets in terms of the Spirit (Rom 2:29; 2 Cor 3:3; Gal 4:6). The second involves sin itself, insofar as God says he will forgive the people's wrongdoings and forget their sins (Jer 31:34) and even save them from their uncleanness (Ezek 36:29). Paul personifies sin reigning in death in Romans 5, and having its reign undone by life—that is, in Pauline thought, something happens to sin itself. The awkward statements in Romans 5–7 regarding Torah's role (see later) amount to a Pauline apology for the Law's incapacity to modify hearts and subdue the power of sin. In Gal

---

22. The divine origin of the Law notwithstanding, Paul must distinguish between the action of God and the Law itself, as, for example, in Rom 8:3a. Indeed, such an inference seems inseparable from his comprehension of Torah's limitations. In other words, obedience to God's written Law is substantially distinct from responding to God's direct intervention into human affairs, even if such intervention is largely consistent with what the Law says about divine action.

23. See the reasoning for continuing exile in this regard in Wright, *Faithfulness*, 139–63.

1:4, Jesus' self-giving is "on behalf of our sins" and "rescues people from the age of the present evil."

Paul identifies with the tradition that revivification comes only by divine intervention, typically through Spirit (Gen 2:7; Exod 8:16-18; Deut 32:39; Isa 57:16; Ezek 37:3-14). The human response to Yahweh in doing Torah can sustain life, but only by God's initiative can the dead be re-enlivened. Hence, Pharaoh's magicians could not make gnats from dust, Habakkuk's only hope was to have faith in God, the dead bones of exiled Israel could only live by the action of Spirit, God was the agent of resurrecting Jesus' crucified body, and, in Paul's context, the Law could not make alive. If it could, Law could rectify (Gal 3:21b).

The attempt to be made alive again, and so be identified as God's people once again on the grounds of observing Torah, confined people to the curse (Gal 3:10). Deuteronomy 27:26 pronounced the curse on those who failed to *do* what the Law dictated; ποιῆσαι αὐτά in Gal 3:10b corresponds to ὁ ποιήσας αὐτὰ in 3:12 reflecting the LXX of Lev 18:5. However, they *had* failed; the curse *had* come upon them, so the ones Paul describes as ὅσοι γὰρ ἐξ ἔργων νόμου (Gal 3:10a), in the age of Messiah, remain cursed.

That this was the case, Paul deems obvious (Gal 3:11a); as Habakkuk foretold, himself frustrated with God because Judah's "deadness" in exile lay inevitably ahead, ὁ δίκαιος ἐκ πίστεως ζήσεται (Gal 3:11b).[24] Even in Habakkuk's context, the Law could not avert the calamity, for Judah's degradation had paralyzed the Law (Hab 1:4).[25] Habakkuk's only assurance was that life, which rectified the deadness of exile, would materialize through faith (Hab 2:4).[26] Where faith was absent and pride persisted, death remained (Hab 2:5).

So Paul introduces Jesus into this chapter of Israel's salvation drama; the curse is broken by the crucifixion; Jesus *became* the curse by embracing *death* (Gal 3:13). Jesus voluntarily suffered the sentence of the rebellious son of Deut 21:18-23 (esp. 21:23).[27] Paul reasoned that Jesus, in voluntarily drawing the curse upon himself, effectively acted as a scapegoat, drawing the curse away from Israel, redeeming her and bringing her into right

---

24. Hab 2:4.

25. The Hebrew implies the Law had been "chilled"; the LXX literally reads that the Law has been scattered abroad, implying has been 'frustrated.'

26. Greek, "my faith" or "faith in me"; Hebrew, "his faith." See exegesis section on Gal 3:11.

27. See further Scott, "For as Many as are of the Works of the Law," 215-16; Wright, *Climax*, 151-53.

relationship with God. The paradigm of Messiah as substitutionary "curse" is reflected in texts like 2 Cor 5:21, though its origins are not clear.[28]

It is worth noting here that scholars should resist the urge to equate the curse of the Law with the Law itself. Wilson's attempt to define "under Law" with "under *the curse* of the Law," whilst innovative, is not ultimately persuasive for two reasons.[29] Firstly, it stalls at Gal 4:21, for Paul can scarcely be asking if anyone wants to be under the curse of the Law. Secondly, Romans 7 proposes a much more sophisticated relationship between Law, death (which is related to curse) and *sin*.

Having drawn the curse of death upon himself in crucifixion, death was nullified by life in resurrection. Though there is no direct mention of resurrection in Gal 3:14, the blessing of Abraham is both identified as Spirit and contrasted with the curse—death. So the Spirit is, for all intents, the *Spirit of life*. This way of viewing Spirit is common in Second Temple Judaism and significant enough for Paul to refer to *Jesus* as a life-giving Spirit in his Adamic Christology (1 Cor 15:45). Resurrection is further implied in Gal 3:14 if we interpret ἐν Χριστῷ as "in the realm of the risen Christ" (see earlier excursus). Jesus was crucified ἵνα εἰς τὰ ἔθνη ἡ εὐλογία τοῦ Ἀβραὰμ γένηται ἐν Χριστῷ Ἰησοῦ.... By this we may understand that the blessing of Abraham, *life*, might be (γίνομαι) to the Gentiles in the realm of the risen Christ. Here, Paul means that life, in the form of the risen life of Jesus, *might become reality* in believers by the action of Spirit. This view tallies with the other key crucifixion passages in Galatians. Paul is *co-crucified* with Christ (2:19) and can thus declare, "Christ *lives* in me" (2:20), before launching into the one thing he wanted to know from the Galatian Gentiles—the origin of *Spirit* (3:2). Gentiles who are "of Christ" have *crucified* the flesh (5:24) and now *live* by virtue of *Spirit* (5:25). The cosmos itself has suffered *crucifixion* (6:14) and given way to *new creation* (6:15) governed by the canon of *Spirit* (6:16; cf. 5:25).[30]

In strategic sequence, Paul then addresses how the giving of the Law is to be construed in light of his theologizing (Gal 3:15–25). For the purposes of the present volume the conclusion of Gal 3:21 is most critical. Performing the Law could not break the curse, because unlike Spirit, *it cannot revivify*. Performing Torah could sustain the post-Exodus generation, but not restore Israel to the fullness of the life that God intended.

---

28. R. Longenecker, *Galatians*, 122. Others have suggested more sophisticated re-readings of the phenomenon, e.g., Girard, *Satan*, 154–60, or attempted to understand it in terms of the *Aqedah*; see Kessler, *Bound by the Bible*, 57–80.

29. Wilson, "Under Law in Galatians," 362–92.

30. Spirit is not mentioned in Gal 6:16, but Paul's use of στοιχέω makes his intentions apparent.

So then, Jesus embraced death, exile and curse; he embraced death by crucifixion, which Paul aligns with Deut 21:23, the hanging of the corpse of an executed capital offender. The context of this practice in Deuteronomy 21 is the rebellious son who must be stoned to death and put out of the community—effectively exiled from the community and even God himself.[31] Interestingly, Luke 7:34 suggests that popular opinion contrasting John the Baptizer to Jesus associates this language of profligacy in Deuteronomy to the latter (Deut 21:20). Israel's exiles were the fulfilment of the threat of curse prophesied in Deuteronomy 30. When Christ was hung upon the tree, he replaced unfaithful Israel as he became the bearer of the Law's curse.[32] The faithful son who had been treated like the rebellious son of Deuteronomy 21 bore the curse.

So through Jesus' resurrection came the great reversal: life came from death, blessing from curse, true restoration from exile. By identifying with Christ in co-crucifixion, Paul dies to Law—he comes away from its jurisdiction, and, therefore, from the possibility of being identified as belonging to God because of it. That is, he has been redeemed from the curse of the Law.[33] Paul entered a new sphere of identity which identified God's people—the "in Christ" sphere. Paul is conscious that he lives in the age before the Parousia whilst the human condition remains susceptible to the effects of sin, that is, in the flesh. *He lives by faith in the Son of God.* There is a distinct tension—Paul is in Christ, in the realm of Christ's risen life, but still prone to the corruptibility of flesh. The contradiction within the apostle's thoughts is evident- for he *lives no longer* (2:20b) . . . but that which he *now lives* he *lives by faith* (2:20d). The originally created Paul, born of his parents and alive by natural biological forces, is dead. A newly created Paul (2 Cor 5:17) is alive by faith in Jesus. Having established a case for Paul's reflections on Deuteronomy, we may now suggest a reading of Gal 3:10–14.

Exegesis of Gal 3:10–14

Gal 3:10

Young suggests that the meaning of almost every phrase in Gal 3:10–14 is disputed.[34] Few scholars accept the so-called "implied premise" of the bib-

---

31. Again, Christian tradition bears witness to this (e.g., citation of Ps 22:1 in Matt 27:46; Mark 15:34). Paul hints at such in 2 Cor 5:21.
32. Caneday, "Redeemed from the Curse of the Law," 205.
33. Note first person plural of Gal 3:13.
34. Young, "Who's Cursed-and Why?" 79.

lical citation in 3:10—the notion that Torah demanded obedience which lay beyond everyone's scope and thus consigned everyone who attempted to keep it perfectly to the realm of curse.[35] The obvious difficulty in Paul's conclusion is that it appears to be arguing backwards. According to Deuteronomy, it is the one *not* remaining in all the Law, who is cursed.[36] However, Paul's contention is that those identifying themselves as the people of God according to Torah's dictates are cursed. He has already alerted his audience to the ἐξ ἔργων νόμου/ἐξ ἀκοῆς πίστεως contrast in 3:2–5, concluding that Spirit is not attained ἐξ ἔργων νόμου. The οἱ ἐκ πίστεως/ἐξ ἔργων νόμου contrast in 3:9–10 is clearly related. One committed to Law in the hope of being rectified is not pointed to faith in Messiah (ergo the warning in 5:4) and so does not find the Spirit who brings life. Israel's dalliances with idolatry resulted in her exile; Israel was under the curse. The *life* which reverses the death of exile, as Ezekiel 37 predicts, comes from Spirit, and is attained through faith. As such, those attempting to identify themselves as God's people by works of Law and not faith in Messiah do not receive, and hence are not identified by, *Spirit*. Such a one is cursed, that is under death, for Spirit makes alive and Law cannot (Gal 3:21).

Gal 3:11

Paul's summary statement, that it is clear (δῆλον) no one is rectified by Torah, is his way of stating that this truth is scripturally blueprinted. However, the verse has two clauses both introduced by ὅτι, the interpretation of which governs how the statement works.

The Greek ὅτι may imply "that" (as a conjunction) or "because." The entire sentence is unintelligible if the ὅτι is translated the same way in each case, so the critical question is which of the two senses of ὅτι is pertinent to the first occurrence and which to the second. Most interpreters read the first ὅτι as "that" and the second as "because." F. Thielman exemplifies the minority stance, rendering Gal 3:11, "But *because* [ὅτι] no one is justified before God by the law, it is obvious *that* [ὅτι] 'the just shall live by faith.'"[37] Though a novel approach, the minority reading is to be rejected on two

---

35. E.g., Schreiner, "Perfect Obedience," 151–60. This *is* the position taken by Lull, however—see Lull, "Law Was Our Pedagogue," 481–98. Braswell does see an important nuance in Lull, though, differentiating "accursed" from "under the curse." See Braswell, "Blessing of Abraham," 74.

36. On these grounds Martyn argues that Paul is reacting to his opponents' use of the text. See Martyn, *Galatians*, 311–12.

37. Thielman, *Paul and the Law*, 127.

counts. Firstly, it has Paul begin with a conclusion and argue *towards* a Biblical intertext rather than *from* it, which effectively extinguishes the force of his point.[38] Secondly, the integrity of 3:12 requires a previous conclusive statement regarding faith, whereas in Thielman's reading, the conclusive statement centres upon *Law*.

So we may consider how Paul argues for a Biblical grounding to his position. The contrast with the Habakkuk citation and Lev 18:5 reinforces the previous point—the life to which doing the Law points is *not* the risen life. However, the co-text of Hab 2:4 reveals more to Paul's rectification as revivification argument reinforcing that one can only share in the risen life of Messiah through faith:

> Therefore the vision is still for a time . . . if it might come late, wait for it . . . If he draws back, my soul will not be pleased in him, but the *righteous one from my faith will live*. But the one being drunk and despising, the bragger, never finishes anything, *Hades and this like death not being filled*, and will gather to himself all the Gentiles and will receive to himself all the peoples (Hab. 2:3–5, LXX).

Habakkuk 2:4b, for all its influence over Reformation theology and significance for understanding rectification, is fraught with interpretive complexities.[39] Paul has not precisely quoted any extant version of the text, though he follows the word order of the LXX. If he has amended the LXX then he has dispensed with the possessive pronoun (*my* faith).[40] Paul's omission of "my" from his citation of Hab 2:4 implies that it is the believer's faith that leads to life. However, even if he had included μου, it could still denote "by faith in me (God)." It is certainly possible that Paul intended to centralize *God's* faithfulness, but it is far more meaningful that he is reinforcing his point about Abraham's faith in God (3:6), especially as references to Abraham frame the entire argument (3:6, 14).

There are two key reasons Paul has cited Hab 2:4; we do not need to succumb to Sanders' fatalistic view that Paul has simply scoured the Bible for a convenient lexical collocation from which to construct proof texts.[41]

First, and most important, is the life-death contrast portrayed by Habakkuk. The prophet likens the greed and arrogance of the Babylonians to Hades' appetite for the dead.[42] In Paul's mind, the actions of his opponents

---

38. Cf. Burton, *Galatians*, 166.
39. See for example Zemek, "Interpretive Challenges," 43–69.
40. The referent of the pronoun is God.
41. Sanders, *Jewish People*, 22.
42. Armerding notes that drunk "is appropriate to the present verse, being

in Galatia make them similarly greedy and arrogant. As Hab 2:5 states, they try to gather the Gentiles—only Paul's opponents are pressurizing Gentiles to Judaize. In so doing, they are drawing them into death (θάνατος).[43] However, those who are in right standing before God will live because they trust him. Whereas Habakkuk linked "by his faith" with "shall live," Paul linked "by faith" with "the righteous."[44] The net effect is the same nonetheless. Second, Paul offers further validation of Abraham as the template for right status—he "lived," that is, was rectified, because of his faith.

Gal 3:12

Preston Sprinkle once referred to Lev 18:5 as the "John 3:16 of early Judaism," suggesting it summarised Torah the way that John 3:16 summarises the gospel for many Evangelicals.[45] That life somehow came from Torah was widely held amongst Jewish communities, quite aside from recourse to Lev 18:5.[46] Various theories about how Paul is using the passage exist; scholarly investigation has tried to isolate (a) what "will live" represents in the apostle's mind; (b) whether Paul's juxtaposition of the passage with the other OT quotes is consistent with some rabbinic hermeneutic methodology which might offer clues to his objectives. With respect to (b), Paul does not seem to follow any known technique with any precision.

With regards to (a) above, S. Gathercole has argued, on the basis of an impressive array of texts which employ Lev 18:5, that the broad picture within Judaism is the "life" which Lev 18:5 often points to, is *eschatological life*.[47] This is contra Dunn, who writes:

> Paul seems to understand the passage in its most obvious sense—that keeping the statutes and ordinances of the law was the way of living appropriate to the covenant . . . Moses did not

---

associated with arrogance, unfulfilled greed and social injustice elsewhere in the OT (e.g., 1 Sam 30:16; 1 Sam. 30:12, 16; Prov 31:4–7; Isa 5:11–12, 22–23; Amos 6:6)." See Armerding, *Habakkuk*, 153.

43. See later on 2 Cor 3:7.

44. Clark and Hatton, *Habakkuk*, 93; the contrast can be seen as "The righteous// shall live by faithfulness" (Habakkuk) as against "The righteous by faith//shall live" (Paul).

45. Sprinkle, "One Who Does These Things."

46. E.g., *Baruch* 4:1.

47. Gathercole, "Torah, Life and Salvation," 126–45; cf. Kaiser, "Leviticus 18:5," 24–25.

say, and Paul did not understand him to say, that keeping the law was a means of earning or gaining life in the future.[48]

The picture is not perfectly even—the context of Lev 18:5 suggests life refers to the immediate blessings of obedience.[49] Though Gathercole's position is initially strong, it seems clear that the ancient authors he cites were re-contextualizing Lev 18:5 to meet their own contemporary situations, which Paul also was doing. Therefore, there is no necessary reason to assume that Paul read the text in precisely the same way as the writers Gathercole names. An increasing number of scholars suggest that Paul's interest in Lev 18:5 is consistent with the prophets who indicted Israel for failing to hold the covenant's expectations. The text is harnessed in Ezek 20:11, 13, 21; Neh. 9:29; *CD III:* 12b–16. The logic is that God promised life through the Law, but precisely because Israel historically did *not* keep the Law, the life was never realised. So as Willits writes:

> Read this way, the contrast between "faith" and "law" implied in 3:11b and 12 is ... between historical periods in salvation history: the period of unrealized covenant potential (3:12) and the period of realized covenant potential (3:11b) ... to be related to the Sinai covenant is to be related to the age ... of unfaithfulness and judgment (covenantal curse).[50]

The readings of Willits, Grindheim, and others are close to my own, but Paul's point is that no law had been given to make alive; as such, it could not be the same life. There are two quite different modes of life at play, not just two periods of history. Galatians 3:12a follows the thought of 3:11b; the essence of reading them together is summed up in 3:21. It follows that:

> The righteous will live by faith
>
> And the Law is not of faith [so the righteous will *not* live by Law]

But, the one doing these things will live in them [*this* life is *not* the life of Hab 2:4]

The use of ἀλλά at the beginning of 3:12b places stress on the disjunction between these two modes of life.

---

48. Dunn, *Romans 9–16*, 612. For an analysis of the contextual dynamics of Lev 18:5, see further Bigger, "Family Laws," 187–203.

49. See esp. Wenham, *Leviticus*, 253.

50. Willits, "Context Matters," 119; see further Grindheim, "Apostate Turned Prophet," 545–65. Grindheim argues that Paul's conversion allowed him to see himself as apostate—as one of those under the curse for failing to hold to the covenant. As such, he aligned himself with the prophetic tradition employing Lev 18:5 to indict Israel. See also Starling, *Not My People*, 46–52.

That there are two modes of life in view is further corroborated by Paul's personal testimony mentioned in the previous chapter—ζῶ δὲ οὐκέτι ἐγώ, ζῇ δὲ ἐν ἐμοὶ Χριστός· ὃ δὲ νῦν ζῶ ἐν σαρκί, ἐν πίστει ζῶ τῇ τοῦ υἱοῦ τοῦ θεοῦ (Gal 2:20). Paul says "I" no longer "live," but later in the clause states that 'that which I now *live*, I *live* by faith in the son of God. The explanatory idea joins the clauses; *Christ lives in me*. Paul is conscious that his former life, lived in obedience to Torah (Lev 18:5), ended in co-crucifixion with Christ. His newly created life is animated by the power of the resurrected life of Jesus.

Gal 3:13–14

It was earlier established that Jesus took on the curse of the Law—death—in crucifixion. That he *became* the curse as opposed to *coming under* the Law's curse is of significance. For in his resurrection, Jesus overcame death and brought forth life.

Recall here the curse of Law is not contrasted with the *blessing of the Law* but rather with the blessing of *Abraham*. *This is a key move in the argument of the letter*; the language of blessing (3:8, 9, 14a) transitions to the predominant language of promise (3:14b, 16, 17, 18, 19, 21, 22, 29; 4:23, 28). The transition in 3:14 renders "blessing of Abraham" and "promise of Spirit" equivalent phrases. Paul treated the curse of the Law as death, so there is clearly a contrasting manner in which the blessing of Abraham is "life"—this pivotal connection will be explored momentarily. However, scholarly readings of Paul's intentions in the somewhat enigmatic conclusive statement of Gal 3:14, are divergent enough to warrant some minimal comment.

For example, Kwon argues that Paul's reference to the Spirit is a new development intended to connect the whole argument (vv. 6–14a) with the fact of the Spirit the Galatians themselves have received (vv. 1–5). He refers to 3:14b as "a somewhat loose addition to the argument proper (vv. 6–14a) to boost the force of his claim of 'by faith,'" and thus, keeps the two statements separate.[51] Chee-Chiew Lee has also recently challenged the broad equation of the promise of Spirit with the blessing of Abraham. She argues rather that *justification* is the blessing of Abraham and the Sprit is both the evidence of and means by which the blessing is perpetuated.[52] Brendan Byrne's suggestion that the Spirit is the promise in the sense of God's guarantee

---

51. Kwon, *Eschatology in Galatians*, 62–63. He does, nonetheless, maintain the grammatical plausibility of taking the two statements as equivalent.

52. Lee, *Blessing of Abraham*, 182–211. Cf. Fung, *Galatians*, 140; Witherington, *Grace in Galatia*, 228.

of eschatological salvation, probably says too much, making corroborative appeal to the "first-fruits" language of Rom 8:23 and "down payment" language in 2 Cor 1:22; 5:5 and Eph 1:14.[53]

The connection is, perhaps, most plausibly explained by Sam K. Williams, who begins by registering that the Gen 15:6 citation is contextually Abraham's response to the promise that his progeny will be as numerous as the stars. This, then, is the initial clue; the "promise of the Spirit" is, initially, the promise of Abraham's paternity over innumerable descendants.[54] This interpretation is possible, Williams notes, because for Paul *the Spirit is the one who begets true children for Abraham*.[55] Furthermore, Williams is correct to point out that in Galatians 3, Paul utterly intertwines being justified and receiving the Spirit.[56] Each implies the other, though they are conceptually distinct. Those persons upon whom God bestows the Spirit are justified; the persons whom God reckons righteous have the Spirit poured out upon them.[57] The work of the Spirit in justification in Williams account is in "making alive"—that which Torah is inept to achieve.[58]

Although the majority of commentators accept that Gal 3:14b is a coordinate purpose clause, restating the purpose clause in 3:14a (such that both refer back to the main clause in 3:13), Williams' observations regarding the connection between "life," Spirit and justification need to be pressed further.[59] A number of key studies have gone on to suggest credible pneumatological frameworks within which to interpret the blessing of Abraham. Most notably, several writers posit an essential echo with the parallelism between "Spirit" and "blessing" in Isa 44:3, which seems quite likely.[60] It is possible, though, to postulate a more immediate pneumatological context for interpreting the blessing of Abraham, which broadens the scope of Paul's biblical appeal to ζάω language in 3:11–12. Following Williams, that, for Paul, the Spirit begets true children for Abraham, (and in his reading more broadly) it seems that the promise-fulfilment narrative in Gal 4:21–31 puts greater weight on the substantive value of promise than Williams allows for. Isaac's birth was according to promise (4:23) insofar as it defied natu-

53. Byrne, *Sons of God*, 156–57.
54. Williams, "Promise in Galatians," 714.
55. Ibid.
56. Williams, "Justification and the Spirit," 97.
57. Ibid.
58. Ibid., 96–97.
59. See deSilva, *Galatians*, 64; Bruce, *Galatians*, 167; Schreiner, *Exegetical*, 218–19; R. Longenecker, *Galatians*, 123.
60. Hays, *Faith*, 182–83; Morales, "Words of the Luminaries," 269–77; Morales, *Spirit*, 110–14; Harmon, *She Must and Shall Go Free*, 146–50.

ral, embryological expectations. Isaac was born because God promised and not because natural, biological channels favoured. *His birth was effectively a revivification miracle.* As such, the promise of the Spirit is not initially the promise of countless descendants, but *the miraculous birth of Isaac.*

With this framework in mind, it is reasonable to assume that if Paul read the curse of Law as death and the blessing of Abraham as life, there is a strong ideological connection between "promise" and "life." The promise Abraham believed which was reckoned to him as right status (Gen 15:6) was the birth of a biological son and heir with his wife.[61] In Gal 4:21–31 Paul couches the narrative in an allegory to explain the full picture, but in essence, *God's promise that Isaac would be born is the promise of Spirit.* Paul declares in 4:29 that Isaac's birth was according to Spirit; that is, *the Spirit brought Isaac to life.* This scheme receives considerable substantiation in Rom. 4:17, which cites an alternative version of the promise from Genesis, where God tells Abraham that he will be a father of many nations (Gen 17:5). Abraham puts his faith in God, τοῦ ζῳοποιοῦντος τοὺς νεκροὺς (the one making alive the dead). Contextually, it is Abraham and Sarah's "dead" reproductive systems that God makes alive. In Rom 4:19, Abraham did not consider his body νενεκρωμένον or Sarah's womb νέκρωσιν. The patriarch was fully convinced of God's power to make alive and, hence, it was reckoned to him as right status.[62] Romans 4:17–21 is an account of *Abraham's faith in the God of resurrection*; Paul continues that because of this (διὸ καὶ) it was reckoned to him as right status.[63] Within Paul's treatment of Gen 15:6, it is faith in God's power to revivify that God regards as right status; Abraham entered into right relation to God *because he trusted that God is able bring life to what is dead. Needless to say, one with faith in the risen Christ demonstrates exactly this principle.* This is also a summary of Hab. 2:4—those in the *right* will *live* because of *faith.*

Romans 4:23–25 indicates the paradigmatic nature of faith in this divine promise; through this God would give birth to his eschatological people.[64] The divine title in Rom 4:24 is reminiscent of the title in Gal 1:1. Notably, in Rom 4:24 Paul directs believers' faith towards God (the one raising Jesus from the dead) rather than Jesus. Like the prescript of Galatians, Rom 4:24–25 emphasises the resurrection as the critical element of

---

61. Gen 15:6 cited in Gal 3:6; cf. Rom 4:3–6, 9, 22.

62. Heb 11:19 attests to the significance of Abraham's faith in God's power to resurrect.

63. Rom 4:22; the καὶ is disputed.

64. For an interesting take on the creation of the people, see Wright, "Paul and the Patriarch," 207–41.

rectification. This view of resurrection is reinforced by referring to God with a resurrection honorific.

Christ, then, subsumed crucifixion death in resurrection life; this risen life indwells those with faith in Christ through Spirit (Gal 3:2–5). In this way, Spirit brings Abraham's spiritual progeny into existence, after the order of Isaac (4:28). The community-creating activity of the Spirit is the birthing of God's people. For the author of Deuteronomy, this blessing of life is the restoration from exile, which itself creates new community. Originally, the birth of Isaac marked the beginning of the nation (Gen 12:1–3) and hence, in Rom 9:7, Paul has Isaac act as a boundary for authentic Israel (Rom 9:6–9).

Having witnessed the God of resurrection literally raise Jesus, Paul reread the passages depicting Israel's restoration as Spirit re-enlivening the dead (esp. Ezek 36–37) in new light. Galatians 3:10–14 demonstrates a harmonization of the Deuteronomic blessing of life (restoration from exile as in Deuteronomy 30) with God's promise to Abraham—Isaac's birth, though he and Sarah were aged (Gen 15:1–6; 18:10–14; 21:1–10; cf. Rom 4:16–25). Both events were new life coming from the dead. Hence, in Gal 3:14 Paul equates the blessing of Abraham with the promise of *Spirit* and in 4:29 Isaac is said to be born κατὰ πνεῦμα.[65] C. Marvin Pate states that Gal 3:13–14

> . . . juxtaposes, in effect, the Deuteronomic curses of this age (cf. Gal 1:4) with the Abrahamic benefits (the Deuteronomic blessings anticipated), which participates in the age to come.[66]

The next section acts as a disclaimer as the inevitable question about the role of the Law looms ever larger. Paul clarifies that the Law is not an obstacle to God's work with a colloquial example and the introduction of the term διαθήκη.

Co-Text: Gal 3:15–18

The general case is in 3:15; covenant stipulations, ratified between two human parties, cannot be altered by the addition of later codicils. Galatians 3:17 applies the general case to Israel's covenantal history—if the terms of a covenant validated by people are unalterable, how much less mutable is a covenant where God is a signatory! The specifications of God's promises to Abraham were not affected by the Torah. Galatians 3:18 points to the

---

65. For an alternative explanation of blessing of Abraham as Spirit see Williams, "Promise in Galatians," 709–20.

66. Pate, *Reverse of the Curse*, 177.

unchangeable nature of God's inheritance promise to Abraham. If the Law altered the promise stipulations, then the scriptural promise is nullified.

There is an obvious tension at work here, which Paul heads off in 3:21 with a trademark μὴ γένοιτο! For his explanation introduces the possibility that Law and promise (Spirit) are at odds. Paul's colloquial example in 3:15–17 is weakened inasmuch as, in a human transaction, prohibiting eleventh hour amendments ensures that the transaction is fair. However, in the present case, *God* made the promises to Abraham *and* God gave the Law. As such, an interlocutor might reasonably posit divine authorization to defend the immutability of the Law. Although Paul's counter clearly implies the superiority of the covenant of Abraham over the Law, this need not necessitate a qualitative superiority. After all, the overarching importance of all divine covenants lies in just that—*they are divine*—and that includes the Sinai covenant. Paul's point is that the Law and the covenant promises had different roles, leading to different effects, and *the effect* of the covenant (right status with God) was superior to the effect of the Law (checking sin until Messiah's advent).

Post-Biblical Jewish writers were aware of this tension—the Abrahamic covenant clearly had temporal priority (Paul's 430 years) and, as White acutely observes, Abraham belonged to a mythical past, prior to the period when Jewish identity was sharpened by the constitutionality of the Mosaic Law.[67] Philo resolved the tension by attempting to equate the law of nature with the Law of Moses; by obeying natural law, Abraham *retroactively* obeyed Torah.[68] The author of *Jubilees* similarly has Abraham celebrating feasts in fact instituted by Moses—he celebrates First-fruits in *Jubilees* 15:1–2 and Tabernacles in 16:20–31.[69] Paul exploits the temporal dissonance between Law and covenant with Abraham to assert the priority of covenant, begging the inevitable question: Τί οὖν ὁ νόμος;

Exegesis of Gal 3:19–25

The question of Paul's position on Torah is, quite possibly, the thorniest debate in Pauline studies. Some propose that Galatians presents a negative view of the Law, which developed into a more sophisticated, positive evaluation by the writing of Romans.[70] Whilst Paul's thought process certainly

67. White, *Apostle of God*, 187.
68. Philo, *De Abrahamo*, 275–76.
69. Cf. Lev 23:34.
70. E.g., Drane, *Paul Libertine or Legalist?*; Hübner, *Law in Paul's Thought*. See further Barclay, "Paul and the Law," 5–15; Moo, "Paul and the Law," 287–307.

evolved, and though both epistles are context specific, Paul's view of Torah in Galatians is only *negative* as far as the temporal limitations he set on its jurisdictional governance represent a demotion. Galatians 3:19–21 suggest only that the Law had a different mandate from faith.

The Law was "added"—(Greek, προστίθημι; BAGD specifies adding to something that is already present or exists)—to the promises to Abraham.[71] It was added on account of the moral imperfections of the elect until Messiah dealt ultimately with sin.

The Law was given on account of *transgressions* as opposed to sin. The four occurrences of παράβασις in Paul's undisputed letters suggest a difference from ἁμαρτία.[72] Transgression would seem to presume the existence of a law to transgress. One might ask what exactly Paul thinks was being transgressed.[73] De Boer reduces the question to whether the Law was added to deal with/identify/restrain transgressions already taking place or to provoke transgressions thereby bringing the reality of sin into the open.[74] Garlington rightly suggests that the correct interpretation is the one which best comports with "until the seed might come."[75] It is, however, important to add that it must also square with ᾧ ἐπήγγελται, the relative pronoun in the dative with the verb in the perfect passive indicative correctly translated "to whom it had been promised." When then we read in 3:22 that συνέκλεισεν ἡ γραφὴ τὰ πάντα ὑπὸ ἁμαρτίαν, ἵνα ἡ ἐπαγγελία ἐκ πίστεως Ἰησοῦ Χριστοῦ δοθῇ τοῖς πιστεύουσιν, it becomes clear that the Law was given on account of transgressions until *the coming Seed gave the Spirit*.[76] The associations earlier drawn between Spirit and life now become clearer—the Law and the promise (Spirit) are not at odds (Gal 3:21a); it is simply that the Law was incapable of generating life—this was always the work of Spirit. Below is an account of Torah's role according to this section of Galatians.

Διαταγεὶς δι' ἀγγέλων (Gal 3:19) has led to all manner of scholarly speculations which need not be discussed here. Though tradition corroborates the involvement of angels in the giving of the Torah (Ps 67:18; CD 5:18; Josephus, *Ant.* 15.5.3. 136; Acts 7:53; Heb 2:2), conjecture surrounds the absence of angels in the Exodus account.[77] An alternative reading is presented

---

71. BAGD, 885.
72. Cf. Rom 2:23; 4:15; 5:14.
73. Rom 4:15 suggests it was not Torah.
74. De Boer, *Galatians*, 230; for various reasons, De Boer opts for the latter.
75. Garlington, *Galatians*, 203.
76. Here, ἡ γραφὴ must equate to the Law.
77. For a useful summary see Wallace, "Crux Interpretum," 240–43.

here, which argues that this phrase in conjunction with ἐν χειρὶ μεσίτου makes a subtler, deeper claim that pervades the rest of Galatians.

The Law being in Moses' hand appears in Exodus (32:15; 34:4, 29) and ἐν χειρὶ Μωϋσέως appears in a number of places in the LXX (e.g., Lev 26:46; Num 4:37; 36:13). Philo writes:

> So Moses, being amazed, and being also constrained by this command, believes those incredible events, and springs down to be a *mediator* and reconciler . . . [78]

The mediator in Gal 3:19 is almost certainly Moses, though it is not initially clear why he is unnamed.[79] What *is* clear is the absence of a definite article in 3:19 ("a mediator") says generally what is explicit in the opening of 3:20 ("the mediator").[80] The giving of the Law through the hands of various agents accentuates the *externality of the written code*—Jeremiah speaks of a time when God would write the Law on people's hearts (Jer 31:33). This is the Law's true destiny—hearts, not stone tablets (cf. 2 Cor 3:3). The Law written on tablets can be passed between hands, emphasising its status as external code. The giving of this external code identified Israel's sins as violations of the divine intentions for humanity—which explains Paul's imprisonment language in 3:22–24. That is, the Law demonstrated that sins were actually transgressions. This was the case until the coming of the *internal* ethical barometer—*Spirit*. Spirit is the Ezekielian language of internalization that corresponds to Jeremiah's prophecy about inscribing the Law on the hearts of the people.[81]

God gave the Law to show Israel their ethical misdemeanours were against the divine order, but after the advent of the Seed who gives the Spirit, it is by the Spirit that people will know that sin is transgression (cf. Rom 8:4).[82] We can thus interpret the hugely confusing sentence in 3:20.

With the question of 3:19 in the foreground, we may understand the reason the Law's role as external code ends in Christ; Spirit becomes an internal index for the community's pattern of life. The Law, however, was given to *Israel*. The *content* of the Law is not at issue, *but the nature of its mediation*—that is, *how* it was given. (Perhaps this is why Moses is referred to as the mediator—to place emphasis on the nature of the act of giving the Law rather than on the Law's content or Moses himself). *It was given only to*

---

78. Philo, *De Vita Mosis* 2.166.
79. Jervis, "Galatians 3:19–25," 287; see further Callan, "Pauline Midrash," 555.
80. In 3:20, ὁ δὲ μεσίτης could be replaced with "And Moses . . ."
81. Esp. Ezek 36:26–27.
82. I associate this idea of internal barometer with the restoration eschatology of Jeremiah and Ezekiel (see later).

Israel, but insofar as there is only one God over all people, as Paul goes on to say, clearly Torah could not be determinative for God's redemptive activity.[83] Again—this is probably why Moses is not named, but called the mediator; to place the emphasis on the nature of the mediation of Torah. Romans 3:29–30 substantiates this view.

This limitation of the Law does not set it against the promise of Spirit (3:21a), but draws a necessary distinction between their roles. Law and Spirit are only at odds for those holding defective views on Torah's role. The complementary nature of Law and Spirit is stated at 3:21a; it is simply the case that the Law cannot make alive, whereas Spirit can. Therefore, the role of the external code of Torah ends in the age of Messiah who gives Spirit to the faithful.

The Law's role is explained using two virtually synonymous verbs, συγκλείω and φρουρέω. Paul states that the Law was given to "lock people up under sin" in order that the promise might be given to them through faith in Christ (3:22); he further argues that Law "holds them in custody, locked up for the faith to be imminently revealed" (3:23). So then, sin was a prison of which the Law was prison-guard; faith is the key to the prison door, held onto by the guard, but only Messiah could turn the key. So Paul was incarcerated under sin, detained by the Law until he was pronounced dead. He was dead in that Torah oversaw him as the hostage of sin but was unable to free him. By submitting to the authority of Law, Paul was "taught" by the Law of its own ineffectiveness to bring him back to life: that is, *through the Law he died to Law* (Gal 2:19). It is in this sense the Law acted as παιδαγωγός. If the Law could have revivified Paul, then right status would have come by Law (3:21b) and Christ would not have had to die (2:21b).

Juxtaposition of Gal 3:22–25 and 2:19–21

By bringing together Paul's broader statements regarding the Law's role alongside the detail of its functionality within his own experience of rectification, which is paradigmatic for believing Jews, we may further elucidate Paul's nomology.

The scriptures (i.e., the Law) "imprisoned" everything under sin in that the codification of God's ethical demands for Israel instantiated her sin as transgression—through holding to the Law, then, Israel may perceive her sin to set her against God. (In line with the earlier comments on Gal 3:19–20, it seems Paul's choice of ἡ γραφὴ instead of the more predictable

---

83. Wright, *Climax* 170; see, however, the critique of Tim Gallant, http://www.biblicalstudiescenter.org/interpretation/gal3_16.htm.

ὁ νόμος accentuates the notion of Law as external code). For Israel, through the Law came death to Law, for as Law awakens Israel to its own estrangement from God because of sin, it points beyond itself to reconcile the gulf. The second half of 3:22 embodies all the elements of that to which in Paul's thought the Law points—promise (Spirit), faith, and Christ. In 3:23, we might read that before the indwelling of Spirit, the Law guarded Israel by demonstrating ethical infractions as transgressions. The Law in 3:24–25 was παιδαγωγός; it stewarded Israel in the knowledge of sin, leaving them dead, but being powerless to revivify them. Those who put their faith in Messiah are set free from this curse of death by being given the blessing of life. Those convinced they are God's people on the grounds of Torah—even if they add faith in Messiah to that fundamental belief—remain cursed. This view of things is validated in the Deutero-Pauline texts.[84]

Romans 5–7 further corroborates this view of the Law's place in Paul's rectification as revivification argument. Romans 7 may come closest to an essential commentary on the Pauline view of Law. It compliments Gal 3:19–25, suggesting why, for Paul, the Law pointed beyond itself to ultimately deal with the problem of sin. The following comments explain briefly how the Romans passages substantiate how Gal 3:19–25 addresses the question Τί οὖν ὁ νόμος;

The most pertinent challenge here is the potentially conflicting and inflammatory relationship between the Law, sin, and death. To this end, Moo rightly draws attention to Paul's belief that the Law brings the sentence of death to Israel collectively, as certain texts imply (1 Cor 15:56b; Rom 2:12; 4:15; 2 Cor 3:6–7).[85] However, as Wright indicates, Romans 7 works as a defense of the Law *against* the suggestion that it is either identical with sin (7:7–12) or, by itself, the ultimate cause of death (7:13–20).[86] The question cannot be simplistically reduced to whether the Law was "a good or a bad thing." On one hand, inferring that the Law is of demonic origin is needlessly melodramatic and demonstrably false.[87] On the other hand, even suggesting in more benign fashion that the Law was given for a negative purpose is potentially misleading, and needs sharpening.[88]

---

84. . . . καὶ ὄντας ἡμᾶς νεκροὺς τοῖς παραπτώμασιν συνεζωοποίησεν τῷ Χριστῷ in Eph 2:5: cf. Col 2:13.

85. Moo, "Israel and Paul," 128.

86. Wright, "Romans and the Theology of Paul," 47.

87. As is the position of Hübner, *Law*, 26.

88. E.g., Schreiner, *40 Questions*, 81–84. Though the relationship between Law and gospel is manifestly complex, Paul is impenitent that the Law is fundamentally good (e.g., Rom 7:12–14).

As above, the Law made sin into transgression—Israel may have succumbed to coveting, but only known it as the *transgression* of coveting because of the Law (Rom 7:7). Sin, seizing upon this, made the commandment into a source of temptation (Rom 7:8a). So the Law on its own is not death, but *apart from Law sin is dead* (Rom 7:8b). So the Law, through which there should have been life (as Lev 18:5), brought death (Rom 7:10). For, like the injunction against coveting which Paul specifically points to in Rom. 7 (citing Exod 20:17/Deut 5:21), the Law forbade allegiance to false deities (Exod 20:3-5/Deut 5:7-9). In Pauline thought, sin manipulated this injunction also, so the Law which was supposed to lead to a life of peace and security (Deut 16:20) actually led to the "death" of exile. Hence, Paul can say that sin killed him (Rom 7:11), by its deceptive interaction with God's good Law (Rom 7:13-14).

Sin and Law lead to death, but Law cannot make alive (Gal 3:21). Wherever Paul depicts the agency of ζωοποιέω, the enlivening agent is always God, Jesus or Spirit. So Law makes sin known, but cannot effectively diffuse sin because of how sin abuses the commandments with respect to weak humanity (Rom 7:14; 8:3). This state is what Paul broadly deems as *death*. Israel's recalcitrant idolatry led to death in exile—Ezekiel (e.g., Ezek 6:9; 11:21) and Jeremiah (e.g., Jer 7:30; 18:15), in particular amongst the Major Prophets, depict Israel's worship of false gods as a perverse lust. Even Terah succumbed to idolatry (Josh 24:2) in the pre-Torah era; however, within Paul's scheme, "sin was in the world until Law, but sin is not registered if no Law exists," (Rom 5:13). Death in Romans 5 is like a contagious disease contracted by exposure to a microbe—*sin*. Adam was the original vector (Rom 5:12), though he was a transgressor, for he violated a direct divine command (Gen 2:16-17). As such, Adam represents sinners who sinned after the giving of the Law (Rom 5:14b). In this analogy, the Law is a diagnostic dye that highlights the presence and pervasiveness of sin (Rom 5:20). People were exposed to this deadly germ by their innate carnal desire; Jesus did not accidentally contract the disease, but willfully exposed himself to the danger zone (he was "made sin" in 2 Cor 5:21 and "became the curse" in Gal 3:13).[89] Accordingly, his death could reconcile people to God (Rom 5:10a). The only cure for death was the divinely bestowed resurrection life— *we are saved by his life* (Rom 5:10b), and the cure was administered by Spirit (Rom 8:11-13; cf. Gal 2:20).

Paul's shift of language from blessing to promise (Gal 3:14), the contrast between the curse of the Law and the blessing of *Abraham* (Gal 3:7-14) and Paul's evaluation that faith in divine power to revivify is what God reckons

---

89. This represents Jesus' submission to death by crucifixion.

as right status (Gal 3:10–14; cf. Rom 4:17–20) all serve to explain why the Law was not given to make alive. *Galatians 3:21 is Paul's way of saying that it was never God's intention to establish the identity of his end-time people on the grounds of a written law. For sin to be ultimately dealt with, and sinners ratified as the people of God, would require the internalization of Spirit, which was procured through faith.*

Now we may consider the similarities between Romans 5/Romans 7 and Galatians 3.[90] The claim that scripture has shut up (συγκλείω) everything under sin (Gal 3:22a) should be read as describing that state of death under sin. For, as 3:22b suggests, this "shutting up" under sin was so the promise of Spirit, that is, the *Spirit of life*, might be given to the faithful. Recalling that the Law was originally given on account of transgressions (Gal 3:19b), we may see how Gal 3:22 corresponds to Rom 7:8–10. The Law was given to register sinful indulgence as violation of the divine intentions for humanity (Gal 3:22); in so doing, sin took advantage of this human propensity for indulgence and rule breaking, so the very instantiation of injunctions luridly instigated a heightened desire to rebel (Rom 7:8–10). Paul captures the notion experientially in Rom 7:19–21, which contrasts the experience of walking in the Spirit (Gal 5:16–17).

Romans 5:20 also answers the question of Gal 3:19a. In Rom 5:20, Paul writes that the Law "slipped in sideways" (παρεισέρχομαι) in order that πλεονάσῃ τὸ παράπτωμα. In Gal 3:19b the Law was added; for the Law to have slipped in, suggests the same thing in more sinister fashion.[91] The Law slipped in that the offence of sin might abound (Rom 5:20)—this further captures the notion of amplified propensity for sin that came with the Law, implied by Rom 7:8–10. It is this complex juxtaposition of sin, law and death that presents such difficulty in comprehending the role of the Law in Paul; the apostle can speak of the Law of sin and death that contrasts the Law of the Spirit of life in Christ (Rom 8:2); he can write elsewhere that the thorn-sting of death is sin and the power of sin is the Law (1 Cor 15:56).

Galatians 3:23 continues the thought of 3:22, though the wording comes precariously close to equating "under sin" with "under Law." Paul has to clarify that this is *not* what he means, by outlining complementarity between Law and promise in Gal 3:21 and exclaiming that Law and sin are not the same in Rom 7:7a. Clearly his reasoning might lead to such a false trail, but Paul will have none of it. That said, it is the Law, having been manipulated by sin, which incarcerates Israel till the revelation of faith. The use of ὥστε to connect Gal 3:23 with 3:24, which portrays Torah as παιδαγωγός, implies logical inference; in other words, it is in this process of

---

90. See Moo, "Israel and Paul," 124.

91. Παρεισέρχομαι in Gal 2:4 describes how the false brothers entered Jerusalem to pressurize Titus.

Law acting to "shut up" and "lock up" that it trains its practitioners, playing the part of pedagogue. The trainer's lesson is harsh; the coming of a "holy, just and good" Law from God accentuates the consciousness of sin, so for all practical intents and purposes, the Law exacerbates human sinfulness! *The Law stewarded Israel by creating the conditions by which the people could be "killed" by their sin* (Rom 7:11).[92] The people "died in jail," prisoners of sin, because the Law awakened the knowledge of sin (Rom 7:8b); but the remedy, the power to make alive, came not from Law, but faith, which came with Messiah.

Romans 7:24 depicts the frustration of someone overwhelmed by sin (cf. Rom 7:15–21), who knows the Law cannot re-enliven him and free him from custody. Note again, the concepts captivity/freedom and death/life, which undergird Pauline teaching on rectification in Galatians and Romans. Paul cries out for the one who will rescue (ῥύομαι) him from this body of death (τοῦ σώματος τοῦ θανάτου τούτου).[93] Paul observed Torah and came to understand both the deceptive nature of sin and the consequent need for an agent of life beyond Torah.

With these correlations in place, we may complete the circle by noting how Paul's personal experience of death to Law in Gal 2:19–20 is substantiated by Romans 7. Romans 7:1 is another of Paul's everyday life analogies of a principle; the contractual obligations of matrimony are dissolved when one party dies. A wife is free from her husband's "law" once he dies (Rom 7:2) and she can marry another (Rom 7:3). Notably, death to Law in Rom 7:4 is διὰ τοῦ σώματος τοῦ Χριστοῦ; in Gal 2:19, death to Law is διὰ νόμου, qualified as co-crucifixion with Christ. Co-crucifixion broadly resonates with "through the body of Christ," but Romans 7 sheds further light on "through Law" as follows.

Paul has clarified for Peter's benefit that rectification is only διὰ πίστεως Ἰησοῦ Χριστοῦ (Gal 2:16). Having torn down the divisive works of the Law with the gospel, to rebuild those walls by demanding that Gentiles observe Torah would be utterly counter-productive (2:18). For, it is διὰ νόμου that Paul died to Torah. Paul cannot reinstate the authority of the Law because it is this very Law that sin exploited to lead to death. Paul sees two things in operation. Firstly, Paul lived once apart from Law (presumably before he became a "Bar Mitzvah"), after which time he received the Law; then sin pounced and he died as a prisoner of sin (Rom 7:9). Secondly, though, dead through Law, Paul believed and was co-crucified with Christ, and shared in the risen life of Christ through Spirit. The elaborations in Rom 7:4 are clearer in view of the above. Having been made dead to Law through the body of Christ, Paul's believing Jewish brethren should literally "become

---

92. Rom 5:12–21.
93. Rom 7:24.

another's," denoting "belong" or "be joined to," another (Jesus)—an appropriate assertion in view of the marital analogy of Rom 7:1–3. Significantly, the writer defines this other one to whom the believers are joined as τῷ ἐκ νεκρῶν ἐγερθέντι (to the one having been raised from the dead). As suggested previously, to "live to God" is to share in the risen life of Christ (Gal 2:19), to live energized by the risen Christ (Gal 2:20) and by implication to live *for* the risen Christ (cf. 2 Cor 5:14–15).

In summation, the revivification text at Gal 3:21 should be read within a co-textual and contextual framework that centralizes the semantics of "life." Chiu correctly states that "the theme of vivification appears essential in order to understand Pauline justification."[94] Similar assertions are made by Lewis and Thiessen.[95] The theme permeates Galatians and is central to its interpretation. A consideration of Paul's arguments in Gal 3:10–14 shows that the vivification theme is scriptural and suggests that God makes alive through Spirit, not Law. Paul equates the blessing of Abraham with the promise of the Spirit, which amounts to the bringing to life those dead in sin and slavery; these become sons for Abraham after the order of Isaac. Paul contrasts this "life" with the curse of the Law—*death*, and thus, constructs a synthesis which is the fulcrum of his argument in Galatians. He exploits the Deuteronomic blessing and curse language; the curse is exile, a punishment for sin that the author of Deuteronomy also depicts as death. The blessing is restoration from exile, which the author also depicts as life. For Paul, the life spoken of by the prophets, (e.g., Deuteronomy, Habakkuk and Ezekiel) has come to fruition in the resurrected life of Messiah, mediated by Spirit to believers. Paul's scheme of rectification then, comes from Paul's re-reading of the relevant texts in light of the resurrection of Jesus. An examination of these intertexts shows how this scheme takes shape.

Intertextual Resonances: "Life" in Galatians and the Prophets

Gal 3:14 and Ezekiel 37

As has already been alluded to, at the heart of the oft-titled scriptural section of Paul's argument in Galatians 3, is how we are to understand the equation of the "blessing of Abraham" and "the promise of Spirit." Firstly, a brief reiteration of the change in language from blessing to promise, which is a turning point in the argument.

---

94. Aguilar Chiu, "Justification and the Spirit in Paul," 363.
95. Lewis, *Looking for Life*, 167–68; Thiessen, *Social Reality*, 159–86.

God promised Abraham a son and heir, despite Abraham and Sarah's advanced years. Paul demonstrates his understanding of Isaac's birth in a number of key statements. Isaac was born through the promise (Gal 4:23, 28); Isaac was born into freedom (Gal 4:22, 24–26); Isaac was born according to Spirit (Gal 4:29); furthermore, Isaac was born because of Abraham's faith in the God that revivifies (Rom 4:16–20); Isaac was the precursor of Israel (Rom 9:6–7; cf. Gen 21:12). For Paul, the promise of Isaac's birth was a promise of life coming forth through faith in divine revivification by the agency of Spirit, which results in freedom.

Paul has already made recourse to the Deuteronomic blessing/curse language; in Deuteronomy 27–30, curse=exile=death and blessing=restoration=life. The author of Deuteronomy articulates exile, the result of sin, as death; freedom is life. Needless to say, restored, freed Israel is in the right before God. It is with this scheme in mind, that Paul has been influenced by Ezekiel 37, which also depicts Israel's restoration from exile as the blessing of life coming to their dead bones under the agency of Spirit resulting in freedom. This is the sense in which Paul equates the blessing of Abraham with the promise of Spirit—*both were the endowment of life based on faith in divine intervention.*

The Law's curse is death; those attempting to be identified as the people of God on the grounds of Law remain in "exile"—estranged from God and not in right relation to him. Those with faith in Christ are made alive by Spirit; that is, they are, like Isaac, born according to Spirit (Gal 4:28–29), and, therefore, free from any master other than God himself. So we turn to *how* Paul drew upon Ezekiel 37.

The question "can these bones live?" (Ezek 37:3) presupposes a yes or no but elicits neither. The implied answer is, of course, no. Ezekiel may have known "raising" stories like the widow of Zarephath's son (1 Kgs 17:17ff) and the Shunammite woman's son (2 Kgs 4:18ff) but as Block notes, those were recent deaths.[96] The bones in the valley were exceedingly dry (ξηρὰ σφόδρα), their situation hopeless and desperate—nothing shy of divine intervention could reverse such devastation. For Paul, as for Ezekiel, liberation necessitates the intervention of Spirit (Gal 4:6–7, 22–31).[97] Only Spirit could end Israel's physical exile and in the same way, for Paul, only Spirit could rectify. So Paul asks, "Having begun in the Spirit, do you now perfect yourself in flesh?"[98] Ezekiel 37 relates how liberation would be accomplished

---

96. Block, *Ezekiel 25–48*, 374.

97. Note here also the connection between Rom 2:29 and Deut 30:6 in terms of Spirit and restoration.

98. Gal 3:3.

by the nation's experience of Spirit. The Galatians had experienced the liberating and rectifying Spirit, but could appeal to anything else enhance their liberation? The implied answer is, again, an unequivocal no. Ezekiel's retort was σὺ ἐπίστῃ ταῦτα. The verb ἐπίσταμαι places the emphasis of knowledge on the process of understanding.[99] This is something *only* YHWH could comprehend; only divine reasoning and intervention, *Spirit*, could free Israel. Only by faith could Spirit be received.

In Galatians, *Isaac*, born κατὰ πνεῦμα, represents freed, restored Israel (Gal 4:29; cf. Rom 4:16–19). The Isaiah 54 citation in Gal 4:27 reinforces the connection between life and freedom, *for it contextualises Isaac's birth as an implicit revivification event*. As Jobes has recounted, barrenness is associated with death in Israel's scriptures.[100] We may note barren Hannah's prayer: "The barren has borne seven, but she who has many children is forlorn. The Lord kills and brings to life; he brings down to Sheol and raises up."[101] Job 3:7 and Prov 30:16 also connect barrenness with death.

Jobes' analysis fits smoothly with the reading outlined in this volume. The crucial stroke in her treatment is the assertion that

> . . . in Paul's thought the historical event which realized Isaiah's prophetic metaphor of a miraculous birth to the barren one [i.e., Isa 54:1] is *the resurrection of Jesus Christ*.[102]

She employs Hays' method of metalepsis, by which a literary echo links the text in which it occurs to an earlier text . . . so the figurative effect of the echo can lie in the unstated . . . points of resonance between the two texts.[103] By showing how Isaiah transforms the theme of barrenness in the OT into a way of speaking about God's future manifestation of power, Jobes argues that Isaiah can speak of the barren one giving birth in Isa 54:1; after all, Isaiah has already merged and transformed Israel's barren matriarch tradition with the female personification of Jerusalem in Isaiah 26:

> *Like a woman with child, who writhes and cries out in her pangs when she is near her time*, so were we because of you, O LORD; we were with child, we writhed, but we gave birth only to *wind*. We have won no victories on earth, and no one is born to inhabit the world. *Your dead shall live, their corpses shall rise*. O

---

99. Louw and Nida, *Lexicon*, 379.
100. Jobes, "Jerusalem, Our Mother," 314.
101. 1 Sam 2:5–6 (NRSV).
102. Jobes, "Jerusalem, Our Mother," 314, emphasis mine.
103. Hays, *Echoes*, 20.

dwellers in the dust, awake and sing for joy! For your dew is a radiant dew, and the earth will give birth to those long dead.[104]

However, contra Jobes, miraculous birth *should* be associated with resurrection in Galatians.[105] She correctly notes there is no *direct* connection, hence, Isaac's birth is not one of the revivification texts in this investigation. However, in Rom 4:16–19, Paul *does* depict Isaac's birth very explicitly as a revivification event through which he explicates rectification apart from Law. Such a position could scarcely apply to Romans and not Galatians. To press the point home, we note the following.

Paul's semantic framework exhibits common ground with Ezekiel— the birth of Isaac and the restoration of Israel both unite the blessing of life with the experience of Spirit. Paul's experience of Jesus' resurrection and his experience of the Spirit suggest that he perceived Jesus' resurrection as the initial concretization and accomplishment of Ezekiel's prophetic resurrection metaphor in Ezek 37:1–14. That Paul sees the raising of Jesus as a preview of the resurrection of believers is implicit in his application of "first-fruits" language to Jesus (1 Cor 15:20, 23) and of those with the Spirit (Rom 8:23). Consequently, the resurrection of Jesus/community experience of Spirit and the prophetic vision of Israel's restoration functioned as mutually interpretive paradigms, by which Paul explains faith-dependent, but Torah-independent rectification. This is clear in how Paul treats Isaac's birth in Gal 4:26–29; the Isaiah 54 citation will show how his birth is a revivification image.

Paul's question in Gal 3:2 bears a striking semantic resemblance to the question that introduces Isa 53:1:

Ἐξ ἔργων νόμου τὸ Πνεῦμα ἐλάβετε ἢ ἐξ ἀκοῆς πίστεως; (Gal 3:2b)

Κύριε, τίς ἐπίστευσεν τῇ ἀκοῇ ἡμῶν; (Isa 53:1).[106]

Scholars rightly infer that in Pauline thought, Gal 3:2—4:27 and Isa 53:1—54:1 are parallel readings of the soteriological significance of Messiah's death; space prevents detailed analysis, but note:

---

104. Isaiah 26:17–19 (NRSV), emphasis Jobes. See Jobes, "Jerusalem, Our Mother," 314. She notes Isaiah's linkage of childbirth, the Spirit, resurrection and rejoicing imagery.

105. Ibid.

106. Morales, *Spirit*, 81–83; Garlington, *Galatians*, 113; Bruce, *Galatians*, 149; Jobes, "Jerusalem, Our Mother," 312–13; see further Kahl, *Reimagined*, 262–63; Paul quotes Isa 53:1 in Rom 10:16.

> καὶ βούλεται κύριος ἀφελεῖν ἀπὸ τοῦ πόνου τῆς ψυχῆς αὐτοῦ, δεῖξαι αὐτῷ φῶς καὶ πλάσαι τῇ συνέσει, δικαιῶσαι δίκαιον εὖ δουλεύοντα πολλοῖς, καὶ τὰς ἁμαρτίας αὐτῶν αὐτὸς ἀνοίσει.

and *the Lord is pleased to take away the strain in his soul,* to *show him light* and to form the comprehension, *to rectify* the righteous being well enslaved to many, and their sins he will carry (Isa 53:10c-11, added emphasis).

Given the death-focused tenor of Isa 53:4–12, especially the two explicit references in 53:9, 12, it is apparent that Paul interpreted God's pleasure to '"take away the strain in [the servant's] soul," "to show him light," and "to rectify" him *as references to Jesus' resurrection*. As becomes apparent from the revivification passages throughout Galatians, rectification is revivification—the already element of salvation history of which the final resurrection is not yet.[107]

In Paul's interpolation of Isa 54:1 in Gal 4:27, we may see why his presentation of barren Jerusalem giving birth is juxtaposed with Isaac's birth— *to demonstrate Isaac's birth is a revivification portrait and hence a portrait of rectification.* It follows that to be born κατὰ πνεῦμα is to be revivified, and hence, freed. This narrative is captured in Ezekiel 37:

> Τάδε λέγει κύριος τοῖς ὀστέοις τούτοις Ἰδοὺ ἐγὼ φέρω εἰς ὑμᾶς πνεῦμα ζωῆς (Ezek 37:5) . . . καὶ δώσω ἐφ' ὑμᾶς νεῦρα καὶ ἀνάξω ἐφ' ὑμᾶς σάρκας καὶ ἐκτενῶ ἐφ' ὑμᾶς δέρμα καὶ δώσω πνεῦμά μου εἰς ὑμᾶς, καὶ ζήσεσθε, καὶ γνώσεσθε ὅτι ἐγώ εἰμι κύριος (Ezek 37:6) . . .
>
> καὶ εἶπεν πρός με Προφήτευσον, υἱὲ ἀνθρώπου, προφήτευσον ἐπὶ τὸ πνεῦμα καὶ εἰπὸν τῷ πνεύματι Τάδε λέγει κύριος Ἐκ τῶν τεσσάρων πνευμάτων ἐλθὲ καὶ ἐμφύσησον εἰς τοὺς νεκροὺς τούτους, καὶ ζησάτωσαν (Ezek 37:9) . . .
>
> καὶ ἐπροφήτευσα καθότι ἐνετείλατό μοι, καὶ εἰσῆλθεν εἰς αὐτοὺς τὸ πνεῦμα, καὶ ἔζησαν καὶ ἔστησαν ἐπὶ τῶν ποδῶν αὐτῶν, συναγωγὴ πολλὴ σφόδρα (Ezek 37:10) . . . καὶ δώσω τὸ πνεῦμά μου εἰς ὑμᾶς, καὶ ζήσεσθε . . . (Ezek 37:14a).[108]

Within Paul's scriptural exegesis, the barren Sarah's delivery of Isaac according to Spirit obliquely addresses Ezekiel's explicit question in Ezek 37:3 much like it addresses the implicit question behind Galatians—how someone is rectified before God—as follows:

---

107. See Rom 4:25 which echoes Isa 52:13—53:12.
108. Cf. Ezek 36:27a.

Can these bones live? Only by God's Spirit, restoring the people, raising them from the necrosis of exile, reversing their estrangement from God, bringing them into a glorious new freedom and empowering them to adhere to his commands. This creates a new community—freed Israel (Ezekiel 37).

How is someone rectified? Only by God's Spirit revivifying people from the deadness of sin, ending their slavery to Law and idolatry and bringing them into a glorious new freedom in Christ. This creates a new community—the end-time people of God (Galatians).

The true exile for Paul was not to be outside Jerusalem, but outside *Christ*; the true restoration was not geographical, but Christological—not restoration in Jerusalem, but *in Christ*.

Ezekiel 37:5-11 are vertebrae in the narrative spine of Galatians. The Spirit of life (Ezek 37:5) is the blessing of Abraham which contrasts the curse of the Law (Gal 3:14) and it is by virtue of Spirit that those of Christ, having crucified the flesh, now live (Gal 5:24-25). Israel will live when God places his Spirit in them (Ezek 37:6, 11; Gal 4:6); moreover, those in the right before God will live from faith (Gal 3:11) for faith is the origin of Spirit (Gal 3:2-5). That the Spirit will blow into the dead ones that they will live (Ezek 37:9) supports Paul's understanding of his own experience—he died in order that he might live to God (Gal 2:19) and ascribed this life to the presence of the risen Christ alive in him (Gal 2:20). Israel came to life and stood upon its feet by the action of the Spirit (Ezek 37:10); this portrayal of Israel's liberation resonates directly with Paul's depiction of the free-born Isaac (Gal 4:21-5:1).

Gal 4:22—5:1 and Ezekiel 36–37

The treatment of Gal 4:21ff above was to unpack the critical transition of blessing to promise in Gal 3:14 and explain *why* Paul equates the blessing of Abraham with the promise of Spirit. The following comments on Gal 4:22—5:1 are to substantiate the principal thematic interface between the pericope and Ezekiel's resurrection prophecy—*Spirit and freedom*.

The section Gal 4:21—5:1 actually reintroduces the issue from 3:7-9— "the sons of Abraham." There, Abraham's *bona fide* heirs are those with faith in Christ. Now, Paul draws Abraham's actual first two sons into the fray, going beyond the "of works" vs. "of faith" contrast of 3:9-10. In this section, the contrast is between "Spirit-Promise-Freedom" vs. "Flesh-Law-Slavery."

In Gal 4:21-31, Paul is trying to gain the theological upper hand by arguing in an unnatural direction. His opponents had the stronger position, because in Gen. 16:6, the *Gentile* Hagar was expelled. Paul's allegorizing allows him to define Isaac as *born according to the Spirit* and determine that his opponents' expulsion from the community is warranted.

Having demonstrated that Spirit is the substance of the Abrahamic promises in Gal 3:14, we may now see the same correspondence of promise and Spirit in Gal 4:23 and 4:29:

ἀλλ' ὁ μὲν ἐκ τῆς παιδίσκης κατὰ σάρκα γεγέννηται, ὁ δὲ ἐκ τῆς ἐλευθέρας δι' ἐπαγγελίας (4:23).

ἀλλ' ὥσπερ τότε ὁ κατὰ σάρκα γεννηθεὶς ἐδίωκεν τὸν κατὰ πνεῦμα, οὕτως καὶ νῦν (4:29).

The child of the slave woman has been born (perfect passive indicative of γεννάω) according to flesh as opposed to the child of the free woman born through promise in 4:23. In 4:29 the one having been born (aorist passive participle of γεννάω) according to flesh persecuted the one born according to Spirit. (In both verses, the verb has to be supplied in the second part of the sentence). The un-named child of the slave woman is Ishmael.[109] Paul wishes to emphasise that Ishmael's birth was according to normal, non-miraculous channels, but also that it happened in contradiction to God's intention that Sarai would bear Abraham's son (Gen 17:15-19). Isaac was the result of God's miraculous intervention allowing the aged Abraham and Sarah to conceive. Similarly, Ezekiel's vision shows Judah's freedom would not arise through any "normal" channels; God intervened miraculously through concern for his tarnished reputation (Ezek 36:12-24).

In his treatment of Spirit as the origin of life, we may reason that Paul would have read Abraham's questions regarding the birth of a legitimate heir (e.g., Gen 15:2; cf. Sarah's questions in Gen 18:12-14) in a similar vein to the questions, "can these bones live" and "how is one rectified?" They all pertain to revivification; as in Rom 4:17-19, these questions all address *the power of the God of Resurrection*. It is God, τοῦ ζῳοποιοῦντος τοὺς νεκροὺς καὶ καλοῦντος τὰ μὴ ὄντα ὡς ὄντα (Rom 4:17), who acts so dead bones can live, aging sexual/gynaecological apparatus can bring forth offspring and those dead in slavery and sin can be rectified and freed. Once more, the answer to these questions is only by *Spirit*, the agent of God's creative intervention.[110]

With this in mind, observe the following corollaries of Paul's case. Ishmael's mother represents the Mosaic covenant, and Isaac's mother, the Abrahamic covenant (αὗται γάρ εἰσιν δύο διαθῆκαι—Gal 4:24). As Hays

---

109. Ishmael is never named in the NT.
110. Rom 8:11-16 makes the role of Spirit more explicit than Gal 4:6-7.

notes, the Abrahamic covenant finds its fulfilment in Christ in Paul's re-reading.[111] Paul is suggesting that, just as Ishmael was born into slavery, his opponents' Gentile converts were being born into slavery by embracing Torah.[112] (There may well have been widespread ill feeling towards Ishmael and his descendants; for example, according to *the War Scroll* the Sons of Light would face off with the sons of Ishmael in an apocalyptic war).[113]

It is not completely clear what Paul is implying by comparing Hagar/Sinai to "the now Jerusalem" in Gal 4:25; is it Paul's description of contemporary Judaism with Jerusalem as its capital (Guthrie)?[114] Did Paul's opponents look to the Jerusalem church to validate their stance (R. Longenecker)?[115] Perhaps it represents Judaism as a whole legal system centralised in Jerusalem (Bruce)[116] or a symbol of the political and religious institution of Judaism (Betz).[117] The precise understanding of τῇ νῦν Ἰερουσαλήμ need not over concern us, because the explanatory γὰρ in 4:25b tells us *how* Hagar "corresponds to" (συστοιχέω) the now Jerusalem—she is in slavery with her children.

By contrast, the Galatian Gentiles were free, for the "above" Jerusalem is their mother.[118] Like Isaac, they were not the product of flesh/Law/slavery; that is, they were not the natural children born of non-miraculous channels, bound to the external Torah and, thus, slaves. Rather, they were "supernaturally" born children, whose faith God had accepted as sonship, born of the same promise that God made to Abraham himself.

Some further comments on Paul's citation from Isa 54:1 will reinforce the thematic importance of Ezek 37:1–14 to Gal 4:21—5:1. Paul is both deeply conversant with and reliant upon Isaiah.[119] As before, the obvious connection between Isa 54:1 and Gal 4:27 is the barrenness of Sarah.[120] Isaiah sets the barren (LXX, στεῖρα) woman in opposition to the woman who

---

111. Hays, *Echoes*, 114.

112. Martyn's suggestion that "bearing children" is a metaphor for gaining converts is certainly correct—see Martyn, *Galatians*, 451–54.

113. 1QM 2:13.

114. Guthrie, *Galatians*, 132.

115. R. Longenecker, *Galatians*, 213.

116. Bruce, *Galatians*, 220.

117. Betz, *Galatians*, 246.

118. For heavenly Jerusalem, see 4 *Ezra* 7:26; 2 *Baruch* 4:2–3.

119. See Oss, "Paul's Use of Isaiah," 105–12; Kwok, "Use of Isaiah"; Shum, *Paul's Use of Isaiah*.

120. So Schreiner, *Galatians*, 304. Schreiner also correctly adds that Sarah's barrenness is no minor theme in Genesis, for her inability to bear children impinges on the fulfilment of God's promise that Abraham would have offspring.

has a husband, but in Genesis, it is Sarah—the *married* woman—who is barren.[121] As we have seen, though, the context of Isaiah 54 illuminates the underlying reasons for Paul's recourse to it.

Like Ezekiel 36–37, Deutero-Isaiah's concern is the restoration of Israel from captivity in Babylon; Israel is likened to a barren woman abandoned by her husband (Yahweh) into exile—Isa 54:5–7. The barren woman is Jerusalem, having been occupied, besieged and pillaged. The woman restored to her husband and now bearing children is the freed Jerusalem, being rebuilt and repaired.

In Galatians, Sarah is the Jerusalem "above;" she bears free children, born according to divine intervention (Spirit). However, as Paul will assert in 6:8, there is a future component to the Spirit's activity in rectification; it seems this is the implication of the *above* Jerusalem.

The apostle's overall position is that *rectification is the true freedom, the real restoration from exile*.[122] Paul wants the Gentiles to know they have been born according to the Spirit. Isaac's birth was because Abraham believed God's promise to give him an heir who would be Israel's progenitor. It is this promise, the promise of life created and granted by God, that Paul sees fulfilled in "Spirit" (Gal 3:14; 4:29). As Schlier notes, "Der Segen Abrahams wird als Geist interpretiert."[123] By faith in Christ, the Gentiles have received the same promise of Spirit (Gal 3:2–6, 14), resulting in the life that comes from God by faith (Gal 3:11; Hab 2:4).

The key connection between Ezek 37:1–14 and Gal 4:21—5:1 is that *when the Spirit imbues life, the result is freedom*. For Ezekiel, the Spirit giving life to the dead bones of Israel and raising them to their feet was a picture of restoration (see esp. Ezek 37:12). Paul, having experienced Jesus' vindication in resurrection, treated the Spirit's life giving action to those with faith in Christ as rectification.

Gal 3:21 and Ezekiel 37

We move to the target revivification text; the question of Ezek 37:3 is answered in the ensuing vision—o*nly Spirit can bring to life what is dead*. For Paul, the prophetic vision of God raising Israel was literalized in Jesus' resurrection. In a previous chapter, ideas of deliverance and vindication were shown to be commonly narrated as "resurrections" in Jewish literature, and a number of Jewish writers confronted with issues of life and death made recourse to the restoration metaphor in Ezekiel 37. Paul certainly appears to have been

---

121. Williams, *Galatians*, 129.

122. As correctly, Wright, *Climax*, 141.

123. Schlier, *Der Brief an die Galater*, 141 cited from Taylor, "Eschatological Interdependence," 302.

inculcated by the prophetic tendency to depict the restoration from Babylon as a *new Exodus* in his rendition of rectification. As such, the emphasis Paul places on the risen Jesus in the opening of the letter and the ensuing condensation of revivification images suggest how Paul evaluated Jesus' resurrection. *Spirit and life being the key terms in Ezekiel 37, and Spirit giving life to what is dead in Ezekiel 37 being the chief metaphor, demonstrate that Paul saw Jesus' resurrection as an eschatological actualization of what Ezekiel captures.* Indeed, confronted with this unprecedented, literal, raising from death, it is difficult to imagine Paul *not* drawing theological significance from Ezekiel 37.

For many Jews, Ezekiel's vision became a picture of the final resurrection, but the resurrection of Jesus radically redrew this overall portrait in Paul. Resurrection was Israel's rectification in Ezekiel 37 and Jesus' rectification in Paul—Paul reasoned that it was also the believers' rectification, as Galatians depicts. Paul's insistence that if a law had been given capable of revivification that right status would come from law makes a direct association between rectification and revivification. As such, God's question to Ezekiel again resonates with the question underlying Galatians. Combatting his opponents in Galatia, the question of how one is rectified became, "how can what is dead be made alive?" Galatians 3:21 answers the question negatively—not by Law. Galatians 5:25 implies an affirmative response—by *Spirit*.

Summary: Gal 3:21—Rectification as Endowment of Life in Galatians

The critical connotation of the biblical tapestry in Gal 3:10–13, and of the conclusive statement in 3:14 which equates the blessing of Abraham with Spirit, is that *rectification results from the life that comes from faith*. The citation from Hab 2:4 in Gal 3:11 allows Paul to make a preliminary statement driven home by Gal 3:21; it is obvious that no one is rectified before God by Law, because the life of the rectified comes from faith (Gal 3:11). If this life originated from Law, then Law would lead to rectification (Gal 3:21).

This "life" is, furthermore, the blessing of Abraham and the promise of Spirit—the life conveyed by Spirit to produce Abrahamic progeny (Gal 3:6, 14; cf. Gal 4:29). This blessing is contrasted with the curse of the Law (Gal 3:9–10); the language of blessing and curse hails from Deuteronomy 27–30, chapters which have clearly influenced Gal 3:10–14. For the author of Deuteronomy, blessing is equated with life and having one's heart inclined towards Yahweh; curse goes hand in hand with banishment to Gentile lands and death. The narrative of exile as death and restoration as life is captured in the metaphorical vision sequence of Ezek 37:1–14, where Spirit initiates this life. This is the backdrop for the pneumatology of Galatians; freedom, life and the birth of the eschatological community are the result of Spirit, as typified by Isaac's birth, in Paul's theologizing. The addition of the external Law code, passed through various hands, does not affect the covenant promise (Gal 3:15-18) because it does not make alive (3:21).

Galatians 3:21 pivotally expresses that constraint upon the Law which underlies Paul's attitude towards it throughout his argument in Galatians. Fee says of 3:21 that it is "no accident that the language reflects Ezekiel's vision of God's people."[124] I would add the following in closing.

Galatians tells us that the Law supervised Israel until Messiah came (3:22-25); now, through faith, Jew and Gentile are sons of God (3:26). They are one people—there is not Jew/Greek, slave/free, male/female (3:27-28). The sons of God are the true seed/sons of Abraham (3:7-9) and heirs according to the promise (of Spirit).

This is reinforced and expanded in 4:1 where ἐπιτρόπους and οἰκονόμους are indicative of the Law's role much like παιδαγωγός in 3:24-25. Galatians 4:1-2 evokes the immaturity of the Exodus generation, who were infant sons of God (Hos 11:1) and needed the Law to survive till they reached maturity. The coming of Messiah marks freedom from the guardianship of the Law and the requisite maturity to receive the inheritance. In this, 3:23-25 says in terms of the coming of faith and the release from the Law's supervision what 4:3-5 says in terms of the coming of maturity and redemption. As above, 3:26-29 is a conclusive section outlining that the sons of God are those with faith in Messiah and thus heirs of the promise to Abraham. These ideas converge strongly in 4:5-7, where those under Law are redeemed and so become sons, receive the Spirit (the Abrahamic promise) and become heirs through God.

This essential narrative is allegorized in 4:21-31: Abraham was brought into right relationship with God through faith and his true children will be related to him by faith. The Abrahamic promise (Spirit/life) will be realized in one sole heir, Messiah—*this life is manifest in his resurrection—this is the meaning of Gal 3:16*. It is this risen life which animates Paul, a life in him by faith (Gal 2:20). *That life predicted by Habakkuk, which comes from faith, is thus understood as the resurrected life of Messiah* (Gal 3:11; Hab 2:4). Those with faith in Messiah inherit the promise, Spirit, who conveys the resurrection life to them. They concomitantly enter a stage of maturity away from the overlord-ship of masters other than God—that is, they are free. Life is from Christ, through Spirit, not Law; Gal 3:21 thus sums up the non-essentiality of Torah for right status.

---

124. Fee, *Galatians*, 132.

5

Revivification Text Four

Galatians 5:24–25: The Crucifixion of the Flesh

Context of Gal 5:24–25; 6:8; 6:14–15: Flesh and Spirit

In Gal 5:24–25, Paul essentially applies to all believers what he has applied to himself in 2:19–20. In each of the final three images, the term σάρξ (flesh) is crucial to the polemic. This chapter will survey the use of σάρξ and demonstrate the points of contact with the revivification imagery. In so doing, the importance of the "life" becomes ever clearer.[1]

Jesus' literal crucifixion of flesh drives the metonymy in 2:19–20 and 5:24–25. Louw and Nida in their analysis of σάρξ in the NT suggest it can be rendered as "flesh," "body," "people," "human," "nation," "human nature," and "human being;" furthermore, there are idiomatic phrases like "thorn in the flesh" (2 Cor 12:7), denoting a severe enduring problem, and "going after strange flesh" (Jude 7), standing for sodomy.[2] The term has considerable semantic elasticity, but the contexts within which Paul employs it exhibit sufficient consistency to comprehend its argumentative functionality in Galatians.

Paul sometimes uses σάρξ relatively innocuously. For example, Barclay draws attention to Gal 2:20, where Paul sees no conflict between living "in faith" and "in flesh."[3] He also raises the question of whether Christians are still associated with flesh in *any* way, for in 5:24 they have crucified the flesh

---

1. For a fuller account see Bruce, *Free Spirit*, 203–11.
2. Louw and Nida, *Lexicon*, 220.
3. Barclay, *Obeying*, 181; see the entire section 178–215 which deals specifically with the flesh-Spirit dichotomy.

but are still susceptible to its desires in 5:13, 16 and in danger of sowing to it in 6:8.⁴ Taking into account the apocalyptic framework within which Paul uses σάρξ, Barclay adds that it reflects that which is merely human.⁵

Alternatively, W. B. Russell III argues that σάρξ and its opposite in Galatians 5–6, πνεῦμα, are theological abbreviations in Paul's argument for two competing identities of the people of God in Galatia.⁶ He notes that the flesh community (Judaizers) is identified with the Law era, characterized by frailty and transitoriness, and not indwelt by Spirit. The Spirit community, on the other hand, is enabled by God's presence and bodily liberated from sin's dominion.⁷

Semantic Analysis of σάρξ

"Flesh" appears eighteen times in Galatians. Broadly speaking, in Galatians, the term should be read as *always* secondary but not *necessarily* pejorative. When Paul writes that at the time "when God was pleased to reveal His Son in me, that I might preach Him among the nations, immediately I did not confer with flesh and blood" (Gal 1:16), Paul is not pejoratively denouncing the physical body. He *is*, however, secondarily implying that seeking human validation for his commission diminishes the directness of divine revelation.⁸

In 2:16 πᾶσα σάρξ simply means "everyone" shall not be rectified through works of Law. However, the clumsy syntax implies a negative tone—Paul might easily have used the adjective "no one" (οὐδείς) rather than negate the verb (no one will be rectified). To state that all flesh will not be rectified (alluding to Ps 143:2) seems to harshly emphasize that there is no exception to this rule—not even adherence to God's Torah.

---

4. Ibid.

5. Ibid., 210.

6. Russell, "Does the Christian Have Flesh," 186.

7. Ibid., 186–87; Russell notes that living according to the rule of Spirit is "the greatest antidote to Judaistic— that is, fleshly—behaviour. Therefore the 'flesh' . . . is the bodily emphasis of the Judaizers. Flesh in this context is that which is merely human and distinctively Jewish." Relating flesh to a Jewish way of life seems to go beyond Paul's intentions.

8. Note Paul's designation of Jesus in Rom 1:2–4, where Jesus' status as God's son according to a spirit of holiness is superior to his status as David's descendant. As in Gal 4:23, 28–29, flesh here represents birth and descent, and as such, Paul clearly saw birth and descent according to flesh as inferior to birth and descent according to Spirit. Within Romans itself, fleshly descent is deemed irrelevant to being the people of God (Rom 9:8). Rom 1:3–4 is another example of σάρξ as secondary but not pejorative.

In Gal 2:20 Paul lives the revivified life ἐν σαρκί. He has revised his eschatological calendar; there is the age before Messiah, the age of rectification by faith in Christ and the final consummation. Though Paul describes his own rectification here as death and rebirth, he is aware that *now* he still lives in an era of imperfection. He shares in the resurrected life of Messiah, but in a world compromised by sin.

The Spirit-flesh dichotomy first appears in 3:2–5; having been rectified through faith in Christ, did the Galatian Gentiles feel that their relation to God needed supplementing "in" or "by" flesh? Gal 3:3b implies "having begun with faith, are you now looking for completion in Law?" That being the case, σάρξ here relates either to the human exertion of doing of the Law, or the appeal to something that relates to the era of flesh, like Law. Certainly in 3:2–3, beginning in Spirit and completing in flesh directly contrasts with the hearing of faith and works of Law. Bruce contends that flesh here is "human nature in its unregenerate weakness, relying on such inadequate resources as were available before the coming of faith."[9] This somewhat obscures the issue—irrespective of the human state, no amount of Law-observance could bring about Spirit possession.

Paul outlines the circumstances by which he first came to preach the gospel in Galatia in 4:13–14, describing the ἀσθένειαν τῆς σαρκὸς the Galatians nursed him through. They did not despise τὸν πειρασμὸν ὑμῶν ἐν τῇ σαρκί μου. Whilst it seems that flesh here merely stands for a physical ailment, Paul uses the phrase τὴν ἀσθένειαν τῆς σαρκὸς ὑμῶν in Rom 6:19 to denote the Romans' pre-Christian susceptibility to lawless acts. Ἐν ᾧ ἠσθένει διὰ τῆς σαρκός in Rom 8:3 suggests that human weakness compromised Torah's ability to deal with sin. Paul's well-known thorn in the flesh of 2 Cor 12:7 was given so Jesus' power was made perfect in Paul's weakness. Therefore, Paul reasoned that he would boast more in (his) weaknesses. It seems when Paul associates σάρξ with ἀσθένεια (and cognates), that despite the apparent innocence of σάρξ as the physical body, there is a note of negativity. This is not the demonization of flesh sometimes associated with "Gnosticising" sects, but Paul does consider the life that predates the Parousia to be inferior.

In 4:21—5:1, the two references to flesh denote the means by which a child is born and the ensuing genealogical legacy.[10] Clearly in these texts, to be born according to Spirit/promise is superior. Σάρξ here depicts frail human reasoning and decision making as with Abraham and Sarah's deci-

---

9. Bruce, *Galatians*, 149.

10. For further evidence of flesh as cipher for descent see Leithart, "Flesh in Galatians."

sion to permit Abraham to copulate with Hagar. In related fashion it also denotes the ordinary, non-miraculous path of childbirth that does not rely on a divine promise.

There is a warning in Gal 5:13 that the freedom afforded by rectification not be used as an "opportunity for the flesh." The wider context of Galatians, the call to freedom in 5:1 and the association in 5:2-4 of circumcision with legal observance suggest that flesh here denotes the decision to be circumcised and embrace Torah.[11] This is confirmed in 5:14, where enslavement to one another fulfils the Law. The remaining occurrences of σάρξ all stand directly in contrast with a reference to Spirit—they are in 5:16, 17, 19, (cf. 5:22), 24 (cf. 5:25), 6:8. The meanings of σάρξ gathered between chapters 1-4 cannot be screened out in the analysis of the σάρξ- πνεῦμα dichotomy.

Verse	Implied Meaning of σάρξ
1:16	Human being
2:16	Humanity
2:20	The physical body in the current age
3:2-3	Human exertion in 'doing' the Law/Law as feature of age of flesh
4:13-14	The physical body susceptible to disease and damage
4:23, 29	Susceptible human decision making/ normal means of child-birth
5:13	Misusing freedom to embrace Torah

If one could postulate some degree of harmony in the above definitions, flesh might be recognised as the *susceptible, external aspect of the human self in the present age*. The Qumran community were close to this view in some of their works:

> As for me, I belong to wicked mankind, to the company of unjust flesh. My iniquities, rebellions, and sins, together with the perversity of my heart, belong to the company of worms and to those who walk in darkness. . . . As for me, if I stumble, the mercies of God shall be my eternal salvation. If I stagger because

---

11. Matera sees this reference and those in 5:16—6:8 as human nature which opposes itself to God through self-seeking. As a broad sweep this has some truth, but specificity here enhances the overall interpretation of the letter; see Matera, *Galatians*, 192.

of the sin of flesh, my justification shall be by the righteousness of God which endures forever.[12]

The *Hodayot* exhibits a similar position on the flesh-Spirit dualism to Galatians (4QH 4:25; 18:25). Flusser concludes that flesh-Spirit dualism in the *Hodayot* is consistent with the NT at large.[13]

In Galatians, circumcising the physical flesh represents embracing Torah. When one considers Paul's view of circumcision "done by the hands" (Rom 2:28; Phil 3:3; cf. Col 2:11; Eph 2:11), it is clear why in his thinking circumcision cut one off from Christ.[14] Though committed to the physical rite, Philo also reckoned that circumcision pointed beyond removing the foreskin. Thus, Abraham's circumcision in Genesis 17 was excision of the lustful passions of the body.[15] The male foreskin was, according to Philo, a symbol of those sense pleasures and impulses.[16] In Philo, circumcision was the putting away of the impious conceit, under which the mind supposed that it was capable of begetting by its own power.[17] In Pauline thought, enforcing circumcision in the Messianic age represented an incorrect, human driven initiative to be identified as the people of God; it was *flesh* because it affected mere externalities. Spirit, then, represents the internalized identity and the commensurate lifestyle (Gal 5:16–17; 5:19, 22; 6:8).

Before returning to Gal 5:24–25, some remarks about the importance of "crucifixion" are necessary. The flesh is not merely destroyed, but *crucified* by the believer, connecting the experience with the Christ event. There is a resonance with Rom 6:6—τοῦτο γινώσκοντες ὅτι ὁ παλαιὸς ἡμῶν ἄνθρωπος (our old man) συνεσταυρώθη (has been co-crucified), ἵνα καταργηθῇ τὸ σῶμα τῆς ἁμαρτίας, τοῦ μηκέτι δουλεύειν ἡμᾶς τῇ ἁμαρτίᾳ. The crucifixion of the believer—Jewish or Gentile—is their participatory inclusion in the crucifixion of Jesus. Rectification is the consequent sharing in the risen life—Paul died to the Law so he might live; believers crucify the flesh and live by virtue of Spirit. Paul's proclamation of Jesus who loved him and gave himself for Paul (2:20) recalls the mission of the risen Jesus who delivers from the present age of evil (1:4). The crucifixion of flesh and revivification by Spirit should be read in the same light. The aorist indicative

---

12. 1QS 11:9ff. (Vermes's translation).

13. Flusser, *Judaism of the Second Temple Period*, 291; see further Maston, *Divine and Human Agency*, 89–92.

14. Gal 5:2–4.

15. *Quaes. Gen.* 3:46–52.

16. Ibid., 3:52.

17. *De Abrahamo* 92.

active tense of this crucifixion-revivification event (contra Schneider) seems to point to baptism.[18]

Co-Text: Gal 5:24–25—Crucifixion and Life

Turning to Gal 5:24–25, the qualifier σὺν τοῖς παθήμασιν καὶ ταῖς ἐπιθυμίαις needs consideration. In 5:19–21a, Paul outlines τὰ ἔργα τῆς σαρκός, a list of (largely) community-destroying vices, which exclude people from inheriting the Kingdom of God (5:19–21). The vice list is contrasted with ὁ καρπὸς τοῦ πνεύματός. Paul suggests with the flesh crucified and life initiated by Spirit, believers can no longer engage in the works of flesh, which must include the passions and lusts of 5:24. The fruit of the Spirit is the evidence that someone has crucified the flesh and been made alive by Spirit. This Spirit-initiated life is the revivified eschatological life celebrated in 3:10–13; it is a new sphere and expression of existence and identity in Christ. This life is begun by (cf. 3:3b) and expressed by the presence of Spirit. The resurrected Christ, who gives the blessing of Spirit to the faithful, delivers them from the present evil age of flesh. This deliverance is transference into Christ, but as Paul says of himself, this life is still lived "in the flesh" (2:20b). Thus for Paul, believers are *primarily* in Christ, identified as such, energised by his risen life and delivered from the dominance of all that belongs to the age of flesh. Yet, they remain susceptible to the corrupting influence of flesh, which is frail, human and concerned with externalities. Just as in the Antioch fellowship in 2:11–14, the contingent from James and those influenced by them exhibited behaviour that suggested they were primarily Jewish and only secondarily in Christ. That is, they were primarily identified by external markers—*flesh*.

By the crucifixion of flesh and concomitant life by Spirit we may understand *the death and re-creation of primary identity*. Rectification identifies people as the eschatological people of God—when the external aspect of humanity (flesh) is crucified, humanity is reborn internally, evidenced by the presence of Spirit. The question in Gal 3:3, which introduces the πνεῦμα-σάρξ dichotomy so pivotal for Galatians 4–6, contains the dative πνεύματι functioning much as it does in 5:25. There, ἐναρξάμενοι πνεύματι implies having been made alive by Spirit, shared in the risen life of Jesus and been established as the people of God on those grounds. The actual query, νῦν σαρκὶ ἐπιτελεῖσθε asks, "are you now trying to establish your identity on the grounds of flesh," which implies circumcision and Law.

---

18. Schneider, "σταυρόω" *TDNT*, 583.

Paul's challenge in 5:25 that those living by Spirit should order [their] steps (στοιχέω) by Spirit is significant for two reasons. Firstly, 5:25 is translated differently depending on how the two occurrences of πνεύματι are treated:

> If we live by the Spirit, let us also be guided by the Spirit (NRSV)
>
> Since we live by the Spirit, let us keep in step with the Spirit (NIV)
>
> If our lives are centred in the Spirit, let us be guided by the Spirit (J. B. Philips)
>
> If we live by the Spirit, let us also behave in accordance with the Spirit (NET)

Burton suggests that the first dative implies the spiritual life being lived in relation to the Holy Spirit.[19] Lightfoot incorrectly notes:

> The "life to the Spirit," of which the Apostle here speaks, is an ideal rather than an actual life; it denotes a state which the Galatians were put in . . . the way of attaining rather than one which they had already attained.[20]

Galatians 3:10–21 has established the Law's incapacity to revivify—this is the work of the Spirit. The dative πνεύματι in 5:25a implies "if we have been made alive by Spirit."[21] We could write, "if the Spirit has given us life, then let the Spirit dictate our ethics." In 5:18 Paul wishes to convey that the Spirit-led ones are not led by the external Torah.[22] It is precisely because the Spirit gives the risen life to those who are of Christ that the Spirit should steer our conduct.[23]

---

19. Burton, *Galatians*,

20. Lightfoot, *Galatians*, 214.

21. As Loubser correctly notes, living in Spirit here is a soteriological statement; see Loubser, "Ethic of the Free," 625.

22. Paul *does* speak of Christians fulfilling the Law; Westerholm surmises, "such fulfilment is not the result of an obligation to observe the demands of the law, but the inevitable outcome of a life lived under the guidance of the Spirit of God." See Westerholm, "Letter and Spirit," 243–44. Westerholm is correct insofar as the Christian's obligation is to imitate Christ's sacrificial love, but to depict it as the *inevitable* outcome of being Spirit led may mistakenly suggest the absence of any human moral effort. Being enslaved to one another (fulfilling Torah in Gal 5:13–14) is an imperative and not a result.

23. See further Bruce, *Galatians*, 257; Matera, *Galatians*, 204.

Further Evidence: Gal 5:24–25 in Relation to 6:16

Secondly, in Gal 6:14–15, Paul describes how the cosmos itself suffers crucifixion and new creation. In this new world, ethnic distinction is divested of significance. In Gal 6:16 Paul pronounces a blessing on all those who 'order their steps' (στοιχέω) in accordance with the rule of new creation. The argument contained in 6:14–15 parallels the argument concluded by 5:24–25.[24] The crucifixion and re-creation of the world is no less than the world's rectification. Classifying the identity of God's people by the external criterion "circumcised" or "not circumcised," a distinction belonging to the former world, is necessarily eradicated.[25] The κανών that governs the new creation is ordering steps by Spirit, which contextually denotes not submitting to the external Torah, another external marker of ethnic exclusivity (i.e. flesh). To order one's steps by Spirit means practically to adhere to the ethical dictates of Spirit, as outlined in Gal 5:22–23.

Intertextual Resonances: Spirit and Life

Galatians 5:24–25 is critical for its association of "Spirit" with "life;" this link, central to Galatians generally, is deeply embedded in Jewish creation ideology. Yates provides a useful survey of Biblical and Post-Biblical traditions to this end.[26] Genesis 2:7 is the obvious starting point for all such investigation, not least of all because it forms part of Paul's own resurrection theology.[27] It is a passage harnessed in a number of early texts to convey the creative activity of God in the world.[28] F. Philip argues that Paul's belief in Spirit bestowal on Gentiles apart from Torah is based on the Damascus experience and on Paul's reflections on texts mentioning the outpouring of Spirit on Gentiles.[29] Levison demonstrates the variety of interpretations of Spirit and life/creation in an array of Jewish and Greco-Roman texts.[30] Lull refers to Gal 5:25, in connection with new life, when discussing Paul's concept of

---

24. Cf. Gal 2:19–20. See Owens, *As it was*, 79.

25. In 2 Cor 5:17, those in Christ are καινὴ κτίσις; 5:14–15 recounts their participation in the Christ event and 5:16 outlines that they are thus no longer *known according to flesh*. The harmony of thought in the section is direct and made more explicit in 5:21 where believers become δικαιοσύνη θεοῦ in Christ.

26. Yates, *Spirit and Creation*, 24–83.

27. 1 Cor 15:45.

28. See esp. *Testament of Reuben* 2:1–9; 2 *Enoch* 30:7; 4 *Ezra* 3:4–6.

29. Philip, *Origins of Pauline Pneumatology*, 27–28.

30. Levison, *Spirit in First-Century Judaism*, 217–35.

Spirit in Galatians.³¹ Malby also references Gal 5:25 to depict Paul's own coming into the new creation, suggesting a parallel with Isaiah's servant being raised (Isa 52:13; 53:10).³²

Nonetheless, the scholarly trend to marginalize resurrection in Galatians has obscured the broader exegesis of 5:24–25.³³ Reading 5:24 and 5:25 together accentuates the centrality of revivification within rectification; believers *live* because, like Messiah, believers are crucified and revivified.

This is a crucifixion of *external self-definition*, or flesh as ὁ παλαιὸς ἡμῶν ἄνθρωπος in Rom 6:6. In Rom 6:5, baptism is expressed as a process by which believers have become σύμφυτοι with the likeness of Jesus' death, denoting "joined together," "identified" or "at one" with. This identification with the likeness of Jesus' death is the crucifixion of the old man, which corresponds directly with the resolution of external identity by crucifixion in Gal 2:19–20; 5:24–25. The revivified people of God are identified by the inner presence of Spirit, showing they are of Christ (5:24–25; cf. 4:6). Those of Christ are those *belonging* to Christ, which incorporates other phrases denoting belonging.³⁴ So in 3:29 those *of Christ* are Abraham's seed and, ergo, heirs of the promise. Since crucifixion of flesh is a crucifixion of *identity*, when the cosmos suffers crucifixion only the *new* creation matters—not the outdated identity distinction circumcised/uncircumcised (6:14–15).³⁵ Living by virtue of Spirit is to live by the canon of the new creation (6:16) as the Israel of God—the Law was given to, and so identifies, *ethnic* Israel only. When Paul narrates his own co-crucifixion with Christ, he aligns it with death to Law—Paul is dead to that which "externally" identified him. This was Paul's own crucifixion of the flesh—a narrative he takes up in Rom 2:25–29.

New life and Spirit in the creation of new identity is not uniquely Pauline. Paul likely drew upon a known ideological norm of Spirit and the creation of new identity within Jewish thought. Two possible examples follow.

---

31. Lull, "Creative Transformation," 41; Lull notes that Paul's identification of the personal presence of God in history as the Spirit of Christ points to the immanence of God *in the special act of the creation of a new structure of human existence, and to its origin in the death and resurrection of Christ* (Lull, "Creative Transformation," 48 emphasis mine).

32. Malby, "Life in the New Creation."

33. Though see the excellent work of Beale, "Fruit of the Spirit," 1–38, esp. 24–25. See further Kim, *Clothing Imagery*, 70.

34. See especially Kushner, "Slavery and Freedom," 284–85.

35. 2 Cor 5:16 suggests that even Jesus' crucifixion incorporates the crucifixion of identity; Paul once knew Christ according to flesh, but no longer. Cf. also Col 3:11.

Spirit/New-Life/New-Identity— Evidence from Joseph and Aseneth

The story of *Joseph and Aseneth* uses the language of Spirit and new life to depict Aseneth's conversion.[36] Joseph states that:

> It is not right for a man who worships God, who with his mouth blesses the living God, and eats the blessed bread of life, and drinks the blessed cup of immortality, and is anointed with the blessed unction of incorruption, to kiss a strange woman ... (*Joseph and Aseneth* 8:5).[37]

Joseph's heart goes out to her and he prays:

> O Lord ... the Mighty One, Who *quickened* all things, and called them from darkness into light ... And from error into truth, and from *death into life*; Do you, O Lord, yourself *quicken* and bless this virgin, And renew her by thy *spirit,* and remould her by your secret hand, And quicken her with thy life ... (*Joseph and Aseneth* 8:10–11).[38]

Joseph and Aseneth 8:10–11 is particularly noteworthy for employing ζωοποιέω ("quickened" above); it is also used in 8:2. *The author also describes conversion as a movement from death to life.* Prior to their nuptials we are told:

> ... they kissed each other for a long time.... And Joseph kissed Aseneth and gave her *spirit of life,* and he kissed her the second time and gave her spirit of wisdom, and he kissed her the third time and gave her spirit of truth (*Joseph and Aseneth* 19:10–11).[39]

It certainly seems like the author of *Joseph and Aseneth* was acquainted with a revivification tradition similar to Paul. It is also attested in the satirical *Testament of Abraham,* which sees God attempt to prepare Abraham for his imminent death, despite the patriarch's apparent reluctance.[40] God even-

---

36. For a fuller treatment of the transformation metaphors in *Joseph and Aseneth* see Hubbard, *New Creation,* 54–78. For Hubbard, Aseneth's conversion is a transforming event whose defining feature is newness. For an elaboration of the death to life metaphor in particular, see Chessnut, *From Death to Life.*

37. Trans. David Cook.

38. Emphasis mine.

39. Emphasis mine.

40. The text exists in two recensions, normally referred to as A and B. The longer form is *Testament of Abraham* A, which is attested to by several Greek manuscripts, largely supported by a Romanian version; the shorter B form, also well attested by a

tually has to send the nonchalantly disguised figure of Death to Abraham as part of a carefully planned ruse to impel Abraham to face the inevitable. The text contains a judgment section where Abraham, seeing the gamut of human sin in a whirlwind tour of the world, initially pronounces a harsh condemnation. During a dialogue with death, Abraham relaxes his position, and we read:

> The righteous Abraham said, Now I know that I have come into indifference of death, so that my spirit fails, but I beseech you, all-destroying Death, since my servants have died before their time, come let us pray to the Lord our God that he may hear us and raise up those who died by your fierceness before their time. And Death said, Amen, be it so. Therefore Abraham arose and fell upon the face of the ground in prayer, and Death together with him, and the Lord sent a *spirit of life* upon those that were dead and they were *made alive* again. Then the righteous Abraham gave glory to God.[41]

Spirit/New-Life/New-Identity: Evidence from Isa 44:1–5

A number of commentators have noted the potential influence of Isa 44:3 in Galatians.[42] Typically, they point to the linkage of "Spirit" and "blessing," which is only here in the OT. Equally interesting is Deutero-Isaiah's use of seed, especially in light of Isa 41:8, where he titles Israel the seed of Abraham.[43] Verse 5 also evidences *Spirit* and *revivification* in the establishment of identity, which may suggest influence over the revivification text in Gal 5:24–25:

> For I will pour water on the thirsty land, and streams on the dry ground; *I will pour my Spirit* upon your *descendants*, and my *blessing* on your *offspring*. They shall *spring up* (ἀνατέλλω) like a green tamarisk, like willows by flowing streams. This one will say, "*I am the LORD's*," another will be called by the name of Jacob, yet another will write on the hand, "The LORD's," and adopt the name of Israel. Thus says the LORD, the King of Israel,

---

number of Greek manuscripts, is on the whole supported by Slavonic, Romanian, Ethiopic, Arabic and Coptic versions.

41. *Testament of Abraham* (A) 18:9–11.

42. E.g., Hays, *Faith*, 82–183; Morales, *Spirit*, 20–22, 110–14; Harmon, *She Must and Shall Go Free*, 146–49.

43. Cf. Gal 3:29.

and his *Redeemer*, (ὁ ῥυσάμενος) the LORD of hosts ... (Isa 44:3–5, NRSV).

Having promised a restorative new Exodus (Isa 43:1–21) and severely rounded upon Israel for her sins, Yahweh changes tone, pledging his commitment to Israel's national renewal. In describing the renewal, Yahweh declares in 43:19 that this new Exodus will "spring forth," using ἀνατέλλω as in 44:4.

The LXX of 44:3 has God pouring out blessing on your children (τέκνα) where the Hebrew text has צֶאֱצָא (offspring). Both terms have significance in Galatians.[44] There is no reason to think that descendants and offspring/children represent different parties—God promises to pour out his Spirit and his blessing upon the future generations of the restored exiles. Blessing and Spirit are equated in Galatians 3; Isaiah, writing a restoration narrative, like Ezekiel, employs a revivification image in 44:4 to illustrate the effects of Spirit.

The resonance with Paul seems clear; *the Spirit revivifies the dead*. Note particularly Isa 44:5—"I am the LORD's" translates the LXX Τοῦ θεοῦ εἰμι; cf. οἱ δὲ τοῦ Χριστοῦ in Gal 5:24. Just as those Paul speaks of live by Spirit, those in view in Isaiah "spring up" after having the Spirit poured out on them.

That "another" will adopt the name of Israel has an interesting resonance with Gal 6:16 (the Israel of God). Scholars debate whether Israel or Gentiles are in view in Isa 44:4–5.[45] Increasingly commentators favour Israel.[46] It is difficult, however, to understand Israel adopting the name Israel.[47] The critical issue is that a renewed people of God spring forth after the action of Spirit. The comparison of Spirit to water poured on the thirsty land (44:3) instantiates the revivification metaphor inherent in vegetation life cycles—just as in Gal 5:24–25, the Spirit is the source of life.

In sum, Paul, like other Jewish writers, understands the Spirit as the source of life. Spirit revivifying crucified flesh in Gal 5:24–25 is explicit revivification language, which like 2:19 and 6:14–15 denotes that an underlying identity change has taken place. This is critical for Paul's argument in Galatians—Gal 3:21b unambiguously asserts that Law is not the source of

---

44. Cf. Gal 4:27–28, 31.

45. Staalduine-Sulman, "Isaiah 44:5," 1–10.

46. This is the position that van Staalduine-Sulman (ibid) takes; see also Grisanti, "Israel's Mission to the Nations," 49.

47. Stuhlmueller, *Creative Redemption*, 130–31; this would seem to be the most immediate difficulty for seeing a reference to Israel. There were Gentiles who adopted Jewish ethno-religious practices even in the exilic periods. See Sommer, "Isaiah," 872; according to Isa 56:3–7, this was one of the prophet's specific concerns.

life. That is, *Law cannot identify people as the end-time community of God.* As such, it is not a prerequisite of rectification and Gentiles are not bound by it. Galatians 5:24–25 expresses that those identified by Christ have put their former identity to death along with its associated baggage; now, made alive by Spirit and identified as God's people, they should live with the Spirit as ethical index.

The following observations reinforce such a reading. Galatians 5:16 commands believers to *walk* πνεύματι and so not fill up the ἐπιθυμίαν σαρκὸς; 5:24–25 dictates that having crucified τὴν σάρκα with the (associated) desires and ἐπιθυμίαις believers *live* πνεύματι. In Gal 5:18 Paul instructs that those *led* πνεύματι *are not under Law.* So then, revivified by Spirit and governed by an "ethics of Spirit," believers have no need to submit to Torah.

Intertextual Resonances: Gal 5:24–25, Spirit Internalization and the New Covenant

The following survey of intertextual influences on Gal 5:24–25 is from the vantage point of *the Spirit's role in the revivification and ethical supervision of the people of God.*

Galatians 5:13–25 outlines the conflict between flesh and Spirit; in vv. 13–14, love is the fulfillment of Torah (πληρόω), for in the context of love God's people should be enslaved to one another. The fulfilment of Law reappears in 6:2, where bearing one another's burdens fulfills completely (ἀναπληρόω) the Law of Christ. Paul's intention in 5:13–14 is to demonstrate that the Gentiles have no need of being circumcised because by mutual enslavement in the context of love they have fully met the demands of the Law. If they keep fighting over their differences, though, they will tear one another to shreds. The change of direction from 5:15 to 5:16 suggests that there was nervousness among the Gentiles about the community's ethical praxis in the absence of Torah. Paul outlines in 5:16–23 that Spirit is the key. Correspondingly, those who restore the ones overtaken in a trespass (6:1), exemplifying bearing one another's burdens and fulfilling Christ's Law (6:2), are ὑμεῖς οἱ πνευματικοὶ.

It is the position of this investigation that Galatians evidences a pneumatological synthesis whose origins lie in the restoration eschatology of Ezekiel and, by extension, Jeremiah. For in Galatians, Spirit is the herald of redemption/freedom (Gal 4:1–9, 21–31), the source of life (2:19–3:14; 5:24–25; 6:8) and the index of community ethics (5:16–23). The revivification portrait at 5:24–25 and its related co-text, point to how these latter two ideas draw upon the prophetic material. In essence, Paul, like Jeremiah and

Ezekiel, speaks of a divinely prompted engagement with God's demands amongst the people. In Galatians, this ideal is articulated in terms of how the Spirit leads the community. Ezekiel also prophesies the day when God will put his Spirit in the people causing them to obey his commands (Ezek 36:27). Jeremiah predicts the time when God would inscribe the Law on the people's hearts (Jer 31:33). Jeremiah refers to this unique, divinely inspired engagement with God's laws as the New Covenant.

Covenant within Galatians is principally associated with Abraham's relation to God. Διαθήκη appears only eight times in the undisputed epistles, and only twice in Galatians (3:15, 17) after which the language of "promise" predominates. Neither of Paul's two references to the "New Covenant" is in Galatians;[48] *yet there is good reason to see Jeremiah's New Covenant prophecy exerting influence on Paul's argument*, as the following will attempt to survey.

"New Covenant" only appears in Jer 31:33 in Jewish scripture, though there are references to an *everlasting* covenant (Isa 55:3; 61:8; Jer 32:40; 50:5; Ezek 16:60; 37:26) and a covenant of *peace* (Isa 54:10; Ezek 34:25; 37:26). The Qumranites, who also saw themselves as the eschatological people of God, (1 QpHab. 7:11–14; cf. 1 Cor 10:11), considered themselves heirs of the New Covenant.[49] Space constraints mean only reasons for *Paul's* acquaintance with Jer 31:33 will be considered.

Jeremiah chides the people for their abject failure to hold to the Torah (Jer 2:8; 6:19; 8:8) and caustically declares that the horrors of exile resulted from it (9:13ff.; 16:11ff.; 26:4ff.). He announces a new state of affairs with people. Under this new covenant, the Law will be inner reality (31:33). L. Beyeler, drawing on the new Exodus traditions in Jeremiah, argues that Jeremiah is the "new Moses" and Paul in Galatians the "new Jeremiah."[50] She proposes that Paul was chiefly concerned in Galatians to present Jesus as the fulfilment of the hope of Jeremiah's long anticipated new Exodus.[51] The conceptualization of this *newness* is one of the problematic areas in interpreting the fulfilment of the New Covenant.

Scholars divide on what the "New Covenant law" could be and how it relates to Torah. Beyeler, who *does* see it as Torah, writes that Jeremiah's New Covenant is the promise of true obedience to the *Shema* by the people of God.[52] F. Adeyemi typifies scholars who argue that new means an ut-

---

48. Cf. 1 Cor 11:25 (Matt 26:28=Mark 14:24=Luke 22:20) and 2 Cor 3:6.

49. E.g., CD 6:19; 19.34–35; 1QpHab. 2.3; see further, Kim, "Concept of Atonement," 98.

50. See Holladay, "Jeremiah's Self-Understanding," 153–64.

51. Beyeler, "Jeremiah's New Exodus in Galatians."

52. Ibid.

terly new entity—not merely a restatement of Torah.[53] This position is also adopted by L. Pettegrew, who cites Von Rad in defence.[54] Calvin, accurately albiet with potentially amorphous terminology, ascribed the newness of the covenant to the "form" and not the "substance" of Law with which the people engaged.[55]

The repositioning of the locus of the Law makes the covenant new. The content of the Law does not differ, only how people engage with it. We need not *over* press the ontological significance of the locus of the Law in the heart—practically it points to the people's acceptance of and compliance with the commands of God, though it goes beyond this. Inscribing the Law on the hearts of the people is the prophet Jeremiah's way of depicting how God changes the covenant people "internally" to make them receptive to his dictates; but it goes beyond a metaphor for compliance. Rather, being transformed by the Spirit, God's commands *become a part of the person's consciousness and thus of the community as a whole*. Inasmuch as Ezekiel's prophecy of the internalization of Spirit is not merely a metaphor for a closer connection with God, Jeremiah's prophecy of the internalization of Law(s) should not be read simply as a metaphor for how people engage with Law. It is this contrast to which Paul points in 2 Cor 3:3; he does not consider obedience to Law under the New Covenant to be a matter of obeying commands inscribed on stone tablets. Rather, it is a matter of changed hearts responding to the Spirit's prompting, so God's demands occur naturally. Hence Jer 31:34—no one will need to teach their neighbour. Consequently, the laws themselves *and* the inclination to default to them become inner actualities. This is further attested in 2 Cor 3:15, another hotly debated passage, about which some brief corroborative comments follow.[56]

One of the key issues in the verse is how the veil moves from Moses' *face* (2 Cor 3:7, 13, citing Exod 34:33–35) to the *hearts* of Paul's opponents (2 Cor 3:15). Given that "when the Old Covenant is read" (v. 14) and "when Moses is read" (v. 15) are clearly equivalent phrases, Paul seems to be reaffirming the same truth in both verses—Israel had failed to comprehend the temporal limits of the Mosaic covenant. However, the reference to the Old Covenant in v. 14 suggests that the veil (clearly the same veil—τὸ αὐτὸ κάλυμμα) is now over the *hearts* because Paul's adversaries cannot perceive the Law as inner reality—the substance of the *New* Covenant. They cannot

---

53. Adeyemi, "New Covenant Law," 312–21.

54. Pettegrew, "New Covenant," 251–70.

55. Calvin, *Jeremiah and Lamentations*, 131–32.

56. Garrett, "Veiled Hearts," 758–59; Scott, *2 Corinthians*, 79; Harris, *Second Epistle to the Corinthians*, 305–6.

comprehend Law as internal code because such comprehension derives from Spirit, which is received when someone turns to the Lord (2 Cor 3:16–18).

Furthermore, the dictates of the Law were a detail specific set of commands (with the Decalogue at their heart) each of which deserved the people's attention. Certainly this seems to have been Paul's view, as Gal 5:3 suggests (cf. Rom 2:25; Jam 2:10). In Ezekiel's terms, the internal presence of Spirit instigates a new impetus to walk in God's *statutes* and *judgments* and do them (36:27). These phrases certainly encapsulate at least God's Torah, but also point to a life that is more broadly consistent with God's requirements, whether or not they are specifically codified in Torah. As such, Ezekiel's prophecy suggests that any external code of conduct would ultimately be compromised by the practitioners' shortcomings. In Rom 2:14–15 Paul mentions Gentiles whose consciences naturally exhibit Torah, writing that they demonstrate τὸ ἔργον τοῦ νόμου γραπτὸν ἐν ταῖς καρδίαις αὐτῶν. Equally significant is the "their God/my people" formula employed in these key internalization sequences (Ezek 36:28; Jer 31:33). Once God has impacted the hearts of the people to submit to his laws, they are identified as his people. It is *because* Spirit is in the hearts that God's Law(s) can become an inner reality, making living as God requires a natural inclination.

The pervasive implications of "Law in the heart" radicalize the newness of the covenant, as Galatians exemplifies, and not some perceived non-alignment with Torah as some suggest. Nonetheless, some argue that the covenant could not be new if in *any* sense it is substantially the Mosaic Law. This, however, necessitates a one-dimensional view of what interiorized Law might practically entail. Given Israel's legacy of obduracy to Torah, a revolutionary way of engaging with it is profoundly new; as Brueggemann writes, obeying will be as normal and as readily accepted as breathing and eating. . . . All inclination to resist, refuse, or disobey will have evaporated.[57] According to M. Greenberg, God will no longer gamble with Israel . . . in the future—no more experiments! God will put his Spirit into them . . . and make it impossible for them to be anything but obedient to his rules and commandments.[58]

Commentators arguing for unbridgeable distance between New Covenant and Torah also point to Jeremiah's statement that the New Covenant "will not be like the covenant that I made with their ancestors when I took them . . . out of the land of Egypt" (Jer 31:32, NRSV). However, this merely compounds the presumption by conjecturing *how* the New Covenant will be unlike the old one. Equally unconvincing are attempts to argue that the

---

57. Brueggemann, *To Build*, 71.
58. Cited by Block, *Ezekiel 25–48*, 356.

semantic range of תּוֹרָה and νόμος means that their use need not necessitate the Mosaic Law. As I have stated, even if we grant that "my laws" means *more* than Torah to Jeremiah's audience, it could scarcely mean less.[59]

Galatians posits interplay between receiving/internalizing Spirit and meeting the requirements of the Law. Interestingly, love is the initial fruit of the Spirit (Gal 5:22), and in (the context of) love, mutual enslavement fulfils the Law (5:14). Spirit permits the essence of Torah to be internalized and followed by entering and transforming the hearts. Below are two lines of evidence in support of the position above, detailing the same association of Spirit and Law, in Romans and 2 Corinthians. Both passages draw upon Exodus and second Exodus traditions and hold "Spirit" and "letter" (γράμμα) in tension.

Heart Circumcision—
Spirit Internalization and Law in Romans 2

Deuteronomy 30 is Moses' review of the ramifications of the covenant demands—obedience leads to the blessing of life and freedom; disobedience, to the curse of exile and death. The people's disobedience seems inevitable; but their freedom will not ultimately result from human impulses—*God will circumcise the hearts of the people* (Deut 30:6–10).

Paul's citation of the "circumcision of heart" tradition in Rom 2:29 reflects the Hebrew of Deut 30:6; the Septuagint translator did not render מול with περιτέμνω but with the future indicative active of περικαθαρίζω, denoting "clean away," or "utterly purge" (cf. Lev 19:23; Isa 6:7). The two other occurrences of heart circumcision in the Hebrew Bible, Deut 10:16 and Jer 4:4, both posit human initiative. Paul's choice to incorporate the meaning of the *Hebrew* of Deut 30:6 is telling.

Paul effectively redefines Jewish identity in Rom 2:29; the "true" Jew has undergone heart circumcision performed by Spirit—a distinction seen in the post-Pauline denunciation of circumcision χειροποίητος in Eph 2:11 and Col 2:11; the latter even speaking of a "circumcision of Christ" (cf. Phil 3:3). Had he opted for the Septuagintal notion of heart purging rather than heart *circumcision*, it would have altered the hermeneutic landscape of Romans 2. The divine origin of the interiorized circumcision implied in Paul suggests Deut 30:6 rather than Deut 10:16 or Jer 4:4 informed his thoughts.[60]

---

59. Wilber Wallis argued that none of the new covenant blessings were new—they were already ratified in the promises to Abraham. Rather, Jeremiah was employing reverse psychology—his argument was ironic; see Wallis, "Irony," 108.

60. See Wells, "Grace," 170–83 for issues directly pertinent to Rom 2:17–29.

In Galatians, there exist only references to *external* circumcision[61]—they connote generic identity markers for Jews/Jewish believers or (in the verb form) the pressure and/or negative implications of Gentile circumcision. Given the associations Paul makes between Jewish identity and circumcision in Galatians (e.g., Gal 5:3), recourse to Romans 2 seems appropriate. From this, readers may surmise that in Pauline thinking *the identity of God's people is not "externally" established*—it is not "according to flesh."

Deuteronomy 30:6 depicts the effects of divine heart circumcision as a restatement of the *Shema*. God circumcises hearts *so that* you will love the Lord your God with all your heart and with all your soul, in order that you may live (30:6b) and that you shall again obey the Lord, observing all his commandments that I am commanding you today. As earlier stated, the author of Deuteronomy treats exile as inevitable, and the heart circumcision, as 30:1–5 suggest, will accompany the restoration from exile. That heart circumcision accompanies the restoration is confirmed by Jer 4:4, a call to repentance demanding an inner, heart level transformation. Though Jer 4:4 accentuates human agency, the inevitability of the people's fate in Jer 4:5–31 is in keeping with Deuteronomy 30. The tension implies that the human impulse to achieve circumcised hearts would always fall short. Only when God reverses the exile will this ideal materialize.[62]

Furthermore, the preponderance of references to "heart" (לֵבָב, καρδία) in Deuteronomy also points to an internalized divine action associated with the end of the exile. There are fifty occurrences of "heart" in Deuteronomy, eight of which appear in chapter 30 alone. In chapter 30, "heart" is peculiarly linked to restoration from exile for it features primarily within the context of (a) having turned one's heart away from Yahweh (e.g., 30:17); (b) turning back to Yahweh with all of one's heart (30:2); (c) loving God with all of one's heart (e.g., 30:6).

Of the fifty-nine instances of καρδία in Paul, only five occur in relation to Spirit. They are Rom 2:29 (Spirit performs heart circumcision); Rom 5:5 (Spirit pours God's love into hearts); 2 Cor 1:22 (Spirit in the heart as a guarantee of salvation); 2 Cor 3:3 (Spirit as the ink with which Christ's letter is written on the heart). The last reference is Gal 4:6, and an interesting correlation emerges. Aside from Rom 5:5, where strictly speaking *love* is ἐν ταῖς καρδίαις rather than Spirit, when Paul speaks of the Spirit in the immediate proximity of the heart, *it is to identify the people of God*. In Rom 2:29, Spirit identifies the true Jew; in 2 Cor 1:22, Spirit is a God-given down payment

---

61. Though it is never specified as external circumcision, Paul endorses inner circumcision, and only external circumcision would cut people off from Christ (Gal 5:3–4).

62. Cf. Raitt, *Theology of Exile*, 176.

that identifies those sealed, established and anointed (2 Cor 1:21) in Christ; 2 Cor 3:3 identifies the church as Christ's letter; Gal 4:6 identifies the sons of God. It appears then, that when Paul reflected upon the restoration prophecies of Jeremiah and Ezekiel, *an interiorized Torah under the auspices of Spirit became an identifying mark for God's people.*

Deuteronomy 30 points to how divine action upon hearts will make the people responsive to the divine commandments, in a way seen in Jeremiah and Ezekiel. Paul's employment of the metaphor in Romans 2, in a section concerned with the true nature of Jewish identity, is especially pertinent. Paul has interpolated a biblical passage depicting transformation in terms of circumcision; in view of comments like Rom 4:9ff (and the related passages in Galatians) the question of community identity is raised.

Despite the remonstrations of M. Thiessen who argues (contra Shaye Cohen and others) that by the Maccabean period conversion to Judaism was not ritually defined as circumcision, it was clearly a significant element of it.[63] Barrett speculates that in Paul's day, Jews saw circumcision as a "passport to salvation."[64] A sufficient body of ancient evidence indicates its importance. After the Ammonite leader Achior informed Israel's leaders of Holofernes' plans to destroy them, we are informed:

> When Achior saw all that the God of Israel had done, he believed firmly in God. So he was circumcised and joined the house of Israel, remaining to this day.[65]

The story of the Royal Family of Adiabene, which has a historical nucleus,[66] is preserved in Josephus (*Ant.* 20.2.1—4.3) and describes how Queen Helena and her son Izates were persuaded by a rabbinic thought school that considered circumcision necessary for conversion to Judaism.[67]

The term "uncircumcised" is used for Gentiles in the biblical text. In light of this, Jeremiah makes an intriguing distinction:

> 25 The days are surely coming, says the Lord, when I will attend to all those who are *circumcised only in the foreskin*: 26 Egypt, Judah, Edom, the Ammonites, Moab ... For *all these nations*

---

63. Thiessen, *Contesting Conversion*, 143; for Thiessen, only Jews circumcised on the eighth day were strictly Jews in many strands of thought—precluding the authenticity of Gentile proselytism. Cf. Frey, "Jewishness of Paul," 78–80.

64. Barrett, *Romans*, 58.

65. *Judith* 14:10.

66. Queen Helena's conversion, journey to Jerusalem and observance of Nazirite vows are mentioned in *Mishnah Nezir* 3:6 and other details are recorded in rabbinic texts.

67. See further 1 *Macc.* 1:14–15.

are uncircumcised, and *all the house of Israel is uncircumcised in heart* (Jer 9:25–26, NRSV).

The Hebrew syntax is awkward, but the prophet intends to treat the uncircumcised and those only *externally* circumcised as equally adrift. Those with uncircumcised hearts are as estranged from Yahweh as the nations who do not acknowledge him.

Though Galatians bears no witness to heart circumcision as in Romans, there are four occurrences of "circumcision" (περιτομή) in Galatians 2, which all act as generic references to Jews. There are only three other appearances in the letter, all of which refer to circumcision in a general context—not directly the circumcision of Galatian Gentiles. The four occurrences of the verb form in Galatians (5:2; 5:3; 6:12; 6:13) are contextually connected with pressure to Judaize and the associated ramifications.

The sole reference to "heart" in Galatians (4:6) depicts the destiny of Spirit and the proclamation of divine fatherhood/sonship. Whilst one should refrain from over-extrapolating a sole reference, Rom 2:29 attests to a Pauline definition of community identity in terms of the action of the Spirit upon the human heart. Given the staunchly ethnic overtones of circumcision, the very notion of heart circumcision introduces the prospect of ethnically classifying someone "in the heart," or just *internally.* Paul's rewriting of the boundaries of Jewish ethnic self-definition in Rom 2:25–29 suggests *the interiorization of ethnic identity* formed part of his thought process. This fits Gal 4:6, where Spirit enters the heart, crying out and proclaiming God as the father of believers; it also explains why there is neither Jew nor Greek in Christ. Rectification does not literally make believers ethno-racially non-descript; empirically, there *were* Jews and Greeks. However, believers are sons of God as Gal 3:26 points out with 4:6, which ties sonship to Spirit. Paul's concept is that *where someone is identified by the internal presence of Spirit, there is not Jew or Greek.* There are Jews and Greeks according to externality or flesh, but according to Spirit there is not Jew or Greek, but the people of God.[68] Naturally, this stance explains Paul's fury at his opponents in Galatia (Gal 5:2–4, 11–12). The identity of God's people was at stake— were he any less stark, this identity could be reduced to ethnic externalities that people could boast in (Gal 6:12–14).

---

68. 1 Cor 10:32; cf. Rom 1:4.

Christ's Letter: Internalization of Spirit and Law in 2 Corinthians

Second Corinthians also has Paul responding to criticism from detractors questioning his apostolic credentials. From 3:1, Paul is charged to validate his ministry with letters of commendation to and from the Corinthians.[69] Paul's counter is that the church is all the recommendation he needs (v. 2). The rest of the defence with its deliberate allusions to key biblical texts is striking.

The Corinthians are "a letter of Christ served by us, written not in ink but in (the) Spirit of (the) living God, not in stony tablets but in fleshly tablets of hearts" (2 Cor 3:3).[70] The Corinthian church is a recommendation letter inscribed on Paul's heart as a constant reminder of his competence as a minister, and a letter all can read. However, rather than compare the church (i.e., Christ's letter) directly to his opponents' recommendation letters, Paul compares it to *the Decalogue*—"stony tablets" (πλαξὶν λιθίναις) is a clear allusion to Exod 31:18, recounting the giving of the Ten Commandments:

> Καὶ ἔδωκεν Μωυσεῖ, ἡνίκα κατέπαυσεν λαλῶν αὐτῷ ἐν τῷ ὄρει τῷ Σινα, τὰς δύο πλάκας τοῦ μαρτυρίου, πλάκας λιθίνας γεγραμμένας τῷ δακτύλῳ τοῦ θεοῦ (Exod 31:18, LXX).

The references to πλαξὶν καρδίαις and πνεύματι θεοῦ ζῶντος bring to mind Jer 31:33 and Ezek 36:26–27. The connection is explicit in 2 Cor 3:6, where Paul and company are ministers of a καινῇ διαθήκῃ, recalling Jer 31:31. For Paul, the New Covenant and end of exile prophecies were finding fulfilment in the Jesus communities in the act of rectification. Second Corinthians 3:1–6 will also be shown to corroborate the notion of the internalization of the Law as evidence of rectification and the true end of the exile.

Paul's competence was questioned earlier in the letter; having celebrated the success of the "tearful letter" (2:3–11), Paul relates his ministry to an aroma (2:14–17). Here, ὀσμή is a keyword; Paul thanks God in 2:14 for revealing the odour of the knowledge of Christ through his ministry; in 2:15 Paul and his team are a sweet odour of Christ to God, because Christ distinguishes between the "saved" and the "lost." Verse 16 implies that the Paul and his team smell like "life" to the saved and "death" to those in perdition.

---

69. Cf. 2 Cor 11:4–5; 12:11–12. Paul's depiction of their message as a "gospel" (11:4; cf. Gal 1:6–9) and the antagonists as false apostles (11:13; cf. Gal 2:4) is reminiscent of the Galatian agitators.

70. Thomas Stegman makes the objective rendering of ἐπιστολὴ Χριστοῦ (a letter about Christ rather than from him) critical for the understanding of 2 Corinthians. See Stegman, *Character of Jesus*, 315–18. For an alternative see Thrall, *2 Corinthians 1–7*, 224.

Paul's contrast between "we" and "many" in 2:17, indicates that his question has two groups in view: himself and his co-workers one one hand, and his opponents in Corinth on the other.[71] The question at the end of 2:16 asks which group is adequate (i.e., qualified) to preach a message that spells life for some and death for others.[72] Turning to 3:3, the "life" aspect of this message is the life-giving power of the Spirit, not writing the external Law on stony tablets, but writing the internal Law on the fleshly tablets of human hearts. Death is adherence to the written code.

As Stegman points out, there are two things being contrasted here—two ministries and two covenants.[73] To insist on submission to the external Torah, as presumably Paul's opponents in 2 Corinthians were doing, was a ministry of death (2 Cor 3:7), corresponding to the Old Covenant.

There is fair scholarly divergence regarding the meaning of "the letter kills but the Spirit makes alive" (2 Cor 3:6). [74] In light of both the reference in v. 3 to the giving of the Law and the Law's inability to revivify in Gal 3:21, "the letter" (τὸ γράμμα) must be related to the Law (though, "Law" is curiously absent in 2 Corinthians). However, the contrast being between the letter and the Spirit as opposed to the Law and the Spirit is reason to pause. For if Paul expects the connection with letter and Law to be implied from resonances of the Old (Sinai) Covenant in 3:1–6, it follows that he would expect a connection between Spirit and Law to be implied by the resonances of the New (end of the exile) Covenant (as per Jer 31:33). All this considered it seems that "letter" reflects the Law as externality to be obeyed and "Spirit" as the internalization of God's Law(s) in the heart.[75] Paul's was a ministry of Spirit not of letter (3:6) which did not seek to tie people to obey an external Law unable to make alive (ζῳοποιεῖ). Paul was a minister of the Spirit that effected the internalization of Law and revivified the faithful. This is consistent with Rom 2:29 where Jewish identity is cast in terms of internalization which is ἐν πνεύματι οὐ γράμματι.[76]

---

71. Gleason, "Covenantal Contrasts," 66.

72. As in Galatians, the Pauline gospel is a message of death and life.

73. Stegman, "'Lifting the Veil," 7.

74. Thrall, *2 Corinthians,* 234–36; Hafemann, *Letter/Spirit,* 334, 446–47; Grindheim, "Law Kills," 97–115; Dunn, "Letter Kills," 163–79.

75. This conclusion also fits with Rom 2:28–29.

76. For a very useful overview of the Spirit-Letter contrast in Rom 2:25–29 see Pate, *Romans,* 59–61.

The Law of Christ

The apparently idiosyncratic term "Law of Christ" (Gal 6:2) should also be understood as the pneumatological internalization process by which God's laws become inner reality.

Todd Wilson's short history of interpretation of Law of Christ argues that the earlier scholarly treatments held that it replaced the Torah, whilst current trends equate it in some way with Torah.[77] Many scholars still hold that Law of Christ is something other than Torah. Bruce describes it as the whole of Jesus' ethical teaching, confirmed by his character and conduct.[78] Hays reads it as Christ's example of burden-bearing, which establishes a normative pattern which all those in Christ are called to fulfil in their relationships with others.[79]

Adeyemi appealed to the similar ἔννομος Χριστοῦ in 1 Cor 9:21 to argue that the Law of Christ and the Law of Moses must be different.[80] However, the terms Paul uses in 1 Corinthians 9 are different from those he employs in Galatians 6—he describes himself in 1 Corinthians 9 as being ἔννομος Χριστοῦ, which may reflect something different from fulfilling τὸν νόμον τοῦ Χριστοῦ. Furthermore, as Winger observes, if ἔννομος Χριστοῦ suggests a law of Christ, then μὴ ὢν ἄνομος θεοῦ suggests a law of God and these can hardly be in conflict. Why change the expression, without elaboration, in the space of six words? Surely, νόμος θεοῦ, without nuance, is likely to be understood as Torah.[81] Indeed this contrast actually supports my position—Paul does not submit to the external Torah, but is not without God's law *because it is in his heart through Spirit*. As such, Adeyemi is ultimately unpersuasive.

Winger suggests that Law of Christ is a metaphor for Spirit.[82] He insists that νόμος in Gal 6:2 refers more loosely to Christ exercising his lordship over believers.[83] Nonetheless, this is still basically replacing one law with another, which forces readers to dissociate the meaning of νόμος too strongly from its previous uses in Galatians.

Other scholars relate the term to Jewish traditions about the role of the Law in the Messianic age. J. Bayes has suggested that the mediator in Gal

---

77. Wilson, "Law of Christ," 123–44 (esp. 134–35).
78. Bruce, *Galatians*, 261.
79. Hays, "Christology and Ethics," 287.
80. Adeyemi, "New Covenant Law," 442–43.
81. Winger, "Law of Christ," 545.
82. Ibid., 537–46.
83. Ibid., 544.

3:19 is not in fact Moses, but *Christ*, and treats Law of Christ as "the Law having originated with Christ." Christ is "the source and goal of the Law" since the Law pointed to him.[84] Though intriguing, his position is difficult to reconcile with the context of Gal 6:2 and his reasons for seeing Christ as the mediator are less than compelling. It is possible, though conjectural, that the phrase originated from Paul's accusers.[85] It is more likely, reading between the lines, that Paul's opponents would have asserted that Christ was Law observant and his disciples obliged to follow suit.

Despite the obvious contentions, Wenham argues that the phrase is a resonance of the Johannine tradition where "loving one another" is the "new commandment" which Jesus issued to his emissaries (John 13:34–35). In Wenham's reading, scholarly oversight of the significance of oral tradition lies at the root of neglect of what is otherwise an evident intertext.[86]

Barclay comes closer—he reads law of Christ as Christ fulfilling the Law in love and a Spirit-led life as a sufficient ethical equivalent to legal observance.[87] Martyn persuasively argues from Paul's other uses of νόμος with a noun in the genitive case that the phrase approximates Law *in the hands* of Christ.[88] The following is the author's proposal.

The charge to resist indulging in empty glory (Gal 5:26) quite likely addresses those most impressed upon by the agitators.[89] Perhaps, having been convinced that circumcision was significant, they believed themselves to be more authentic children of Abraham than those uncircumcised, provoking the uncircumcised and instigating a misplaced envy in them (5:26).

Therefore, those enticed by the false gospel are examples of people overtaken in a trespass (6:1). Those spiritual ones were to restore the overtaken ones whose actions took them backwards to the realm of "flesh." In restoring them, the spiritual fulfil the Law of Christ; they have shown themselves mutually enslaved to their brothers in the context of love, for the Law is in their hearts through Spirit.

The clue lies in the opening of Galatians 6.[90] The conjunctive phrase καὶ οὕτως attaches the imperative first half of 6:2 with the inferential future indicative second half—carry one another's burdens *and in this way* you will

---

84. Bayes, *Weakness of the Law*, 171–72.
85. Betz, *Galatians*, 300.
86. Wenham, "Critical Blindness," 183–203.
87. Barclay, *Obeying*, 141–44.
88. Martyn, *Galatians*, 554–58.
89. The tensions here are the same ones reflected in Gal 5:15 (see above).
90. Winger is not *totally* accurate when he describes the phrase as "without explanation" in the opening sentence of his paper—the context does offer the tiniest window of explanatory clue.

fulfil the law of Christ. The encouragement to so assist one another originates in 6:1, where Paul urges that if a fellow Christian is caught out in some wrong-doing, that they should be restored by ὑμεῖς οἱ πνευματικοί—you the spiritual ones. Paul's choice of προλαμβάνω here supports my reading, for the connotation of being "caught out" or "overtaken" is appropriate for a group coaxed by a rival message. The spiritual ones are those made alive by Spirit and so ordering their steps by Spirit (5:24–25). Taking Gal 6:1 and 6:2 together, those spiritual ones, gently restoring the transgressors, carry their brethren's burden and exemplify fulfilling completely[91] the law of Christ.[92]

How, one might ask, is the law of Christ fulfilled by "being spiritual?" The answer is once more the pneumatological internalization of Law (cf. Rom 7:14). The completion of the Law is the moment when the Spirit makes the Law an inner code; the Law of Christ is the Torah in the hearts of believers under the auspices of Spirit. In Rom 8:2, the Law of the Spirit of life in Christ frees from the Law of sin and death. This approximates Gal 6:1–2—the spiritual ones filling up completely the Law of Christ. The "Laws," whether "of Christ" as Gal 6:2 or "of the Spirit of life" as Rom. 8:2, express the same ideal captured by the prophetic statement of Jeremiah. That is, the internalization of the divine Law and the writing of the Law on the hearts, which brings the love command to its fullest expression. As such, Paul delights in God's Law κατὰ τὸν ἔσω ἄνθρωπον (Rom 7:22).[93]

Within Paul's wider polemic, the phrase Law of Christ makes rhetorical capital gain. Though initially awkward, for Paul to depict the internalization of divine Law as the Law of Christ would have been an argumentative master-stroke for the following reasons.

Firstly, the heart of the Law was love (Deut 6:4–5; Lev 19:18; cf. Mark 12:28–34)—if Paul could argue that Spirit and Law would ultimately work in harmony, then his gospel was the means by which Gentiles could enter into the heart of the Law (cf. Mic 4:2). Moreover, this understanding of an internalized Law explains why Paul readily substantiates his ethical imperatives by recourse to Torah.

---

91. Πληρόω in Gal 5:14 denotes the cohesive love of the community as a *future* fulfilment of the Mosaic Law (Lev 19:18). Paul's use of ἀναπληρόω in 6:2 seems apt to reflect what this prophesied love looks like in practice.

92. Strelan asserts that 6:1–2 do not form a unit on the grounds that there is no connecting particle, focusing attention rather on Gal 6:2–3 which are conjoined with a γάρ. However, 6:1 continues the thought of 5:19; the charge in 5:26 is based on the challenge to walk in the Spirit. Those who are spiritual in 6:1 are those who walk in the Spirit and so have the Law of Christ in their hearts. Thus, the absence of a conjunctive particle between 6:1 and 6:2 is inconsequential. See Strelan, "Burden-Bearing," 266.

93. Cf. *1QH* 4:10–12.

Secondly, Paul has also managed to demonstrate that Torah has an enduring *legacy*, though not an endurng role, when understood in a way that is complementary with faith and Spirit (cf. Gal 3:21a).

Thirdly, within the situational context of Galatians itself, such an understanding of Law of Christ allows Paul to demonstrate how correctly comprehending Torah unites a community in love. Reconfiguring the role of the Law is one aspect of Paul's solution to the conflict erupting in Galatia; designating the completed Law as inner reality and not external Jewish code levels the playing field by removing the need to commit to Torah.

Summary: Gal 5:24–25—Life by Virtue of Spirit

So far we know the following: humanity is being rescued by participation in the Christ event. For Israel this means co-crucifixion with Christ, death to Law and the resultant life to God conveyed by Spirit. Paul's focus is largely on Israel's rectification until Gal 3:26 (twenty-one of thirty-two occurrences of "law" in Galatians are before 3:26); the destiny of Gentiles then comes to the fore. The Law is fulfilled in love in 5:14; 5:15 suggests that a group loyal to Paul's view of the Law is at odds with a group inclined towards his opponents' view (cf. 5:26). In 5:16, Paul's command implies that the tension between the groups stems in part from confusion over how people who sit loose to the Law conduct themselves practically. He effectively answers by recourse to one term—Spirit, culminating in Gal 5:25.

The revivification texts at 5:24–25 and 6:8 directly invoke the Spirit-flesh dichotomy and 6:14–15 does so in oblique fashion. Paul's uses of σάρξ in Galatians, though not uniform, exhibit enough consistency to define it as the external aspect of human identity, which is natural, physical and susceptible. In contrast, Spirit implies that which is internal, of divine origin and thus central to both the ultimate will of God and the ultimate expression of his identity. This forms a critical backdrop for the trajectory of the argument. For Gal 5:24 speaks of flesh being crucified along with the lusts and passions—the marks of fragile human identity (especially 5:19–21a). Now made alive by Spirit, the community is identified by the internal presence of Spirit; they are "of Christ," "in Christ," and "Abraham's seed" (5:24–25; cf. 3:26–29). As such, the community's ethical direction should be Spirit governed (Gal 5:25; cf. 5:18).

Galatians 5:24–25 for the second time in the letter draws together the themes of crucifixion, life and Spirit, which first arose in 2:19–3:5. Once again Spirit initiates life in those co-crucified with Jesus—in Gal 5:24, this is crucifixion of flesh. They are a new people whose identity and social praxis has a new index—Spirit. The Pauline stance on the work of the Spirit in revivification, and the concomitant motivation to satisfy God's ethical demands, can be shown to originate from the restoration eschatology of Ezekiel and Jeremiah. The influence of these prophetic voices on Paul is further substantiated by the associations of Spirit and Law in Romans 2 and 2 Corinthians 3 and in the contextual understanding of Law of Christ in Gal 6:2.

6

Revivification Text Five

Galatians 6:8: The Spirit and Eternal Life

The noun "life" only appears at 6:8 in Galatians, in the composite expression ζωὴν αἰώνιον, which typically connotes eschatological salvation.[1] Paul also revisits the πνεῦμα-σάρξ dichotomy for the last time in 6:8. Interpreting "sowing to" Spirit or flesh, therefore, must be in keeping with the thrust of the dichotomy so far, and the proximity with Gal 5:24–25.

The main difficulty in interpreting this revivification text lies in the apparently disconnected co-textual subject matter.[2] Once more, though, methodologically pursuing lexical connections in the co-text illuminates Paul's aims.

As already argued, it makes most orderly sense to treat 5:26—6:5 as context specific, and see in view two groups—those loyal to Paul's rendition of the gospel and those enticed by his rivals. Note, Gal 5:1–2; 6:1–10 and Paul's view that a Gentile's total acquiescence to the rival position cuts them off from Christ (5:4) raises doubts that those persuaded by Paul's rivals had actually undergone circumcision. This is reflected in the addition in most English translations of Gal 5:4 of *trying* to be justified by Law or *wanting* to be justified by Law; the italicised words do not appear in the Greek text. The in-fighting implied by 5:15 and 5:26 points to a group who were at least *theoretically* convinced that Paul's gospel was incomplete and circumcision was necessary—even if they had not yet performed the rite.

With this in mind, the co-text can be explained along the lines of personal responsibility for eschatological salvation—*the net effect of 6:8 is to*

---

1. Rom 2:7; 5:21; 6:22–23; cf. 1 Tim 1:16; 6:19.
2. Particularly, 6:6 appears to introduce unrelated issues.

*connect the end time resurrection event (judgment) with the now time resurrection event (rectification).*³

Contextual and Co-Textual Issues—Gal 6:1–6

In the present age, the Law of Christ is completely fulfilled by carrying one another's burdens (6:1-2). Here, βαστάζω ("carry") is in the present imperative active ("carry one another's burdens"). After commenting that the self-important are self-deceived, Paul warns each person to evaluate his own work (6:4a). He cleverly employs ἔργον—denoting the outcome of one's actions, it looks ahead to the sowing-reaping metaphor, but also addresses all involved in the Galatian crisis. Those seduced by the troublemakers have engaged in *works* of Law, but the Spirit has *worked* powerful deeds in the faithful (3:5) and faith *working* through love characterises the new community (5:6). The author continues—self-examination makes someone the sole audience for their own boast (6:4b), which contrasts those insisting on Gentile circumcision in 6:13 in order to boast in their proselytising successes. The reason for self-evaluation and having only a self-boast is in 6:5—each one will carry (βαστάσει) his own load.

Scholarly opinion is divided regarding 6:5. Kuck writes that the text hinges on whether it invokes future divine judgment or simply refers to a burden encountered in everyday life.⁴ R. Longenecker treats it as a general maxim to support Paul's statement in 6:4 that each one should test his own actions.⁵ Betz is adamant that the phrase should be interpreted within the context of gnomic literature, stressing the future tense is gnomic and not eschatological.⁶ Though Bruce similarly sees a common maxim here, he notes that in the day of Christ Paul would not be compared with Peter; his καύχημα would be the quality of those who had been won for Christ through his own ministry, suggesting Paul *employs* it eschatologically.⁷ Kuck suggests that Paul uses the idea of a final judgment of individual Christians in the passage to bring a rhetorical climax to the admonitions of Gal 6:1–5 concerning the role of individual self-regard in the community. He sees an apocalyptic motif at play here similar to 1 Cor 3:5—4:5 and Rom. 14:1–12, where such language encourages Christians to see their accomplishments in light of the

---

3. Strictly speaking, this text is a *resurrection* text.
4. Kuck, "Each Will Bear," 289.
5. Longenecker, *Galatians*, 278.
6. Betz, *Galatians*, 304.
7. Bruce, *Galatians*, 263.

final judgment and so enable them to contribute to the church.[8] Jewett also reads the future of βαστάζω as a reference to the last Judgment.[9] It strikes me that however one interprets the future "will carry" in 6:5, (*should* carry, *must* carry), in light of 6:2 the only burden which no one else can carry for you is the ultimate responsibility to God at the Judgment. The change to the future indicative of βαστάζω reflects the change in responsibility for the outcome of the final resurrection. Each person will be responsible for his or her *own* fate at the Judgment, though clearly what transpires in the present will influence the outcome. The condensation of terms stressing *personal* responsibility in 6:3–8 (ἑαυτόν in 6:3; ἑαυτοῦ ... ἕκαστος ... ἑαυτὸν in 6:4; ἴδιον in 6:5; ἑαυτοῦ in 6:8) underscores that no one will carry this burden for you.

Though making a relatively simple point in its own right, the pertinence to 6:6 of the wider issues in Galatians is not easily established. Were Paul conscious that some of his supporters had indeed gently restored some of their wayward brethren (6:1), he may have been simply encouraging the restored to show their gratitude in some way. However, the saying does suggest another instantiation of the sowing-reaping idea—if one teaches what is good, it warrants a share in the good things that arise.[10]

Exegesis of Gal 6:7–8

> 7 Μὴ πλανᾶσθε, θεὸς οὐ μυκτηρίζεται. ὃ γὰρ ἐὰν σπείρῃ ἄνθρωπος, τοῦτο καὶ θερίσει· 8 ὅτι ὁ σπείρων εἰς τὴν σάρκα ἑαυτοῦ ἐκ τῆς σαρκὸς θερίσει φθοράν, ὁ δὲ σπείρων εἰς τὸ πνεῦμα ἐκ τοῦ πνεύματος θερίσει ζωὴν αἰώνιον.

The NT, Post-Biblical literature and ancient secular texts are replete with maxims akin to the agriculturally inspired dictum of Gal 6:7.[11] It stipulates that all actions have appropriate, predictable consequences. Manifestly, the warning not to deceive oneself and so mock God in 6:7a frames the proverb as an austere warning to anyone trying to bear fruit from seed they have not sown. Paul disabuses readers of such an assessment. Linguistically, the recurrence of the Spirit-flesh contrast places 6:7–8 within the wider interpretation of 5:16—6:10, and thus, our conclusions from the previous section need consideration.

8. Kuck, "Each Will Bear," 289–97.
9. Jewett, "Agitators," 211.
10. Cf. 1 Cor 9:11; 2 Cor 9:6, 10.
11. See Garlington, *Galatians*, 371; Bruce, *Galatians*, 264; R. Longenecker, *Galatians*, 280.

Sowing and Reaping as Revivification Metaphor

Paul opts to cite a sowing-reaping metaphor here because it is ostensibly a *dying and rising* metaphor, and *Paul ultimately associates sowing to Spirit with rectification*. He does not merely quote a maxim of personal responsibility—he applies the language of sowing and reaping to the flesh-Spirit contrast. Paul can use the metaphor more generally (1 Cor 9:11; 2 Cor 9:6), but in resurrection based contexts, more is implied—as in 1 Cor 15:36–37, 42–44, and in the present text. It is not simply that "you get out what you put in"—*it is that final resurrection depends on present revivification*.

Examples of this sowing and reaping as death-life metaphor abound[12]—the Johannine Jesus asserts that a grain of wheat must fall to the ground and die to bear fruit.[13] Several scholars note how traditions of dying and rising gods within ancient Greco-Roman religion were typically expressions of agrarian harvest cycles.[14] In Ugaritic mythology, Baal, the overseer of the harvest cycle, suffers "death and resurrection." His death was marked by drought and his rebirth by the restoration of rain and crops. Paul's appropriation of the sowing-reaping mataphor has exegetical resonances with the Psalmist's.

The Psalmist applies the metaphor directly to the joyful hopes of Judah's restoration from exile:

> Restore our fortunes, O LORD . . . May those who sow in tears reap with shouts of joy. Those who go out weeping, bearing the seed for sowing, shall come home with shouts of joy, carrying their sheaves.[15]

The sow-reap metaphor appears to work in reverse in Psalm 126, but the contrast is in *how* the sower sows and reaps, not *what* he sows and reaps. There are both syntactical and hermeneutical questions which affect the context of Psalm 126, most particularly the time frames associated with vv. 1–3 with respect to vv. 3–6 and how v. 4 relates to v. 1.[16] The broad scholarly position is that 126:1–3 recollects the joy of the people's release and immediate return to the homeland. Psalm 126:4–6 is a plea amidst the prevailing despondency at the magnitude of the rebuilding work that faced the

---

12. Paul employs the metaphor as a portrait of the nature of body in eschatological judgment in 1 Cor 15:42–44; for potential influences on Paul regarding this portrait, see Singh, "Semen, Philosophy, and Paul," 32–45.
13. John 12:24.
14. McKenzie, *Pagan Resurrection Myths*, 42.
15. Ps 126:4–6, NRSV.
16. Beyerlin, *We are like Dreamers*, 23.

restored people.[17] Corresponding passages like Hag 1:1–11 validate such a stance. Though mystery shrouds why the farmer sows in tears (Ps 126:5), the broader point seems clear—the Psalmist has faith that God can restore his fortunes based on past experience (vv. 1–3) and the natural routine of life (v. 4).[18] As such, the contrast is consistent with the principle behind the sowing-reaping metaphor. If the people sow faithfully, they reap abundantly, *even if it is painful to sow*. This approach also comports with the nature of divine intervention in restoration; even in the bleakest scenario, God's intercession brings about so complete a change, it is like life coming from death.

Paul is sensitive to the notion that when God reverses very dire situations the people must be responsible in playing their part, however difficult; this fits with the overall emphasis on *personal responsibility* in Gal 6:1–8. The sower's tears may reflect a famine context where the farmer must make the painful choice of whether to use the seed to feed a starving family now, or plant it in the hope of a successful future crop.[19] *The sower plays his part sowing the seed*, the difficulty evidenced by his tears, and God ensures a crop is joyfully harvested. Paul actually uses the metaphor *twice* in Gal 6:8–10; in both instances, the "harder part" played by the people works in conjunction with God's action to bring about the harvest.

Firstly, sowing to the Spirit, as discussed below, relates to identifying with the crucified Christ and resisting circumcision—the harder choice, for it incurs persecution (Gal 6:12; cf. 5:11). Secondly, Gal 6:9–10 promises a reaping of the right harvest if believers do not tire of doing good to all people—again, this is the difficult choice, for the implication is that Paul's loyalists must persist in goodness to those siding with his detractors. The author of Psalm 126 in using a sowing-reaping metaphor, like Ezekiel and the author of Deuteronomy, employs a new life image to reflect restoration from exile.[20]

Crucial to texts like Psalm 126 and Ezekiel 37 is the divine impetus behind new life. In Gal 5:24, Paul speaks of believers themselves actively crucifying the flesh—he uses a passive term of his own "crucifixion." This need not present an interpretive obstacle—the personal decision to trust in Messiah and the divinely prompted transformative action exerted upon the believer operate in tandem.

---

17. Flesher, "Psalm 126," 434–35.

18. Ibid., 435.

19. Bratcher and Reyburn, *Psalms*, 1070; Jenkins, "Next Christendom," 118; cf. Ps 30:5.

20. Ezek 20:23; 22:15 both evidence Ezekiel's reference to Israel's scattering among the nations as "sowing."

If one crucifies the flesh, the Spirit brings the believer into the risen life. The believer is identified as belonging to Christ (οἱ τοῦ Χριστοῦ) because the Spirit revivifies. What Gal 6:8 implies is that rectification in the present is the precursor of resurrection in the future—hence the mockery injunction—it is an affront to God to imagine that one can attempt to establish their identity on the grounds of flesh now (circumcision) and be identified as God's people in the eschaton.

Sowing to the Flesh/Spirit

The proverbial statement in Gal 6:7 is directed at those who would venture after the false teaching—sowing to the flesh approximates to pursuing the agitators' message and being circumcised. Luhrmann writes that when it comes to the relationship between flesh and Spirit, God does not "play games."[21] Paul later associates his opponents' message with the flesh; the agitators have dishonourable motives wishing to "look well *in the flesh*" and circumvent persecution for the cross (6:12).[22] Following Paul's thought, "sowing to the flesh" meant being circumcised and identifying *with an external expression of identity*—a soft option, avoiding the harder choice. There is little to be gained speculating about the nature of persecution in Galatia for our purposes here; Hardin's emphasis on it is most helpful. Paul, the church's persecutor, had become Paul, the church's persecuted apostle (1:13-14; 2:19-3:1; 5:11); 5:11 confirms this picture, implying that those preaching circumcision could bypass persecution.[23] This seems to be what lies behind the accusation of 6:12; Jewett's hypothesis that Jewish Christian hardliners in Judea pressurized Gentiles into circumcision to avoid reprisals from Jewish militants suspicious of fraternization with Gentiles, could be justified by 6:12-13.[24] Perhaps one might avoid persecution by remaining under the synagogue's umbrella and being externally identified as Jewish. If circumcision cuts one off from Christ and grace (5:2-4), resisting is to remain in grace but invoke persecution. It was to make the painful choice, but those sowing to Spirit will reap eternal life.

There is little scholarly consensus on the precise meaning of Gal 6:8. In De Boer's reckoning, sowing in Paul's metaphor denotes "indulgence" and

---

21. Lührmann, *Continental*, 117.

22. "Look well in the flesh" translates εὐπροσωπῆσαι ἐν σαρκί; those so wishing were trying to compel Gentiles to be circumcised.

23. Hardin, *Imperial Cult*, 101-2.

24. Bruce, *Galatians*, 269; see Jewett, "Agitators," 205. For a refutation, see Fung, *Epistle*, 6-7; Barclay, "Mirror-Reading," 88.

reaping approximates "obtaining." As such, sowing to flesh (an evil impulse that destroys human existence) is engaging in a pattern of life (which probably includes circumcision) whereby one thumbs their nose at God. To sow to the Spirit is to "align one's life with Spirit" (5:25) so as to obtain eternal life.[25] De Boer does not see choices to make in Gal 6:8, but two modes of being—one sows to the flesh "before and apart from Christ."[26] This seems to divorce the passage from the co-text and is difficult to reconcile with what Paul depicts as an ongoing conflict between flesh and Spirit (e.g., Gal 5:17). Matera holds that Paul is contrasting reliance—sowing to flesh is relying on circumcision and Law whilst sowing to Spirit implies reliance on the power of the Holy Spirit.[27] Matera also helpfully draws attention to exegetes who do *not* read Gal 6:7–8 independently of 6:6—Erasmus says of the teachers mentioned in v. 6 that one who hands down a carnal teaching will reap, for his carnal seed, a fruit which will perish and one who imparts a spiritual teaching will gain eternal life.[28] For Schreiner, the distinction is one of the ages referred to in the letter—sowers to flesh belong to the present evil age and will perish; sowers to Spirit are part of the new creation and so receive eternal life. Strictly, Schreiner treats sowing to Spirit as walking with, being led by or keeping in step with the Spirit (5:16, 18, 25 respectively).[29]

Whilst *some* overlap exists across some of the interpretations, it seems to that *any* correct reading of Gal 6:8 must satisfy the following: (i) the context of Galatians; (ii) the co-textual issues; (iii) the broader meaning behind the flesh-Spirit dichotomy; (iv) the specific flesh-Spirit contrast in 5:24–25, both for its proximity to 6:8 and for the connection between ζάω/ζωή and πνεῦμα. In what follows, the reading presented here will be shown to satisfy (i)-(iv) above.

To sow to the Spirit is to identify with the crucified Christ; in so doing, believers resist the urge to Judaize and are marked by the internal presence of Spirit. (i). Contextually this accords with Paul's objective to dissuade Gentiles from Judaizing and directly addresses how the people of God are identified. (ii). Though the co-text is not easily reconciled, there is an underlying thread in 6:1–8—*responsibility and consequence*. The disciples' responsibility to carry each other's burdens which fills up Christ's Law (6:1–2); the responsibility of self-examination resulting in one having a self-boast and

---

25. De Boer, *Galatians*, 388.

26. Ibid., 388–89.

27. Matera, *Galatians*, 216; cf. Dunn, *Galatians*, 330; Dunn emphasizes the ethnic element of flesh implied by circumcision.

28. Matera, *Galatians*, 222.

29. Schreiner, *Galatians*, 369.

obtaining salvation (6:3–5); the instructor teaching the word and so being justly entitled to a share in the good things (6:6). (iii). Throughout the letter, flesh is associated with externality, susceptibility and death, which is consistent with "corruption" in 6:8. Correspondingly, sowing to Spirit is consistent with Spirit internalization and "making alive." For those revivified by Spirit in this life will receive eternal life through Spirit at the end of the age. (iv). With respect to 5:24–25, it was previously argued that crucifixion of the flesh and life by Spirit denotes a *reconfiguration of identity*. This reinforces my understanding of Paul's flesh-Spirit duality—those identified as God's people are those who will share in eternal life.

The wording of 6:8 initially appears ungainly; literally, "the one sowing to the flesh of himself from the flesh will reap corruption and the one sowing to the Spirit will from the Spirit reap life eternal." However, if sowing to flesh is to accentuate an externally determined identity through circumcision and Law, Paul's statement that the attempt to be externally identified as God's people reaps corruption makes sense, for it implies a continued alienation from God in the next age. It also tallies with my assertion regarding the divine impetus behind revivification. If one sows to the flesh, it is *from the flesh* corruption ensues; but in sowing to Spirit, it is *from* Spirit that eternal life springs forth. The five occurrences of "corruption" (φθορά) in the Pauline corpus all exist in eschatological contexts (Rom 8:21; 1 Cor 15:42, 50; Gal 6:8; Col 2:22) and all but the Colossians reference in resurrection contexts.[30]

The implication of Gal 6:7–8, then, is that to attempt to identify oneself as God's people externally alienates one from God now and continuing into the eschaton. Rectification encompasses identifying with Spirit; the revivification event of the present age, rectification, initializes the revivification event of the final age, eschatological resurrection. The verdict of judgment day has been declared in the present.[31] We may confidently surmise that Gal 6:8 serves to connect rectification, the now time death-to-life movement, with resurrection, the end time death-to-life movement. For the same Spirit who revivifies in the now time is guarantor of the life to come. The question of Gal 3:3 aptly asks "having begun in Spirit, do you now perfect yourself in flesh?" That is, having begun in the life of Spirit will you become complete with something other than Spirit?

---

30. Μὴ πλανᾶσθε also occurs in 1 Cor 15:33; 6:9 in eschatological contexts.
31. Bird, "Raised for Our Justification," 43.

Intertextual Resonances: The Spirit of Life—Gal 6:8 and Ezekiel 37

Following on from 5:24–25, 6:8 has at its heart the connection between *Spirit* and *life*. Sowing to the flesh is directly connected with circumcision and the external component of identity. Yet Paul's pervasive connection of Spirit and life reflects Ezekiel, who also treats the internalization of Spirit as the epochal moment of identification as the people of God (Ezek 36:27–28; 37:12–14; cf. 39:29).

The Spirit-life relationship is explicit in Ezekiel 37; God's Spirit is the "Spirit of Life" (Ἰδοὺ ἐγὼ φέρω εἰς ὑμᾶς πνεῦμα ζωῆς, Ezek 37:5b, LXX).[32] The parallelism of Ezek 37:5 and 37:6 equates πνεῦμά μου with πνεῦμα ζωῆς. In Galatians, the Spirit of God is the agent of life-giving in believers (Gal 5:25); furthermore, it is from Spirit that believers will reap the eschatological blessing of life (Gal 6:8) and hope for it before the end (5:5). The Spirit is the source of life now and in the final age.

The semantically proximal phrase πνοὴ ζωῆς from Gen 2:7 becomes significant in Ezek 37:9–10. In Gen 2:7 God "formed the man from the heaped up earth, and blew (ἐνεφύσησεν) into his face a *spirit of life* and the man became a living soul." In Ezek 37:9, the prophet is commanded: "prophesy to the Spirit and say to the Spirit, come from the four winds and blow (ἐμφύσησον) into these dead ones and let them live." The verb 'blow' (ἐμφυσάω) evidences Ezekiel's ideological position. In the creation narrative, God "blows" Spirit into the inanimate earth and the man lives. Ezekiel summons Spirit to blow into inanimate (dead) Israel that she may live. Paul knows that God supplies the Spirit, as Gal 3:5a, where God must be the subject of ἐπιχορηγέω and ἐνεργέω. As the question posed in Ezek 37:3 implies, the dead can only live if Spirit intervenes. God's creative energy in Spirit revivifies the dead—thus, faith in Messiah, the origin of Spirit, rectifies. As many have noted, life was the experience within the covenant, which was mediated by the Law, as a number of Jewish texts depict (e.g., *Pss. Sol.* 14:2; *Sir.* 17:11–12).[33] Paul debates how this life was never fully realized because of the compromising weakness of sin in Romans 7–8, as I mentioned earlier. However, we must stress the other consistent aspect of Ezekiel's influence on Paul's pneumatology—"life" can only be realized fully by the action of Spirit. Galatians 6:8 expresses how that Spirit-triggered life in the current age persists to the final age.

---

32. Cf. Ezek 1:20–21; 10:17; for further uses of "Spirit of Life," especially in the creation motif in ancient Jewish texts see the extensive analysis in Yates, *Spirit and Creation*, 35–63.

33. For an excellent summary see Bertone, *Law of the Spirit*, 157–69.

Summary: Gal 6:8—Life Now, Life Everlasting

The previous revivification text, by drawing together crucifixion of flesh and life from Spirit, points to a change of identity—the referents are "of Christ" (Gal 5:24) and are now, therefore, Abraham's eschatological children (3:29).[34] The final stages of Paul's argument are concerned with the eschatological dimension of rectification. There will be a final resurrection bringing everlasting life for those identified by Spirit and thus belonging to Christ. Paul describes these as the ones sowing to Spirit in 6:8. Having been identified as God's people in the present age by the internal Spirit received through faith, they will be identified as God's people in the final age by the presence of the same Spirit. Those relying on external identity markers, or flesh, (contextually, circumcision, implying Torah), will be destroyed. These ones, Paul styles as sowing to flesh in 6:8. Once again, the overarching Ezekielian narrative of Spirit as harbinger of life takes centre stage; those imbued with the life of Spirit now in rectification, will live eternally through Spirit in resurrection.

---

34. The figure of Abraham is most central to the articulation of the identity of God's people in Paul, despite the subversion of physicality within Paul's determination of lineage. See Punt, "Hermeneutics in Identity Formation," 846–48.

7

Revivification Text Six

Galatians 6:14–15: A Newly Created Cosmos

Context: Closing Sentiments of Galatians

This final revivification text occurs in the closing unit of the epistle. Betz writes that Gal 6:11–18

> contains the interpretive clues to the understanding of Paul's major concerns in the letter as a whole and should be employed as the hermeneutical key to the intentions of the Apostle . . . [1]

J. Weima notes that final sections are not merely conventional in nature, but rather are

> carefully constructed units, shaped and adapted in such a way that they relate directly to—sometimes, in fact, even summarize—the major concerns and themes previously addressed in the body sections of their respective letter.[2]

This final revivification text embodies one of two references to "new creation" in Paul, within what is effectively a rehearsal of all the key themes raised, as the scholars above observe. Tolmie adds that in 6:11–18 Paul was adapting the letter closing for a final refutation of his opponents.[3] It is crucial to point out, however, that Gal 6:11–18 demonstrates conclusively something which has been apparent from the beginning: the crisis in the Galatian Jesus assemblies was a social and religious eruption along a pre-

---

1. Betz, *Galatians*, 313.
2. Weima, "Pauline Letter Closings," 198.
3. Tolmie, *Persuading*, 232.

existent fault-line. Behind this story of competing visions of the gospel, lay a wider, farther reaching meta-narrative of *how the Christ event had altered the world*.

The eschatological community was no longer the "world," but a newly formed entity predicated on a new set of governing principles. Martyn writes:

> Here Paul speaks . . . of two different worlds. He speaks of an old world, from which he has been painfully separated, by Christ's death, by the death of that world, and by his own death; and he speaks of a new world, which he grasps under the arresting expression, New Creation.[4]

Galatians 6:14–15 portrays the rectification of the cosmos—Martyn's "antidote to what is wrong with the world that lies beyond the world."[5] Paul has alerted readers to his crucifixion, by which he lived to God, and the crucifixion of believers leading to Spirit-initiated life. In the letter's final use of σταυρόω it is appropriate to read καινὴ κτίσις as the "life" component of a revivification image. As the last revivification text, closing with a more all-embracing portrait of revivification seems fitting.

However, as Moo has shown, new creation presents a complex constellation of issues in ancient Jewish apocalyptic.[6] The term is absent from the OT and infrequent in other texts. Creation language in general is common, but is applied in numerous divergent contexts.[7] Moo's conclusion that 'new creation' in Gal 6:15 refers to the radically new state of affairs that Christ's death has inaugurated is only part of the story. It relies heavily on a sketchy picture of Jewish apocalyptic and what Moo judges to be the broader apocalyptic context of the letter.[8] He too hastily screens out ideas like internal transformation, such as espoused by Hubbard, on these grounds.[9] With such sparse information to go on, it makes best sense rather than any interpretation should focus principally on the internal details of Galatians.

The central section of the closing is riddled with controversial and exegetically complex formulations; for the purposes of this analysis, we will proceed in two ways. Firstly, the way the co-textual data in Gal 6:12–13 sets

---

4. Martyn, "Apocalyptic Antinomies," 412.

5. Martyn, "Apocalyptic Gospel," 255.

6. Moo, "Creation and New Creation," 44–47; Moo, however, downplays resurrection in his reading of Gal 6:14–15.

7. Moo draws some general conclusions based on the occurrences in *Jubilees* 1:29; 4:26; *1 Enoch* 72:1; *1QS* 4:25; *2 Bar.* 44:12.

8. Ibid., 51.

9. Hubbard, *New Creation*, 224.

up the revivification passage will be evaluated. Secondly, the co-text will be read in juxtaposition with the co-text of Gal 5:6, which makes a virtually identical claim to 6:15 about circumcision.

Co-Text: Gal 6:12–13

The world had suffered crucifixion to Paul according to Gal 6:14–15 and resurfaced as something newly created. Galatians 6:12 suggests how preaching circumcision could sidestep the persecution associated with the cross; in 6:13, Paul adds further condemnatory detail, rhetorically creating a contrast between flesh/circumcision and the cross.

The elasticity of the term "flesh" allows Paul to zero in on the key point in 6:12–13. Those imposing circumcision on Gentiles, did so *in order that they might boast in your flesh* (6:13). "Boasting in your flesh," signals "boasting that we (the agitators) were instrumental in marking you (the Gentiles) with the external mark of Jewish identity." This corresponds to *looking well in the flesh* (6:12), implying "make a good public show." Paul's contempt for boasting in flesh (external identity) is generously documented—Rom 2:17, 23; 3:27; 4:2; 11:18; 1 Cor 4:7; 5:6; 2 Cor 10:15–16; 11:17–18.[10] Galatians 6:12a corresponds to 6:13b; looking well in the flesh depicts maintaining public (external) appearances and boasting in flesh, a self-congratulatory attitude towards circumcising Gentiles. *The flesh/circumcision—cross contrast sets up the revivification motif in 6:14b–15.* In 6:12–13, *Paul derides externality*—he condemns making a good *outward* show by a rite which *outwardly* exemplifies Jewish ethnicity.

The world suffered crucifixion and was newly created just as Jesus (3:13), Paul (2:19–20) and all believers (5:24–25) were subjected to crucifixion and reconstitution into a new mode of existence. Paul is dead to the old world and it is dead to him—it no longer informs his understanding of reality, with its validation of superficial markers of identity, like those in which his opponents boast. Paul boasts in the cross, *through which* he was co-crucified with Christ and the world's inverted value systems were shattered.[11]

The annihilation of ethnic division in 6:15 is broadly equivalent to the first of the three couplets in Gal 3:28 and directly equivalent to Gal 5:6, where Paul writes that "neither circumcision nor un-circumcision has any

---

10. For a nuanced picture of "Israel's boast" about which Paul was trying to correct his diatribe partner in Romans, see Gathercole, *Where is Boasting?*

11. It makes better sense that the cross, rather than Jesus himself, is the referent of δι' οὗ in 6:14.

strength, but faith working through love." A brief look at the setting of 5:6 will elucidate its continuity with 6:15. The interpretive key lies in Paul's portrayal of self-sacrificial *love* as the fulfillment of the external Law—as such, Gal 5:13–14 is critical to shaping this argument.

Exegesis of Gal 6:14–15

The double occurrence of "neither circumcision nor uncircumcision has any strength, but ... " in 5:6; 6:15, points to a similar correlation to the references of "truth of the gospel" in Gal 2:5, 14. With the co-textual considerations of Gal 6:12–13 in place, we may proceed to navigate 6:14–15 in light of 5:6 and the connected sentiments in 5:13–14.

Galatians 5:5–6 and 5:13–14 draw together both objectives of the argument of the letter—*articulating the identity of God's people* and *re-contextualizing Torah*—in one central matrix: ἀγάπη. In the former text, love is the context in which faith overrides circumcision/non-circumcision. In the latter, love fulfills Torah.

Galatians 5:5 concludes 5:2–4 and 5:6 offers a broader legitimation, setting this conclusion within the context of articulating the identity of God's people. Similarly, 5:13 concludes 5:7–12 and 5:14 reinforces the conclusion with a view to re-contextualization of the Law. Both 5:5–6 and 5:13–14 form dual conclusive statements signalled by a γὰρ that grounds the preceding statements:

5 ἡμεῖς γὰρ πνεύματι ἐκ πίστεως ἐλπίδα δικαιοσύνης ἀπεκδεχόμεθα.

6 ἐν γὰρ Χριστῷ Ἰησοῦ οὔτε περιτομή τι ἰσχύει οὔτε ἀκροβυστία ἀλλὰ πίστις δι' ἀγάπης ἐνεργουμένη.

13 Ὑμεῖς γὰρ ἐπ' ἐλευθερίᾳ ἐκλήθητε, ἀδελφοί· μόνον μὴ τὴν ἐλευθερίαν εἰς ἀφορμὴν τῇ σαρκί, ἀλλὰ διὰ τῆς ἀγάπης δουλεύετε ἀλλήλοις.

14 ὁ γὰρ πᾶς νόμος ἐν ἑνὶ λόγῳ πεπλήρωται, ἐν τῷ· ἀγαπήσεις τὸν πλησίον σου ὡς σεαυτόν.

5:2—circumcision nullifies the victory of Christ, by committing someone to do the entire Law (5:3); 5:4—commitment to attaining right status by Law leads to falling away from grace. Thus, we may understand 5:5–6 as follows:

First Conclusive Statement: For *it is* through the Spirit *we received from* faith *that we have confidence about the eschatological finality (hope) of right status* (5:5).

Second Conclusive Statement: For in Christ, *the external expression of your human identity is immaterial; you are identified by* Spirit through faith *in the context of* love (5:6).

Note, the second conclusive (5:6) explains the first (5:5), so legitimizing the claims of 5:2–4. The Spirit gives believers confidence about salvation because *Spirit marks them out as God's people.* That which marks *internal* identity, one's identity as God's people, gives confidence about eschatological salvation, not that which marks our *external*, ethnic designation. The γὰρ in 5:6 introduces the reason for what Paul claims in 5:5. The term "love" in 5:6 functions as it does in 2:20, where Paul lives by faith in the son of God who *loved* him. *It is within the context of Jesus' loving act of self-giving that believers' faith "works."*

Galatians 5:7—certain Gentiles were out of step with the truth of the gospel; 5:8—God had not called Gentiles to obey Torah; 5:9—rather, a rogue teacher was responsible; by coercing one person into circumcision, he was corrupting the community; 5:10—as such, he will be judged; 5:11–12 Paul may have preached this message of circumcision once, but no more and wishes those doing so now would cease. We may understand 5:13–14 as follows:

First Conclusive Statement: For, brothers, *the one who called you to freedom did not persuade you to be circumcised, establishing your identity externally on the grounds of Law.* Rather, with love as governing principle, be enslaved to one another.

Second Conclusive Statement: For a community where imitating Christ's self-sacrificial love inspires us to become one another's slaves, is one where the Law is fulfilled.

Once more the second conclusive explains the first, validating the preceding verses. It is because (hence, the γὰρ in 5:14) a loving community where people are one another's servants evidences the completion of the Law's role, becoming the servant of the Law is nonsensical. The true gospel is Law fulfilled in love—a "gospel" preaching circumcision is retrograde and confused.

So we return to 6:15 in the light of the parallel construction in 5:6 and the related issue of community love in 5:13–14. In the context of Christ's love, faith works to bring forth the Spirit, the internal mark of identity by which believers receive eschatological salvation. In light of this, external identity markers (circumcision or uncircumcision) are irrelevant. So once freed, those with faith should not use said freedom for flesh—that is, believers should not be circumcised and reinforce external identity markers which have been rendered irrelevant because of Spirit. Rather, in the context of Christ's sacrificial love we are enslaved to one another, fulfilling the Law's central objectives and removing any need to Judaize. This loving act (δι' ἀγάπης in 5:6) is recalled in 5:13 (διὰ τῆς ἀγάπης)—Paul sees Jesus' vicarious crucifixion as the definitive example of the loving one's neighbour, and, therefore, as the template for love within the community, as Gal 5:13-14 captures. Believers must imitate the sacrificial love of Christ for mankind, demonstrated through his crucifixion, in their love for one another. It is this intra-community devotion that Paul describes as mutual enslavement (Gal 5:13c). It is probably not accidental that the first fruit of the Spirit is love (Gal 5:22). Of course, Paul's own faith in the Son of God who loved him and sacrificed himself on Paul's behalf, is the power by which Paul lives (Gal 2:20); faith which Paul articulates is the precursor for Spirit possession (3:2-5).

The act of circumcision runs directly counter to this scheme. The rite obligates people to the prescriptions of the written code (5:3) and disconnects people from the grace offered by virtue of Christ's act of sacrifice (5:4). As such, those insisting on the rite for salvation prove they do not operate in love. Imitating Christ's self-giving love fulfils Torah (5:14), so the agitators show that they themselves misappropriate Torah's demands (6:13). They act not in love but out of the desire to boast, presumably, in front of Jewish communities regarding their success at compelling Gentiles to Judaize. As Paul implies in 3:3, the Gentiles who began in Spirit are on the verge of being completed in flesh by the circumcisers.

However, to use one's freedom in Christ to permit circumcision, reinforces external, ethnic identity, and is tantamount to a denial of the Spirit who marks out God's people. So Paul boasts in the cross, the locus of the crucifixion of Jesus' flesh. The cross is where Jesus' loving act of sacrifice was manifested and the arena where faith brings forth Spirit. With this in mind, we may fully reconnect Gal 5:5-6, 5:13-14 and 6:12-14. Through the cross the world has been crucified to Paul, which as in 2:19 and 5:24, denotes destroyed with a view to revivification. Here, κόσμος refers to the world, but interestingly, the same term denotes outward adorning.[12] The author of 1 Peter warns against women defining beauty by the braiding of hair, the wearing of gold jewellery or ἐνδύσεως ἱματίων κόσμος (the putting on of garments of adornment). It is possible that Paul intended some hint of this aspect of κόσμος, for in this context it represents that sphere where externalities have value. However, on the cross, Jesus' sacrificial love created the conditions for faith to work, bringing forth the Spirit, who enters the

---

12. BAGD, 561.

hearts of the faithful. So to Paul (representative of all believers here) the old world is no more, and with it, the merit once attached to ethno-racial classification; *both* circumcision *and* uncircumcision are inert as identity markers or indices of value (5:6; 6:15).

Paul appropriately recalls his own crucifixion in this context; ἐμοὶ κόσμος ἐσταύρωται κἀγὼ κόσμῳ. For Paul acknowledges in Gal 2:19 that, co-crucified with Christ, he is now alive in a new way. He titles this "living to God," which in juxtaposition with 6:14, depicts "no longer lives to the world."

Within Paul's scheme, what matters is new creation. Paul's disdain for emphasizing the external marks of ethnic identity in the refrain found in Gal 5:6 and 6:15 obliquely invokes his pneumatological stance. That is, new creation parallels faith working in the context of love. In Gal 5:6, it is because of Christ's loving act of sacrifice that faith in him becomes the source of Spirit, who emblematizes the people of God. In 6:15 (6:14–16), Spirit is the "canon," or guiding principle of the new creation. External ethnic classification is irrelevant because of the internal mark of Spirit, which, as per our previous remarks, is the arena in which "there is not Jew or Greek." The invocation of the "neither circumcision nor uncircumcision" refrain in 1 Cor 7:19 *may* reflect the wider pneumatology of 1 Corinthians, inasmuch as all, whether Jew or Greek are baptized by the Spirit into the body (1 Cor 12:13) and so do God's will by Spirit. It is more likely a recollection of Gal 6:15–16, suggesting that keeping God's commands within the new creation meant following the canon of Spirit.

Intertextual Resonances

Internalization and Community Formation

It was shown, based on Gal 5:24–25, that those with crucified flesh have entered a new sphere of identity. The revivifying Spirit acts as ethical barometer, so the practical life of the community is evidence of the community's identity. Spirit, then, is an internal identity marker. Galatians 5:16–23 expresses the ethical superiority of the Spirit-*dictated* life; vv. 24–25 rationalize how the Spirit-dictated life originates from a Spirit-*initiated* life. Paul depicts the Galatian Jesus communities as Spirit-created entities, energized by Spirit to live in a fashion acceptable to God. Paul's portrait of community originates from the prophetic foretelling of a post-exilic community—*a people established by the work of Spirit in making the statutes of God an inner reality*. The process of internalization detectable in Jeremiah's New Covenant prophecy and Ezekiel's Spirit prophecy resonate strongly with Gal 6:14–15, housed as it is in the context of Paul's derision of externality and championing of an internal index of identity. Furthermore, Paul's new creation orders its steps by the canon of Spirit and not Law. We observe the following.

There is a prevailing fatalism among the deportees in Babylon, suggesting exile was punishment for the crimes of a bygone generation. Both Jeremiah and Ezekiel cite and refute the same proverb:

> In those days they will not say again, *the fathers have eaten sour grapes, And the children's teeth are set on edge*. But everyone will die for his own iniquity; *each man who eats the sour grapes, his teeth will be set on edge* (Jer 31:29–30, NRSV).

> What do you mean by using this proverb concerning the land of Israel, saying, *the fathers eat the sour grapes, But the children's teeth are set on edge*. As I live, declares the Lord God, you are surely not going to use this proverb in Israel anymore (Ezek 18:1–2, NRSV).[13]

Nonetheless, both prophets testify to a qualitative difference between the New Covenant and the Sinai covenant; it will guarantee Israel's perpetual fidelity to its stipulations.[14]

> I will give them one heart and one way, that they may fear me for all time . . . I will make an everlasting covenant with them . . . and I will put the fear of me in their hearts, so that they may not turn from me (Jer 32:39–40; cf. Ezek 36:26–27 above).

The end of captivity is heralded by the divine action upon the hearts of the people creating a community with an irrevocable allegiance to God's dictates. One *leitmotif* truly bears the weight of the concept of covenant-community identity.

Yates observes:

> The recurring use of the "my people/their God" formula (Jer 30:22; 31:1, 33; 32:38) highlights the covenant theme in this section. For this relationship as the original goal or intent of the first Exodus, see Jer 7:23; 11:4; 13:11 (cf. also Exod 6:7; Lev 26:12; Deut 27:9; 29:12 for the influence of the earlier Exodus traditions). This phrase has a similar usage elsewhere in the prophets (Ezek 11:20; 14:11; 36:28; 37:23, 27; Zech 8:8).[15]

---

13. For the conflict between notion of personal versus generational responsibility, see Joyce, *Divine Initiative*, 36–47; Brownlee, *Ezekiel*, 282–93; Tuell, *Ezekiel*, 119–20.

14. Yates, "People Have Not Obeyed," 234.

15. Ibid., 234 n. 98.

The term is especially noteworthy in Jer 31:33; 32:38; Ezek 11:20 and 36:28, where it is connected to statements attesting God's spiritual heart surgery. As earlier proposed, it is *because* God has acted to change the hearts of the people they become fit to be his people and call him their God.

So we may understand that the divine interiorization which accompanied the end of exile had the combined effect of instigating obedience in the people's hearts and establishing them as God's people.

Pettegrew notes that for some OT scholars, the key provision of the New Covenant is the new heart (Jer 24:4–7; 31:31–34; 32:37–41; Ezek 11:17–21; 36:22–32). Yahweh promises, "I will give them a heart to know me, for I am the Lord; and they will be My people, and I will be their God, for they will return to me with their whole heart" (Jer 24:7).[16]

Readers should recall those passages which treat the Exodus as the moment Israel was created as a nation (e.g., Exod 3:10; Num 22:5). As such, the greater Exodus to which Galatians points may be seen as creating a "greater" Israel in Paul's thought—the Israel of God (Gal 6:16). There are a few reasons for making this connection. Firstly, the flight from Egypt and the restoration from Assyrian/Babylonian captivity are resurrection moments which led to the creation of Israel; it is reasonable, then, that rectification, the now-time resurrection moment, should create Israel. Paul's apparent separation of Israel into historical and eschatological realities in Romans 9–11 reinforces this.[17] Secondly, if Paul understands Spirit as the pillar of fire that led Israel, the creation of the "Israel of God" which orders its steps by the canon of Spirit, is fitting. Thirdly, Gal 6:15 points to a new creation, annihilating Israel's standard ethnic bifurcation of the world. A fourth, co-related idea is how ἐν Χριστῷ Ἰησοῦ in Galatians typically depicts ethnic inclusivity (see above on Ἐν Χριστῷ). In some ancient manuscripts, Gal 6:15 begins ἐν γὰρ Χριστῷ Ἰησοῦ, which, though almost certainly an insertion based on 5:6, rightly envisions how the text was understood. Ἐν Χριστῷ Ἰησοῦ appears in 2:4 to show the freedom that circumcised *and* uncircumcised believers share. Galatians 3:14 suggests the blessing of Abraham will come to Gentiles so *all* believers receive the Spirit. In 3:26, *all* are sons of God through faith ἐν Χριστῷ Ἰησοῦ; 3:28 states that there is not Jew or Greek *in Christ Jesus*; 5:6 parallels 6:15 in nullifying the circumcised/not circumcised distinction. The new creation in Galatians comprises the "in Christ" community—a new entity beyond ethnic classification (see below).

---

16. Pettegrew, "New Covenant," 255.
17. See Dinkler, "Historical and Eschatological Israel," 109–27.

Further Evidence: The Israel of God

My reading of Gal 6:14-15 is corroborated by the inclusive interpretation of "the Israel of God." A. J. Köstenberger is essentially correct concluding that the

> "Israel of God" represents all believers regardless of their ethnic provenance who follow Paul's "new rule" of a Spirit-led life by faith in the crucified Christ.[18]

This rule of Spirit is the internal impetus to obedience to God through the Spirit, operating over and against another rule—the observance of the external Torah. The substance of this rule is apparent from Paul's use of the verb στοιχέω in 6:16, also used in 5:25, and substantiated by his use of the noun, στοιχεῖον in Galatians 4, which shall now be reconsidered.

Generally, στοιχεῖον denotes "what belongs to a series."[19] According to G. Delling, five different but related meanings from this same period are detectable: "the length of a shadow on the sundial," "part of a syllable or a word," "the essential elements of the cosmos," "smallest parts (of anything) which stand in relation to one another," and "astral bodies as elements of fire."[20] Having already suggested that the term in Galatians refers to enslaving powers, we need only add the following.

Paul's choice of verb here, in light of στοιχεῖα in chapter 4, cannot be accidental. The στοιχεῖα, by enslaving people, gave structure and order to the world. For Paul, the old world rested upon this underlying principle of people held down by slave-masters.[21] The crucifixion of Jesus shattered this sequence—hence Paul speaks of the *freedom* we have in Christ (Gal 2:4). The world itself suffered crucifixion to the believer, suggesting the order of their world was destroyed. Crucifixion in Galatians implies death as precursor of revivification; in Gal 6:15, this is the new creation, shattering the previous order where uncircumcised and circumcised had meaning. With the στοιχεῖα shattered, people are called στοιχεῖν by Spirit.

We may now turn to "the Israel of God." Galatians 6:16 presents a number of syntactical problems.[22] Most notoriously, the second καὶ leaves

---

18. Köstenberger, "Identity," 4. For the view that the phrase refers to Paul's on-going mission to the Jews, see Eastman, "Israel and the Mercy of God," 367-95. Eastman argues that Paul invokes peace on those who live according to the new creation, and mercy on unbelieving Israel.

19. Delling, "στοιχεῖον," *TDNT*, 670

20. Ibid., 670-82; see Schweizer, "Slaves," 455-68.

21. Cf. Martyn, *Theological Issues*, 115-16 on apocalyptic antinomies.

22. Kostenberger, "Identity," 9-11.

open whether Israel of God refers to the same group ordering their steps by this rule, includes them but points to the wider Christian community, or refers to another group entirely. The question is unresolvable grammatically. If a purely syntactical decision was unavoidable, the usual translation of καὶ is preferred. Then, the Israel of God would be a different group altogether and Gal 6:16 would express "peace" to "those who will order their steps according to this rule" on one hand, and "mercy" to "the Israel of God" on the other. There are a few reasons, however, why the term must be an inclusive term for the Spirit community irrespective of their ethnic designation.

Firstly, Israel is mentioned only here in Galatians, in a phrase unprecedented in Paul, the NT or any Second Temple Literature; Paul's introduction of such a phrase at this late stage of the letter is a piece of deliberate paradox. This would undermine the scholars who favour excluding Gentiles from the Israel of God on the grounds that "Israel" is never used in Biblical literature in the sense of a multi-ethnic people of God.[23]

Secondly, Paul's sustained anti-Judaizing polemic renders a sudden shift in his argument in Gal 6:16b (suddenly pronouncing a blessing on literal Israel) implausible.[24]

Thirdly, Gal 6:14–15 seems to have been influenced by Jer 9:23–26:

> 23 Thus says the Lord: Do not let the wise boast in their wisdom, do not let the mighty boast in their might, do not let the wealthy boast in their wealth; 24 but let those who boast, boast in this, that they understand and know me . . . 25 The days are surely coming . . . when I will attend to all those who are circumcised only in the foreskin: 26 Egypt, Judah, Edom, the Ammonites, Moab, and all those with shaven temples who live in the desert. For all these nations are uncircumcised, and all the house of Israel is uncircumcised in heart (NRSV).

Jeremiah's indictment stipulates that the only appropriate grounds for boasting are the understanding and knowledge of Yahweh. Paul cites Jer 9:24 more directly in 1 Cor 1:31; nonetheless, the principle seems clearly applicable in Gal 6:14, for Paul will not boast in anything but the cross of *the Lord*. The cross is the locus of God's intervention to rectify humanity. So people may boast of God's great act, but no act of human impulse is cause for boasting. Jeremiah then proceeds to register God's indifference to circumcision with all those nations (listing Judah in and amongst Egypt, Edom, Ammon and Moab) who practice the external rite without internal reformation. In Jer 9:26, the *uncircumcised* nations are the same as Israel

---

23. E.g., Johnson, "Paul and The Israel of God," 183–94.
24. Köstenberger, "Identity," 3.

who is physically circumcised, but uncircumcised of heart. Again, it seems most reasonable to assume that Paul follows Jeremiah in eliminating the privilege of one group to pronounce favour on another. Both writers discount boasting privileges on grounds of personal success (for Jeremiah, wisdom, might and riches; in Paul's context, circumcising Gentiles). The authors both express how neither circumcision nor uncircumcision affords privilege—what matters is responsiveness to God's commands (Jeremiah's heart circumcision) and new creation (Paul).[25] Having so leveled the playing field, for Paul to unbalance it again in the space of one verse by separating the Israel of God from the ones ordering their steps by the canon of Spirit, seems contradictory.[26]

Fourthly, the term "Israel" is a loaded term in its own right for it refers to the ethnic people chosen by God. Adding τοῦ θεοῦ has the effect of intensifying the exclusivity of the group (this is not just Israel, but the Israel *of God*). If the negation of the circumcision/uncircumcision distinction is to be considered meaningful, especially given the association of circumcision with ethnic Judaism (and proselytism) in the letter, it is difficult to accept τὸν Ἰσραὴλ τοῦ θεοῦ as a reference to ethnic Israel. If *neither* circumcision nor its opposite are anything, and ethnic Israel is "the circumcision," (e.g., Gal 2:7–9, 12), how could the Israel *of God* be ethnic Israel? How could a more restrictive term apply if the distinction has been collapsed? Furthermore, just as the "newness" of διαθήκην καινήν in Jer 31:31 corresponds to the engagement with God's Law (what Ezek 36:26–27 defines as Spirit-governed), the *new* aspect of καινὴ κτίσις in Gal 6:15 is *how* Spirit (a) makes ethnic distinction irrelevant and (b) becomes the community's ethical invigilator by making Law an inner reality. Inasmuch as God's Law is not different, only engaged with differently, *Israel is still God's people—only defined by Spirit, not flesh.*

So Paul's Israel of God is a newly created community that lives by the rule of Spirit. In Jeremiah's oracle, a "divine way," a "fear," and the Law itself are placed in the heart so the people do not depart from Yahweh and are established as his people. In Ezekiel's prophecy, the people are given a new heart and are imbued with Spirit resulting in an unparalleled responsiveness to the commandments. Paul synchronises Israel's redemption with the Spirit entering the hearts and marking them out as the sons of God (Gal 4:6). He further articulates how the people's life in Spirit encourages resistance against unethical conduct (5:16–17) without Torah (5:18). Indeed, Paul did not point the community to the performance of any Law, but to completely

---

25. Cf. 1 Cor 7:19.
26. Cf. Matera, *God's Saving Grace*, 148–50.

filling up Christ's Law—those who achieved this are οἱ πνευματικοὶ (6:1–2). The spiritual ones are those with the Law as internal reality through Spirit. In sum, the evidence of Galatians (cf. Romans 7–8) is that Paul's vision of a New Covenant people of God was shaped by his appreciation of the prophetic insight of Jeremiah and Ezekiel.

Even with this emphasis on the correlation between the new creation and the newly formed community, Adams correctly asserts that Paul is not saying that the community of Christ *is* the new creation, but belongs to it.[27] The debate as to whether Paul intends καινὴ κτίσις to refer to the individual believers themselves, the community at large or a new cosmic order, rages on.[28] The community concerns of Gal 5:16–6:18 more broadly, and the specificity of 6:16a particularly, suggest that whatever Paul has in focus, the social and practical implications of new creation upon the believing community cannot be ignored.[29]

Further Evidence: Ephesians 2:11–18

The author of Ephesians may have been cognizant of Galatians. There certainly seems to be a correlation between Eph 2:11–18 and Gal 6:8–16 as the following suggest:

1. *Circumcision/uncircumcision* (Gal 6:15/Eph 2:11)

2. *External circumcision* as "flesh" (Gal 6:12–13/Eph 2:11)

3. *An unprecedented composite phrase for Israel*—τὸν Ἰσραὴλ τοῦ θεοῦ (Gal 6:16) and τῆς πολιτείας τοῦ Ἰσραὴλ (Eph 2:12)[30]

4. *A third entity that is neither circumcision nor uncircumcision* (Eph 2:14; Gal 6:15)

5. *New creation* (Eph 2:15/Gal 6:15); in Ephesians, the newly created entity is explicitly "man" (καινὸν ἄνθρωπον), in whom is the resolution of peace between Jew and Gentile

6. *Peace* (Gal 6:16/Eph 2:14)

7. *Spirit* (Gal 6:8/Eph 2:18).

Again, one key theme of Galatians is articulating the identity of God's people, an agenda also present in Romans 9–11 and Philippians 3, and one

---

27　Adams, *Constructing the World*, 228.

28.　Hubing, *Crucifixion and New Creation*, 311–421.

29.　Cf. τοὺς οἰκείους τῆς πίστεως in Gal 6:10.

30.　The reference to Israel in Ephesians is clearly ethnic Israel.

in which the term Israel occasionally appears in somewhat cryptic fashion within Paul's theologizing (Gal 6:16; Rom 9:6; 11:26). Whilst no major scholarly consensus on Paul's vision for Israel's ongoing role in the divine economy of salvation is forthcoming, we may speculate from the available data, that Paul engaged in some conceptual renegotiation of "Israel."[31] If the Israel of God is indeed an ethnically indistinct "Spirit-initiated" and "Spirit-directed" community, consistent with a new creation, then Eph 2:11–18 offers a contextually nuanced parallel portrait of this community with resemblances to the restored community depicted (principally) by Jeremiah and Ezekiel.

Indifference to Circumcision—We have discussed the interface between Jeremiah's comments in Jer 9:23–26 and Gal 6:12–15. Jeremiah's pronunciation indicates the futility of a community with circumcised foreskins, for other Gentile nations engaged in the same practice. If Israel's commitment to the covenant was no greater than circumcised pagans, then the ritual was null. In Ezekiel's castigation of the people for desecrating the temple, his indictment includes that they admitted " . . . foreigners, uncircumcised in heart and flesh, to be in my sanctuary, profaning my temple when you offer to me my food, the fat and the blood . . . " (Ezek 44:7). The author of Ephesians specifies that those called the circumcision (Eph 2:11; cf. Gal 2:12), who, themselves cast the Gentiles as uncircumcision, have only a circumcision of flesh performed by hands (περιτομῆς ἐν σαρκὶ χειροποιήτου). The heart circumcision God demands is by Spirit (Rom 2:29; cf. Phil 3:3; Col 2:11). The annihilation of the circumcised/uncircumcised distinction within Paul's new creation ideology crystallizes the prophetic ambivalence towards the external ritual in the absence of internal transformation. The "new creation community" parallels the restored "New Covenant community," having undergone the divine process of internalization (Jer 31:33; Ezek 36:27; 37:14). Paul has no time for boasts tied to externalities (Gal 6:12–13), for the Israel of God walks by the canon of the internalized Spirit (Gal 6:16) and is identified by the presence of that same Spirit in the hearts, declaring Yahweh as Father (Gal 4:6; cf. Ezek 37:14).

Two Become One—Ezekiel's acted symbol of the reunification of the northern and southern kingdoms follows the dry bones drama. That the unity and oneness of the restored community is the central issue of the symbol is reflected in ten occurrences of the Hebrew אֶחָד (Ezek 37:16–24b). There are a number of divergences of detail between the Greek and Hebrew renditions of the pericope which are beyond present concerns.[32] However,

---

31. See Merkle, "Romans 11," 707–22; Schreiner, "Church as the New Israel," 17–38.

32. E.g., the Greek suggests the unification of two *sceptres*; interpreters speculate that

once restoration is achieved, Yahweh's attention turns to reunification. There will not be two nations or two kingdoms, but one, with one king (37:22) and the cessation of idolatry implies the people's devotion to one God.[33] Oneness is a clear concern in Eph 2:14–18, though it is the unification of Jew and Gentile the author expounds upon. Jesus is our peace, the one making both groups *one* (Eph 2:14); who in himself from the two creates *one* new man (Eph 2:15); reconciling both into *one* body (Eph 2:16); and through whom both by *one* Spirit have access to the father (Eph 2:18).[34] The comparable prominence of "two" and "both" (Eph 2:14, 15, 16, 18) emphasizes the separation and division of Jew and Gentile in the writer's mind.[35] In Galatians, Paul, in registering the invalidity of the circumcised/uncircumcised demarcation within the new creation, resolves Jew and Gentile into one unprecedented entity that is ethnically neither.

Newness—Jeremiah profoundly declares the ratification of a *new* covenant (Jer 31:31); Ezekiel speaks of the *new* heart and *new* spirit God will bestow on the people (Ezek 11:19; 18:31; 36:26);[36] the deutero-Pauline author of Ephesians has one *new* man created from the two (Eph 2:15; cf. 4:24); Paul introduces the notion of a *new* creation (Gal 6:15; cf. 2 Cor 5:17). Hafemann rightly concludes that Jeremiah's New Covenant inaugurates the new creation.[37] Wright opines that when God fulfils the covenant through the death and resurrection of Jesus and the gift of the Spirit, this both deals with sin and procures forgiveness and brings forth God's intention of a multi-ethnic Abrahamic family.[38]

In his analysis of Christian identity Saucy writes:

> The believer is part of the "new creation" (2 Cor 5:17). He has put off the "old man" and put on the "new man" (Col 3:9–10; cf. Rom 6:6). This transition refers to the believer's transference from the old corporate humanity under the headship of Adam to the new humanity with Christ as Head.[39]

---

the idea of making one title deed from two lies behind the Hebrew text. See Zimmerli, *Ezekiel 25–48*, 273–74.

33. Cf. Jer 32:39 for the "oneness" of the direction of the new covenant community.
34. Cf. Eph 4:4–6; 5:31.
35. Greek for "both" in Eph 2:14, 16, 18 is ἀμφότεροι.
36. Cf. Jer 24:7.
37. Hafemann, *Letter/Spirit*, 429–36; cf. Polhill, *Letters*, 267; Elias, *Remember*, 192–96.
38. Wright, *Perspectives*, 37.
39. Saucy, "Sinners," 402.

A more involved foray into the concept of newness would take its theological cue from the perspective that the created order will eventually be resolved in a new heavens and a new earth (Isa 65:17; 66:22; cf. *1 Enoch* 45:4–5; *2 Apoc. Bar.* 32:6; *4 Ezra* 7:75). Paul's invocation of a newness formula with its emphasis on Christ and Spirit in Galatians, has strong enough resonances with the newness themes in Jeremiah and especially Ezekiel, reflected in Ephesians 2, to postulate that, for the apostle, new creation summed up how God's Spirit renewing men's hearts was the central aspect of the New Covenant.

Spirit—Block correctly sees Ezek 37:1–14 as resumption of 36:26–27.[40] Ezekiel essentially recapitulates the Jeremianic New Covenant ideal in terms of Spirit. As Thorsell writes:

> The prediction of an eschatological covenant between Yahweh and Israel is not limited to Jeremiah 31 but is a common theme in the OT. One prominent element of this predicted covenant is that of moral transformation, an element that Paul dwells upon in some of his references to the New Covenant.[41]

Paul's New Covenant pneumatology in Galatians suggests that he reckoned texts like Ezek 36:27 and 37:14 as equivalent clauses, pointing to the *epochal moment of Spirit internalization*:

καὶ τὸ πνεῦμά μου δώσω ἐν ὑμῖν καὶ ποιήσω ἵνα ἐν τοῖς δικαιώμασίν μου πορεύησθε καὶ τὰ κρίματά μου φυλάξησθε καὶ ποιήσητε (Ezek 36:27).

καὶ δώσω τὸ πνεῦμά μου εἰς ὑμᾶς, καὶ ζήσεσθε, καὶ θήσομαι ὑμᾶς ἐπὶ τὴν γῆν ὑμῶν, καὶ γνώσεσθε ὅτι ἐγὼ κύριος λελάληκα καὶ ποιήσω, λέγει κύριος (Ezek 37:14).[42]

Ezekiel's prophecy of internalization is in terms of Spirit, by which the restored community will obey God's laws. Paul's use of στοιχέω (Gal 5:25; 6:16) points to Spirit as the governing canon of the new creation. Ephesians 2:18 intimates that, through Jesus, both Jew and Gentile have access to God by the one Spirit. This one Spirit, by whom both groups come to the Father, permits their access on the basis of the "dividing wall of partition" having been destroyed in his (Jesus') flesh (Eph 2:14).[43] Ephesians 2:15 makes an

---

40. Block, "Beyond the Grave," 133; cf. Ezek 11:19.

41. Thorsell, "Spirit in the Present Age," 400.

42. Cf. Διδοὺς δώσω νόμους μου εἰς τὴν διάνοιαν αὐτῶν in Jer 31:33.

43. The temple imagery of Eph 2:21 suggests that the author was thinking about the wall separating the Gentile court from the inner section of the temple when he employed the μεσότοιχον τοῦ φραγμοῦ metaphor.

indirect, albeit unambiguous, association between this dividing wall and the Mosaic Law (τὸν νόμον τῶν ἐντολῶν ἐν δόγμασιν); the combined effect is that the crucifixion of Jesus makes Jew and Gentile one new entity by bringing the age of Torah's supervisory function to an end. The defining emblem of the new age is Spirit, who founds the new family of God (Eph 2:19–22; cf. Gal 4:4–7). Ezekiel, Paul and the author of Ephesians all treat Spirit as the initiator of a new potentiality for being God's people. For Ezekiel, Spirit transforms the people's hearts to receive God's demands as an inner reality which they respond to. Paul takes up this theme such that he can speak of the Spirit as ethical overseer of a community in a salvation-historical contrast with Law. In Ephesians, Spirit grants the newly created people access (προσαγωγή) to God—in other words causes them to become the family of God (cf. Isa 44:3; Joel 2:28–29).

Peace—The Ezekielian portrait of the reunification of the house of Israel involves the cutting of a covenant of *peace* (Ezek 37:26) which corresponds to Jeremiah's cutting of a new covenant (Jer 31:31). Indeed, Jeremiah bemoans the counterfeit peace proclaimed by bogus prophets (Jer 4:10; 6:14; 8:11, 15; 9:8; 38:22)—true peace will accompany the divinely instigated rebuilding of Judah (Jer 33:6, 9). As above, the Pauline benediction of peace and mercy is upon all who walk by the rule of Spirit (Gal 6:16). According to the author of Ephesians, Jesus is 'our peace' because his crucifixion ended the fractious Jew-Gentile relationship by making them one new people (Eph 2:14)—an act by which hostility ceased and peace was forged (Eph 2:15). The writer sees this harmony as fulfillment of Isaiah's prediction (Eph 2:17; cf. Isa 57:19).[44]

Summary: Gal 6:14–15—The Eschatological People of God

The final revivification text contains the final reference to crucifixion in the letter and corresponds to σταυρόω in 2:19 and 5:24. The "life" component in Gal 6:14–15 is new creation. In this final pericope, Paul brings a number of the foundational themes of the letter to a head, most notably the fact that externally marked identity is mere technicality within God's new creation. For this reason, the identity of God's people effectively transcends ethnic distinction.[45] The annihilation of this distinction marks the community of

---

44. See further Martin, *Reconciliation*, 190.

45. Contra Hodge, *If Sons then Heirs*, 117–35. Johnson Hodge, amongst others, argues against the idea that Paul advocates the effective collapsing of ethnic difference into one Christian identity—what she refers to as fusion theory.

the new creation. The final part of Paul's argument is that within the new creation is a community formed and identified by the internalization of Spirit. The Jeremianic and Ezekielian foreshadowing of internalization, both of Spirit and impetus to obey God, is captured in Paul's thoughts here. The divine interiorization which accompanied the end of exile had the combined effect of instigating obedience in the people's hearts and establishing them as the people of God. Paul's closing sentiments in Galatians revolve around a people who having been created by Spirit, order their steps by Spirit (Gal 6:14–16). It is this combination of creation by Spirit, establishing the identity of a people of God and a Spirit-instigated ethics that points to the influence of Ezekiel and Jeremiah on Paul. The thematic and intertextual interface outlined here demonstrates that Paul understood rectification before God as the true restoration from exile. This interface evidences the following: Spirit changed the hearts of the restored people to receive the commands of God—Paul pronounced his blessing upon all who walk by the canon of Spirit; as a result of the intervention of Spirit and the people's new-found commitment to God's laws, the freed people were fit to be a people of God, seen in the repeated refrain "they will be my people and I will be their God." The rectified community was the Israel of God, a component of the new creation where the standard Jewish ethnic bifurcation of the world was erased. The above receives support from Eph 2:11–18, which draws together a very similar collocation of themes and key terms as Ezekiel/Jeremiah and Gal 6:8–16.

8

Thesis Conclusions and Summation

Outline of Argument and Controlling Theory of Thesis

This volume presents the following understanding of Paul's argument in Galatians: "co-crucifixion with Christ," "crucifying the flesh," and "crucifixion to/of the world" are tightly correlated phrases by which we may approximate the revivification motifs—"life to God;" "life initiated by Spirit;" "new creation."[1] Crucifixion in Galatians stands specifically for death as prelude to revivification. The primordial revivification event is the death and resurrection of Jesus—his rectification (vindication) and restoration (after having become the curse). Having encountered rectification and restoration as resurrection in Jesus, Paul outlined the rectification of believers and the world itself as eschatological, participatory immersion in the Christ event. Consequently, Paul's gospel and ministry in Galatians is both cast and explicated within the contextual and semantic matrix of resurrection.

God *raised* Jesus from among the dead (Gal 1:1) so the risen Christ could orchestrate mankind's rescue from the present evil age (1:4). Paul (as all Jewish believers) was rectified by *co-crucifixion* with Christ/*death* to Law in order to *live* to God (2:19–20); Gentile believers are rectified in the *crucifixion* of flesh and being *made alive* by Spirit (5:24–25); the cosmos is rectified by *crucifixion* and *new creation* (6:14–15); rectification is effected by faith, the origin of Spirit. Law is *not* the source of Spirit and so cannot

---

1. As Yates aptly notes: "'the new creation depends on the resurrection of Christ, as is evident in 2 Cor 5:14–17; it is, therefore, right to speak of new creation and resurrection in the same breath." See Yates, *Spirit and Creation*, 121.

make alive (3:21); the *revivified life* kindled by Spirit in this age is the precursor for sharing in the *risen life* of the age to come (6:8).

This preponderance of death-life imagery allows us to treat Paul's view of rectification as an *inaugurated eschatological revivification event*. Rectification is the first step to being raised in the final resurrection—Judgment is the *consummated eschatological revivification event*, where the "already but not yet," becomes here and now; where the hope of righteousness (5:5) is hope realized. This brings us to the fulcrum of Galatians: what instigated Paul to frame his explanation of attaining right covenant status with God in resurrection language, within a letter written to counteract a false thesis regarding the role of Torah? Why has Paul opted to depict rectification as revivification in Galatians?

As I have argued, Gal 3:10–13 makes apparent Paul's Deuteronomic view of Israel's unfolding history. For the author of Deuteronomy, the language of death (curse) and life (blessing) metaphorizes exile and restoration, respectively. Ezekiel's portrait of restoration employs the same metaphor—*adding that Spirit is the architect of this resurrection-restoration* (Ezek 37:1–14).

Consequently, the "life from death" lexicon we encounter in Galatians points to the following: confronted with the resurrected Jesus, the *literal* resurrection of this individual before the eschaton, Paul determined two things. Firstly, that Jesus was Israel's prophesied Christ;[2] secondly, that the curse had been undone. Jesus had physically embodied what these great prophetic traditions had foretold.[3] Jesus' literal movement from death to life had *actualized* what the prophets *symbolized* as a movement from exile to restoration; Jesus personified the foretelling of Israel's destiny. Paul viewed Jesus' death as vicarious—he lovingly gave himself over on Paul's own behalf (Gal 2:20); he took on the curse for Israel (3:13); Paul writes that Jesus became the curse, for unlike Israel who had been "locked up under sin by the Law and died," Jesus gave himself over to death.

Yet God raised Jesus from death (1:1) and imbued him with the end-time life in the present. The blessing of life had subsumed the curse of death—or in Deuteronomic terms, the blessing of restoration ended the curse of exile. Thus, *in Christ*, Israel's exile was finally over—those incorporated into Christ participated in the death-to-life movement epitomized

---

2. Many scholars posit that Paul's change in direction stems from the impact of the risen Jesus. See Allison, *Resurrecting Jesus*, 263–68; Licona, *Resurrection of Jesus*, 302–3; Hyam Maccoby writes that the Jerusalem leaders did not sever their links with Judaism, but regarded themselves as essentially believers in Judaism who also believed in the resurrection of Jesus, a human Messiah figure—see Maccoby, *Mythmaker*, 14–18.

3. For the bodily nature of the resurrection of Jesus see Wright, *Resurrection*, 215.

by Jesus. Jews in Christ died to slavery to Law, Gentiles died to slavery to counterfeit deities and both were revivified. That is, they were rectified—by sharing in the experience of Christ they too were brought back from their exile, their estrangement and alienation from God. Rectification, the inaugurated eschatological revivification event, is the true end of the exile. I further maintain that Paul, with the risen Christ as interpretive grid, understood the biblical restoration from exile prophecies, couched as they were in revivification language, as a prophetic eschatological revivification event.

Historical Event	Associated Eschatological Revivification Event
The Resurrection of Jesus	*Primordial*
Physical Relocation to Holy Land	*Prophetic*
Rectification	*Inaugurated*
The Final Resurrection	*Consummated*

The six revivification texts I have outlined act as a dialogical bridge between Paul's account of the conflict in Galatia and the divine restoration of Israel and the world through Christ. By illustrating how rectification is actually revivification, Paul can explain why circumcision has no soteriological value.

Paul had his narrative outlook shaped by the account of Israel's destiny in the closing chapters of Deuteronomy.[4] He was most profoundly shaped, however, by his encounter with the resurrected Jesus. The death-life imagery with which Paul contextualizes the debacle in the Galatian Jesus assemblies, points to one way the resurrection of Jesus shaped his thinking. As Spaulding rightly suggests, God's character is on display through the resurrection.[5] Thus, Paul defines God in terms of Jesus' resurrection in Gal 1:1. To give life was how God "put things right."[6] To be set right before God was to share in the experience of Jesus' resurrection and, consequently, be freed from captivity to sin, which Paul saw as the true captor. To be freed from captivity was to be made alive by Spirit, as per the Ezekielian vision. This begins with rectification; people in the exile of sin and the consequent alienation from God (Gal 4:8) were restored, not in a geographical homeland, but *in Christ*. In Christ, they received the identity of God's eschatological people, the seed

---

4. See the useful introductory comments in Waters, *End of Deuteronomy*, 1–3.
5. Spaulding, "Resurrection in Pauline Literature."
6. Cf. Rom 4:17.

of Abraham. It ends with reaping eternal life in the consummated revivification event, the Judgment.

This Spirit formed/led community *summarizes part of what Galatians contributes to what might cautiously be called a "theology of Paul."* Hafemann writes of 2 Cor 3:3 that believers' existence is a result of the Spirit's work in their hearts which is an expression of the fulfilment of Ezekiel's prophecy.[7] Galatians points implicitly to this core element of Pauline thought. Galatians reveals how the prophetic restoration oracles inform its narrative—the raising of Jesus is the finality of God's saving work and the blueprint of how his people engage with that work. The Spirit brings to life a community by indwelling the hearts of the faithful, so provoking them to obedience, made manifest in a life characterised by love.[8]

Paul's rhetorical strategy in Galatians was to re-appropriate the role of Torah, demonstrating that faith was the only indispensable component of right status. This re-appropriation was consistent with the statements Jeremiah and Ezekiel made about God's Law and commands. In the context of Galatians, the Law reached fulfilment in the context of love (Gal 5:14)— what Paul meant by *the Law of Christ*.[9] It is precisely because the community was impelled by Spirit to obey the commands (as spoken through the prophets) that the people will be freed from any other masters. Paul can say that the Spirit-led are not under Law because community life is aroused by Spirit—not by devotion to any law or any idol.[10]

The critical move in the argument is the contrast of the *curse of the Law* with the *blessing of Abraham*, and the equation of the blessing of Abraham with the *promise of Spirit*. The Law's curse is summed up as *death* and the contrasting promise of Spirit, as *life*. This promise is expounded in Paul's harnessing of Gen 15:6 (Gal 3:6; cf. Rom 4:3, 20–22). The promise was specifically the miraculous birth of Isaac against all gynaecological odds. Abraham trusted God despite the deadness of his own and Sarah's reproductive apparatus (Rom 4:18–19; cf. Heb 11:11) and God treated Abraham's trust as a kinship bond. Within Jewish ideology, originating from man's very inception (Gen 2:7), Spirit is the origin and creative power of *life*. Paul, therefore, understands the miraculous birth of Isaac from his parents dead reproductive systems, as birth according to Spirit (Gal 4:29). Furthermore, he treated birth according to Spirit as the substantive element of rectification by faith. Once life is understood as the power with which dead things are made alive

7. Hafemann, *Suffering and the Spirit*, 213.
8. This thread runs through Romans 5–8, Galatians 3–4 and 2 Corinthians 3–5.
9. Gal 6:2.
10. Gal 5:18.

(Rom 4:17), Paul could say that the heir of this promise is Messiah (Gal 3:16). He could assert this because he encountered the resurrected Messiah, whom God had imbued with new life after the crucifixion—God had raised him from the dead (Gal 1:1). *The risen life of Messiah is mediated by Spirit to those with faith in Messiah—for, just as Abraham had faith in the God who revivifies, to have faith in the risen Messiah is indicative of the same paradigm.* God treats this faith as kinship bond, so those with faith in Christ are both Abraham's seed and sons of God (Gal 3:6-9, 26-29; 4:6). Paul saw prophetic validation for the paradigm that life results from faith in Hab 2:4.

This reading of Galatians takes a different direction from other readings in the following ways. Firstly, it foregrounds resurrection as pivotal for understanding Galatians rather than treating it as background noise in the letter, with the implicit assumption that Paul, his readers and his opponents simply agreed upon it. This idea is seen in the second notion broadly missed in scholarship—rectification is Jesus' risen life mediated by Spirit to believers. Galatians is, therefore, undergirded by a thoroughgoing Spirit-life soteriology. Thirdly, "life" is what connects the blessing of Abraham and the promise of Spirit, as seen in the birth of Isaac. The birth of Isaac is the miracle of the God who makes alive; with this in mind, Paul is able to (a) treat the "life" of Ezekiel's restoration prophecy and the life from faith in Habakkuk 2 as premonitions of the risen life of Jesus and (b) establish that Messiah is the sole heir of the Abrahamic promise. It is this life that makes sons of Abraham after the order of Isaac. Fourthly, the narrative of Ezekiel 37—Spirit bringing the people of God to life (with Isaac as type)—is the key narrative backdrop for Galatians. This is the thing that the Law cannot do.

Bibliography

Abegg, Martin G. "4QMMT C 27, 31 and 'Works Righteousness.'" *Dead Sea Discoveries* 6.2 (1999) 139–47.

Adams, Edward. *Constructing the World: A Study in Paul's Cosmological Language.* Edinburgh: T&T Clark, 2000.

———. "Paul's Story of God and Creation." In *Narrative Dynamics in Paul: A Critical Assessment,* edited by Bruce W. Longenecker, 19–43. Louisville: Westminster John Knox, 2002.

Adeyemi, Femi. "The New Covenant Law and the Law of Christ." *BibSac* 163 (2006) 438–52.

———. "What is the New Covenant 'Law' in Jeremiah 31:33?" *BibSac* 163 (2006) 312–21.

Aguilar Chiu, J. E. "Justification and the Spirit in Paul: Is there a Relationship?" *AnBib* 165 (2007) 357–78.

Alexander, T. D. "Jonah and Genre." *TynBul* 36 (1985) 35–59.

Allison, Dale. *Resurrecting Jesus: The Earliest Christian Tradition and Its Interpreters.* New York: T. & T. Clark, 2005.

Anderson, Jr. R. Dean. *Ancient Rhetorical Theory and Paul.* Kampen: Pharos, 1996.

Arichea, Jr. Daniel C., and Eugene A. Nida. *Galatians: A Translator's Handbook on Paul's Letter to the Galatians.* New York: United Bible Societies, 1976.

Armerding, C. E. *Habakkuk.* Grand Rapids: Zondervan, 1985.

Arndt, William F., et al. *A Greek-English Lexicon of the New Testament and other Early Christian Literature.* Chicago: University of Chicago Press, 2000.

Arnold, Clinton E. "Returning to the Domain of the Powers: 'Stoicheia' as Evil Spirits in Galatians 4:3, 9". *NovT* 38 (1996) 55–75.

Aune, Daivd E. *The New Testament in Its Environment.* Philadelphia, PA: Westminster, 1987.

———. *The Westminster Dictionary of New Testament and Early Christian Literature and Rhetoric.* Louisville: Westminster John Knox, 2003.

Bahnsen, Greg L. "The Encounter of Jerusalem with Athens." *Ashland Theological Journal* 13 (1980) 7–40.

Balch, David L, Everett Ferguson, and Wayne A. Meeks. *Greeks, Romans, and Christians: Essays in Honor of Abraham J. Malherbe.* Minneapolis: Augsburg Fortress, 1991.

Barclay, John M. G. "Mirror-Reading a Polemical Letter: Galatians as a Test Case." *JSNT* 31 (1987) 73–93.

———. *Obeying the Truth: A Study of Paul's Ethics in Galatians.* Edinburgh: T. & T. Clark, 1988.

———. *Paul & the Gift.* Grand Rapids: William B Eerdmans, 2015.

———. "Paul and the Law: Observations on Some Recent Debates." *Themelios* 12 (1986) 5–15.

Barrett, C. K. *A Commentary on the Epistle to the Romans.* New York: Harper & Row, 1957.

———. "New Testament Eschatology." *SJT* 6.2 (1953) 136–55.

Barry, John D. *The Resurrected Servant in Isaiah.* Colorado Springs: Paternoster, 2010.

Bayes, Jonathan F. *The Weakness of the Law: God's Law and the Christian in New Testament Perspective.* Milton Keynes: Paternoster, 2000.

Beale, Gregory K. *A New Testament Biblical Theology: The Unfolding of the Old Testament in the New.* Grand Rapids: Baker Academic, 2011.

———. "The Old Testament Background of Paul's Reference to 'the Fruit of the Spirit' in Galatians 5:22." *BBR* 15.1 (2005) 1–38.

Beare, Francis W. *A Commentary on the Epistle to the Philippians.* New York: Harper Collins College Division, 1959.

Berchman, R. M. "Galatians 1:1–5: Paul and Greco-Roman Rhetoric." In *The Galatians Debate: Contemporary Issues in Rhetorical and Historical Interpretation*, edited by Mark D. Nanos, 60–72. Peabody, MA: Hendrickson, 2002.

Bertone, John A. *The Law of the Spirit: Experience of the Spirit and Displacement of the Law in Romans 8:1–16.* New York: Peter Lang, 2005.

Best, E. *One Body in Christ: A Study in the Relationship of the Church to Christ in the Epistles of the Apostle Paul.* London: SPCK, 1955.

Betz, Hans D. *Galatians: A Commentary on Paul's Letter to the Churches in Galatia.* Philadelphia: Fortress, 1979.

———. "The Literary Composition and Function of Galatians." In *The Galatians Debate: Contemporary Issues in Rhetorical and Historical Interpretation*, edited by Mark D. Nanos, 3–28. Peabody, MA: Hendrickson, 2002.

———. Review of *Dying and Rising with Christ: A Study in Pauline Theology*, by Robert C. Tannehill. *JBL* 86.3 (1967) 349–51.

Beyeler, Lisa. "Jeremiah's New Exodus in Galatians" Online: http://www.leithart.com/pdf/Beyeler_Galatians_FinalPaperREVISED_2009_0322.pdf.

Beyerlin, Walter. *We are like Dreamers: Studies in Psalm 126.* Edinburgh: T. & T. Clark, 1982.

Bigger, Stephen F. "The Family Laws of Leviticus 18 in Their Setting." *JBL* 98.2 (1979) 187–203.

Bird, Michael F. "'Raised for Our Justification': A Fresh Look at Romans 4:25." *Colloquium: Australian and New Zealand Theological Review* 35.1 (2003) 31–46.

———. *The Saving Righteousness of God: Studies on Paul, Justification and the New Perspective.* Eugene: Wipf and Stock, 2007.

———. "Thoughts on Gal. 1:4." In *Euangelion: A Post-Post-Modern Blog on Scripture, Faith and Following Jesus.* Online: http://www.patheos.com/blogs/euangelion/2011/12/thoughts-on-gal-14/.

Black, David A. "Discourse Analysis, Synoptic Criticism and Markan Grammar: Some Methodological Considerations." In *Linguistics and New Testament Interpretation: Essays on Discourse Analysis,* edited by David A. Black, Katherine G. L. Barnwell, and Stephen L. Levinsohn, 90–99. Nashville: Broadman, 1992.

Block, Daniel I. "Beyond the Grave: Ezekiel's Vision of Death and Afterlife." In *BBR* 2 (1992) 113–41.

———. *The Book of Ezekiel Chapters 25–48.* Grand Rapids: Eerdmans, 1998.

———. "The Prophet of the Spirit: The Use of *RWH* in the Book of Ezekiel." In *JETS* 32.1 (1989) 27–49.

Boakye, Andrew. Review of *The Spirit and the Restoration of Israel: New Exodus and New Creation Motifs in Galatians,* by Rodrigo Morlales. *EvQ* 84.1 (2012) 83.

Bonneau, Normand. "The Logic of Paul's Argument on the Curse of the Law in Galatians 3:10–14." *NovT* 39.1 (1997) 60–80.

Bowers, W. P. "Mission." In *The Dictionary of Paul and His Letters,* edited by Gerald F. Hawthorne, Ralph P. Martin and Daniel Reid, 608–19. Downers Grove, IL: InterVarsity, 1993.

Boyarin, Daniel A. *A Radical Jew: Paul and the Politics of Identity.* Berkeley: University of California Press, 1997.

Braswell, Joseph P. "The Blessing of Abraham Versus the Curse of the Law: Another Look at Gal 3:10–13." *WTJ* 53.1 (1991) 73–91.

Brondos, David A. *Paul on the Cross: Reconstructing the Apostle's Story of Redemption.* Minneapolis: Fortress, 2006.

Bronner, Leila L. "The Resurrection Motif in the Hebrew Bible: Allusions or Illusions?" *Jewish Bible Quarterly* 30.3 (2002) 143–54.

Bronson David B. "Paul, Galatians and Jerusalem." *JAAR* 35.2 (1967) 119–28.

Brooke, George J. "Shared Intertextual Interpretations in the Dead Sea Scrolls and the New Testament." *International Symposium on Biblical Perspectives: Early Use and Interpretation of the Bible in Light of the Dead Sea Scrolls.* Online: http://orion.mscc.huji.ac.il.

Brownlee, William H. *Ezekiel 1–19.* Waco, TX: Word Books, 1986.

Bruce, F. F. "The Curse of the Law." In *Paul and Paulinism. Essays in Honour of C.K. Barrett,* edited by Morna D. Hooker and Stephen G. Wilson, 27–36. London: SPCK, 1982.

———. "Galatian Problems 4: The Date of the Epistle." *Bulletin of the John Rylands Library Manchester* 54.2 (1972) 250–67.

———. *Galatians: A Commentary on the Greek Text.* Grand Rapids: Eerdmans, 1982.

———. *Paul: Apostle of the Free Spirit.* Exeter: Paternoster, 1977.

Brueggemann, Walter. *To Build, To Plant: A Commentary on Jeremiah 26–52.* Grand Rapids: Eerdmans, 1991.

Bryant, Robert A. *The Risen Crucified Christ in Galatians.* Atlanta: Society of Biblical Literature, 2001.

Bullock, C. Hassell "Ezekiel, Bridge Between the Testaments." *JETS* 25.1 (1982) 23–31.

Bundrick, David R. "Ta Stoicheia Tou Kosmou in (Gal. 4:3)." *JETS* 34.3 (1991) 353–64.

Burke, Trevor J. *Adopted Into God's Family: Exploring a Pauline Metaphor.* Downers Grove, IL: InterVarsity, 2006.

Burton, Ernest De Witt. *A Critical and Exegetical Commentary on the Epistle to the Galatians.* Edinburgh: T. & T. Clark, 1921.

Byrne, Brendan. *Sons of God, Seed of Abraham: A Study of the Sonship of God of All Christians in Paul Against the Jewish Background*. Rome: Biblical Institute, 1979.

Callan, Terrance. *Dying and Rising With Christ: The Theology of Paul the Apostle*. Mahwah, NJ: Paulist, 2006.

———. "Pauline Midrash: The Exegetical Background of Gal 3:19b." *JBL* 99 (1980) 549–67.

Calvert Koyzis, Nancy J. *Paul, Monotheism and the People of God: The Significance of Abraham Traditions for Early Judaism and Christianity*. London: T. & T. Clark International, 2004.

Calvin, John. *Commentaries on the Book of the Prophet Jeremiah and Lamentations*. Grand Rapids: Eerdmans, 1950.

Campbell, Douglas A. *The Deliverance of God: An Apocalyptic Rereading of Justification in Paul*. Grand Rapids: Eerdmans, 2009.

———. "Romans 1:17: A *Crux Interpretum* for the ΠΙΣΤΙΣ ΧΡΙΣΤΟΥ Dispute." *JBL* 113 (1994) 265–85.

Caneday, Ardel. "Redeemed from the 'Curse of the Law': The Use of Deut. 21:22–23 in Gal. 3:13." *Trinity Journal* 10 (1989) 185–209.

Carter, Warren. "Paul and the Roman Empire: Recent Perspectives." In *Paul Unbound: Other Perspectives on the Apostle*, edited by Mark D. Given, 7–26. Peabody, MA: Hendrickson, 2010.

Charlesworth, James H. "Challenging the Consensus Communis Regarding Qumran Messianism (1QS, 4QS, MSS)." In *Qumran-Messianism: Studies on the Messianic Expectations in the Dead Sea Scrolls*, edited by James H. Charlesworth, Hermann Lichtenberger and Gerbern S. Oegema, 120–34. Tübingen: Mohr Siebeck, 1998.

Chessnut, Randall D. *From Death to Life: Conversion in Joseph and Aseneth*. Sheffiled: Sheffiled Academic, 1995.

Choi, Hung-Sik. "'The Truth of the Gospel': An Exegetical and Theological Study of the Antitheses in Galatians 5.2–6". PhD diss., University of Durham, 2002.

Choi, S. "PISTIS in Galatians 3:5–6: Neglected Evidence for the Faithfulness of Christ." *JBL* 124 (2005) 467–90.

Churchill, Timothy W. R. *Divine Initiative and the Christology of the Damascus Road Encounter*. Eugene: Pickwick, 2010.

Ciampa, Roy E. *The Presence and Function of Scripture in Galatians 1 and 2*. Tübingen: Mohr Siebeck, 1998.

Clark, David J. and Howard A. Hatton. *A Translator's Handbook on the Book of Habakkuk*. New York: United Bible Societies, 1989.

Clifford, Richard J. "The Exodus in the Christian Bible: The Case for 'Figural' Reading." *TS* 63 (2002) 345–61.

Clifton Black II, C. "Pauline Perspectives on Death in Romans 5–8." *JBL* 103.3 (1984) 413–33.

Collins, John J. *Daniel: A Critical & Historical Commentary on the Bible*. Minneapolis: Fortress, 1993.

———. "Jesus, Messianism and the Dead Sea Scrolls." In *Qumran-Messianism: Studies on the Messianic Expectations in the Dead Sea Scrolls*, edited by James H. Charlesworth, Hermann Lichtenberger, and Gerbern S. Oegema, 100–19. Tübingen: Mohr Siebeck, 1998.

———. *The Sceptre and the Star: Jewish Messianism in Light of the Dead Sea Scrolls*. New York: Doubleday, 1995.

Cook, David. "The Prescript as Programme in Galatians." *JTS* 43.2 (1992) 511–19.

Cosgrove, Charles H. *The Cross and the Spirit: A Study in the Argument and Theology of Galatians*. Georgia: Mercer University Press, 1988.

Cranfield, C. E. B. "The Works of the Law in the Epistle to the Romans." *JSNT* 43 (1991) 89–101.

Crawford, Sidnie White. "Reading Deuteronomy in the Second Temple Period." In *Reading the Present in the Qumran Library: The Perception of the Contemporary by Means of Scriptural Interpretations*, edited by Kristin De Troyer and Armin Lange, 127–40. Leiden & Boston: Brill, 2005.

Dabney, D. Lyle. "Justified by the Spirit: Soteriological Reflections on the Resurrection." *International Journal of Systematic Theology* 3.1 (2001) 46–69.

Dahl, Nils A "The Future of Israel." In *Studies in Paul: Theology for the Early Christian Mission*, edited by N. A. Dahl, 137–58. Minneapolis: Fortress, 1977.

Das, A. Andrew. *Galatians*. St. Louis: Concordia, 2014.

Davies, W. D. "Paul: From the Jewish Point of View." In *The Cambridge History of Judaism. Volume Three: The Early Roman Period*, edited by William Horbury, W. D. Davies, and John Sturdy, 678–730. Cambridge: Cambridge University Press, 1999.

Davis, Anne K. "Israel's Inheritance: Birth-right of the Firstborn Son." In *Chafer Theological Seminary Journal* 13 (2008) 79–94

De Boer, Martinus C. *Galatians: A Commentary*. Louisville: Westminster John Knox Press, 2011.

deSilva, David A. *Galatians: A Handbook on the Greek Text*. Waco: Baylor University Press, 2014.

Dinkler, E. "The Historical and the Eschatological Israel in Romans Chapters 9–11: A Contribution to the Problem of Pre-Destination and Individual Responsibility." *Jrel* 36.2 (1956) 109–27.

Donaldson, Terrance. *Paul and the Gentiles. Remapping the Apostle's Convictional World*. Minneapolis: Fortress, 1997.

Downing, F. Gerald, *Cynics, Paul and the Pauline Churches*. London: Routledge, 1998.

Drane, John. *Paul Libertine or Legalist?* London: SPCK, 1975.

Dunn, James D. G. "4QMMT and Galatians." *NTS* 43 (1997) 147–53.

———. *The Epistle to the Galatians*. London: A & C Black, 1993.

———. "In Quest of Paul's Theology: Retrospect and Prospect." In *Pauline Theology Volume IV: Looking Back, Pressing On*, edited by Jouette M. Bassler, E. Elizabeth Johnson and David M. Hay, 95–115. Atlanta: Scholars, 1997.

———. *Jesus, Paul and the Law: Studies in Mark and Galatians*. Louisville: John Knox, 1990.

———. "The Letter Kills, but the Spirit gives Life (2 Cor. 3:6)." *Pnuema* 35.2 (2013) 163–79.

———. *Romans 9–16*. Waco, TX: Word, 1988.

———. "Works of the Law and the Curse of the Law (Galatians 3:10–14)." *NTS* 31 (1985) 523–42.

Dupont, Jaques. "The Conversion of Paul, and Its Influence on His Understanding of Salvation by Faith." In *Apostolic History and the Gospel: Biblical and Historical Essays Presented to F. F. Bruce*, edited by W. Ward Gasque and Ralph P Martin, 176–94. Exeter: Paternoster, 1970.

Easley, Kendell H. *User-Friendly Greek: A Common Sense Approach to the Greek New Testament*. Nashville: Broadman & Holman, 1994.

Easter, M. C. "The Pistis Christou Debate: Main Arguments and Responses in Summary." *CBR* 9 (2010) 33–47.

Eastman, Susan. "Israel and the Mercy of God: A Re-reading of Galatians 6.16 and Romans 9–11." *NTS* 56 (2010) 367–95.

Elias, Jacob W. *Remember the Future: The Pastoral Theology of Paul the Apostle.* Harrisonburg, VA: Herald, 2006.

Elledge, Casey D. "Resurrection of the Dead: Exploring Our Earliest Evidence Today." In *Resurrection: The Origin And Future of a Biblical Doctrine,* edited by James H. Charlesworth, et al., 32–52. New York: T. & T. Clark, 2006.

Elliott, Neil. "The Anti-Imperial Message of the Cross." In *Paul and Empire: Religion and Power in Roman Imperial Society,* edited by Richard A. Horsley, 167–83. Harrisburg, PA: Trinity International, 1997.

———. *The Arrogance of Nations: Reading Romans in the Shadow of Empire.* Minneapolis: Fortress, 2008.

Emmrich, Martin. *Pneumatological Concepts in the Epistle to the Hebrews: Amtscharisma, Prophet and Guide of the Eschatological Exodus.* Lanham, MD: University Press of America, 2003.

Engberg-Pedersen, Troels. *Paul and the Stoics.* Edinburgh: T. & T. Clark, 2000.

Esler, Philip F. *Galatians.* London: Rouledge, 1998.

Evans, Craig A. "Aspects of Exile and Restoration in the Proclamation of Jesus and the Gospels." In *Exile: Old Testament, Jewish and Christian Conceptions* edited by James M. Scott, 299–328. Leiden: Brill, 1997.

———. "Messianic Hopes and Messianic Figures in Late Antiquity." In *Journal of Greco-Roman Christianity and Judaism* 3 (2006) 9–40.

Everts, J. M. "Conversion and Call of Paul." In *Dictionary of Paul and His Letters,* edited by Gerald F. Hawthorne, Ralph P. Martin, Daniel G. Reid, 156–63. Downers Grove, IL: InterVarsity, 1993.

Fairbairn, Patrick. *Ezekiel, and the Book of His Prophecy: An Exposition.* Edinburgh: T. & T. Clark, 1855.

Fee, Gordon D. *Galatians: Pentecostal Commentary.* Dorset: Deo, 2007.

———. *God's Empowering Presence: The Holy Spirit in the Lettes of Paul.* Peabody, MA: Hendrickson, 1994.

Finlan, Stephen F. "Can We Speak of Theosis in Paul?" In *Partakers of the Divine Nature: The History and Development of Deification in the Christian Traditions,* edited by Michael J. Christensen and Jeffrey Wittung, 68–80. Grand Rapids: Baker Academic, 2007.

Fitzmyer, Joseph. "Qumran and the Interpolated Paragraph in 2 Cor. 6:14–7:1." *The CBQ* 23 (1962) 271–80.

———. *Romans: A New Translation with Introduction and Commentary.* New York: Doubleday, 1993.

Flesher, Leann Snow. "Psalm 126." *Interpretation* 60 (2006) 434–36.

Flusser, David. *Judaism of the Second Temple Period: Qumran and Apocalypticism.* Grand Rapids: Eerdmans, 2007.

Forbes, C. "Comparison, Self-Praise and Irony: Paul's Boasting and the Conventions of Hellenistic Rhetoric." *NTS* 32 (1986) 1–30.

Frey, Jörg. "The Jewishness of Paul." In *Paul: Life Setting, Work, Letters,* edited by Oda Wischmeyer, 57–96. London: T. & T. Clark, 2012.

Frick, Peter. *Paul in the Grip of the Philosophers: The Apostle and Contemporary Continental Philosophy.* Minneapolis: Fortress, 2013.
Fuller, Michael E. *The Restoration of Israel: Israel's Re-gathering and the Fate of the Nations in Early Jewish Literature and Luke-Acts.* Berlin: de Gruyter, 2006.
Fung, Ronald Y. K. *The Epistle to the Galatians.* Grand Rapids: Eerdmans, 1988.
Gaffin, Richard B. "Life-Giving Spirit: Probing the Centre of Paul's Pneumatology." *JETS* 41 (1998) 573–89.
———. "Redemption and Resurrection: An Exercise in Biblical-Systematic Theology." *Themelios* 27.2 (2002) 16–31.
———. *Resurrection and Redemption: A Study in Paul's Soteriology.* Phillipsburg, NJ: P&R, 1987.
Gage, Warren A. *Milestones to Emmaus: The Third Day Resurrection in the Old Testament.* Fort Lauderdale, FL: Warren A. Gage, 2011.
Gallant, Tim. "What Saint Paul Should Have Said: Is Galatians a Polemic Against Legalism?" In *Rabbi Saul.Com: Studies in Paul and Second Temple Judaism.* Online: http://www.rabbisaul.com/articles/shouldhave.php.
Garland, David. E. *2 Corinthians.* Nashville: Broadman & Holman, 1999.
Garlington, Don. *An Exposition of Galatians: A Reading from the New Perspective.* Eugene, OR: Wipf and Stock, 2007.
Garrett, Duane A. "Veiled Hearts: The Translation and Interpretation of 2 Corinthians 3." *JETS* 53.4 (2010) 729–72.
Gathercole, Simon J. "Torah, Life and Salvation: Leviticus 18:5 in Early Judaism and the New Testament." In *From Prophecy to Testament: The Function of the Old Testament in the New,* edited by Craig A. Evans, 126–45. Peabody, MA: Hendrickson, 2004.
———. *Where is Boasting? Early Jewish Soteriology and Paul's Response in Romans 1–5.* Grand Rapids: Eerdmans, 2002.
Gaventa, Beverley R. "Galatians 1 and 2: Autobiography as Paradigm." *NovT* 28.4 (1986) 309–26.
Gilbert, George H. "The Hellenization of the Jews between 334 B. C. and 70 A. D." *The American Journal of Theology* 13.4 (1909) 520–40.
Girard, René. *I See Satan Fall Like Lightning.* New York: Orbis, 2001.
Gleason, Randall C. "Paul's Covenantal Contrasts in 2 Corinthians 3:1–11." *BibSac* 154 (1997) 61–79.
Goodrich, John K. "Guardians, not Taskmasters: The Cultural Resonances of Paul's Metaphor." *JSNT* 32 (2010) 251–84.
Gorman, Michael J. *Death of the Messiah and the Birth of the New Covenant: A (Not-So) New Model of the Atonement.* Eugene: Cascade, 2014.
———. *Inhabiting the Cruciform God: Kenosis, Justification, and Theosis in Paul's Narrative Soteriology.* Grand Rapids: Eerdmans, 2009.
Gorman, Robert. "Poets, Playwrights, and the Politics of Exile and Asylum in Ancient Greece and Rome." *International Journal of Refugee Law* 6.3 (1994) 402–24.
Grassi, J. A. "Ezekiel 37: 1–14 and the New Testament." *NTS* 11 (1965) 162–164
Grayston, Kenneth. *Dying, We Live: A New Enquiry into the Death of Christ in the New Testament.* London: Darton, Longman and Todd, 1990.
Grebe, Sabine. "Why Did Ovid Associate His Exile with a Living Death?" *Classical World* 103.4 (2010) 491–509.
Gregerman, Adam. "The Lack of Evidence for a Jewish Christian Countermission in Galatia." *Studies in Jewish Christian Relations* 4 (2009) 1–24.

Grindheim, Sigurd. "Apostate Turned Prophet: Paul's Prophetic Self-Understanding and Prophetic Hermeneutic with Special Reference to Galatians 3.10–12." *NTS* 53.4 (2007) 545–65.

———. "The Law Kills but the Gospel Gives Life: The Letter-Spirit Dualism in 2 Corinthians 3.5–18." *JSNT* 84 (2001) 97–115.

———. "Not Salvation History, but Salvation Territory: The Main Subject Matter of Galatians." *NTS* 59 (2013) 91–108.

———. Review of *The Spirit and the Restoration of Israel: New Exodus and New Creation Motifs in Galatians*, by Rodrigo Morlaes. *Review of Biblical Literature*, March 2012. Online: http://www.bookreviews.org/pdf/7939_8797.pdf.http://www.bookreviews.org/pdf/7939_8797.pdf.

Grisanti, Michael A. "Israel's Mission to the Nations in Isaiah 40–55: An Update." *The Master's Seminary Journal* 9.1 (1998) 39–61.

Guthrie, Donald. *Galatians*. London: Thomas Nelson and Sons, 1969.

Hafemann, Scott J. "Paul and the Exile of Israel in Galatians 3–4." In *Exile: Old Testament, Jewish and Christian Conceptions*, edited by James M. Scott, 329–71. Leiden: Brill, 1997.

———. *Paul, Moses, and the History of Israel: The Letter/Spirit Contrast and the Argument from Scripture in 2 Corinthians 3*. Waynesboro: Paternoster, 2005.

———. *Suffering and the Spirit: An Exegetical Study of 2 Cor. 2:14–3:3 within the Context of the Corinthian Correspondence*. Tübingen: Mohr Siebeck, 1986.

Hardin, Justin K. *Galatians and the Imperial Cult: A Critical Analysis of the First-Century Social Context of Paul's Letter*. Tübingen: Mohr Siebeck, 2008.

Harink, Douglas. *Paul Among the Postliberals: Pauline Theology Beyond Christendom and Modernity*. Grand Rapids: Brazos, 2003.

———. "Setting it Right." *The Christian Century* 122.12 (2005) 20–25.

Harmon, Matthew. *She Must and Shall Go Free: Paul's Isaianic Gospel in Galatians*. Berlin: Walter de Gruyter GmbH, 2010.

Harris, Martin J. *The Second Epistle to the Corinthians: A Commentary on the Greek Text*. Grand Rapids: Eerdmans, 2005.

Harrison, J.R. "Why did Josephus and Paul Refuse to Circumcise?" *Pacifica* 17 (2004) 137–58.

Harvey, John D. "The 'with Christ' Motif in Paul's Thought." *JETS* 35.3 (1992) 329–40.

Hayes, Elizabeth R. "The Influence of Ezekiel 37 on 2 Corinthians 6:14–7:1." In *The Book of Ezekiel and Its Influence*, edited by Henk Jan de Jonge and Johannes Tromp, 123–36. Hampshire: Ashgate, 2007.

Hays, Richard B. "Christology and Ethics in Galatians: The Law of Christ." *CBQ* 49 (1987) 268–90.

———. "Crucified with Christ: A Synthesis of the Theology of 1 and 2 Thessalonians, Philemon, Philippians, and Galatians." In *Pauline Theology, Volume I: Thessalonians, Philippians, Galatians, Philemon*, edited by Jouette M. Bassler, 227–46. Minneapolis: Fortress, 1994.

———. *Echoes of Scripture in the Letters of Paul*. New Haven, CT: Yale University Press, 1989.

———. *The Faith of Jesus Christ: The Narrative Substructure of Galatians 3:1—4:11*. Grand Rapids: Eerdmans, 1983.

———. "Psalm 143 and the Logic of Romans 3." *JBL* 99.1 (1980) 107–15.

Herczeg, Rabbi Yisrael I.Z. *Rashi: Commentary on the Torah Vol. 2.* Brooklyn, NY: Mesorah, 1999.
Hester, James D. "Placing the Blame: The Presence of Epideictic in Galatians 1 and 2." In *Persuasive Artistry: Studies in New Testament Rhetoric*, edited by G. A. Kennedy, 281–307. Sheffield: JSOT 1991.
Holladay, William L. "The Background of Jeremiah's Self-Understanding." *JBL* 83 (1964) 53–164.
Hooker, Morna. "ΠΙΣΤΙΣ ΧΡΙΣΤΟΥ." *NTS* 35 (1989) 321–42.
Horne, Charles M. "The Meaning of the Phrase 'And Thus All Israel will be Saved' (Romans 11:26)." *JETS* 21.4 (1978) 329–34.
Hubbard, Moyer V. *New Creation in Paul's Letters and Thought.* Cambridge: Cambridge University Press, 2002.
Hubing, J. S. *Crucifixion and New Creation: The Contribution of Galatians 6:11–17 to an Understanding of the Situation and Message of Galatians.* Chicago: Pro Quest, 2007.
Hübner, Hans. *Law in Paul's Thought.* Edinburgh: T. & T. Clark, 1984.
Hultgren, Stephen J. "2 Cor. 6.14–7.1 and Rev. 21.3–8: Evidence for the Ephesian Redaction of 2 Corinthians." *NTS* 49 (2003) 39–56.
Hunn, Debbie. "ΠΙΣΤΙΣ ΧΡΙΣΤΟΥ in Galatians 2:16: Clarification from 3:1–6." *TynBul* 57.1 (2006) 23–33.
Hutson, Christopher R. "The Cross as Canon: Galatians 6.16." *Leaven* Vol. 12.1 (2004) 48–53.
Ianziti, Gary. "A Life in Politics: Leonardo Bruni's Cicero." *Journal of the History of Ideas* 61.1 (2000) 39–58.
Irons, Charles Lee. *The Righteousness of God: A Lexical Examination of the Covenant-Faithfulness Interpretation.* Tübingen: Mohr Siebeck, 2015.
Jackson, T. Ryan. *New Creation in Paul's Letters: A Study of the Historical and Social Setting.* Tübingen: Mohr Siebeck, 2010.
James, Montague R. *The Apocryphal New Testament: Being the Apocryphal Gospels, Acts, Epistles, and Apocalypses.* Oxford: Clarendon, 1924.
Jassen, Alex P. "Religion in the Dead Sea Scrolls." *Religion Compass* 1.1 (2007) 1–25.
Jenkins, Philip. "The Next Christendom: The Coming of Global Christianity." *The Religious Educator* 8.3 (2007) 113–25.
Jervis, L. Ann. "Galatians 3:19–25 as an Argument for God's Faithfulness: Reading Paul's Rhetoric in Light of His Strategy." *Word and World* 20.3 (2000) 281–89.
Jewett, Robert. "The Agitators and the Galatian Congregation." *NTS* 17 (1971) 198–212.
Jobes, Karen. H. "Jerusalem, Our Mother: Metalepsis and Intertextuality in Galatians 4:21–31." *WTJ* 55 (1993) 299–320.
Johnson, S.L. "Paul and 'The Israel of God': An Exegetical and Eschatological Case-Study." In *Essays in Honour of J. Dwight Pentecost*, edited by Stanley D. Toussaint and Charles H. Dyer, 181–96. Chicago: Moody, 1986.
Johnson Hodge, Caroline. *If Sons, Then Heirs: A Study of Kinship and Ethnicity in the Letters of Paul.* Oxford: Oxford University Press, 2007.
Joyce, Paul M. *Divine Initiative and Human Response in Ezekiel.* Sheffield: Almond, 1989.
Judge, E. A. "The Decrees of Caesar at Thessalonica." *Reformed Theological Review* 30 (1971) 71–78.

Juncker, Günther H. "Children of Promise: Spiritual Paternity and Patriarch Typology in Galatians and Romans." *BBR* 17.1 (2007) 131–60.

Kahl, Brigitte. *Galatians Re-imagined: Reading with the Eyes of the Vanquished.* Minneapolis: Fortress, 2010.

Kahn, Yoel. *The Three Blessings: Boundaries, Censorship, and Identity in Jewish Liturgy.* New York: Oxford University Press, 2011.

Kaiser, Walter C. "Leviticus 18:5 and Paul: Do This and You Shall Live (Eternally?)." *JETS* 14 (1971) 19–28.

Käsemann, Ernst. "The Righteousness of God in Paul." In *NT Questions of Today*, edited by Ernst Käsemann, 168–82. Philadelphia: Fortress, 1969.

Keesmaat, Sylvia C. "Paul and His Story: Exodus and Tradition in Galatians." *Biblical Theology* 18.1 (1996) 138–61.

Keil, Carl F. and Delitzsch, Franz. *Commentary on the Old Testament.* Peabody, MA: Hendrickson, 1996.

Kennedy, George A. *New Testament Interpretation through Rhetorical Criticism.* Chapel Hill: University of North Carolina Press, 1984.

Kern, Philip H. *Rhetoric and Galatians: Assessing an Approach to Paul's Epistle.* New York: Cambridge University Press, 1998.

Kessler, Edward. *Bound by the Bible: Jews, Christians and the Sacrifice of Isaac.* Cambridge: Cambridge University Press, 2004.

Kim, J. H. *The City in Isaiah 24–27: A Theological Interpretation in Terms of Judgment and Salvation.* Stellenbosch: University of Stellenbosch Press, 2008.

———. "The Concept of Atonement in the Qumran Literature and the New Covenant." *Journal of Greco-Roman Christianity & Judaism* 7 (2010) 98–111.

———. *The Significance of Clothing Imagery in the Pauline Corpus.* New York: T. & T. Clark International, 2004.

Kim, Seyoon. *The Origin of Paul's Gospel.* Grand Rapids: Eerdmans, 1982.

Kirk, J. R. Daniel. "Appointed Son(s) An Exegetical Note on Romans 1:4 and 8:29." *BBR* 14.2 (2004) 241–41.

———. *Unlocking Romans: Resurrection and the Justification of God.* Grand Rapids: Eerdmans, 2008.

Kline, Meredith G. *The Holy Spirit as Covenant Witness.* Philadelphia: Westminster Theological Seminary, 1972.

Knibb, M. A. "Life and Death in the Old Testament." In *The World of Ancient Israel: Social, Anthropological and Political Perspectives*, edited by Ronald E. Clements, 395–415. Cambridge: Cambridge University Press, 1989.

Kohn, Risa Levitt. *A New Heart and a New Soul: Ezekiel, the Exile and the Torah.* Sheffield: Sheffield Academic Press, 2002.

Koptak, Paul D. "Rhetorical Identification in Paul's Autobiographical Narrative." *JSNT* 40 (1990) 97–113.

Köstenberger, A. J. 'The Identity of ΙΣΡΑΗΛ ΤΟΥ ΘΕΟΥ in Gal. 6:16." Online: http://www.biblicalfoundations.org/pdf/galatians_6.pdf.

Kuck, David W. "Each Will Bear His Own Burden: Paul's Creative Use of An Apocalyptic Motif." *NTS* 40 (1994) 289–97.

Kushner, Mario. "Slavery and Freedom in the Epistle to the Galatians." *KAIROS—Evangelical Journal of Theology* 5.2 (2011) 271–89.

Kwok, Hon Lee. "Use of Isaiah in the Pauline Letters: with Special Reference to his Self-Conception of being an Apostle to the Gentiles." PhD diss., University of Edinburgh, 2009.
Kwon, Yon-Gyong. *Eschatology in Galatians: Rethinking Paul's Response to the Crisis in Galatia.* Tübingen: Mohr Siebeck, 2004.
Lakoff, George, and Mark Johnson. *Metaphors We Live By.* Chicago, IL: Chicago University Press, 1980.
Lee, Chee-Chiew. *The Blessing of Abraham, the Spirit and Justification in Galatians.* Eugene, OR: Wipf and Stock, 2013.
Lee, Jae Hyun. "Against Richard B. Hays's 'Faith of Jesus Christ.'" *Journal of Greco-Roman Christianity and Judaism* 5 (2008) 51–80.
Leithart, Peter J. "Flesh in Galatians." *Leithart.* November 19, 2010. Online: http://www.leithart.com/2010/11/09/flesh-in-galatians/.
Lemke, Jay L. "Semantics and Social Values." *Word* 40 (1989) 37–50.
Levenson, Jon D. *Resurrection and the Restoration of Israel: The Ultimate Victory of the God of Life.* New Haven, CT: Yale University Press, 2006.
Levison, John R. *The Spirit in First-Century Judaism.* New York: Brill, 1997.
Lewis, John G. *Looking for Life: the Role of "Theo-Ethical Reasoning" in Paul's Religion.* New York: T. & T. Clark International, 2005.
Liantonio, R. "Saved By His Life: Resurrection and Justification in Romans." Online: http://www.richardliantonio.com/richardliantonio.com/Projects_files/Saved%20By%20His%20Life%20Draft.pdf Missouri, 2007.
Licona, Michael. *The Resurrection of Jesus: A New Historiographical Approach.* Downers Grove, IL: InterVarsity, 2010.
Lightfoot, Joseph B. *St. Paul's Epistle to the Galatians: A Revised Text with Introduction, Notes, and Dissertations.* London: Macmillan, 1874.
Lincicum, D. "Paul and the Testimonia: Quo Vademus?" *JETS* 51.2 (2008) 297–308.
———. "Paul's Engagement with Deuteronomy: Snapshots and Signposts." *CBR* 7.1 (2008) 37–67.
Longenecker, Bruce W. "Narrative Interest in the Study of Paul: Retrospective and Prospective". In *Narrative Dynamics in Paul: A Critical Assessment,* edited by Bruce W. Longenecker, 3–18. Louisville: Westminster John Knox, 2002.
Longenecker, Richard N. *Galatians.* Dallas, TX: Word, 1990.
Lopez, Davina C. *Apostle to the Conquered: Reimagining Paul's Mission.* Minneapolis: Fortress, 2008.
Loubser, G. M. H. "The Ethic of the Free: A Walk According to the Spirit! A Perspective from Galatians." *Verbum et Ecclesia* 27 (2006) 614–40.
Louw, J. P., and E. A. Nida. *Greek-English Lexicon of the New Testament: Based on Semantic Domains.* New York: United Bible Societies, 1996.
Lührmann, D. *A Continental Commentary: Galatians.* Minneapolis: Fortress, 1992.
Lull, David J. "The Spirit and the Creative Transformation of Human Existence." *JAAR* 47.1 (1979) 39–55.
Luther, Martin. *Commentary on Galatians.* Wheaton, IL: Crossways, 1998.
Maccoby, Hyam. *The Mythmaker: Paul and the Invention of Christianity.* New York: Barnes & Noble, 1998.
Malby, D. S. "Life In The New Creation: The Eschatological Character of Paul's Ministry and Theology in Galatians." Online: http://www.rts.edu/Site/Virtual/Resources/Student_Theses/Mably-Life_in_the_New_Creation.pdf

Malherbe, Abraham J. *Paul and the Popular Philosophers.* Minneapolis: Fortress, 1989.

Manning, Gary T. *Echoes of a Prophet: The Use of Ezekiel in the Gospel of John and in Literature of the Second Temple.* New York: T. & T. Clark International, 2004.

Marshall, I. Howard. *Aspects of the Atonement: Cross and Resurrection in the Reconciling of God and Humanity.* Milton Keynes: Paternoster, 2007.

———. *The Gospel of Luke: A Commentary on the Greek Text.* Exeter: Paternoster, 1978.

Martin, Ralph P. *Reconciliation: A Study of Paul's Theology.* Atlanta: John Knox, 1981.

Martyn, John Louis. "Apocalyptic Antinomies in Paul's Letter to the Galatians." *NTS* 31.3 (1985) 410–24.

———. "The Apocalyptic Gospel in Galatians." *Interpretation* 54 (2000) 246–66.

———. *Galatians: A New Translation with Introduction and Commentary.* New Haven, CT: Yale University Press, 1997.

———. *Theological Issues in the Letters of Paul.* Edinburgh: T. & T. Clark, 1997b.

Maston, Jason. *Divine and Human Agency in Second Temple Judaism and Paul.* Tübingen: Mohr Siebeck, 2010.

Matera, Frank J. *Galatians.* Collegeville, MN: Liturgical, 1992.

———. *God's Saving Grace: A Pauline Theology.* Grand Rapids: Eerdmans, 2012.

McCann, Jr., Clinton. *A Theological Introduction to the Book of Psalms: The Psalms as Torah.* Nashville: Abingdon, 1993.

McCant, Jerry W. *2 Corinthians.* Sheffield: Sheffield University Press, 1999.

McComiskey, D. S. "Exile and the Purpose of Jesus' Parables (Mark 4:10–12; Matt 13:10–17; Luke 8:9–10)." *JETS* 51.1 (2008) 59–85.

McKenzie, Leon. *Pagan Resurrection Myths and the Resurrection of Jesus: A Christian Perspective.* Charlottesville, VA: Bookwrights, 1997.

McKnight, Scot. "The Ego and 'I': Galatians 2:19 in New Perspective." *Word & World* 20.3 (2000) 272–80.

Merkle, Ben L. "Romans 11 and the Future of Ethnic Israel." *JETS* 43.4 (2000) 707–22.

Metzger, Bruce M. *A Textual Commentary on the Greek New Testament.* New York: United Bile Societies, 1994.

Minear, Paul S. "Some Pauline Thoughts on Dying: A Study of 2 Corinthians." In *From Faith to Faith: Essays in Honor of Donald G. Miller on his Seventieth Birthday,* edited by Dikran Y. Hadidian, 91–106. Pittsburgh: Pickwick, 1979.

Mitchell, Margaret M. "Peter's 'Hypocrisy' and Paul's: Two 'Hypocrites' at the Foundation of Earliest Christianity?" *NTS* 58 (2012) 213–34.

Moltmann, Jurgen. *The Spirit of Life: A Universal Affirmation.* Minneapolis: Fortress, 1992.

Moo, Douglas J. "Creation and New Creation." *BBR* 20.1 (2010) 39–60.

———. "Israel and Paul in Romans 7:7–12." *NTS* 32 (1986) 122–35.

———. "Justification in Galatians". In *Understanding the Times: New Testament Studies in the 21st Century: Essays in Honour of D. A. Carson on the Occasion of His 65th Birthday,* edited by Andreas Köstenberger and Richard W. Yarbrough, 160–95. Wheaton, IL: Crossway, 2011.

———. "Paul and the Law in the Last Ten Years." *STJ* 40 (1987) 287–307.

Morales, Rodrigo J. *The Spirit and the Restoration of Israel: New Exodus and New Creation Motifs in Galatians.* Tübingen: Mohr Siebeck, 2010.

———. "The Words of the Luminaries, The Curse of the Law and the Outpouring of the Spirit in Gal. 3:10–14." *Zeitschrift für die neutestamentliche Wissenschaft und die Kunde der älteren Kirche* 100 (2009) 269–77.

Munck, Johannes. *Christ & Israel: An Interpretation of Romans 9–11*. Philadelphia: Fortress, 1967.

Mussner, Franz. *Der Galaterbrief*. Freiburg: Herder, 1974.

Nanos, Mark. *The Irony of Galatians: Paul's Letter in First-Century Context*. Minneapolis: Fortress, 2002.

———. "Paul and Judaism: Why Not Paul's Judaism?" In *Paul Unbound: Other Perspectives on the Apostle*, edited by Mark Given, 117–60. Peabody, MA: Hendrickson, 2010.

Nelson, R. D. "Response to Thomas Römer." In *In Conversation with Thomas Römer. The So-Called Deuteronomistic History: A Sociological, Historical And Literary Introduction*, edited by Raymond F. Person, 36–49. London: T. & T. Clark, 2005.

Newman, Carey C. "Transforming Images of Paul: A Review Essay of Alan Segal, Paul the Convert." *EvQ* 64.1 (1992) 61–74.

Nickelsburg, George W. E. *Resurrection, Immortality and Eternal Life in Intertestamental Judaism and Early Christianity*. Massachusetts: Harvard University Press, 2006.

Nida, Eugene A. "The Role of Context in the Understanding of Discourse." In *Discourse Analysis and the New Testament: Approaches and Results*, edited by Stanley E. Porter & Jeffrey T. Reed, 20–27. Sheffield: Sheffield Academic Press, 1999.

Nixon, R. E. *The Exodus in the New Testament*. London: Tyndale, 1962.

Novenson, Matthew V. *Christ among the Messiahs: Christ Language in Paul and Messiah Language in Ancient Judaism*. Oxford: Oxford University Press, 2012.

O'Brien, M.A. "The 'Deuteronomistic History' as a Story of Israel's Leaders." *ABR* 37 (1989) 14–34.

Oh, Myeong Hwan. "The Relationship Between the Individualism of Jeremiah and that of Ezekiel." PhD. diss., New Orleans Baptist Theological Seminary, 2005. Online: http://proquest.umi.com/pqdlink?did=1221658241&Fmt=2&clientId=79356&RQT=309&VName=PQD.

Omanson, Roger L., and John Ellington. *A Handbook on Paul's Second Letter to the Corinthians*. New York: United Bible Societies, 1993.

Oropeza, B. J. *Exploring Second Corinthians: Death and Life, Hardship and Rivalry*. Atlanta: SBL, 2016.

Oss, Douglas A. "A Note on Paul's Use of Isaiah." *BBR* 2 (1992) 105–12.

Owens, Mark D. *As It Was in the Beginning: An Intertextual Analysis of New Creation in Galatians, 2 Corinthians, and Ephesians*. Eugene: Pickwick, 2015.

Parsons, Michael. "'In Christ' in Paul." *Vox Evangelica* 18 (1988) 25–44.

Pate, C. Marvin. *The Reverse of the Curse: Paul, Wisdom and the Law*. Tübingen: Mohr Siebeck, 2000.

———. *Romans*. Grand Rapids: Baker, 2013.

Peace, Richard V. *Conversion in the New Testament: Paul and the Twelve*. Grand Rapids: Eerdmans, 1999.

Pettegrew, Larry. "The New Covenant." *The Master's Seminary Journal* 10.2 (1999) 251–70.

Philip, Finney. *The Origins of Pauline Pneumatology: The Eschatological Bestowal of The Spirit upon Gentiles in Judaism and in the Early Development of Paul's Theology*. Tübingen: Mohr Siebeck, 2005.

Piper, John. *The Future of Justification: A Response to N. T. Wright*. Wheaton, IL: Crossway, 2007.

Pitre, Brant. "The Lord's Prayer and the New Exodus." *Letter & Spirit* 2 (2006) 69–96.

———. "The 'Ransom For Many,' The New Exodus, and the End of the Exile: Redemption as the Restoration of All Israel (Mark 10:35-45)." *Letter & Spirit* 1 (2005) 41–68.

Plutarch. *The Life of Cicero* V4; xxiv–xxv. Warminster: Aris and Philips, 1988.

Polhill, John B. *Paul and His Letters*. Nashville: Broadman & Holman, 1999.

Pollard, Paul. "The 'Faith of Christ' in Current Discussion." *Concordia Journal* 23 (1997) 213–28.

Potter, H. D. "The New Covenant in Jeremiah XXXI 31–34." *VT* 33.3 (1983) 347–57.

Punt, Jeremy. "Hermeneutics in Identity Formation: Paul's Use of Genesis in Galatians 4." *HTS Theological Studies* 67.1 (2011) 846–54.

Rata, Cristian G. "Some Reflections on Life and Death from the Old Testament." *Torch Trinity Journal* 12.1 (2009) 8–24.

Raitt, Thomas M. *A Theology of Exile: Judgment and Deliverance in Jeremiah and Ezekiel*. Philadelphia: Fortress, 1977.

Reed, Jeffrey T. "The Cohesiveness of Discourse: Towards a Model of Linguistic Criteria for Analysing New Testament Discourse." In *Discourse Analysis and the New Testament: Approaches and Results*, edited by Stanley E. Porter and Jeffrey T. Reed, 28–46. Sheffield: Sheffield Academic Press, 1999.

———. "Discourse Analysis as New Testament Hermeneutic: A Retrospective and Prospective Appraisal." *JETS* 39.2 (1996) 223–40.

Reist, I.W. "The Theological Significance of the Exodus." *JETS* 12.4 (1969) 223–32.

Reumann, J. "Justification and Justice in the New Testament." *Horizons in Biblical Theology* 21 (1999) 26–45.

Richardson, Peter. "Pauline Inconsistency: 1 Corinthians 9:19–23 and Galatians 2:11–14." *NTS* 26 (1980) 347–62.

Ridderbos, Hermann. *When the Time Had Fully Come: Studies in New Testament Theology*. Ontario: Paideia, 1982.

Robinson, A. "Cicero's References to His Banishment." *The Classical World* 87.6 (1994) 475–80.

Robson, James. *Word and Spirit in Ezekiel*. New York: T. & T. Clark, 2006.

Russell, Walter B. "The Apostle Paul's Redemptive-Historical Argumentation in Galatians 5:13–26." *WTJ* 57 (1995) 333–57.

———. "Does the Christian Have Flesh in Gal. 5:13–26?" *JETS* 36.2 (1993) 179–87.

———. "Rhetorical Analysis of the Book of Galatians Part 1." *BibSac* 150 (1993) 341–58.

Sabou, Sorin. *Between Horror and Hope: Paul's Metaphorical Language of Death in Romans 6:1–11*. Waynesboro: Paternoster, 2005.

Sanders, E. P. *Paul and Palestinian Judaism: A Comparison of Patterns of Religion*. Philadelphia: Fortress, 1977.

———. *Paul: The Apostle's Life, Letters, and Thought*. Minneapolis: Fortress, 2015.

———. *Paul, the Law and the Jewish People*. Philadelphia: Fortress, 1983.

Saucy, Robert. "Sinners Who Are Forgiven, or Saints Who Sin?" *BibSac* 152.608 (1995) 400–12.

Sawyer, James F. "Hebrew Words for the Resurrection of the Dead." *VT* 23.2 (1973) 218–34.

Schlier, H. *Der Brief an die Galater*. Göttingen: Vandenhoeck & Ruprecht, 1989.

Schmisek, Brian. "Paul's Vision of the Risen Lord." *Biblical Theology Bulletin* 41 (2011) 76–83.

Schmithals, Walter. *Paul and the Gnostics*. Nashville: Abingdon, 1972.

Schneemelcher, William. *New Testament Apocrypha, Vol. 2: Writings Relating to the Apostles, Apocalypses, and Related Subjects*. Translated by Robert McLachlan Wilson. Tübingen: J.C.B. Mohr, 1989.

Schneider, J. "σταυρόω." In *Theological Dictionary of the New Testament Vol. 7*, edited by Gerhard Kittel, Geofrrey W. Bromiley and Gerhard Friedrich, 572–84. Grand Rapids: Eerdmans, 1964.

Schnelle, Udo. *Apostle Paul: His Life and Theology*. Grand Rapids: Baker, 2005.

Schottroff, L. "ζάω." In *Exegetical Dictionary of the New Testament Vol. 2*, edited by Horst R. Balz and Gerhard Schneider, 106–9. Grand Rapids: Eerdmans, 1990.

Schreiner, Thomas A. *40 Questions about Christians and Biblical Law*. Grand Rapids: Kregel, 2010.

———. "The Church as the New Israel and the Future of Ethnic Israel in Paul." *StudBT* 13 (1983) 17–38.

———. *An Exegetical Commentary on the New Testament: Galatians*. Grand Rapids: Zondervan, 2010.

———. "Is Perfect Obedience To The Law Possible? A Re-Examination of Galatians 3:10." *JETS* 27.2 (1984) 151–60.

———. Review of *The Spirit and the Restoration of Israel: New Exodus and New Creation Motifs in Galatians*, by Rodrigo Morlales. Online: http://thegospelcoalition.org/themelios/review/the_spirit_and_the_restoration_of_israel_new_exodus_and_new_creation_motifs.

———. "Works of the Law." In *Dictionary of Paul and his Letters*, edited by Gerald F. Hawthorne, Ralph P. Martin, and Daniel G. Reid, 975–79. Downers Grove, IL: InterVarsity, 1993.

Schweizer, Eduard. "Slaves of the Elements and Worshipers of Angels: Gal. 4:3, 9 and Col. 2:8, 18, 20." *JBL* 107.3 (1988) 455–68.

Scott, James M. *Adoption as Sons of God: An Exegetical Investigation into the Background of υἱοθεσία in the Pauline Corpus*. Tübingen: Mohr Siebeck, 1992.

———. "Exile and Restoration." Online: https://impact.twu.ca/images/twu/ExileAndRestoration.pdf.

———. "Paul's Use of Deuteronomic Tradition." *JBL* 112.4 (1993) 645–65.

Segal Alan F. *Paul the Convert: The Apostolate and Apostasy of Saul the Pharisee*. New Haven, CT: Yale University Press, 1990.

Seifrid, Mark A. "Paul, Luther, and Justification in Gal. 2:15–21." *WTJ* 65 (2003) 215–30.

———. "Paul's Use of Righteousness Language Against Its Hellenistic Background." In *Justification and Variegated Nomism Volume 2: The Paradoxes of Paul*, edited by Donald A. Carson, Peter T. O'Brien, and Mark A. Seifrid, 39–75. Tübingen: Mohr Siebeck, 2004.

Shum, Shiu Lun. *Paul's Use of Isaiah in Romans: A Comparative Study of Paul's Letter and the Sibylline Qumran Sectarian Texts*. Tübingen: Mohr Siebeck, 2002.

Singh, Yii Jan. "Semen, Philosophy, and Paul." *Journal of Philosophy and Scripture* 4.2 (2007) 32–45.

Skjoldal, Neil O. "The Function of Isaiah 24–27." *JETS* 36:2 (1993) 163–72.

Sloan, Robert B. "Paul and the Law: Why the Law Cannot Save." *NovT* 33.1 (1991) 35–60.

Snodgrass, Klyne R. "Introduction to a Hermeneutics of Identity." *BibSac* 168 (2011) 3–19.

Soards, Marion L. *1 Corinthians*. Grand Rapids: Baker, 1999.

Soding, T. *Die Freiheit des Glaubens*. Online: www.rub.de/nt.

Sommer, B. D. "Isaiah." In *The Jewish Study Bible,* edited by Adele Berlin, and Marc Zvi Brettler, 780–916. New York: Oxford University Press, 1985.

Spaulding, Mike. "Resurrection in Pauline Literature: Did Paul Incorporate Greco-Roman Apotheosis Mythologies?" Online: http://www.cclohio.org/Articles/Resurrection.

Sprinkle, Preston. "Why Can't the One who does these Things Live by them? The Use of Leviticus 18:5 in Galatians 3:12." In *Early Christian Literature and Intertextuality: Volume 2: Exegetical Studies,* edited by Craig A. Evans and H. Daniel Zacharias, 126–37. New York, T. & T. Clark, 2009.

Staalduine-Sulman, E. V. "Isaiah 44:5: Textual Criticism and Other Arguments." *Textual Criticism: A Journal of Biblical Textual Criticism* 16 (2011) 1–10.

Stanley, Christopher. *Paul and the Language of Scripture: Citation Technique in the Pauline Epistles and Contemporary Literature*. Cambridge: Cambridge University Press, 1992.

Stanley, David M. *Christ's Resurrection in Pauline Soteriology*. Rome: Pontifical Biblical Institute, 1961.

Starling, David I. *Not My People: Gentiles as Exiles in Pauline Hermeneutics*. Berlin: Walter de Gruyter Gmbh, 2011.

Steck, Odil H. *Israel und das gewaltsame Geschick der Propheten: Untersuchungen zur Oberlieferung des deuteronomistischen Geschichtsbildes im Alten Testament, Spiitjudentum und Urchristentum*. Neukirchen-Vluyn: Neukirchener Verlag, 1967.

Stegman, Thomas D. *The Character of Jesus: The Linchpin to Paul's Argument in 2 Corinthians*. Rome: Pontifical Biblical Institute, 2005.

———. "'Lifting the Veil': The Challenges Posed by 2 Corinthians 3." *Studies in Christian-Jewish Relations* 4 (2009) 1–15.

Stendahl, Krister. *Paul Among Jews and Gentiles and Other Essays*. Philadelphia: Fortress, 1976.

Stockhausen, Carol Kern. *Moses' Veil and the Glory of the New Covenant: The Exegetical Substructure of 2 Cor. 3:1—4:6*. Roma: Editrice Pontificio Istituto Biblico, 1989.

Strelan, J. G. "Burden-Bearing and the Law of Christ: A Re-Examination of Galatians 6:2." *JBL* 94.2 (1975) 266–76.

Street, Andrew. *The Vine and the Son of Man: Eschatological Interpretation of Psalm 80 in Early Judaism*. Minneapolis: Fortress, 2014.

Strine, Casey. "The Role of Repentance in the Book of Ezekiel: A Second Chance for the Second Generation." *JTS* 64 (2012) 467–91.

Stuhlmueller, Carroll. *Creative Redemption in Deutero-Isaiah*. Rome: Biblical Institute, 1970.

Stutzman, Robert. *An Exegetical Summary of Galatians*. Dallas, TX: SIL International, 2008.

Suh, Robert H. "The Use of Ezekiel 37 in Ephesians 2." *JETS* 50.4 (2007) 715–33.

Sumney, Jerry L. "Paul and the Christ-Believing Jews Whom he Opposes." In *Jewish Christianity Reconsidered: Rethinking Ancient Groups and Texts,* edited by Matt Jackson-McCabe, 57–80. Minneapolis: Fortress, 2007.

Surburg, Mark P. "Rectify or Justify? A Response to J. Louis Martyn's Interpretation of Paul's Righteousness Language." *CTQ* 77 (2013) 45–77.
Tannehill, Robert C. *Dying and Rising with Christ: A Study in Pauline Theology*. Verlag Alfred Töpelmann: Berlin, 1967.
Taylor, John W. "The Eschatological Interdependence of Jews and Gentiles in Galatians." *TynBul* 63.2 (2012) 291–316.
Taylor, Walter F. *Paul: Apostle to the Nations*. Minneapolis: Fortress, 2012.
Thiessen, Gerd. *Social Reality and the Early Christians: Theology, Ethics, and the World of the New Testament*. Edinburgh: T. & T. Clark, 1992.
Thiessen, Matthew. *Contesting Conversion: Genealogy, Circumcision and Identity in Ancient Judaism and Christianity*. Oxford: Oxford University Press, 2011.
Thielman, Frank. *From Plight to Solution: A Jewish Framework to Understanding Paul's View of the Law in Galatians and Romans*. Leiden: E. J. Brill, 1989.
———. *Paul and the Law: A Contextual Approach*. Downers Grove, IL: InterVarsity, 1994.
Thompson, Michael B. *The New Perspective on Paul*. Cambridge: Grove, 2002.
Thorsell, Paul R. "The Spirit in the Present Age: Preliminary Fulfilment of the Predicted New Covenant According To Paul." *JETS* 41.3 (1998) 397–413.
Thrall, Margaret E. *2 Corinthians 1–7*. New York: T. & T. Clark, 1994.
Tolmie, D. Francois *Persuading the Galatians: A Text-Centred Rhetorical Analysis of a Pauline Letter*. Tübingen: Mohr Siebeck, 2005.
———. "Research on the Letter to Galatians: 2000–2010." *Acta Theologica* 32.1 (2012) 118–57.
———. "The Spirituality of the Letter to the Galatians." *Acta Theologica Supplementum* 15 (2011) 167–82.
Trafton, Joseph L. "The Psalms of Solomon in Recent Research." *Journal for the Study of the Pseudepigrapha* 12 (1994) 3–19.
Trench, Richard C. *Synonyms of the New Testament*. New York: Cosimo, 2007.
Tuell, Stephen. *Ezekiel*. Peabody, MA: Hendrickson, 2009.
———. "True Metaphor: Insights into Reading Scripture from the Rabbis." *Theology Today* 67 (2011) 467–75.
Turner, David L. "Paul and the Ministry of Reconciliation in 2 Cor 5:11—6:2." *Criswell Theological Review* 4.1 (1989) 77–95.
Tyson, Joseph B. "'Works of Law' in Galatians." *JBL* 92.3 (1973) 423–31.
Vanlaningham, Michael G. "Romans 11:25–27 and the Future of Israel in Paul›s Thought." *The Master's Seminary Journal* 3.2 (1992) 141–74.
Vermes, Geza. *The Dead Sea Scrolls in English*. Sheffield: Sheffield Academic Press, 1995.
Voelz, J. W. "Multiple Signs, Levels of Meaning and Self as Text: Elements of Intertextuality." *Semeia* 69.70 (1995) 149–64.
Vos, Johan S. "Paul's Argumentation in Galatians 1–2." *HTR* 87.1 (1994) 1–16.
Wagner, J. Ross. *Heralds of the Good News: Isaiah and Paul in Concert in the Letter to the Romans*. Leiden: E. J. Brill, 2003.
Wallace, Daniel B. "Galatians 3:19–20: A Crux Interpretum for Paul's View of the Law." *WTJ* 52 (1990) 225–45.
Wallis, Ian G. *The Faith of Jesus Christ in Early Christian Traditions*. Cambridge: Cambridge University Press, 1995.
Wallis, Wilber B. "Irony in Jeremiah's Prophecy of a New Covenant." *JETS* 12.2 (1969) 107–10.

Waters, Guy. *The End of Deuteronomy in the Epistles of Paul.* Tubingen: Mohr Siebeck, 2006.

Watson, Francis. "By Faith of Christ: An Exegetical Dilemma and its Scriptural Solution." In *The Faith of Jesus Christ: Exegetical, Biblical and Theological Studies,* edited by Michael F. Bird and Preston M. Sprinkle, 147–64. Peabody, MA: Hendrickson, 2009.

———. *Paul and the Hermeneutics of Faith.* New York: T. & T. Clark International, 2004.

———. *Paul, Judaism and the Gentiles.* Cambridge: Cambridge University Press, 2007.

Wedderburn, A.J.M. *Baptism and Resurrection: Studies in Pauline Theology against Its Greco-Roman Background.* Tübingen: Mohr Siebeck, 1987.

———. "Some Observations on Paul's Use of the Phrases 'In Christ' and 'With Christ.'" *JSNT* 25 (1985) 83–97.

Weima, Jeffrey A. D. "The Pauline Letter Closings: Analysis and Hermeneutical Significance." *BBR* 5 (1995) 177–98.

———. "What Does Aristotle Have to Do with Paul? An Evaluation of Rhetorical Criticism." *CTJ* 32 (1997) 458–68.

Wells, Kyle B. "Grace, Obedience, and the Hermeneutics of Agency: Paul and his Jewish Contemporaries on the Transformation of the Heart." PhD diss., University of Durham, 2010. Online: http://etheses.dur.ac.uk/190/

Wenham, David. "Critical Blindness, Wise Virgins and the Law of Christ." In *The Message of Jesus: John Dominic Crossan and Ben Witherington III in Dialogue,* edited by Robert B. Smith, 183–203. Minneapolis: Fortress, 2013.

Wenham, Gordon J. *The Book of Leviticus.* Grand Rapids: Eerdmans, 1979.

Westerholm, Stephen. "Justification by Faith is the Answer: What is the Question?" *Concordia Theological Quarterly* 70.3 (2006) 197–217.

———. *Justification Reconsidered: Rethinking a Pauline Theme.* Grand Rapids: Eerdmans, 2013.

———. "Letter and Spirit: the Foundation of Pauline Ethics." *NTS* 30.2 (1984) 229–48.

White, John L. *The Apostle of God: Paul and the Promise of Abraham.* Peabody, MA: Hendrickson, 1999.

Wilder, William N. *Echoes of the Exodus Narrative in the Context and Background of Galatians 5:18.* New York: Peter Lang, 2001.

Williams, Sam K. *Galatians.* Nashville: Abingdon, 1997.

———. "Justification and the Spirit in Galatians." *JSNT* 29 (1987) 91–100.

———. "Promise in Galatians: A Reading of Paul's Reading of Scripture." *JBL* 107.4 (1988) 709–20.

Willits, Joel. "Context Matters: Paul's Use of Leviticus 18:5 in Galatians 3:12." *TynBul* 54.2 (2003) 105–22.

Wilson, R. M. "Gnostics: In Galatia?" *Studia Evangelica, Texte und Untersuchungen zur Geschichte der altchristlichen Literatur* 4 (1968) 358–67.

Wilson, Todd A. "The Law of Christ and the Law of Moses: Reflections on a Recent Trend in Interpretation." *CBR* 5 (2006) 123–44.

Winger, Michael. "The Law of Christ." *NTS* 46.4 (2000) 537–46.

Witherington, Ben. *Grace in Galatia: A Commentary on St. Paul's Letter to the Galatians.* Grand Rapids: Eerdmans, 1998.

Wolff, Hans Walter. *Jonah: Church in Revolt.* St. Louis: Clayton, 1978.

Woodhouse, John. "The Spirit in the Book of Ezekiel." In *Spirit of the Living God*, edited by B. G. Webb, 1–22. Sydney: Lancer, 1991.
Wright, Benjamin G. "Qumran `Pseudepigrapha in Early Christianity: Is 1 Clem. 50:4 a Citation of *4QPseudo-Ezekiel* (4Q385)?" Online: http://orion.mscc.huji.ac.il/symposiums/.
Wright, N. T. *The Climax of the Covenant: Christ and the Law in Pauline Theology*. London: T. & T. Clark, 1991.
———. "Gospel and Theology in Galatians." In *Gospel in Paul: Studies on Corinthians, Galatians and Romans for Richard N. Longenecker*, edited by L. Ann Jervis and Peter Richardson, 222–39. Sheffield: Sheffield Academic Press, 1994.
———. *Jesus and the Victory of God*. London: SPCK, 1996.
———. *Justification: God's Plan & Paul's Vision*. London: SPCK, 2009.
———. "The Letter to the Galatians." In *Between Two Horizons. Spanning New Testament Studies and Systematic Theology*, edited by Max Turner and Joel B. Green, 206–36. Grand Rapids: Eerdmans, 2000.
———. *The New Testament and the People of God*. London: SPCK, 1992.
———. *Paul and the Faithfulness of God*. Minneapolis: Fortress, 2013.
———. "Paul and the Patriarch: The Role of Abraham in Romans 4." *JSNT* 35.3 (2013) 207–41.
———. *Paul: Fresh Perspectives*. London: SPCK, 2005.
———. "Paul in Current Anglophone Scholarship." *The Expository Times* 123 (2012) 367–81.
———. *The Resurrection of the Son of God*. London: SPCK, 2003.
———. "Romans and the Theology of Paul." In *Pauline Theology, Volume III*, edited by David M. Hay and E. Elizabeth Johnson, 30–67. Minneapolis: Fortress, 1995.
Yates, Gary E. "The People Have Not Obeyed: A Literary and Rhetorical Study of Jeremiah 26–45." Online: http://digitalcommons.liberty.edu/cgi/viewcontent.cgi?article=1025&context=fac_dis
Yates, John W. *The Spirit and Creation in Paul*. Tübingen: Mohr Siebeck, 2008.
Young, Norman H. "Who's Cursed-and Why? (Galatians 3:10–14)." *JBL* 117.1 (1998) 79–92.
Zemek, George J. "Interpretive Challenges Relating to Habakkuk 2:4b." *GraceTJ* 1.1 (1980) 43–69.
Ziesler, John A. *The Epistle to the Galatians*. London: Epworth, 1992.
———. *The Meaning of Righteousness in Paul: A Linguistic and Theological Enquiry*. Cambridge: Cambridge University Press, 2004.
Zimmerli, W. *Ezekiel 2: A Commentary on the Book of the Prophet Ezekiel Chapters 25–48*. Philadelphia: Fortress, 1983.
Zoccali, Christopher. "'And So All Israel will be Saved': Competing Interpretations of Romans 11.26 in Pauline Scholarship." *JSNT* 30.3 (2008) 289–318.

Author Index

Adams, Edward, 208
Adeyemi, Femi, 172, 181
Aguilar, Chiu, J. E., 148
Alexander, Philip, 11

Barclay, John M. G., 22n89, 80, 169, 169n3, 170, 182
Barrett, Charles K., 177
Barry, John D., 31
Bayes, Jonathan F., 181
Beale, Gregory K., 34, 34n129, 167n33
Beare, Francis W., 23
Betz, Hans D., 2, 2n7, 3, 15, 16, 78, 91n39, 94, 94n2, 155, 187, 196
Bird, Michael F., 24
Black, David A., 17n75
Block, Daniel I., 68, 68n256, 112, 112n71, 149, 211
Boakye, Andrew K., 9n38
Brondos, David A., 109n65
Bronner, Leila L., 125, 125n18
Bruce, Frederick F., 84, 89, 91n39, 121n2, 155, 161, 181, 187
Brueggemann, Walter, 174
Bryant, Robert A., 79
Bundrick, David R., 71, 71n269
Burton, Ernest D. W., 71, 100, 165
Byrne, Brendan, 136

Callan, Terrence, 15–16

Campbell, Douglas A., 24, 104, 104n47
Charlesworth, James H., 40n153
Choi, H. S., 99
Ciampa, Roy E., 54
Clifford, Richard J., 57
Collins, John J., 38
Cook, David, 79
Cosgrove, Charles, 2, 7
Cranfield, Charles, E. B., 103n41
Crawford, Sidnie W., 123

Dabney, Lyle D., 111n70
Das, A. Andrew, 21n89
Davies, W. D., 45, 46, 96
Davis, Anne K., 55
De Boer, Martinus C., 71, 72n270, 100, 106, 141, 141n74, 191, 192
Delitzsch, Franz, 55
Dunn, James D.G., 3, 4, 24, 94n2, 103, 103n39, 103n40, 103n41, 104, 109n65, 121n2, 134, 192n27
Dupont, Jacques, 97

Easley, Kendell H., 17n77
Eastman, Susan, 205n18
Esler, Philip F., 94n2
Everts, J. M., 83

Fee, Gordon D., 4, 111n70, 158
Finlan, Stephen F., 14n62

Flusser, David, 163
Fung, Ronald Y. K., 94n2

Gaffin, Richard B., 111n70
Gage, Warren A., 47
Gallant, Tim, 80
Garlington, Don, 141
Gathercole, Simon J., 134, 135, 198n10
Gaventa, Beverley R., 78
Gorman, Michael J., 12–14, 66n249, 109n65
Grassi, J. A., 62
Grayston, Kenneth, 95
Grebe, Sabine, 43
Gregerman, Adam, 1n1
Grindheim, Sigurd, 3n11, 10, 135, 135n50
Guthrie, Donald, 94n2, 155

Hafemann, Scott J., 5–9, 217
Halliday, Michael, A. K., 17
Hardin, Justin K., 191
Harink, Douglas, 66
Harrison, J. R., 98n22
Hayes, Elizabeth R., 63
Hays, Richard B., 88n31, 93, 104, 105, 109n65, 122, 123, 150, 154, 181
Hooker, Morna D., 104, 109n65
Hubbard, Moyer, V., 168n36, 197
Hübner, Hans, 144n87
Hunn, Debbie, 104

James, Montague R., 61
Jewett, Robert, 188, 191
Jobes, Karen H., 150, 151, 151n104
Johnson Hodge, Caroline, 212n45
Joyce, Paul, 113
Juncker, Günther, 89

Kahl, Brigitte, 54
Käsemann, Ernst, 35
Keesmaat, Sylvia C., 6, 45n181
Keil, Karl F., 55
Kern, Philip F., 2n7
Kirk, J. Daniel, 13, 24, 89, 90
Kline, Meredith G., 51
Koptak, Paul D., 78
Köstenberger, Andreas J., 205

Kuck, David W., 187
Kwon, Y. G., 136

Lee, C. C., 136
Lemke, Jay L., 17
Levenson, Jon D., 33, 33n124, 60
Levison, John R., 166
Lewis, John G., 148
Lightfoot, Joseph B., 71, 83n19, 165
Longenecker, Bruce W., 93
Longenecker, Richard N., 94n2, 107, 130n28, 155, 187
Loubser, G. M. H., 165n21
Louis Martyn, John, 3, 3n12, 20, 22n89, 25, 54, 121n2, 132n36, 155n112, 182, 197
Louw, J. P., 159
Lührmann, D., 191
Lull, David J., 132n35, 166, 167n31

Maccoby, Hyam, 215n2
Malby, D. S., 167
Manning, Gary T., 63
Marshall, I. Howard, 51n198, 92
Matera, Frank J., 162n11, 192
McCant, Jerry W., 63n242
McKnight, Scot, 108
Minear, Paul S., 14n62
Moo, Douglas J., 94, 144, 197, 197n6, 197n7
Morales, Rodrigo J., 9–10, 36n134, 126
Mussner, Franz, 58

Nanos, Mark D., 1n1, 97n16
Nelson, R. D., 124
Nida, Eugene A., 83n19, 159
Nixon, R. E., 51
Noth, Martin, 124
Novenson, Matthew V., 115

Oakes, Peter, 103n38
Oh, Myang H., 68

Parsons, Michael, 115n78
Pate, C. Marvin, 139, 180n76
Peace, Richard V., 83
Pettegrew, Larry, 173, 204
Philip, Finney, 70n265, 166

Piper, John, 11n44
Potter, H. D., 75

Rata, Cristian, G., 113
Reed, Jeffrey T., 16–17
Russell, Walter B., 20, 160n7

Sanders, Ed P., 19, 103n38, 109n65, 115, 133
Schlier, H., 156
Schmisek, Brian, 83n19
Schmithals, Walter, 1n1
Schnelle, Udo, 99n24
Schreiner, Thomas R., 10, 94, 155n120, 192
Scott, James M., 5–6, 5n20, 8n36, 9, 122, 122n8
Segal, Alan F., 83
Seifrid, Mark A., 94
Sloan, Robert B., 120n1
Snodgrass, Klyne R., 106
Soards, Marion L., 18n79
Soding, T., 106
Spaulding, Mike, 216
Sprinkle, Preston M., 134
Stanley, Christopher, 123n12
Stanley, David M., 14–15
Stegman, Thomas D., 179n70, 180
Stendahl, Krister, 83, 83n20
Strelan, J. G., 183n92
Strine, Casey, 113
Stuhlmueller, Carroll, 170n47
Suh, Robert H., 61, 62
Sumney, Jerry L., 99

Tannehill, Robert C., 15, 109n65
Thielman, Frank, 132, 133
Thiessen, Gerd, 148

Thiessen, Matthew, 177, 177n63
Thompson, Michael, 11
Thorsell, Paul R., 211
Tolmie, D. Francois, 2n3, 121n2, 196
Tuell, Stephen, 61, 113
Tyson, Joseph B., 103

Vermes, Geza, 38, 39, 40
Von Rad, Gerhard, 173
Vos, Johan S., 78

Wallis, Wilber B., 175n51
Watson, Francis, 104, 104n47, 123
Wedderburn, A.J.M., 13n54
Weima, Jeffrey A. D., 3n7, 196
Wells, Kyle B., 175n60
Wenham, David, 182
Westerholm, Stephen, 22n89, 165n22
White, John L., 140
Wilder, William N., 6, 51, 52
Williams, Sam K., 95, 105, 137
Willits, Joel, 135
Wilson, Todd A., 70n266, 130, 181
Winger, Michael, 181, 182n90
Witherington, Ben, 24
Woodhouse, Richard, 68, 68n257
Wright, N.T., 9, 10–12, 10n44, 19n80, 23, 41, 46, 109n65, 128n23, 138n64, 144, 210, 215n3

Yates, Gary E., 203
Yates, John W., 166, 194n32, 214n1
Yoder, J. H., 66
Young, Norman H., 131

Ziesler, John A., 107
Zoccali, Christopher, 116

Subject Index

Abraham, 1, 18, 57, 88, 89, 104, 110, 111, 117, 120–24, 130, 132n35, 133–34, 136–41, 138n62, 139n65, 145, 148–49, 153–58, 161–63, 167, 168–69, 172, 175n59, 182, 184, 195, 195n34, 204, 210, 217–18
Abraham, promises, 7, 137, 139–41, 153–55, 155n120
Abraham, sons of, 8, 20, 58, 104, 114, 121–22, 148–49, 153–54, 158
Adam, 24, 119, 130, 145, 210
Adiabene, 177
apocalyptic, 3, 3n10, 3n11, 3n13, 20n85, 25, 29, 54, 79, 80, 83, 115, 155, 160, 187, 197, 197n4, 197n5, 205n21
apostleship, 3, 77, 78, 80, 82
Assyria, 8, 37, 56, 204
Augustus, 43

Babylon, 8, 11, 44, 49, 51, 52, 53n204, 56, 62n237, 71, 133, 156, 157, 203, 204
baptism, 18, 19, 26, 38, 46, 58, 59, 59n255, 60, 92, 117, 164, 167, 202
blessing, 4, 5, 9, 40, 41, 53n204, 55, 67, 72, 89, 104, 111, 114, 120, 122–26, 130, 131, 132n35, 135, 136, 136n52, 137, 138, 139, 139n65, 144, 145, 148, 149, 151, 153, 157, 164, 166, 169, 170, 175, 175n59, 194, 204, 206, 213, 215, 217, 218

Carson, Don A., 10, 10n43
Christ, 1n1, 6, 8, 11, 12, 13, 15, 19, 20, 21, 23, 24, 27, 34, 41, 46, 48n187, 50, 54, 57, 58, 59, 62, 63, 64, 65, 66, 79, 79n7, 81, 81n15, 82–92, 93, 97n16, 99n23, 100, 105, 106, 108, 109, 109n65, 110, 111, 111n69, 112, 114, 115, 116, 116n83, 117, 118, 131, 136, 139, 143, 144, 147, 150, 153, 158, 163, 164, 165n22, 166n25, 167, 167n31, 167n35, 171, 176, 176n61, 177, 179, 179n70, 181, 182, 183, 184, 186, 190, 191, 192, 195, 197, 198, 200, 201, 202, 205, 208, 210, 211, 214, 214n1, 215
Christ, faith in/of, 3, 21, 23, 36, 55, 58, 71, 74, 75, 84–85, 86, 88, 92, 95, 100, 101, 103, 104, 104n47, 105n50, 105n52, 107, 110, 111, 112, 114, 115n79, 118, 119, 124, 130, 132, 139, 143, 144, 149, 153, 156, 158, 161, 194, 202, 205, 218

243

SUBJECT INDEX

Christ, in, 6, 12, 13, 14, 16, 21, 23, 45, 53, 58–59, 62, 85, 86, 93, 99, 100, 105, 106, 107, 115, 115n78, 115n80, 116, 117, 131, 138, 142, 153, 155, 164, 166n25, 177, 178, 181, 183, 184, 200, 201, 204, 205, 215, 216
Christ, life of, 15, 21, 91, 114, 147, 148
Christ, of, 18, 29, 78, 84, 108, 116, 117, 130, 153, 165, 167, 171, 175, 179, 181, 181n77, 181n81, 182, 183, 183n92, 184, 185, 187, 195, 199, 201, 208, 217
Christ, Spirit of, 3, 146, 167n31
Christology, 119, 130
Cicero, 43–44
circumcision, 23, 52, 74, 78, 89, 96, 97, 98, 98n22, 99, 100, 101, 102, 116, 122, 162, 163, 164, 166, 167, 171, 175, 176, 176n61, 177, 177n63, 178, 182, 186, 187, 190, 191, 191n22, 192, 192n27, 193, 194, 195, 198, 199, 200, 201, 202, 204, 205, 206, 207, 208, 209, 210, 216
covenant, 4, 7, 7n30, 8, 9, 12, 22, 22n89, 69, 83, 97n16, 98, 99, 103, 103n39, 104, 122, 127, 128, 134, 135, 135n50, 139–40, 154, 155, 158, 172, 173, 174, 175, 180, 194, 203, 209, 210, 211, 212, 215
curse, 6, 9, 12, 32, 46, 47, 49, 54, 104, 110, 113, 114, 121, 121n2, 122–32, 131n32, 131n34, 132n35, 135, 135n50, 136, 138, 139, 139n66, 144, 145, 148, 149, 153, 157, 175, 214, 215, 217

death, 2, 2n2, 4, 8, 9, 10, 12, 14, 14n62, 15, 19, 21, 22, 23, 23n65, 25, 26–30, 31, 32, 33, 33n125, 34, 37, 38, 40, 41, 42–51, 42n161, 42n163, 43n169, 54, 59, 59n223, 59n225, 60–66, 60n229, 66n249, 75, 76, 79, 80, 84, 85, 86, 87, 88, 92, 93, 105, 106, 107, 108, 109, 110, 112, 113, 113n76, 114, 119, 123, 125–34, 125n18, 136, 138, 144–52, 144n89, 156, 157, 161, 164, 167, 167n31, 168, 168n36, 169, 171, 175, 179, 180, 180n72, 183, 184, 189, 193, 197, 210, 214, 215, 217
death as crucifixion, 4, 12, 18, 29, 33, 92, 109, 110, 136, 139, 167, 205, 214
death-to-life movement, 15, 21, 23, 26, 49, 60, 63, 75, 85, 86, 91, 92, 104, 136, 168, 190, 193, 215
deliverance, 13, 24, 32, 33, 36, 38, 45, 54, 58, 86, 92, 156, 164
Deuteronomist History, 67, 113, 122, 123, 124, 116, 117, 128, 139, 148, 149, 215
Discourse Analysis, 16–20

Egypt, 8, 45, 47–59, 81, 91, 124, 126, 127, 174, 204, 206
Egyptian, 47, 48, 49, 59, 72
Epictetus, 44–45
eschatology, 12, 13, 22, 24, 25, 28, 29, 33, 34, 38, 60, 66, 68, 69, 70, 73, 75, 76, 79, 85, 86, 89, 91, 96, 98n21, 100, 101, 107, 108, 112, 113, 115, 116, 122, 126, 134, 137, 138, 142n82, 157, 161, 164, 171, 172, 185, 186, 187, 189n12, 193, 193n30, 194, 195, 197, 200, 204, 211, 212, 214, 215, 216
Euripides, 45
exile, 5, 8, 9, 11–12, 33, 37, 41, 42, 43, 44, 44n173, 44n176, 45, 46, 47, 50, 54, 64, 67, 75, 76, 113, 114, 119, 122, 124, 125, 126, 127, 128, 128n23, 129, 131, 132, 139, 145, 148, 149, 153, 156, 157, 170, 172, 175, 176, 179, 180, 189, 190, 203, 204, 213, 215, 216
Exodus, narratives, 5, 5n22, 6, 8, 9, 18, 19, 20, 33, 36, 45, 45n181, 46–58, 56n215, 60, 72, 73, 113, 127, 130, 141, 142, 157, 158, 175, 203, 212
Exodus, new, 5, 6, 7, 54, 56, 59, 91, 170, 172, 175
Ezekiel, 19, 20, 36, 60, 61, 62, 63, 64, 66, 67, 68, 68n257, 69, 72, 74, 75,

SUBJECT INDEX

112, 112n71, 113, 114, 119, 128, 142, 142n82, 145, 148, 149, 150, 151, 152, 153, 154, 156, 157, 158, 170, 171, 172, 173, 174, 177, 185, 190, 190n20, 194, 195, 203, 207, 208, 209, 210, 211, 212, 213, 213, 215, 216, 217, 218

faith, 3, 9, 10, 12, 13, 16, 19, 23, 23n95, 36, 40, 52, 58, 71, 84, 88, 89, 95n8, 101, 104, 105, 108, 110, 114, 117, 119, 120, 121, 121n2, 122, 127, 128, 129, 129n26, 131, 132, 133, 134, 134n44, 135, 136, 137n60, 138, 138n62, 141, 143, 144, 145, 146, 147, 149, 150, 151, 153, 155, 156, 157, 158, 159, 161, 169m42, 184, 187, 190, 195, 199, 200, 201, 214, 217

faith in/of Christ (see Christ, faith in/of)

faith, justification/rectification by, 9, 25, 75, 125, 126, 161, 217

first-fruits, 86, 137, 140, 151

flesh, 10, 13, 16, 18, 23, 29, 38, 41, 70, 79, 112, 118, 131, 149, 153, 155, 159, 159n3, 160–64, 160n6, 160n7, 160n8, 161, 161n10, 166, 171, 182, 184, 188–89, 191–95, 191n22, 192n27, 198, 200–201, 207, 208, 209, 211

flesh, according to, 7, 8, 89, 90, 92, 154, 166n25, 167n35, 176, 178

flesh, crucifixion of, 18, 27, 29, 85, 108, 130, 153, 159, 162–64, 167, 170, 184, 186, 188, 190–91, 195, 202, 214

forensic, 2, 6, 20, 21, 25, 78n1

freedom, 8, 11, 20, 21n88, 24, 33, 37, 40, 41, 45, 46, 53, 58, 59, 60, 65, 67, 68, 70, 71, 73, 75, 76, 100, 112, 119, 147, 149, 150, 153, 154, 156, 157, 158, 162, 171, 175, 200, 201, 204, 205

Gentile, 1, 1n1, 3, 6, 7, 7n30, 20, 22, 28, 30, 53, 57, 58, 62, 66, 71, 72, 72n270, 73, 74, 75, 78, 82, 83, 84, 85, 86, 88n31, 89, 94, 95, 96, 97, 97n16, 98, 98n22, 99, 99n24, 100, 101, 102, 102n35, 103, 105, 106, 108, 109, 110, 111, 112, 116, 117, 118n84, 121, 122, 123, 127, 130, 133, 134, 147, 154, 155, 156, 157, 158, 161, 163, 166, 170, 170n47, 171, 174, 176, 177, 177n63, 178, 183, 184, 186, 187, 191, 199n22, 192, 198, 200, 201, 204, 206, 207, 208, 209, 210, 211, 211n43, 212, 212, 214, 216

Gnosticism, 1n1, 161

God, 2, 3, 4, 6, 7, 8, 9, 11, 12, 14, 16, 20, 20n86, 21, 21n89, 22, 23, 25, 26, 27, 28, 29, 30, 32, 33, 34, 35, 36, 37, 38, 39, 40, 41, 44, 45, 46, 47, 48, 49, 50, 51, 52, 53, 54, 55, 55n211, 56, 56n215, 57, 58, 59, 60, 61, 64, 64n246, 65, 66, 67, 68, 68n257, 69, 70, 72, 73, 74, 75, 78, 79, 80, 81, 81n15, 82, 82n16, 83, 84, 85, 86, 87, 88, 89, 90, 90n38, 91, 92, 94, 95, 96, 97, 97n15, 97n16, 98, 100, 101, 102, 103, 103n39, 104, 105, 106, 107, 107n63, 108, 109, 110, 111, 111n68, 112, 113, 114, 115, 116, 117, 118, 119, 120, 121, 121n2, 122, 123, 124, 125, 126, 127, 128, 129, 130, 131, 132, 133, 133n40, 134, 135, 136, 137, 138, 138n62, 139, 140, 142, 143, 144, 145, 146, 147, 148, 149, 150, 152, 153, 154, 155, 155n20, 156, 157, 158, 160, 161, 162, 162n11, 166, 167n31, 168, 169, 170, 171, 172, 173, 174, 175, 176, 177, 178, 179, 180, 181, 183, 184, 185, 188, 190, 191, 192, 193, 194, 200, 202, 203, 204, 205, 206, 209, 210, 211, 212, 213, 214, 215, 216, 217, 218

God, Israel of, 167, 170, 204–7, 209, 213

God, Kingdom of, 39, 164

God, life/living to, 13, 27, 29, 59n226, 84, 107, 108, 110, 114, 116, 148, 153, 184, 197, 202, 214

God, people of, 2, 4, 5, 7n30, 8, 10n44,
    18, 22, 23n95, 58, 62, 66, 68,
    70, 71, 89, 91, 96, 101, 117, 118,
    122, 124, 126, 128, 128n22, 129,
    131, 132, 139, 144, 146, 149,
    153, 158, 160, 160n8, 163, 164,
    166, 167, 170, 171, 176, 177,
    178, 191, 192, 193, 194, 195,
    195n34, 199, 200, 201, 202, 204,
    206, 207, 208, 212, 213, 216
God, promises of, 105, 138, 139,
    155n20, 156
God, righteousness of, 22n89, 23, 24, 35,
    36, 163
God, son of, 57, 67, 69, 71, 73, 84, 86,
    89, 90, 90n38, 91, 104, 112, 118,
    131, 136, 160n8, 200, 201
God, sons of, 55, 58, 69, 70, 71, 117,
    118, 158, 177, 178, 204, 207, 218
God, Spirit of, 34, 52, 67, 71, 75,
    68n257, 90, 91, 111n68, 153,
    165n22, 194, 211
Gospel, 1, 2, 7, 9, 10, 25, 26n104, 39,
    62, 64, 66, 78, 79, 82, 83, 84, 89,
    91, 92, 95, 96, 97, 98, 99, 100,
    101, 109, 112, 113, 121, 122,
    134, 144n88, 147, 161, 179n69,
    180n72, 182, 183, 186, 197, 199,
    200, 214
grace, 53, 74, 85, 85n27, 86, 100, 103,
    191, 199, 201

Hades, 32, 38, 41, 46, 133
Hagar, 154, 155, 162
heart, 8, 9, 14, 41, 58, 64, 65, 66, 67, 68,
    69, 70, 71, 75, 91, 98, 109, 112,
    125, 127, 128, 142, 157, 162,
    168, 172–83, 183n92, 202, 203,
    204, 206, 207, 209, 210, 211,
    212, 213, 217
heirs, 7, 18, 57, 67, 89, 104, 121, 153,
    158, 167, 172
Hellenism, 2n7, 19, 19n81, 31, 83

idolatry/idols, 6, 11, 52, 53, 55, 56, 63,
    64, 66, 72, 73, 74, 75, 109, 112,
    113, 126, 127, 128, 132, 145,
    153, 210, 217

inheritance, 6, 7, 7n30, 57, 70, 73, 82,
    101, 140, 158, 164
internalization, 64, 65, 66, 67, 68, 69, 71,
    75, 114, 119, 142, 146, 163, 171,
    173, 174, 175, 176, 179, 180,
    181, 183, 193, 194, 202, 209,
    211, 213
Isaac, 7, 8, 55, 137, 138, 139, 148–56,
    158, 217, 218
Ishmael, 7, 8, 47, 154, 154n109, 155
Israel, 1, 4, 5, 6, 7, 8, 16, 18, 19, 20, 22,
    23, 23n95, 30, 32, 33, 37, 39, ,
    41, 46, 48, 49, 50, 51, 52, 54, 55,
    56, 56n214, 56n215, 57, 58, 59,
    60, 62, 64, 65, 66, 67, 69, 70, 71,
    72, 73, 74, 83, 92, 107, 109, 113,
    114, 116, 116n83, 120, 122, 123,
    124, 126, 127, 128, 129, 130,
    131, 132, 135, 135n50, 139, 142,
    143, 144, 145, 146, 147, 149,
    150, 151, 153, 156, 157, 158,
    167, 169, 170, 170n47, 173, 174,
    177, 178, 184, 190, 190n20, 194,
    198n10, 203, 204, 205, 205n18,
    206, 207, 208, 208n30, 209, 211,
    212, 213, 215, 216
Israelite, 7, 8, 18, 46, 48, 51, 59, 98, 124

James, 81, 94, 96, 96n12, 97, 97n13, 98,
    99, 99n24, 118, 164
Jeremiah, 4, 19, 20, 49, 68, 69, 69, 70, 71,
    73, 74, 75, 76, 83n20, 128, 142,
    142n82, 145, 171, 172, 173, 174,
    175, 175n59, 177, 183, 185, 202,
    203, 206, 207, 208, 209, 210,
    211, 212, 213, 217
Jerusalem, 62, 70, 71, 78, 80, 94, 97,
    97n13, 112, 146n91, 150, 152,
    153, 155, 155n118, 156, 177n66,
    215n2
Jesus, 1, 4, 5, 10, 11, 12, 13, 14, 15, 16,
    18, 19, 20, 22, 23, 23n95, 24, 25,
    26, 26n104, 27, 28, 29, 30, 32,
    33, 38, 40, 41, 44, 45, 46, 51, 52,
    53, 54, 56, 57, 58, 59, 60, 62, 63,
    68, 69, 70, 73, 73n272, 79, 80,
    81, 81n15, 82, 82n16, 83, 84, 85,
    86, 87, 88, 89, 90, 91, 92, 93, 95,
    96, 97, 97n16, 98, 99, 102, 105,

105n52, 107, 109, 109n65, 110,
111, 111n67, 111n70, 112, 113,
114, 116, 117, 119, 120, 125,
126, 129, 130, 131, 136, 138,
139, 145, 145n89, 148, 150, 151,
152, 156, 157, 159, 160n8, 161,
163, 164, 167, 167n35, 172, 179,
181, 182, 184, 189, 196, 198,
198n11, 200, 201, 202, 204, 205,
210, 211, 212, 214, 215, 215n2,
215n3, 216, 217, 218
Jew/Jewish, 1, 1n1, 10, 11, 12, 16, 19,
22, 23, 28n106, 30, 33, 37, 49,
51, 53, 57, 58, 58, 60, 66, 71, 72,
75, 76, 82, 83, 89, 94, 94n2, 95,
95n9, 96, 97, 97, 98, 98n22, 99,
99n24, 100, 102, 102n35, 103,
103n39, 106, 107, 108, 112, 113,
116, 117, 118n84, 123, 134, 140,
143, 147, 156, 157, 158, 160n7,
164, 166, 167, 170, 170n47, 172,
175, 176, 177, 177n63, 178, 180,
181, 184, 191, 194, 194n32, 197,
198, 201, 202, 204, 205n18, 208,
210, 211, 212, 213, 214, 216, 217
Josephus, 32, 44, 44n176, 95n9, 98n22,
121, 177
Judah, 19, 21, 49, 52, 67, 70, 72, 112,
119, 129, 154, 177, 189, 206, 212
judgment, 8, 13, 21, 61, 66, 122, 135,
169, 187, 188, 189n12, 193, 215,
217
justification, 10, 12, 14, 15, 20, 21, 24,
25, 66, 95, 96, 100, 136, 137,
148, 163

Kennedy, Matt, 10
kinship, 54, 58, 69, 70, 104, 217, 218

law, 2, 3, 4, 4n14, 8, 9, 10, 14, 16, 22,
23, 25n101, 29, 31, 32, 34, 36,
45n181, 46, 47, 51, 53, 56, 57,
58, 64, 65, 67, 68, 69, 69n259,
70–73, 78, 82, 84, 85, 88, 92,
96, 97, 98, 100, 101, 102, 103,
105, 106, 107–110, 112, 114,
115, 116, 117, 118, 119, 120–24,
120n1, 121n2, 127, 128, 128n22,
129, 129n25, 130, 130n29, 132,
132n35, 132n37, 133, 134,
135, 136, 139, 140, 140n70,
141, 141n76, 142, 143, 144–49,
144n87, 144n88, 151, 153, 155,
157, 160, 161, 162, 163, 164,
165, 165n22, 167, 170, 171, 172,
173, 173n53, 174, 175, 179–85,
180n74, 181n77, 181n80,
181n81, 182n84, 183n91,
183n92, 186, 187, 192, 193, 194,
194n33, 199, 200, 201, 203, 207,
208, 211, 212, 213, 214, 215,
216, 217
law, curse of, 6, 12, 32, 46, 47, 104, 110,
122, 123, 124, 126, 130, 131,
131n32, 136, 138, 148, 149, 153,
217, 218
law, works of, 3, 9, 10, 36, 94, 103,
103n39, 103n41, 103n45, 104,
110, 118, 129n27, 132, 147, 161,
187
life, 13, 14, 14n62, 15, 16, 17, 18, 19,
21, 23, 25n103, 26, 27, 27n105,
28, 29, 30, 32, 34, 36, 37, 38, 40,
41, 42, 43, 44, 45, 46, 47, 48, 49,
51, 52, 59, 60, 61, 62, 63, 64, 65,
65n248, 68n287, 73, 75, 76, 77,
79, 80, 83, 84, 86, 88, 91, 92, 94,
95, 98, 102, 104, 106, 107, 108,
109, 110, 111, 111n69, 112, 113,
113n76, 114, 116, 118, 120, 123,
125–39, 125n18, 134n47, 141,
143, 144, 145, 146, 147, 148,
148n95, 149, 150, 151, 153, 154,
156, 157, 158, 159, 160n7, 161,
164, 165, 165n22, 166, 167n32,
168, 168n36, 169, 170, 171, 174,
175, 179, 180, 180n72, 182, 183,
184, 189, 190, 192, 193, 194,
194n32, 195, 197, 202, 205, 207,
212, 214, 215, 216, 217, 218
life, eternal, 27, 28, 186, 191, 192, 193,
217
life, new, 12, 26, 37, 46, 59, 59n226, 63,
75, 87, 92, 106, 118, 139, 166,
167, 168, 169, 190, 218

life, resurrected/risen, 10, 13, 15, 20, 23, 26, 75, 88, 91, 95, 107, 108, 110, 112, 114, 117, 118–19, 120, 126, 130, 131, 133, 136, 139, 145, 147, 148, 158, 161, 163, 164, 165, 191, 218

love, 13, 20, 40, 42, 53, 68, 70, 101, 109, 110, 163, 165n22, 171, 175, 176, 182, 183, 183n91, 184, 187, 199–202, 215, 217

Maccabean, 31, 177
maturity/immaturity, 20, 57, 58, 73, 158
Messiah, 12, 23n95, 25, 39, 46, 55, 64, 74, 77, 82, 85, 91, 95, 98, 102, 104, 104n47, 106, 107, 109, 114, 116, 117, 118, 119, 125, 129, 130, 132, 133, 140, 141, 143, 144, 147, 148, 151, 158, 161, 167, 190, 194, 215n2, 218

Moses, 7, 8, 18, 32, 48, 52, 54, 55, 56, 60, 122, 123, 134, 140, 142, 142n80, 143, 172, 173, 175, 181, 182

Nebuchadnezzar, 50
New Covenant, 4, 5, 7n30, 8, 9, 56, 64, 65, 66, 66n249, 67, 68n256, 69, 72, 74, 75, 83, 171–74, 175n59, 179, 202, 203, 204, 208, 209, 210, 210n33, 211, 212
New Creation, 7n30, 22, 23, 27, 52, 53, 79, 106, 130, 166, 167, 192, 196, 197, 202, 203, 204, 205, 205n18, 207, 208, 209, 210, 211, 212, 213, 214, 214n1
New Perspective, 10, 10n43, 21, 22n89, 24

Ovid, 42–43

Parousia, 13, 108, 131, 161
participation, 12, 19, 21, 23n95, 59, 109, 109n65, 166n25, 184
Passover, 48, 62n237
Peter (Cephas), 61, 81, 94, 94n2, 96, 97, 99, 99n24, 100, 101, 101n34, 102, 102n35, 103, 105, 106, 117, 118, 118n84, 147, 187

Pharaoh, 13, 48, 49, 54, 55, 129
Pharisees, 23, 83
Philo, 140, 142, 163

Quintillian, 2
Qumran, 38, 49n153, 61, 103, 123, 162, 172

reconciliation, 14, 14n59, 63, 66, 212n44
rectification, 9, 10, 12, 13, 16, 18, 19, 20, 21, 21n88, 21n89, 22, 23, 26, 27, 29, 36, 41, 45, 51, 57, 58, 60, 74, 75, 77, 84, 85, 86, 87, 88, 89, 91, 92, 93, 95, 96, 103, 104, 105, 106, 107, 108, 109, 110, 111, 112, 114, 117, 118, 119, 122, 125, 133, 139, 144, 147, 148, 151, 152, 156, 157, 161, 162, 163, 164, 166, 167, 171, 178, 179, 184, 187, 189, 191, 193, 195, 197, 204, 213, 214, 215, 216, 217, 218
redemption/redemption history, 5, 6, 7, 9, 11, 16, 19, 19n81, 20, 32, 37, 46, 47, 56, 57, 58, 60, 66, 69, 69, 70, 71, 72, 86, 92, 93, 107, 124, 129, 131, 143, 158, 170, 171, 207
reformation, 133
restoration, 5, 8, 9, 11, 19, 20, 29, 30, 33, 35n130, 37, 39, 40, 41, 42, 44, 44n176, 46, 47, 56, 60, 64, 67, 68, 69, 75, 76, 91, 92, 112, 114, 120, 124, 125, 131, 139, 142n82, 148, 149, 149n97, 151, 153, 156, 157, 170, 171, 176, 177, 185, 189, 190, 204, 210, 213, 214, 215, 216, 217, 218
resurrection, 2, 4, 5, 8, 9, 10, 12, 13, 14, 14n59, 15, 18, 19, 21, 22, 23, 23n95, 24, 25, 25n101, 25n102, 26, 27, 27n105, 29, 30, 31, 32, 33, 33n124, 34, 37, 38, 39, 40, 41, 45, 46, 47, 49, 51, 54, 58, 59, 60, 61, 62, 63, 64, 64n244, 76, 77, 78, 79, 80, 81, 82, 84, 85, 86, 88, 89, 90, 90n38, 91, 92, 93, 95, 105, 107, 108, 109, 114, 116, 117, 118, 119, 125, 125n18, 129,

130, 131, 136, 138, 138n62, 139,
    145, 148, 150, 151, 151n314,
    152, 153, 154, 156, 157, 158,
    161, 164, 166, 167, 167n31, 187,
    187n3, 188, 189, 191, 193, 195,
    197n6, 204, 210, 214, 214n1,
    215, 215n2, 216, 218
revivification, 2n2, 4, 9, 10, 13, 14, 21,
    21n88, 22, 23, 26, 27, 29, 30, 31,
    35, 36, 38, 40, 45, 46, 47, 51, 52,
    54, 58, 59, 60, 65, 66, 75, 76, 77,
    84, 85, 86, 88, 92, 93, 94, 95, 102,
    106, 109, 110, 111, 112, 113,
    115, 117, 118, 120, 122, 125,
    126, 128, 129, 30, 133, 138, 144,
    145, 148, 149, 150, 151, 152,
    153, 154, 156, 157, 159, 163,
    164, 165, 167, 168, 169, 170,
    171, 180, 184, 185, 186, 189,
    193, 195, 196, 197, 198, 201,
    202, 205, 212, 214, 215, 216, 217
rhetoric, 2n7, 16, 18, 21, 24, 27, 54, 63,
    64, 73, 78, 78n1, 79, 91, 102,
    110, 117, 183, 187, 198, 217
rhetoric, forensic, 2, 78n1
right status, 21, 21n89, 34, 73, 88, 92,
    100, 103, 105, 109, 110, 111,
    112, 114, 118, 120, 121, 126,
    134, 138, 140, 143, 146, 157,
    158, 199, 200, 215
righteousness, 9, 14, 20, 21, 23, 24, 31,
    35, 36, 38, 39, 111, 121, 163, 215

Sadducees, 33, 107
salvation, 15, 29, 40, 82, 86, 114, 119,
    122, 123, 129, 135, 137, 152,
    162, 176, 177, 186, 193, 200,
    201, 209, 212
Scripture, 4, 6, 7, 8, 16, 21, 61, 88n31,
    89, 116, 121, 122, 123, 143, 146,
    150, 172
Second Temple, 11, 123, 163, 206
sin, 3, 6, 7, 14, 26, 38, 46, 47, 54, 62, 68,
    73, 74, 86, 87, 89, 92, 105, 107,
    111, 114, 117, 119, 128, 129,
    130, 131, 140, 141, 142, 143,
    144, 145, 146, 147, 148, 152,
    153, 154, 160, 161, 162, 163,
    169, 170, 183, 194, 210, 215, 216
slave/slavery, 3n11, 6, 8, 9, 19, 21, 41,
    45n181, 46, 48, 52, 53, 54, 57,
    58, 59, 60, 62, 67, 68, 70, 71, 72,
    73, 75, 89, 107, 112, 148, 152,
    153, 154, 155, 158, 162, 165,
    171, 175, 182, 200, 201, 205, 216
soteriology, 4, 18, 20, 21, 25, 76, 77, 86,
    87, 109, 119, 151, 165n21, 216,
    218
Spirit, 1, 2n4, 3, 4, 7–8, 7n31, 9, 9n38,
    10, 10n40, 10n41, 11, 14, 15, 16,
    18, 20, 21, 23, 29, 34, 34n127,
    35–36, 36n134, 38, 39, 40, 47,
    51–53, 57, 58, 63–76, 65n248,
    68n255, 68n256, 65n257,
    70n265, 73n272, 79, 88, 89, 90,
    90n38, 91, 91n39, 92, 92n40,
    100, 107, 108, 109, 110, 111,
    111n68, 111n70, 112, 114, 115,
    118, 119, 120–22, 126n19, 128,
    129, 130, 130n30, 132, 136,
    137, 137n56, 137n60, 138,
    139, 139n65, 140–58, 148n94,
    149n97, 151n94, 151n96,
    154n110, 159, 159n1, 159n3,
    160–67, 165n22, 166n26,
    166n30, 167n31, 167n33, 169,
    170, 171–85, 180n74, 180n76,
    183n92, 186, 187, 188, 189, 190,
    191, 192–95, 194n32, 194n33,
    200, 201–213, 210n37, 211n41,
    214, 214n1, 215, 217, 217n7, 218
Spirit, according to, 89, 92, 138, 138,
    149, 154, 156, 160n7, 160n8,
    178, 217
Spirit, birth by, 7, 8, 138, 217
Spirit, Holy, 52n201, 56, 56n213, 90n38,
    165, 192
Spirit, life by/through/in, 4, 9, 18, 20, 21,
    26, 27, 29, 34, 52, 63, 65n248,
    75, 88, 91, 92, 95, 108, 109, 111,
    112, 114, 117, 118, 119, 130,
    132, 146, 147, 148, 154, 156,
    157, 163, 164, 165, 165n21, 167,
    168–71, 180, 183, 184, 191, 194,
    197, 216, 218

seed, 18, 89, 90, 117, 125, 141, 142, 158, 167, 169, 184, 188, 189, 190, 192, 216, 218
Stoicheia, 6, 71, 72, 205

Teacher of Righteousness, 38
Torah, 20, 21, 30, 31, 36, 46, 51, 52, 62n237, 67, 68, 69, 70, 72, 74, 78, 82, 84, 85, 94n2, 95, 97, 97n16, 98, 99, 101, 102, 103, 104, 105, 106, 107, 112, 113, 117, 118, 125n18, 126, 128, 128n22, 129, 130, 132, 134, 136, 137, 139, 140, 141, 141n73, 143, 144, 145, 146, 147, 151, 155, 158, 160, 161, 162, 163, 165, 165n22, 166, 171, 172, 173, 174, 175, 177, 180, 181, 183, 184, 195, 199, 200, 201, 205, 207, 212, 215, 217
transgression, 62, 86, 128, 141, 142, 143, 144, 145, 146
truth, 38, 74, 95, 96, 97, 99, 100, 101, 104, 168, 173, 199, 200

vindication, 29, 30, 31, 32, 35n130, 36, 92, 114, 156, 214

world, 1, 3, 4, 6, 7, 25, 27, 31, 38, 43, 47, 60, 61, 80, 122, 145, 150, 161, 166, 169, 197, 198, 201, 202, 204, 205, 208, 213, 214, 216

zeal, 97, 97n17, 98, 98n22, 100, 102

Scripture Index

Hebrew Bible (Old Testament)

Genesis

1–3	52
1:2	53
1:27	53
2:7	48, 127, 166, 194, 217
2:16–17	145
9:4	49
12:1–3	139
12:3	111
15:1–6	139
15:2	154
15:6	111, 121, 137, 138, 138n61, 217
16:6	154
17	163
17:5	138
17:15–19	154
18:10–14	139
18:12–14	154
18:18	111
21:1–10	139
21:12	149
22:17–18	111
23:6–19	113
37:35	47
46:3	47

Exodus

3:8	58, 58n221
3:10	18, 58, 204
4:22	54, 55, 56
4:22–23	55
6:6	46
6:7	56n214, 72n271, 203
7:5	72
7:14–25	47
7:16	55
7:17	72n271
7:21a	48
8:1	55
8:16–18	129
8:20	55
9:1	55
9:1–3	48
9:4	48
9:6	48
9:13	55
9:16	13
10:2	72n271
10:28	48
11:5	48
12	48
12:7	48

Exodus (continued)

12:12–13	48n187
12:27	46
12:30	49
12:33	49n189
13–14	18
13:21–22	52
14:4	72
14:11	49n190
14:14	56
14:18	72
14:19	52
14:24	52
14:30	59n227
14:48	37n140
15:13	46
16–17	18
18:8–10	46
19:1—24:11	69
20:2	54
20:3–5	145
20:17	145
28:1–3	52
29:46	54, 72
30:30–35	52
31:1–6	52
31:3	52
31:4	52, 52n202
31:18	179
32:1	36n135
32:15	142
34:4	142
34:29	142
34:33–35	173

Leviticus

17:11	49
17:14	49
18:5	51, 127, 128, 129, 133, 134, 135, 135n50, 136, 145
19:18	183, 183n91
19:23	175
19:36	54
23:34	140n69
25:38	54
25:55	54
26:1	64
26:11–12	63
26:12	64, 203
26:13	54
26:45	54
26:46 (LXX)	142

Numbers

4:37 (LXX)	142
11:25	52
14:2	49n191
15:41	54
21:5	49n191
22:5	58. 204
22:10	18
25:11–13	98
36:13 (LXX)	142

Deuteronomy

1:30–31	126
4:1	127, 128
4:1–4	127
4:12–19	127
4:20	18, 59, 126
4:26–28	127
4:32–39	127
4:37	36n135, 126
4:45	126
5:6	54, 126
5:7	127
5:7–9	145
5:15	126
5:21	145
5:33	127, 128
6	127
6:4–5	67, 183
6:12	126
6:14–15	127
6:20–25	60n228, 126
7:1–12	127
7:4	127
7:8	126
8:1	127n21
8:11–14	126

8:11–20	127	28:27	50, 126
8:19	127	28:32–68	50
9:5	66	28:36	127
9:6	66	28:49–68	126
9:7–12	126	28:60	126
9:12	36n135	28:64	127
9:26	126	28:68	50n193, 126
10:16	175	29:2	126
11:10	126	29:12	203
11:13–16	127	29:13	126
11:16	127	29:25	126
11:28	127	29:26	127
11:31	127n21	30	8, 75, 125, 131, 175, 176, 177
12:10	127n21	30:1	125, 125n17
12:23	49	30:1–5	128, 176
12:29	127n21	30:1–6	127
13:1–8	127	30:2	176
13:2–7	127	30:6	127, 128, 149n97, 175, 176
13:5	126	30:6b	176
13:10	126	30:6–10	175
13:12	127n21	30:15	125, 125n17
13:13	127	30:17	127, 176
15:15	126	30:19	125, 125n17
16:1	54, 126	30:2	67n252
16:3	126	30:14	67n252
16:6	126	31:18	127
16:12	126	31:20	127
16:20	127n21, 145	31:29	127
17:3	127	32	54, 122, 125
18:20	127	32:1–43	55
20:1	126, 127	32:5	55
21	131	32:5–6	55
21:18–23	129	32:6	54
21:20	131	32:6b	55
21:23	98, 113, 129, 131	32:15–17	55
24:18	126	32:18	54, 55
26:1	127n21	32:39	125, 125n18, 126, 129
26:1–10	86		
26:8	126		
27–30	11, 75, 123, 126, 149, 157		
27:9	126, 203		Joshua
27:10–15	127		
27:26	129	24:2	145
28:9	126	24:23	67n252
28:13–15	127		
28:14	127		
28:26	113		

Judges

2:10	73
6:8	54

1 Samuel

2:5–6	150n101
10:6	52
10:18	54
30:12	134n42
30:16	134n42

1 Kings

8:48	67n252
8:51	18, 59
9:9	54
17:17	149

2 Kings

4:18	149
10:16	98
18:21	49n192

1 Chronicles

17:21	18, 59

2 Chronicles

7:22	54

Nehemiah

9:12	51n200
9:20	51n200
9:26	124
9:29	135

Job

3:7	150
14:14	44n175
16:16	30

Psalms

15:9–11 (LXX)	41
16:9–11	41n156
18:4–5	37n140
22:1	131n31
32:6	37n140
51:11	56n213
67:18	141
69:1–2	37n140
69:9	98
70:20 (LXX)	35
79:2	113
79:6	73
79:18 (LXX)	35
80:8	18, 59
81:10	54
84:5–6 (LXX)	35
89:27–28	56n218
95:10	73
104:30	34n129
114:1	18, 59
116:3	30
119:53	98
126	189, 190
126:1	189
126:1–3	189, 190
126:4	189, 190
126:4–6	189, 189n15
126:5	190
137:7 (LXX)	35
142 (LXX)	35
142:2 (LXX)	36
142:3 (LXX)	36
142:7 (LXX)	36
142:9 (LXX)	36
142:10 (LXX)	36n134
142:10c (LXX)	36
142: 10–11 (LXX)	35
142:11 (LXX)	36
142:11c (LXX)	36
143	35, 35n132
143:2	160
145:14	39n151
146	40, 41
146:6–7	39
146:7–8	39
1467–9b	40

146:8b	39

Proverbs

9:10	72
30:16	150
31:4–7	134n42

Isaiah

5:11–12	134n42
5:22–23	134n42
6:7	175
9:2	30
11:1	90n36
11:9	72
11:10	90n36
24–27	33, 33n121
25:8	33, 46
26	150
26:17–19	37, 151n104
26:19	33
30–31	49n192
40:9	11n46
40–55	11
41:8	169
43:1–21	170
43:2	37n140, 51n199, 59
43:16	51n199
43:19	51n199, 170
44:1–5	169
44:3	137, 169, 170, 212
44:3–5	169–70
44:4	39n152, 170
44:4–5	170
44:5	170
48:12	51n199
52:7	11n46
52:12	51n199
52:13	167
52:13—53:12	152n107
53:1	151, 151n106
53:1—54:1	151
53:4–12	152
53:9	152
53:10	31, 167
53:10c–11	152
53:12	152
54	150, 151, 156
54:1	150, 152, 155
54:5–7	156
54:10	172
55:3	172
56:3–7	170n47
57:15–16	34
57:15–19	34
57:16	34n129, 129
57:19	212
61	40
61:1	39, 40
61:4a	39
61:8	172
61:11	39
63	56n213
63:7–10	56
63:7–16	55
63:8	56n214
63:10	56
63:10–11	56
63:11–14	51
63:12	56
63:14	52, 56
63:16	55, 56
65:17	211
66:22	211

Jeremiah

1:5	83n20
2:8	73, 172
3:6–10	70n262
3:17	70n263
3:18	70n264
3:19	70
4:4	175, 176
4:5–31	176
4:10	212
5:4	74
5:4–5	71
5:5	74
5:6	71
5:7	71, 74
6:14	212

Jeremiah (continued)

6:19	172
7:23	203
7:30	145
8:8	172
8:11	212
8:15	212
9:6	73
9:8	212
9:13ff.	172
9:23–26	206, 209
9:24	72, 206
9:25–26	177–78
9:26	206
10:25	73
11:4	54, 203
13:11	203
16:11ff.	172
18:15	145
22:16	72
23:5–6	90n36
24:4–7	204
24:7	72, 74n277, 204, 210n36
26:4ff.	172
30:22	203
31	8, 65, 76, 211
31:1	56, 203
31:9	56, 70
31:20	70
31:27	70
31:29–30	203
31:31	56, 69, 70, 207, 210, 212
31:32	36n135, 69, 174
31:33	68, 69, 70, 74, 128, 142, 172, 174, 179, 180, 203, 204, 209, 211n42
31:31–34	68, 204
31:34	37n138, 72, 73, 128, 173
32:37–41	204
32:38	74n277, 203, 204
32:39	210n33
32:39–40	203
32:40	172
33:6	212
33:9	212
34:13	54
38:22	212
42	49–50
42:1–6	49
42:7	49
42:8–9	49
42:10–14	49
42:15–21	49, 50
42:16	49
42:17	49
42:18	49
43–44	50
43:11–13	50
44:12–14	50
44:27	50
50:5	172

Ezekiel

1	61
1:4–28	61
1:20–21	194n32
6:7	72n271
6:9	145
6:10	72
6:13	72n271
6:14	72
7:4	72n271
9:2	61
10	61
10:17	194n32
11:10	72n271
11:12	72n271
11:17–21	204
11:19	210, 211n40
11:20	203, 204
11:21	145
12:15	72
14:11	203
16:60	172
18	113
18:1–2	203

18:31	210		148, 149, 152, 153, 156, 157, 190, 194, 218
20	113		
20:1–31	113		
20:11	135	37:1–2	62
20:13	135	37:1–14	8, 30, 37, 47, 60, 62, 63, 63n241, 64, 75, 119, 151, 155, 156, 157, 211, 215
20:21	135		
20:23	190n20		
22:15	190n20		
24:7	72		
25:11	72	37:3	60, 114, 149, 152, 156, 194
26:6	72		
29:12	50	37:3–14	129
30:4	50	37:5	153, 194
30:6	50	37:5b	194
30:8	50	37:5–6	75
30:11	50	37:5–10	62
30:16	50	37:5–11	153
33	113	37:6	75, 152, 153, 194
34:23–24	90n36	37:6b	75
34:24	74n277	37:7	62
34:25	172	37:9	52, 75, 152, 153, 194
36	8		
36–37	4, 65–66, 75, 76, 139, 153, 156	37:9–10	194
		37:10	75, 153
36:1—37:14	119	37:11–14	63
36:12–24	154	37:12	62, 75, 156
36:17–19	114, 119	37:12b	62
36:21–23	35	37:12–13	62
36:22–23	66	37:12–14	194
36:22–28	66, 75	37:14	75, 209, 211
36:22–32	204	37:14a	152
36:24	67	37:16–24b	209
36:25	66	37:22	210
36:26	67, 210	37:23	74n277, 203
36:26–27	66, 68, 71, 119, 142n81, 179, 203, 207, 211	37:24	115
		37:26	64, 172, 212
		37:27	63, 64, 64n246, 74n277, 203
36:26–28	75		
36:27	34, 35, 67, 68, 115, 119, 172, 174, 209, 211	39:29	194
		44:7	209
36:27a	152n108		
36:27–28	67, 68, 75, 194	## Daniel	
36:28	67, 174, 203, 204	7:9–10	61
36:29	128	9:15	54
36:32	35n133	10:5	61
37	33, 61, 62, 63, 65, 112, 113, 132,	12:6–7	61

Hosea

4:1	73
5	37
5:13	37
6:1	37
6:1–3	8, 47
6:2	37
6:3	37
6:6	72
11:1	6, 57n219, 73n273, 158
11:1–4	8
13	32
13:14	33n125, 37, 46
13:14b	32
14:8	37, 37n139

Joel

2:28	52
2:28–29	212

Amos

4:10	48n186
6:6	134n42

Jonah

2:3 (LXX)	38n142
2:7 (LXX)	38

Micah

4:2	183
4:12	73

Habakkuk

2	218
2:3–5	133
2:4	104, 104n47, 129, 129n24, 133, 135, 138, 156, 157, 158, 218
2:4b	133
2:5	129, 134
2:14	72

Haggai

1:1–11	190
2:4–5	51
2:5	52

Zechariah

8:8	74n277, 203

Malachi

2:10	55n211

Apocrypha

Judith

9:4	98
14:10	177, 177n65

Wisdom of Solomon

3:1–4	32
3:2	50
7:5–6	50

Sirach

17:11–12	194
44:19	121

Baruch

1:18–19	124
4:1	134n46

1 Maccabees

1:14–15	177n67
2:24–27	98
2:44	102n36

2 Maccabees

6:13	98n21
7:9	31
7:22–23	31
14:36	31
14:38	31n113

Pseudepigrapha

2 Baruch

4:2–3	155n118
32:6	211
44:12	197n7

1 Enoch

45:4–5	211
72:1	197n7

2 Enoch

30:7	166n28

4 Ezra

3:4–6	166n28
7:26	155n118
7:75	211

3 Maccabees

3:3–4	95n9

4 Maccabees

7:18–19	107
16:25	108
18:16–19	60–61

Apocalypse of Peter

	61

Assumption of Moses

9:6—10:1	32

Joseph and Aseneth

7:1	95n9
8:2	168
8:5	95n9, 168
8:10–11	168
12:5	95n9
19:10–11	168

Jubilees

1:29	197n7
4:26	197n7
15:1–2	140
16:20–31	140
22:16	95n9
23:23–24	102

Psalms of Solomon

1:1	102n36
2:1	102n36
11	11
14:2	194

Sibylline Oracles

2.1.220	61

Testament of Abraham

18:9–11	169, 169n41

Testament of Judah

25:4	31

Testament of Naphtali

1:1	51, 51n196

Testament of Reuben

2:1–9	166n28

New Testament

Matthew

11:5	40n154
12:39–41	38n144
16:4	38n144
26:28	172n48
27:46	131n31
27:51	62
27:51–53	62
27:52	62
27:53	62

Mark

12:28–34	183
14:24	172n48
15:34	131n31

Luke

7:22	40n154
7:34	130
9:30–31	50
11:29–32	38n144
15:32	41
20:37–38	108
20:38	107n63
22:20	172n48

John

3:16	134
5:25–28	62
6:53–54	49n188
12:24	189n13
13:34–35	182
20	63
20:22	63

Acts

7:53	141
9:3–9	82n17
15	97n13
15:24	97n113
22:6–11	82n17
26:11	101
26:12–21	82n17

Romans

1	73
1:1	89
1:2	89
1:2–4	160n8
1:3–4	89, 92, 160n8
1:3–4a	90
1:4	89, 90, 178n68
1–5	24
1:17	28n106
1:21	73n274

SCRIPTURE INDEX

1:21–32	73n275	5	63, 119, 128, 145, 146
1:28	73n274		
2	175, 176, 177, 185	5–7	128, 144
2:7	186n1	5–8	217n8
2:12	144	5:5	176
2:14	102n35	5:10	86, 119
2:14–15	174	5:10a	145
2:17	198	5:10b	145
2:17–29	175	5:12	145
2:23	141n72, 198	5:12–21	14, 21, 147n92
2:25	174	5:13	107, 145
2:25–29	167, 178, 180n76	5:14	141n72
2:28	163	5:14b	145
2:28–29	180n75	5:17	28
2:29	128, 149n97, 175, 176, 178, 180, 209	5:18	27n105, 28, 119n85
3:20	35	5:20	145, 146
3:20b	107	5:21	186n1
3:23–25	15, 25	6	46, 59n223
3:24	86	6:1–7	38n141
3:26	24	6:1–11	59
3:27	198	6:3	59n225
3:29–30	143	6:3–4	37n140, 92
4	89	6:3–6	26
4:2	198	6:4	59, 59n225, 80
4:3	217	6:4a	59
4:3–6	138n61	6:4–8	114
4:9	138n61, 177	6:5	59, 167
4:15	141n72, 144	6:6	114, 163, 167, 210
4:16–19	150, 151	6:8	65
4:16–20	149	6:10	107
4:16–25	104, 139	6:10–11	108
4:17	14n61, 56, 80, 111, 138, 154, 216n6, 218	6:14	70
		6:15	70
		6:17	108
4:17–19	154	6:19	161
4:17–20	145	6:22–23	186n1
4:17–21	138	7	130, 144, 145, 146, 147
4:18–19	217		
4:19	138	7–8	194, 208
4:20–22	217	7:1	147
4:22	138n61, 138n63	7:1–3	148
4:23–25	138	7:2	147
4:24	56, 82, 111, 138	7:3	147
4:24–25	138	7:4	147
4:25	12, 86, 87n30, 92, 152n107	7:5	46
		7:6	67
		7:7	145

Romans (continued)

Reference	Pages
7:7a	146
7:8a	145
7:8b	145, 147
7:7–11	107n62
7:7–12	144
7:8–10	146
7:9	147
7:10	145
7:11	145, 147
7:12–14	144n88
7:13–14	145
7:13–20	144
7:14	145, 183
7:15–21	147
7:19–21	146
7:22	183
7:24	32n118, 47, 147, 147n93
8:2	46, 67, 112, 146, 183
8:3	145, 161
8:3a	128n22
8:4	142
8:10	111, 119
8:11	12, 15, 56, 82, 90, 111, 119
8:11–13	145
8:11–16	154n110
8:12–13	26
8:13	108
8:14	51, 56n216, 70
8:15	15, 73n272
8:17	14
8:21	193
8:23	137, 151
8:29	90
9:6	209
9:6–7	149
9:6–9	139
9:7	139
9:8	160n8
9:13–17	89
9:17	13
9:26	28n106
9–11	8, 116, 204, 208
10:4	107
10:5	28n106
10:9	86, 111
10:16	151n106
11	63
11:14–15	109
11:18	198
11:25	116
11:26	32n118, 116, 209
12:1	28n106
14:1–12	187
14:7–8	108
14:7–9	14n59
14:9	80
14:11	28n106
15:4	88n31
15:31	32n118

1 Corinthians

Reference	Pages
1:13	18
1:14	18
1:15	18
1:16	18
1:17	18
1:21	73n274
1:31	206
3:5—4:5	187
4:7	198
5:6	198
5:6–8	45n182
5:7	48n187
6	24
6:9	193n30
6:14	13, 119
7:19	202, 207n25
7:39	28n108
8:3	74n276
9	181
9:11	188n10, 189
9:14	28
9:20	70
9:21	181
10:1	45n182
10:1–6	56n216
10:2	18, 46
10:5	18
10:7–12	18

10:11	172
10:17	18
10:32	18, 178n68
11:25	172n48
12:12–13	58, 59
12:13	18, 58, 202
15	13, 24, 25, 86
15:3–4	86
15:4	37n137
15:15	111
15:19	27n105, 28
15:20	45n182, 86, 151
15:22	111
15:23	86, 151
15:26	33
15:29	18
15:33	193n30
15:39–45	81
15:35–50	13
15:35–54	21
15:36–37	189
15:42	193
15:42–44	189, 189n12
15:43	114
15:45	28n107, 33, 80, 109, 111, 130, 166n27
15:50	193
15:54–57	46
15:55	32
15:56	46, 146
15:56b	144

2 Corinthians

1:8	28n107
1:8–10	30n111, 108
1:9	13, 56, 82
1:9–10	86
1:10	32n118, 46
1:21	177
1:22	64, 137, 176
2:3–11	179
2:14	179
2:14–17	179
2:15	179
2:15–16	108
2:16	64, 180
217	180
3	8, 185
3–5	217n8
3:1	179
3:1–6	179, 180
3:1–7	45n182
3:2	64, 179
3:2–3	64
3:3	28n107, 128, 142, 173, 176, 177, 179, 180, 217
3:6	64, 108, 111, 172n48, 180
3:6c	63n241
3:6–7	144
3:7	108, 134n43, 173, 180
3:13	173
3:14	173
3:15	173
3:16–18	174
3:17	67
3:17–18	111n67
4:7–14	64n244
4:10	26
4:10–12	109
4:14	13, 82
5:5	137
5:11	74n276
5:12	64
5:12–15	64
5:14	64, 65
5:14–15	148, 166n25
5:14–17	214n1
5:15	64
5:15–19	63
5:16	166n25, 167n35
5:17	106n55, 131, 166n25, 210
5:21	130, 131n31, 145, 166n25
6	64
6:3–4	64
6:9	64
6:11	64
6:14–16	64
6:14—7:1	63

2 Corinthians *(continued)*

6:16	28n107, 63, 64
6:16b	63, 64n246
7	65
7:1	65
7:2	63
7:3	65, 109
9:6	188n10, 189
9:10	188n10
10:15–16	198
11:4	179n69
11:4–5	179n69
11:13	179n69
11:17–18	198
11:23–28	25
12:7	159, 161
12:9	14
12:11–12	179n69
13:4	28, 90n38, 119

Galatians

1–2	78, 94n2
1–4	162
1:1	14, 26, 27, 29, 32, 40, 53, 54, 58, 59, 80, 81, 82, 85, 87, 89, 91, 111, 114, 138, 214, 215, 216, 218
1:1b	87
1:1–2	78n1
1:1–4	91
1:1–5	16, 77, 79, 91
1:2–3	85
1:2–4	81, 85
1:3	53
1:3–4	78n1
1:4	20, 32n119, 53, 54, 58, 80, 85, 86, 87, 89, 114, 119, 129, 163, 214
1:4a	85, 86, 87
1:4b	5, 87
1:4c	85, 87
1:5	78n1
1:6–9	179n69
1:6–10	91, 100
1:10	78
1:11	84n25
1:11–12	78
1:11—2:10	79
1:12	82, 83n18, 84, 91, 114
1:12a	82, 83
1:12b	83
1:12c	83
1:13	97, 98
1:13–14	96, 191
1:13–17	82
1:13–20	96, 102
1:14	97, 101n32
1:15	83n20, 84
1:16	82, 82n16, 83, 84, 91, 114, 160, 162
1:18–19	96
1:20	100
1:22	116
2	97
2:1–5	100
2:1–9	96, 102
2:1–10	97n13
2:3	101
2:4	97, 98, 100, 116, 146n91, 179n69, 204, 205
2:4–5	99
2:5	99, 100, 199
2:6	96
2:6b	97n15
2:7–9	207
2:9	96
2:11	96
2:11–12	96
2:11–14	94, 94n2, 96, 102, 164
2:12	99, 207, 209
2:12b	96, 97
2:13	96
2:14	26, 28, 94n2, 95, 99, 100, 101, 102n35, 118n84, 199
2:14b	96
2:14–21	94n2

SCRIPTURE INDEX

2:15	94n2, 95, 102	3:1	26, 88n31, 94n2, 99, 109, 110
2:15–16	9		
2:15–17	94n2	3:1–2	2
2:15–21	10, 22n89, 94, 94n2, 95, 96, 102	3:1–5	112, 114, 136
		3:1–14	118, 121
2:16	35, 36, 103, 110, 117, 147, 160, 162	3:2	2, 92, 110, 130, 151
2:16a	102	3:2b	151
2:17	94n2, 105, 116, 117	3:2–3	161, 162
		3:2–5	71, 88, 110, 119, 121, 132, 139, 153, 161, 201
2:18	105, 117, 147		
2:19	13, 14, 26, 59n226, 65, 84, 85, 87, 92, 105, 106, 109, 109n65, 110, 114, 118, 130, 143, 148, 153, 170, 201, 202, 212	3:2–6	156
		3:2—4:7	151
		3:3	149n98, 164, 193, 201
		3:3b	161, 164
		3:4	14
		3:5	187
		3:5a	194
2:19–20	14, 15, 16, 51, 84, 86, 87, 88, 93, 102, 104, 105, 107, 112, 113, 116, 117, 118, 120, 147, 159, 166n24, 167, 198, 214	3:6	58, 88, 104, 110, 111, 120, 121, 133, 138n61, 157, 217
		3:6–9	114, 121, 218
		3:6–14a	136
		3:6—4:7	79
		3:7	121
2:19–21	29, 110, 119, 143	3:7–9	153, 158
2:19—3:1	191	3:7–14	145
2:19—3:5	75, 184	3:8	121, 136
2:19—3:14	171	3:9	2, 104n46, 121, 123, 124, 136
2:20	13, 15, 26, 87, 92n40, 109, 111, 114, 118, 119, 130, 136, 145, 148, 153, 158, 159, 161, 162, 163, 200, 201, 215	3:9–10	104, 132, 153
		3:9–14	123
		3:10	110, 123, 124, 129, 131, 132
		3:10a	129
2:20a	118	3:10b	129
2:20b	118, 131, 164	3:10–13	114, 157, 164, 215
2:20c	118	3:10–14	75, 120, 122, 123, 131, 139, 146, 148, 157
2:20d	131		
2:21	26, 87, 88, 94n2, 109, 110, 114, 119	3:10–21	165
		3:11	26, 28, 123, 129n26, 132, 153, 156, 157, 158
2:21b	87, 88, 109, 143		
2:21—3:5	108		
3	57, 104, 114, 146, 148, 170	3:11a	129
3–4	217n8	3:11b	129, 135

Galatians *(continued)*

3:11–12	137
3:11–13	86
3:12	26, 28, 123, 127, 129, 133, 134, 135
3:12a	135
3:12b	135
3:13	25, 32n120, 46, 98, 123, 124, 129, 131n33, 137, 145, 198, 215
3:13–14	57, 88, 136, 139
3:14	57, 111, 114, 116, 120, 123, 130, 133, 136, 139, 145, 148, 153, 154, 156, 157, 204
3:14a	136, 137
3:14b	136, 137
3:15	139, 172
3:15–17	140
3:15–18	5, 139, 158
3:15–25	130
3:16	136, 158, 218
3:17	136, 139, 172
3:18	136, 139
3:19	88, 92, 136, 141, 142, 182
3:19a	128, 146
3:19b	128, 146
3:19–20	143
3:19–21	29, 141
3:19–25	106, 120, 140, 144
3:20	142
3:21	9, 14, 16, 21, 26, 34, 36, 51, 88, 111n66, 112, 119, 120, 130, 132, 135, 136, 140, 145, 146, 148, 156, 157, 158, 180, 215
3:21a	141, 143, 184
3:21b	9, 85, 87, 88, 109, 110, 114, 128, 129, 143, 170
3:22	136, 141, 143, 144, 146
3:22a	146
3:22b	146
3:22–24	142
3:22–25	107, 119, 120, 143, 158
3:23	70, 71, 143, 144, 146
3:23–25	158
3:24	146
3:24–25	107, 144, 158
3:26	55, 58, 116, 117, 121, 158, 178, 184, 204
3:26–27	58
3:26–29	7, 58, 117, 158, 184, 218
3:26–4:7	57
3:27	58
3:27–28	158
3:27–29	117
3:28	14, 22, 52, 53, 58, 116, 198, 204
3:29	7, 18, 121, 136, 167, 169n43, 195
3–4	5, 8
4	65, 76, 205
4–6	164
4:1	158
4:1–2	5, 57, 158
4:1–7	5, 7, 20, 57, 73
4:1–9	171
4:1–11	11
4:3	6, 57, 71, 72
4:3–5	158
4:4	69, 70
4:4–5	69, 70
4:4–6	57, 75
4:4–7	68, 69, 70n265, 75, 212
4:5	7, 46, 56, 57, 69, 70, 72, 112
4:5–6	71
4:5–7	70, 158
4:6	34, 34n129, 57, 66, 67, 68, 69, 73n272, 91, 112, 128, 153, 167, 176, 177, 178, 207, 209, 218
4:6–7	75, 149, 154n110

4:6–8	66	5:2–4	162, 163n14, 178, 191, 199, 200
4:6–9	75		
4:7	7, 67, 70, 112	5:2–6	
4:7a	67	5:3	174, 176, 178, 199, 201
4:7–9	112		
4:8	71, 102n35, 216	5:3–4	176n61
4:8b	71	5:4	132, 186, 199, 201
4:8–9	6, 73, 74, 75	5:5	194, 199, 200, 215
4:9	72, 73, 74	5:5–6	199, 201
4:11	14	5:6	116, 187, 198, 199, 200, 201, 202, 204
4:13–14	161, 162		
4:13–15	100		
4:16	99, 100	5:6a	53
4:17	102	5:7	99, 100, 101, 200
4:17a	100	5:7–12	199
4:17–18	101n32	5:8	101, 200
4:21	70, 130, 153	5:9	101, 200
4:21–25	68	5:10	101, 200
4:21–30	8	5:11	97n16, 190, 191, 200
4:21–31	20, 68, 75, 89, 112, 137, 138, 153, 158, 171		
		5:11–12	178, 200
		5:13	160, 162, 198, 201
4:21—5:1	70, 153, 155, 156, 161	5:13c	201
		5:13–14	53, 68, 165n22, 171, 199, 200, 201
4:22	149		
4:22–31	149	5:13–25	171
4:23	136, 137, 149, 154, 160n8, 162	5:13–6:10	79
		5:14	20, 162, 175, 184, 199, 200, 201, 217
4:24	154		
4:24–26	149	5:15	171, 182n89, 184, 186
4:25	155		
4:25b	155	5:16	20, 70, 160, 162, 171, 184, 192
4:26	68		
4:26–29	151	5:16–17	69, 146, 163, 207
4:27	150, 152, 155	5:16–23	75, 171, 202
4:27–28	170n44	5:16–25	112
4:28	68, 136, 139, 149	5:16—6:8	162n11
4:28–29	149, 160n8	5:16—6:10	188
4:28–31	75	5:16—6:18	208
4:29	55, 68, 138, 139, 149, 150, 154, 156, 157, 162, 217	5:17	162, 192
		5:18	52, 56, 69, 70, 112, 165, 184, 192, 207, 217n9
4:30	68		
4:31	68, 170n44	5:18a	36
5–6	10, 160	5:19	162, 163, 183n92
5:1	162	5:19–21	164
5:1–2	186	5:19–21a	164, 184
5:2	178, 199	5:22	34, 162, 163, 175, 201

Galatians (continued)

5:22–23	69, 166
5:24	26, 28, 130, 159, 162, 164, 167, 170, 184, 190, 195, 201, 212
5:24–25	14, 15, 16, 29, 34, 85, 99, 106, 108, 112, 116, 153, 159, 163, 164, 166, 167, 169, 171, 183, 184, 186, 192, 193, 194, 198, 202, 214
5:25	18, 26, 28, 53, 75, 108, 111, 112, 130, 157, 162, 164, 165, 167, 184, 192, 194, 205, 211
5:25a	165
5:26	75, 182, 183n92, 184, 186
5:26—6:5	186
6	181, 182
6:1	171, 182, 183n92, 188
6:1–2	183, 183n92, 187, 192, 208
6:1–5	187
6:1–6	187
6:1–8	190, 192
6:1–10	186
6:2	171, 181, 182, 183, 183n91, 183n92, 185, 187, 217n9
6:2–3	183n92
6:3–5	193
6:3–8	188
6:4a	187
6:4b	187
6:5	187, 188
6:6	181n2, 188, 192, 193
6:7	188, 191
6:7a	188
6:7–8	188, 192, 193
6:8	16, 26, 29, 75, 112, 159, 160, 162, 163, 171, 184, 186, 191–95, 208, 215
6:8–10	190
6:8–16	208, 213
6:9–10	190
6:10	208n29
6:11–18	79, 196
6:12	101, 178, 190, 191, 198
6:12a	198
6:12–13	191, 197, 198, 199, 208, 209
6:12–14	178, 201
6:12–15	209
6:13	178, 187, 198, 201
6:13b	198
6:13–14	75
6:14	26, 130, 198n11, 202, 206
6:14–15	16, 22, 29, 159, 166, 167, 170, 184, 196, 197, 197n6, 198, 199, 203, 205, 206, 212, 214
6:14b–15	198
6:14–16	14, 52, 85, 202, 213
6:15	22, 52, 116, 130, 197, 198, 199, 200, 202, 204, 205, 207, 208, 210
6:15a	53
6:15–16	202
6:16	18, 53, 130, 130n30, 166, 167, 170, 204, 205, 206, 208, 209, 211, 212
6:16a	208
6:16b	206
6:17	25

Ephesians

1:13	101
1:14	137
1:15	101n33
1:19–20	23n92
2	61, 211
2:1	62
2:1–6	62
2:1–10	62
2:5	62, 144n84
2:6	13, 62
2:11	163, 175, 208, 209
2:11–18	208, 209, 213
2:12	208
2:14	208, 210, 210n35, 211, 212
2:14–18	210
2:15	208, 210, 211, 212
2:16	210, 210n35
2:17	212
2:18	208, 210, 210n35, 211
2:19–22	212
2:21	211n43
4:4–6	210n34
4:24	210
5:31	210n34

Philippians

1:21	29, 119
1:22	28
2:15	55
2:16	27n105, 28
3	208
3:2–7	98n20
3:3	23, 163, 175, 209
3:5, 9	23n94
3:9–11	119
3:10–11	23
3:11	24
4:3	27n105, 28

Colossians

1:5	101
1:13	32n118
2:11	163, 175, 209
2:12	13, 38n141, 86
2:13	144n84
2:20	65
2:22	193
3:1	13
3:3–4	114
3:4	111n69
3:9–10	210
3:11	58, 167n35
4:5	101n33

1 Thessalonians

1:1	53n205
1:9	28n107, 64n247
1:9–10	109
1:10	32n118, 86, 111
3:8	28
4:3–5	102n37
4:14–17	86
4–5	25, 73n274
4:15	28n107, 28n108
4:7	28n107
5:10	114

2 Thessalonians

3:2	32n118

1 Timothy

1:13	97n14
1:16	186n1
3	24
6:19	186n1

2 Timothy

1:8–10	109
2:11	65, 114
2:18	13n55
3:11	32n118
4:17, 18	32n118

Titus

1:16	73n274
2:14	32n118

Hebrews

2:2	141
11:11	217
11:19	138n62
11:22	50

James

2:10	174

1 Peter

3:20–22	38n141

2 Peter

1:15	50

Jude

1:7	159

Revelation

11:2	62
21:2	62
21:11	62
22:19	62

Dead Sea Scrolls

1QH

4:10–12	183n93
11:19–23	38n148
18:14–15	11
19:10–14	38

1QM

2:13	155n113

1QpHab

2:3	172n49
7:11–14	172

1QS

4:25	197n7
9:22	98n21
11:9	162–63, 163n12
4Q521	39–41, 53

4QMMT

	103

4Q Pseudo-Ezekiel

	61

11QMelch

	11

Damascus Document

3:12b–16	135
5:18	141
6:19	172n49
19:34–35	172n49

Hodayot

4QH 4:25	163
4QH 18:25	163

Ancient Jewish Writers

Josephus

Against Apion

2:29–30	113
2:218	32
2:258	95n9

Antiquities

1.165–68	121n3
2.66	44n176
4.189	51n196
9.3.9	44n176
15.5.2 (136b)	141
20.2.1–4:3	177

Life

112–13	98n22

Philo

De Abrahamo

92	163n17
275–76	140n68

De Vita Mosis

2.166	142, 142n78

Quaestiones et Solutiones in Genesin

3:46–52	163n15
3:52	163n16

Virtues

77	51n196

Rabbinic Writings

Amidah — 40–41

Babylonian Talmud

Megillah

31a	62n237

Menahot

43b	53n204

Sanhedrin

91b	125n18

Tosefta Berakhot

6:18	53

Mishnah

Nezir

3:6	177n66

Greco-Roman Writings

Cicero

Ad Atticum
6:6   44n172

Diodorus Siculus

Bibliotheca Historia
34:1:2   96n10

Epictetus

Discourses
2.1.13   45n178
2.16.19   45n179

Enchiridion   44n177

Euripides

The Medea   45

Ovid

Epistulae ex Ponto   42
1.2 26–27   42n162

2.2. 9–14   42n58
2.2 9–72   42n160

Tristia   42
2.207   42n159
3.3.56   42n164
5.7.54   42n165
5.10.37   43n165

Philostratus

Vita Apollonii
5:33   96n10

Plutarch

Life of Cicero
143   43n170

Tacitus

History
5:5   96n10

Early Christian Writings

Eusebius

Praeparatio Evangelica
9:8   121n3
9:17–18   121n3

Justin Martyr

Dialogue with Trypho
105   51n196
138:1–2   38n141